CURRENT GLOBAL IDEAS AND MOVEMENTS CHALLENGING CAPITALISM

CURRENT GLOBAL IDEAS AND MOVEMENTS CHALLENGING CAPITALISM

By Duan Zhongqiao

Translated by Fan Haixiang

CANUT INTERNATIONAL PUBLISHERS
Berlin, London

Originally published as Contemporary Western Social Thoughts in 2001 and 2010 by China Renmin University Press.

Original Chinese Edition Copyright © 2001

ISBN: 978-7-300-11682-2

All rights reserved. No part of this book may be used or reproduced in any manner whatsoever without the written permission of the publisher.

English Print edition: Current Global Ideas and Movements Challenging Capitalism

ISBN: 978-3-942575-06-5

English Digital Edition:

ISBN: 978-3-942575-08-9

Published by
Canut International Publishers
Yorck Street. 66
10965 Kreuzberg Berlin-Germany

Canut International-London
12a Guernsey Road E11
London 4BJ –England-U.K
URL: http// www.canut.us
E-Mail: canut@gmail.com

CONTENTS

Foreword	vii
Acknowledgements	ix

CHAPTER I
FUTURISM — 11

1.1 Science, Sustainable Development and Futurism	14
1.2 Convergence Hypothesis: Social History School	19
1.3 Toffler's Hypothesis: "The Third Wave"	24
1.4. Naisbitt and "Information Society"	29
1.5 Rational Factors in Futurism	33

CHAPTER II
NEO-LIBERALISM — 45

2.1 Revival of Neoliberalism in the 1970s	48
2.2 Basic Ideas and Main Schools of Neoliberalism	59
2.3 A General Evaluation of Neo-liberalism	86

CHAPTER III
POST-MODERNISM — 91

3.1 Origins and Development of Postmodernism	94
3.2 Representatives of Post-modernism	107
3.3 Rationality and Limitations of Post-modernism	125

CHAPTER IV
POST-COLONIALISM — 133

4.1 Rise of Post-colonialism	136
4.2 Main Contents of Post-colonialism	148
4.3 General Evaluation of Post-colonialism	166

CHAPTER V
ANALYTICAL MARXISM 171

5.1 Historical background of Analytical Marxism   *174*
5.2 General Features of Analytical Marxism   *178*
5.3 Cohen, Roemer, Wright   *184*
5.4 Evaluation of Analytical Marxism   *203*

CHAPTER VI
ECO-SOCIALISM 207

6.1 Rise and Development of Eco-socialism   *210*
6.2 Basic Ideas of Eco-socialism   *224*
6.3 Evaluation of Eco-socialism   *241*

CHAPTER VII
SOCIALIST FEMINISM 247

7.1 The Rise of Socialist Feminism   *250*
7.2 Views of Socialist Feminism   *260*
7.3 Evaluation of Socialist Feminism   *275*

CHAPTER VIII
MARKET SOCIALISM THEORIES 279

8.1 Origin and Evolution of Thoughts of Market Socialism   *282*
8.2 Miller, Roemer, Schweickert   *288*
8.3 Evaluation on Market Socialism Trends   *307*

CHAPTER IX
THE THIRD WAY 311

9.1 Reasons for the Rise of "The Third Way"   *314*
9.2 Basic Ideas of "The Third Way"   *329*
9.3 Evaluation of 'The Third Way'   *339*

About the Authors   *349*

FOREWORD

This book was written in a time when the world stood at a crossroads. At the turn of the century, neo-liberalism still prevailed and the U.S new economy seemed strong which pushed economic globalization vigorously, left and socialist forces were reviewing and reflecting on the changes caused by the great upheaval in Soviet Union and Eastern Europe. Social democracy was seeking new ways and new social subjects to recover public support under the conditions of low-economic growth and high-unemployment, while trade-unions were losing power. Critical voices on post-modernism were becoming louder, marking the beginning decline of this trend of thought. North and south disparity grew rampantly causing a gross unrest among wide circles of the population in developing countries which triggered neo- nationalism and Islamist political movements. The crisis of planetary sustainability, environmental disasters have expanded capitalism critic and part of the green movement had opted for eco-socialism which was well-blessed globally. New sufferings in women's conditions; un-employment, low-wage jobs and neo-liberalism aggravating discrimination in labor market have mobilized socialist feminists to blaze a new trail for gender equality.

In such a background Duan Zhongqiao, the renowned Beijing based philosophy scholar and his colleagues, have analyzed the nine influential trends and movements of the times keenly observing how their prominent representatives have reflected on manifold problems of capitalism. With an original exegesis they have delved into the inner logic of those thoughts and thrown light on the major counterpoints in them. These trends in the spheres of philosophy, economics, politics, sociology and Marxist theory have shaken and challenged academy, parties, governments and peoples' lives, some of them defending the existing capitalist system, others sought how to transform to socialism and some tried to conserve it further by reforms.

Current situation in the world especially the great financial crisis, increasing unemployment and growth hitting bottoms in the main centers of capitalism call for new changes and bring forth new questions for all the movements and trend of thoughts. And people all around the world seek alternatives and strive for subsistence, development, peace and more democracy. Marxists value these appeals highly, especially when social ferment for revolution is not full-blown.

The book was written by a group of scholars from Philosophy Department and researchers in the Marxism Institute in Renmin University of China. Duan Zhongqiao has edited and compiled the whole book; chapters on analytical Marxism and market socialism were written by him; futurism by Zhang Yunfei, neo-Liberalism by Zhang Xu, post-modernism by Xu Fei, post-colonialism by Zhang Libo, ecological socialism by Han Haitao, socialist feminism by Liu Jianjun and the Third Way by Qin Xuan.

The book reflects the recent courage and optimism in Chinese academia to bring forth creativity in Marxist narration and offers a creative methodology on how to evaluate emerging new thoughts from variety of aspects and reveal their complex links with real contradictions and human lives. If this book is anything to go by, we can look forward to further persuasive works from them.

Lastly, I would like to thank Prof. Xu Ruizhi and Prof. Gao Zilong for their precious contribution for the realization of this book.

Cem Kızılcec

Berlin, March 2011

ACKNOWLEDGEMENTS

The Chinese edition of this book was designed and edited by Duan Zhongqiao. He has written the Chapters 5 and 8 on Analytical Marxism and Market Socialism. I would like to thank my colleagues who have co-authored the following parts: Chapter 1: Futurism, Zhang Yunfei; Chapter 2, Neo-liberalism, Zhang Xu; Chapter 3, Post-modernism, Xu Fei; Chapter 4, Post-colonialism, Zhang Libo; Chapter 6, Ecological Socialism, Han Haitao; Chapter 7, Socialist Feminism, Liu Jianjun; Chapter 9, "The Third Way", Qin Xuan.

I would also thank Institute of Marxism Studies in Renmin University of China and China Renmin University Press who have generously contributed in the realization of this book. Finally we would like to express our gratitude to Xu Ruizhi and Gao Zilong who have offered their precious advice and suggestions.

Zhang Yunfei

CHAPTER II

FUTURISM

1 *Science, Sustainable Development and Futurism*
2 *Convergence Hypothesis: Social History School*
3 *Bell and Post-Industrial Society*
4 *Toffler's Hypothesis: "The Third Wave"*
5 *Naisbitt and "Information Society"*

CHAPTER ONE

INTRODUCTION

Futurism is a social trend of thought engaged in the study and prediction of social development in the future. It has originated in some advanced capitalist countries in Western world between the end of 1960s and the beginning of 1970s. Generally speaking, futurism generally closely interacts with two schools, namely, Social History School (Annales School) and Ecological School. The former, focusing on the study and foresight of social changes brought by new scientific revolution, and holds the view that with the progress of new scientific revolution, a new social form will replace of the existing social systems, transcending both capitalist and socialist ones. The latter emphasizes balance between of the environment and development, focuses on the research of the negative impacts and consequences of science and technology, particularly explores in a critical manner the impact that global environment and economic development ensues on the social progress. Although those two schools display differences in many aspects, they share several common aims and ideas. That is, they are both oriented on the study of the future, and focus on the new scientific revolution; They apply modern science and technology in designing and predicting the future, and enthusiastically highlight the impacts of new scientific revolution on the future development of human society; and they both aim to predict and design future human society to emancipate human beings out of current extrication.

14 CURRENT GLOBAL IDEAS AND MOVEMENTS CHALLENGING CAPITALISM

1.1 SCIENCE, SUSTAINABLE DEVELOPMENT AND FUTURISM

Futurism focuses on the development issues of the times and efforts that human beings have made to explore the future. It came into being on the basis of people's reflection upon the social impact of science and technology and issues of global environment and development. It has also incorporated a lot from related social trends of thoughts and scientific achievements.

1.1.1 THE SOCIAL BACKGROUND OF FUTURISM

Researchers generally assert that, it was historically inevitable for Futurism to come into being in the 1960s due to two tremendous changes, the new scientific revolution and the emerging global environment problems, which has radically effected social development after in the post- World War II era, and triggered a series of significant social problems in the 1960s. Therefore, Futurism emerged in an attempt to tackle those problems.

1.1.1.1 PREDICTING THE OUTCOMES OF THE NEW SCIENTIFIC REVOLUTION

To cure the destruction of war and revive the economy rapidly, a new scientific revolution sprung up worldwide after the World War II.

In 60 ties, the human society, especially the advanced countries, have encountered deep changes, owing to the establishment of new sciences, such as relativity, quantum mechanics, molecule biology, ecology and system sciences, and new and high-techs, like Information technology, electronics, biology, space technology, marine technology, advanced materials technology, new energy resources and environmental protection. Those changes could be summarized as follows: (1) Elements of productive forces have changed: Knowledge, especially science and technological knowledge, has gradually shifted from an adherent factor of productive forces to a separated one, owing to the application of advanced information technology and artificial intelligence. As a result, production automation was greatly improved; and the material exchanges between human society and nature turned to information technology. (2) Changes in the industrial structure. In the 1960s, 60% of the labor force in the United States was engaged in service industry, which increased to 70% or so in the 1980s. Furthermore, the number of employees engaged in information industry occupied a large proportion of thi service sector. (3) Adjustments of labor structure. In the history of industrial civilization, it was the first time that the number of white-collar workers in the United States had surpassed blue-collar workers in 1956. This was due to knowledge playing the key part in production and also reflected the above change in the industrial structure. From then on, this ratio has steadily increased. Most surprisingly, the growth rate of scientists and engineers in the United States was double the average of the total labor force. Obviously, the speedy development of new scientific revolution had not only triggered a series of significant changes in social structure, but also shortened the process of social transformation. It had injected fresh energy into the industrial society, leading the industry to a new stage. Thus, people excitingly needed to understand and master the new social changes and trends, so that they could foresee the future.

1.1.1.2 RELATIONSHIP BETWEEN GLOBAL ENVIRONMENT AND DEVELOPMENT

With the social development rapidly propelled forward by science and technology, a series of negative problems have surfaced, like population explosion, resource exhaustion, environment pollution, and energy crisis. Consequently, all of those, together with other problems, turned out to be global issues of environment and therefore development, too. It could be said that those problems had already existed at any time in the history. However, they have become global issues only after the 1960s, the reasons for which lay in the following aspects: (1) Complexity: new problems emerging and occurring possess complex causes; which are mutually dependent, and interactive. They form a complex and intertwined integrity, one rising and other subsiding. For instance, due to population expansion, resources, environment, and energy resource problems have intensified. And the increasing tensions related resources, environment and energy challenges improvement of human life. (2) Increased threats and risks: Global environment and development is a threat existing objectively. No one can overlook it, and no one can escape from being punished by it. If not settled appropriately, it might bring severe and irretrievable losses for the whole humankind. It can not only worsen human living conditions and decrease the production capability, but can also ruin human civilization. Human beings have already suffered a heavy loss for it. (3) Cooperative action: to settle the problem of global environment and development rationally and effectively, it is necessary that all countries should seek common ground and leave aside differences thus cooperate for survival. And it is also necessary for governments of all countries', country groups' and international organizations' coordinated actions and establish a worldwide cooperation. Because the real scope of the global problems have transcended both political and geographical range. For instance, due to ultraviolet radiation caused by the depletion of the ozone layer and rising sea level, their consequences effect equally every country and every region, with no regional solution for them. The evolution of global problems, especially environment and development, reveal that environment and development issues should be dealt with a global aspect so that mankind can lead a sustainable development.

16 CURRENT GLOBAL IDEAS AND MOVEMENTS CHALLENGING CAPITALISM

In all, in the 1960s, either capitalism or socialism were faced with the challenges of new scientific revolution and global environment and development. It was deemed necessary to holistically consider both positive and negative effects of social development brought by science and technology in a holistic approach. This ideology gave birth to Futurism.

1.1.2 THEORETICAL SOURCES OF FUTURISM

Futurism did not emerge groundlessly, but mainly on the basis of social trends of thought and Scientific Achievements, such as Futurology, Scientific Determinism, Convergence Hypothesis, System Dynamics and Ecology. All these sciences and methodologies constitute the theoretical sources for Futurism.

1.1.2.1 FUTUROLOGY, A DISCIPLINARY MATRIX, FOR FUTURISM

The term Futurology, was coined by German professor Ossip K. Flechtheim in 1934. During the 1960s and the 1970s, Futurology expanded into a new and complex branch of knowledge that integrated natural science, social science, and science of management. Loosely speaking, Futurology is the study of future. It studies manufacturing modes of large-scale industry and influences of new scientific revolution on social development. Futurology also studies the various [choices that human beings make to achieve their goals, and people's prediction and explanation of the development trends of the future as well. What futurists took in from Futurology were:

(1) Scientific prediction was seen as credible and convinced people that the study on future could become a science. Application of science together with technology, could produce scientific knowledge on the laws of social development, and therefore make this field of study a science. In other words studies on the future based on scientific predications; by employing science and technology as tools could be a science.

(2) The study of future was closely related to social development, and the prediction of the future could be used as reference for people's action. Additionally, Futurology provides a kind of scientific foresight, which could predict how people would react to the given situation and what might affect their ability to make the correct choices Consequently, the insight into the future could be beneficial, wherein possible actions that can be taken and their respective impacts could be weighed. Thus destructive or harmful situations could be avoided to a great deal, thereby helping solve problems of the present and also those of the future.

1.1.2.2 SCIENTIFIC DETERMINISM, A DIRECT THEORETICAL SOURCE OF FUTURISM

Scientific determinism (also known as technocracy) is a kind of social trend of thought that was born in the United States in the 1920s. Its founder is believed to be the US sociologist Thorstein Veblen (1857-1929) With the development of new scientific revolution after the World War II, scientific determinism spread widely in the Western part of the world and caused a great influence on social life at all levels. What Futurism has borrowed from scientific determinism can be summarized as follows:

(1) Science and technology is a crucial factors that dominate the development of modern society. With [developments in science and technology, social differences could be eliminated and the shortcomings of all current social systems could be improved. For example, in Thorstein Veblen's opinion, revolutions had taken place in the military and political forms in the 19th century. However, in the 20th century, social revolutions and disturbances were hindered by the large industrial, scientific and social advancements In other words, just by industrial means, could any significant and efficient transformation be realized or held back. (The word "industrial" means "technological" or, "belonging to science and technology).

(2) Since scientists and technicians are in the middle of all scientific and technological advancements –on which the social development depends greatly- and are capable of overcoming social disadvantages by foreseeing the possible future, they should be the rightful rulers of the society. This idea is supported by reasoning that scientists and technicians are rational, unselfish human beings who are concerned about the social welfare and progress.

(3) Science and technology are independent of any conflicting group. The essential reason why science and technology could be able to become a combined dominant factor over any other factor lay in the fact that they were separated from the social structures, and joined their forces (science+technology) to become an independent structure.

1.1.2.3 CONVERGENCE HYPOTHESIS, AS THE SOURCE OF FUTURISM

Convergence, is originally a biological term, meaning that the heterogeneous organisms possess nearly identical characteristics and functions in structure because they live in or share the same circumstances. This term was transplanted into social politics in 1961 by a Dutch economist, Jan Tinbergen, to illustrate on the relationship between capitalism and socialism. Thus had the convergence hypothesis emerged as a particular social trend of thought. Its contributions to Futurism were as follows: (1) capitalism and socialism are definitely two opposite poles.

18 CURRENT GLOBAL IDEAS AND MOVEMENTS CHALLENGING CAPITALISM

Both have advantages and disadvantages, and they cannot be perfect. (2) In the process of social development, capitalism and socialism supplements each other, and learn from each other. Therefore, they could depart from their original poles, and may form series of identical characteristics and functions. That is, capitalist ownership has undergone a qualitative change. As a result, the distinction between public ownership and private ownership has blurred up. The combination of planned economy and market economy was adopted by both capitalism and socialism. The poverty of the proletariat does not exist any longer, and income distribution in capitalist societies tends to be equalized. Consequently, the differences between classes disappear and the struggle of the proletariat against the bourgeoisie has lost its ground and lost its significance. The conflict between Marxism and non-Marxism has faded away, and these two social systems coexist and progress forward with parallels beyond consciousness. The accumulation of these similar characteristics and functions that both socialism and capitalism shares would lead to synthesization, hatching a new social form. Consequently, the future of human society would neither be capitalism nor socialism, but a new social form combining merits of the two.

1.1.2.4 SYSTEM DYNAMICS AS THE METHODOLOGY OF FUTURISM

System dynamics was established in 1956 by Jay Wright Forrester, professor at the MIT Sloan School of Management. He had used computer simulations to analyze large and complex systems, like modern science, economy, society and environment, and applied computer analysis to make decisions. Its principles, methods and requirements can be summarized as follows: (1) In the traditional management model, using the real world as object, and applying information feedback, people could make a comparison between the complex and changeable social phenomenon such as movement of fluids. That general principle and method could be inherited and incorporated to describe the structure of social system in the way similar to hydrodynamics. (2) With the aid of powerful memory and speedy calculation of the computers, the change of the real social system can be traced, and the simulated experiment can be done time and again. As a result, it can be feasible to use computers to study strategies of the large social system. After system dynamics was created, it was widely used in several spheres of social systems. It has made great influence on two schools of Futurism, Social History School and Ecological School.

1.1.2.5 ECOLOGY, AS THE SCIENTIFIC BACKGROUND OF FUTURISM

The term ecology was coined by the German biologist Ernst Haeckel in 1866. It was the scientific study on the interactions between organisms and their environment. As the global problems went increasingly worse, ecology started to rise in the 20th century, and became a strong trend amidst new scientific revolution in sixties. What ecology has contributed to the social development ideas can be summarized as follows: (1) The relationship between human society and natural ecological system is identical to that between organisms and environment. Both of them contain material exchange, through which they form a whole – ecological system. Therefore, it is necessary to combine environment with development as a whole body. (2) Due to the existence of system relation (e.g. food chain), any inappropriate action will destroy ecological system, which in turn will hold back social development. Therefore, people should pay due attention to this problem.. (3) Ecology is a science of managing the earth as well. A harmonious ecological system can finally appear through human mastery and exertion of ecological rules. Thus, it is utterly possible to have a sustainable social development. And the research on global environment and development should be carried out right on the basis of ecology.

In all, Futurism has borrowed social trends of thought and scientific achievements that are mentioned above. And with this theoretical framework, it has become a social trend of thought internationally.

1.2 CONVERGENCE HYPOTHESIS: SOCIAL HISTORY SCHOOL

Annales (Socio-economic history) History School born in France, basing itself theoretically on scientific determinism, has established convergence hypothesis through the analysis of the social changes brought by science and technology. They held the view that with the advance of new scientific revolution, the status of science and technology and intellectuals would increasingly grow dominant in the process of social development. As a result, a series of changes would take place in social structures, especially class structures. And human society could step into a new stage. This new stage, replacing the existing social systems, capitalism and socialism, would combine merits of the two, and discard their demerits. There has been many scholars illustrating on such a theoretical basis, like Daniel Bell's "Post-Industrial Society", Alvin Toffler's "The Third Wave", and John Naisbitt's "Information Society".

1.2.1 BELL AND POST-INDUSTRIAL INDUSTRY

Futurism, especially Social History School, was theoretically based on the concept of post-industrial society. This idea was first raised in 1959 by Daniel Bell, the US. Sociologist and political philosopher. According to his central-axle technique (also known as central-axle principle), Bell held the view that both capitalism and socialism were outcomes of social industrialization and bureaucratic collectivization. They would both move to post-industrial society, and the future society would integrate those two social characteristics and functions. His ideas are as follows:

1.2.1.1 TECHNICAL CENTRAL-AXLE PRINCIPLE

As for social history, Bell held the view that technology was the primary force that dominated change of social forms. According to variations in technology, he divided the history of social development into three stages, pre-industrial society, industrial society and post-industrial society. He employed the notion of central-axle in his analysis of social structure and forms. In his opinion, there existed two different central-axle principles. One principle uses the criteria of ownership of means-of-production as the central-axle. According to this principle, social development is divided into three stages: feudalism, capitalism and socialism. The other principle utilizes productive forces as the central-axle. In his view, the rule to distinguish modern society lay in productive force rather than the ownership of means of production. Productive force was the central-axle in modern society. And distinctions between pre-industrial society, industrial society and post-industrial society lay in nowhere but their unique productive labor. That is, in pre-industrial society, the central-axle was of traditionalism, considering the limit of land and resources. In industrial society, the central-axle was economic growth, with the emphasis on the state's or individual's control over decision of investments. However, in post-industrial society the central-axle becomes knowledge. Knowledge has risen to be social primary resource, and scientists and researchers have mounted up to be social rulers. Thus in his analysis, relations and differences between capitalism and socialism does not seem all too revealing; since he has observed the productive forces isolated from production relations; although the two form — as an organic whole— the economic base of any social formation. Seen from the Marxist view in they should be always be studied in a certain stage of development and also as a organic whole.

And we can explicitly see that: if we compare the evolution from industrial society to post-industrial society, and the change from capitalism to socialism or bureaucratic collectivism, those two have moved on entirely different central-axles.

1.2.1.2 NEW CHANGES IN CAPITALISM AND HISTORICAL TREND TO SOCIALISM

Observing the new changes in capitalism, and analyzing the changes in social structure, class structure and cultural conflicts, Bell has given a negative answer to the historical certainty of socialism replacing capitalism.

1.2.1.2.1 The New Mode of Capitalism

In order to test his hypothesis on social development, Bell made a textual research of Marx's theories on social development. He has argued that Marx had raised two different modes of capitalist development in his work "On Capital." The first mode was exposed in the Volume One of this book. That is, with the development of capitalist production mode, landed class and bourgeois would gradually merge into one, leaving only two classes in the society, capitalists and proletariat. The contradictions between socialized production and private ownership of means of production would certainly lead to perishing of capitalism and victory of socialism replacing the former. However, Bell held the view that the first mode Marx had exposed was just the "pure capitalism". In reality, capitalism did not enter in such a mode, but existed in the second mode, that is, as socialization of capital, separation of capital ownership with management and thus resulting an independent management transcending the private capital and resulted as the expansion of white-collar workers. Marx was sharply aware of those new changes occurring in capitalist social structure, and thus studied and exposed "the second mode" of capitalism in his book On Capital: Volume III. Marx's ideas can be explained in detail as the following: (1) With the establishment of a new banking and credit system, capital accumulation depends on the savings of the whole society rather than on raising money through individuals' thrift and savings of the enterprisers. Thus capital accumulation tends to be socialized. (2) The occurrence of stock company form separates the right of ownership (of capital) from its management rights, producing a new profession, labor-commanding management. (3) The expansion of banking system, credit system, and boom of stock companies had necessarily led to increase of office staff and white-collar workers. As a result, a new stratum has emerged in the old society. In Bell's view, the second mode Marx brought forward was much more significant, but was little known. If that was well noticed and associated with the hypothesis on the future of capitalism in the first half of the 20th century, it could easily be grasped that almost all theories on social development were having a dialogue with Marx's second mode. And for Bell, the existing two social systems were learning from each other in the three aspects, as I have mentioned above, and thus a trend of convergence had emerged.

1.2.1.2.2 The New Stratum in Capitalist Society

Bell has argued that with the progress of modern technology, blue-collar workers would become minority, while white-collar workers would grow into majority and will become a dominant power either in the developed industrial society or in the post-industrial society. Although they have not formed into a new class yet, they have turned into a power, which will rise to be a ruling class in the post-industrial society. They have two common characteristics, that is, they are outcomes of the new system, in which their power is based and have attained a higher social status by their special technological knowledge. And they have common spiritual quality on the basis of new values. In order to depict post-industrial society, Bell has discarded the factor of ownership of means of production, and established his "new" understanding of classes. He demonstrated that to suit the contemporary world, the definition of class should be given on the basis of a certain systemized social structure. Only this kind of social structure can be the basis that differentiates social status, influence of power (authority) and rewards.. This definition should also integrate cultural perspectives of a group (that keeps various perspectives consistent.) and the common consciousness (amidst which legalization of class itself should embrace to some extend). To put it in a nutshell, as long as there was social commonwealth, integrity of institutionalized benefits and tenets(or behavioural principles), that were universally accepted by its social members, that group could form a "class". On the prerequisite of removing economic contents of "class", Bell put forth his hypothesis on the class structure of post-industrial society: the specialists class on the basis of knowledge rather than property will in the leading place in the new society. The system supporting the society would be the political order rather than professional class, which is inherited generation after generation. The intellectual class was likely to rise to the top in the new society. In all, in his opinion, the conflict that Marx assumed between bourgeoisie and proletariat would perish. Therefore, that class foundation, on which socialism would replace capitalism, does not exist any longer.

1.2.1.2.3 Cultural Contradictions in Capitalist Development

Since a series of significant and essential changes have emerged in social structure, including class structure, are there still any contradictions in capitalist society? If any, how do they demonstrate themselves ? Bell has argued that the major contradiction of capitalism focuses on culture. In his opinion, capitalist society is composed of three spheres as well: economy, politics and culture. The three move around their own central-axle. Efficiency principle is the central-axle in economy; equality principle as the central-axle of politics; individualism, as the central-axle of culture. Because individual hedonism is wide-spread, it is bound to produce frictions even conflicts with efficiency and equality principle. As a result, the contradictions urged by capitalist culture is unavoidable. The culture, in Bell's view, was neither human nature as the Ancient Greeks had considered, nor human history as Hegel thought, nor reflection of economic base as Marx had believed. In his view, it was just a humanly situation faced by difficulties, and he has described this "practical" problem as follows: when a person is born into the world (in spite of his will or not), he starts to be aware of such a difficulty and tries to give some answers. The core of these answers constitute the human culture. And, Bell, has traced back to human history to seek a solution for the problem.. It was on such a point that Bell had discovered that the post-industrial society would be a society of knowledge. Under those prerequisites, Bell has argued that the opposite ideology to capitalism is not the socialist thought of working class, but values of the rising new class. Therefore, the values of post-industrial society rather than socialist thought can replace the capitalist ideology. As a result, ideology progresses to an end, and cultural motivation to produce socialism does not exist any longer.

1.2.1.2.4 Post-Industrial Society; Capitalism; Socialism

The new changes in capitalism caused by technological development indicates that a new social form, post-industrial society was gestated in capitalist society. (1) Post-industrial society would be the outlook of future human society because it can be able to merge and replace the current capitalism and socialism. Post-industrial society is a society, which shifts from manufacture-centeredness to service orientation. In post-industrial society, most labor is engaged in service industry, like trade, finance, transport, health care, entertainment, research, education and management, and not in agriculture or manufacture any longer. (2) Post-industrial society is a society that shifts from entrepreneurship orientation to scientist centeredness. In this society scientists and researchers become the ruling class. They exert their power by means of balancing powers between technology and politics, and suffrage and other rights. It will be a society under the rule of "talents." The term "talents" should be understood in a best sense. It refers to those who deserves to be praised and they were appreciated to be excellent by people in their respective field. (3) Theoretical knowledge will become the core of society and foundation for social innovation and policy-making. In post-industrial society, the nature of knowledge itself changes, that is, theoretical knowledge becomes primary, compared with empirical knowledge. Additionally, after knowledge is encoded into a symbolic system, it can be used like any law to explain empirical knowledge in various fields. Post-industrial society will be organized with knowledge as the core, which aimed at social management, and guiding innovation and transformation. In turn, it will produce new social relations and structures. And all of those will become issues under political management. (4) Technological development will be planned and controlled, and technological assessment becomes vitally important. At present, technology has brought great social progress, but has produced negative effects as well, and even unimaginable consequences that are overlooked. The causes of these problems lay in that people do not give assessment on technology. However, in post-industrial society, technological progress could be planned and controlled. At present, the problems to be settled was how to urge political structure allow such research and formulate norms to supervise new technology. (5) In post-industrial society, policies should be regulated through intelligence technology. Intelligence technology uses rules or systems (rules to settle problems) and avoids subjective judgments. These rules or systems could be set in the automatic device, or a computer program, or a set of statistical or mathematical command. The statistical knowledge and logic technology might be utilized to deal with "organized complexity" of the social system, and a set of decision rules could thus be formulated. He has certainly believed that such a new social form could eliminate demerits of the current two social systems.

In Bell's view: (1) Capitalism and socialism were both two ways progressing to the future; (2) But, there has emerged a "new" way which combines capitalism with socialism, "Post-industrial society as a new social system will combine the two like bureaucratic collectivism, rather than inherit capitalism and/or socialism."[1]

1.3 TOFFLER'S HYPOTHESIS: "THE THIRD WAVE"

Alvin Toffler, US futurologist has divided human society into three stages: agrarian wave, industrial wave and knowledge wave according to the role that industrial structure, particularly technology, plays in social development. He argued that the new civilization in the Third Wave stage would be "Practopia" (which differed from Utopia)..

Capitalism and socialism, as the outcome of industrialization, would both transfer toward "Practopia". Below, I will review his ideas:

1.3.1.1 SOCIAL DEVELOPMENT PUSHED FORWARD BY TECHNOLOGY WAVES

Toffler held the view that technology was the driving power for the progress of human society. In his eyes, there always six interrelated spheres in all civilized societies, technology, sociology, information, biology, power and psychology. These six spheres constitute the essential elements of the social nature, with the integration of all social processes and aspects.

Interaction of the six spheres would result in the progress of human society. Basically, any significant change in technology would cause responding changes in the other spheres of the society. As a result, it would trigger a chain reaction with ripples passing through the whole social structure, pushing the society forward. The term "wave" was employed just to illustrate sharp social transformations brought by innovation of technology. A diachronic review of human history has revealed that it had turbulent waves piling or clashing each other in the past. Human civilization has gone through two waves, and now it is entering the third. The agrarian revolution which was an innovative change in human history, was the first wave, with the tool of the hoe as a symbol. More than 300 years ago, the industrial revolution that took place in the United Kingdom,which was the second wave, symbolically represented by assembly line production mode. In the 1950s, the social change caused by key breakthrough in technology and knowledge is the

---

1   Bell, Daniel: *The Coming of Post-Industrial Society*, p. 534-535, Beijing, Commercial Press, 1986.

Third Wave of human society, marked with the dawn of the computer. The three waves mentioned above have pushed forward piles after piles, marking the past, present and future of human society. Nowadays, the conflict between knowledge wave and industry wave constituted the theme of social development. The second wave has adopted the six basic principles, namely, standardization, specialization, synchronization, concentration, maximization (infatuation with massiveness and growth), centralization of power; but they have brought a stagnation in the social development. On the other side the Third Wave uses principles, like intellectualization, diversification, miniaturization, individualization, decentralization, and Production-Marketing Integration, which will surely propel human society into an age of growth and prosperity. Toffler, with his concept of "wave" has predicted the future of social development with the combination of structure and process, highlighting inner linkage of unrelated affairs and trends, and foreseeing the consequence of technological innovation. Obviously, Toffler's view on social development belonged to scientific determinism, which is also a branch of historical socialism.

1.3.3.2 INDUSTRIALIZATION: IDENTITY OF CAPITALISM AND SOCIALISM

Toffler has discussed the issues of capitalism and socialism under the framework of his second wave concept, highlighting the identical characteristics of the two (identity); but he has left aside social systems, particularly the ownership of the means of production, His ideas will be given below.

1.3.3.3.1 Homology of Capitalism and Socialism

Only discussing the establishment of socialism from the angle of technology and industry, Toffler has argued that capitalism and socialism were outcomes of the Second Wave. In his eyes, there was no essential difference between the Russian, October Revolution in 1917 and the bourgeois revolutions like the American Civil War and the Japanese Meiji Reforms in Japan. All of these revolutions had taken with the purpose of industrialization and civilization according to the Second Wave. "The Revolution in 1917 was a copy of the US Civil War in Russia." The Revolution had occurred with the aim of industrialization rather than communism just as it was taken for. Having abolished slavery and feudal imperialism, the Bolsheviks, had put agriculture in the second place, speeded up industrialization. As a result, they had become the ruling party in the Second Wave."[2] Therefore, Toffler has blurred up the distinction between specific historical conditions, where the two social systems were established, and regarded them as different social forms that synchronically exist and belong to the same paradigm.

---

2   Toffler, Alvin: *The Third Wave*, p. 20. Beijing: Xinhua Press, 1996.

26   CURRENT GLOBAL IDEAS AND MOVEMENTS CHALLENGING CAPITALISM

1.3.3.3.2 Homogeneous Structure of Capitalism and Socialism

In an attempt to understand the structure of capitalism and socialism, Toffler has argued that, "six principles like standardization, specialization, synchronization, concentration, maximization (infatuation with massiveness and growth.), and centralization of power, were simultaneously applied in the two wings of industrial society – capitalism and socialism."[3]

It is so because: (1) Management of Taylorism which originated from capitalist society, which was not only praised by capitalist enterprisers but also warmly welcomed by Bolsheviks. Lenin had clearly claimed that Taylorism should also be applied in the socialist production. It can be seen that Lenin was also an industrialization advocator and an enthusiastic believer of it first, and then secondly a communist. (2) Not only in capitalist society the division of social labor had become more and more complicated, but also in a socialist society. The development of specialization reached the peak because socialists have elevated political propaganda into a special profession. As a matter of fact, Lenin was a politician who had advocated that experts should be the ruling class of the society. The mere difference is that the experts he mentioned should be "red", for he stressed that without the help of the experts, the masses could not go on with revolution. (3) Either in capitalist or socialist society, people are bounded by timetables that was identically formulated. They were required to work or lead such an ordinary life and plus giving a birth to a child in the same time. (4) Either in capitalism or socialism, the principle of concentration was widely applied in many aspects, such as energy, population, labor, education or economic organizations. Not only in capitalist conditions, monopoly brings the forth concentration, but also the presidents or managers in the socialist society hold the view that concentration is the necessary guarantee for production efficiency. Lenin was also an advocator of concentration because he had once stated that in Russia all the citizens should be cultivated into a big Syndicate-national staff. (5) Maximization (the more the better) is not only the value advocated by capitalism but also the aim to be achieved by socialism. Marx had advocated the combination of the scale expansion of industrial construction and maximization of material development.

What's more, Lenin, had spared no efforts to push forward the advance of big enterprises in Russia, believed that large enterprises, trusts and syndicates could maximize the utility of manufacturing technology in a large scale. Stalin, however, -with violence- had forced to advance industrialization in a large scale, which had resulted in escalation of ecological as well as social risks (6) It was the same strategy for both capitalism and socialism to push forward the industrialization by means of centralization. The discrepancy of the two lay in the following: in capitalist society, particularly the US have cleverly established the centralization in the

---

3   *Ibid.* p. 60.

form of legal Constitution and advanced it further by economic means through the central bank. However, in a socialist society, centralization was pushed forward roughly, with Russia going too excessively. If explored, the origin of which, lay in the mechanism of centralization by the state. Bureaucratic policy had born and grown herein. By the comparison above, Toffler has drawn the conclusion that the six principles were the common "program" and aim for both capitalism and socialism.

1.3.3.3.3 Identity of Capitalist Contradiction and Socialist Contradiction

In Toffler's eyes, though there indeed exist struggles between capitalism and socialism, it is merely a " minor struggle", but in the process towards the Third Wave, the struggle between the new civilization and the industrial civilization will be a "big struggle" a "supper struggle". Consequently, the conflict between capitalism and socialism will be lowered to a secondary position. They are both confronted with the issue to end the industrial society and enter the Third Wave. Therefore, what they are faced is the same contradiction. Currently, one side of the struggle was the defenders and beneficial owners of the old industrial society complex. They want to keep the social order. The other side is the advocator of the Third Wave. Numerous severe problems in the world today (food, energy, arms race, population, poverty, resource, ecology, climate, aging, urban disintegration, production necessity and, wages, etc.) are extremely difficult to solve in the existing structure of industrial society, and could only be tackled smoothly in the course of transformation towards the Third Wave. Finally, the struggle between the Second Wave and the Third Wave goes far beyond the struggle between capitalism and socialism.

1.3.2.3 THIRD WAVE: NEW SOCIAL FORM SURPASSING INDUSTRIAL SOCIETY

Toffler has argued that the occurrence of the Third Wave civilization would result in the convergence of capitalism and socialism based on series of totally new characteristics: (1) Knowledge becomes the source of wealth creation. Knowledge mentioned here refers not only to some common items like science, technology and education, but also other social symbolized products, such as information, data, imagery, attitude and norm of values, etc. "What is vitally important in contemporary economy is the rise of a new system for wealth creation. This system is based on brain (brainwork) rather than muscle (physical labor)."[4] (2) As knowledge becomes part of production factors, a capital revolution is triggered. Knowledge capital has turned out to be new form and intangible form of capital. (3) To meet the needs of various choices that customers make, technology

---

4   Toffler, Alvin: *Powershift*, p. 9-10. Beijing: Xinhua Press, 1996.

starts to change towards ingenious and adaptable production. Small-scale production enriches the varieties of the products. Componentization (individual order, small-scale production) is the characteristic of the new the production model, and it starts to expand into other fields as well. As a result, it brings revolutionary changes in the economic system: a shift from homogeneity to the extreme heterogeneity. (4) With the development of new economy, the ratio between flexible labor and inflexible labor, direct labor and indirect labor has changed significantly. What increasingly needed is staff engaged in unchangeable labor and in highly specialized technological spheres (5) With the increase of economic globalization and international competition, innovation is constantly becoming more important. Invention and innovation has become more and more important in the Third Wave. Under such conditions, the new conception had to embrace many fields like product, technology, arts and crafts, sales, finance, etc. Therefore, it is necessary to motivate people to inspire ingenuity and creativity, putting forward new ideas, and even break up conservatism (if necessary indeed). (6) Large-scale enterprises gradually tend to get smaller, while small-scale enterprises increasingly becomes multi-functionalized. (7) Due to the quick changes in the markets, the standard identical model becomes less important than flexibility and mobility. Instead, matrix organizations like Special Project Team, Profit Center, varieties of Strategic Alliances, Joint-venture Enterprises, and Multinational companies have started to display enormous vitality and vigor.. Among those new organizations, many of them are international groups belonging to not one but various nations –multinationals. (8) Complex problems occurring in the economic system need to be settled by means of integrated measures and specialized management. (9) Electronic information network is the basic facility, which the economic system of the Third Wave civilization is based on. The electronic infrastructure of the advanced countries is characterized by six aspects: man-machine interaction, mobility, transferability, connectivity, ubiquity and globalization. (10) Time becomes a key factor. Economy of speed, emphasizing efficiency, takes the place of scale economy.

All in all, in Toffler's eyes, the reason why the Third Wave can merge the two social systems lay in the following two aspects (trends): First. is the aid provided by technology to social development and its growth and propagation with the advance in technology which can be summarized as technicization of social development. When this real revolution occurs in high-tech countries, those still staying in the process of industrialization have become groups going against the tide. Therefore, with the progress of high tech, the Third Wave would merge the two systems. The second, lay in globalization of social development. On the basis of the world history – globalization- created by industrialization and marketization, unprecedented advance in technology and the new economy has accelerated historical course of globalization. Under such circumstances, it has become necessary to surpass the distinction of the two social systems, and merge them into one. "Globalism, or at least super-nationalism, is the natural representation of the new economy that needs to cross the borders in this rapidly developing process."[5] Consequently, Toffler has argued that the Third Wave provides a positive and revolutionary choice.

1.4. NAISBITT AND "INFORMATION SOCIETY"

Naisbitt, U.S. social predictor, divided human society into three stages, based on a society's reliance on information,: agrarian society, industrial society and information society. He has argued that the gap between the two social systems (socialism and capitalism) would bridge up on the basis of information prevalent in the society. At the same time, judging from the reforms made in the socialist economic system and adjustments in capitalist economic system, he has drawn a conclusion that the two social systems are heading towards privatization. His viewpoint can be summarized as follows:

1.4.1.1 MEGA-TRENDS IN FUTURE SOCIAL DEVELOPMENT

Based on his analysis of 'news hole', Naisbitt has discovered that information becomes increasingly important in the process of social development, and it is the United States leading us out of the industrial society into a new stage – information society. The term "news hole" refers to that the layout size of a newspaper cannot not be enlarged at will, but is fixed due to economic restrictions at a particular time. Therefore, when something new is being introduced, something could be subtracted or omitted. Therefore, the process of preserving and discarding the old is a reality reflected in social changes.

Naisbitt held the view that information society had started from the 1950s on the basis of two significant events that had globally impacted the social development. One was the significant adjustments in the employment structure, with the number of white-collar workers surpassing that of blue-collar workers for the first time in the United States in 1956, due to the development of technological progress. The other was the launch of satellites for the first time in the world by the former U. S. S. R. in 1957, opening a new era of global communication, and the concept of "the global earth village" coming into being. In the transition from industrial society to the information society, five important things must be born in mind: (1) Information society is the existence of real economy rather than abstract idea. (2) Inventions in telecommunication and the computer will greatly shorten the time to transmit information, which quickens the change process. (3) New information technology will be primarily applied to solve problems and tasks that the old industry could not overcome, and then gradually be utilized to create new activities, generate new methods and offer new products. (4) In the information

---

5   Toffler, Alvin: *Powershift*, p. 379. Beijing: Xinhua Press, 1996.

society,, basic skills, like reading and writing, would become even more important than ever. However, the current educational system increasingly deteriorates with the quality of students going down incessantly. (5) Technology of the new info era would not be absolutely safe. Whether it would be successful or not will be finally determined by balance of high tech and high touch. Thus, the negative effect of science and technology could be avoided, while the progress made in the field of science and technology should be utilized in the process of development for the benefit of mankind. Under such circumstances, information becomes the most important social resource, and "knowledge productive force has turned out to be the key factor that determines productive forces, competition capability and economic achievements. Knowledge industry has become the most important industry providing the vitally central resources, which is necessary for production."[6] Shortly to say, the tendency in the US towards development partly reflects that of the whole world. Regarding social development, the United States has regained its leading position in the world.

1.4.1.2 PRIVATIZATION: COMMON FUTURE OF CAPITALISM AND SOCIALISM

Based on his observation on socialist reforms and political adjustments in the welfare states, Naisbitt argues that privatization has become a global trend. Under such conditions, socialism would converge towards capitalism by means of market mechanisms. He has expounded that on the basis of the following two aspects. (1) Certainty of the emergence of free-market socialism: Naisbitt has held the view that reforms are going on in all socialist countries, and economy under the control of the state is bygone. This reveals that the traditional socialism disappears, which was caused by the following aspects: 1) Formation of a global economy and the process of globalization. In the course of economic globalization, any isolated state cannot preserve its closed and self-sufficient economy, but had to merge itself into the global economy, with no exceptions: capitalist or socialist countries. Due to the comparatively high-efficient economy of capitalist countries, they could better adjust themselves and have joined the world economic commonwealth. However, there are lots of problems in socialist countries. It is necessary for socialist countries to reform their structure so that they can better prepare to join the world economy. (2) Progress of new and high technology. Telecommunication helped in the dawn of a unified global economy and now has sped up its development. Financial institutes have become advanced leading departments in the global economy. Their progress was more closely associated with electronic technology rather than financial industry or service industry. Although the financial industry and service industry had existed for a long time in economic history, only after the advent of the telecommunication technology, could they improve a lot, and were able to do more than the financial institutions and service

---

6   Naisbitt, John: *Megatrends*, p. 14-15. Beijing: China Social Science Press, 1984.

institutions of the old days (3) Failure of centralization. Up till now, there was not any successful case for a centrally planned economy. In his eyes, a controlled economy led by a central authority was a catastrophe, at least in Stalin's time. Nearly everyone knows great strides were made in the world regions where policies were carried out in decentralized ways, like scattering economy, enterprise-independent economy and market economy. Nowadays, socialism, which once seemed to surpass capitalism, is strongly challenged and is facing an indecisive choice– reform or perish. (4) High costs in socialist welfare system. Nearly none of the countries whose social welfare was offered by the central government could afford those related heavy costs. And many of them were at their last gasp because of the heavy burden. Ministers and premiers in charge of social welfare are worried about the collapse of the economy. With the number of retiring people sharply increasing, warnings are clear about the increasing growth of public expenditures. People cannot not help asking, how could the government be responsible for the welfare of people without a deficit in the state bank or budget ? (5) Changes in manpower structure. Blue-collar workers were the foundation of the labor unions and socialism. But their number are decreasing now all over the world. Labor theory of value had led to the establishment of socialism, but its inception meant its end. Ratio of manpower in production tends to be zero in the future, and a new economic theories are needed. (6) Individuals' role has become increasingly important. The essential characteristic of the new information economy lay in the shift of the social orientation from the state to individuals. Computers has strengthened individual's power, but has weakened the role of the governments. With the deepening economic globalization, individual's role will be even more important than it had been at the era of industrialization. In Naisbitt's eyes: "it is really surprising to witness individual values are placed above the state or the collectivity and this is becoming true in socialist countries". He believed that the interaction between the six factors mentioned above have jointly led socialism to a dilemma: either re-structuring it or discarding it.

1.4.1.2 PRIVATIZATION OF WELFARE STATE

Observing the whole world, Naisbitt has held the assumption that the key factor causing the socialist countries and welfare states to turn to reforms lay in that they have adopted the successful models of the U. K., with the promotion of de-nationalization or privatization of state-owned enterprises and privatization of their stocks. While the reforms in socialist countries were going on, welfare states have set off a wave of privatization. In those welfare states, the basic change was the shift from centralization to private ownership. And these changes are generally summarized as follows: (1) shift from renting public real estate to promoting private real estate in housing (2) from medical service offered by the state to a variety of choices offered by private medical institutions; (3) from government control to market economy; (4) from welfare aids to job provision, (5) from government monopoly to enterprise competition, (6) from the state-owned enterprise to the private enterprise, (7) from the state-run enterprise to the individuals owning stocks in the large enterprises, (8) from the government social insurance plan to the private insurance and investment institutions for the older ages, (9) from heavy taxes to tax cuts or tax exemptions. Naisbitt has claimed that the development of capitalist private enterprises advocated by Social Democratic parties have indeed promoted the economic development.

In all, "The core of socialist economics is the government-owned means of production and government-controlled production. However, socialist countries all over the world are losing control.. Actually they are changing patterns of possessing means of production through privatization and leasing methods. Regardless of their outcome, these reforms are not socialism in a strict sense. For more than hundred years in the past, ideological competition in the industrial age has been that between Marxism and capitalism. Should we follow the capitalist road, or the Marxist road? But now, the industrial age is bygone and is behind us. Today an unusual re-construction and re-structuring is rapidly developing; we will hear more about 'Free-market Socialism'. Of course, this is not what socialism has strived for."[7] Obviously, in Naisbitt's view, the market economy is evaluated as equivalent to capitalist economy, while planned economy is equaled to socialist economy.

I can say that it is obvious that he could not see that the market and plans both are the ways of allocating resources.

1.4.1.3 INFORMATION SOCIETY: THE FUTURE SOCIAL FORM

In John Naisbitt's eyes, with a series of brand-new characteristics, information society could be a future social form. Its characteristics are summarized as follows: (1) Knowledge becomes an important resource, and knowledge production turns out to be a significant industry. In information society, knowledge production will be systematized, and will enhance the human brain. Nowadays, knowledge can be produced in a large scale, and its outcome is that it becomes the driving force in economic sphere. In this sense, information society will be a knowledge-based society. (2) Knowledge turns out to be the resource of value. At present, value of a product does not increase according to the increase of labor, but appreciated with the high content of knowledge in it. Therefore, Naisbitt argues that "'the labor theory of value' was born in the preliminary stage of industrial economy, and was bound to be replaced by 'the knowledge theory of value' established recently."[8] Information society will be an intellect-intensive society. The new rights will not be authorized to those who have the money in their hands, but to those who possess information. As a result, what works or matters in information society will

---

7 Naisbitt, John: *Mega-trends* 2000, p. 101. Beijing: Economic Daily Press, 1990.
8 Naisbitt, John: *Mega-trends*, p. 15-16.

be information rather than capital. (4) Information society will be a community focusing on the future. Agrarian society was centered mainly on „the past", and industrial society on „now", while information society looks forward to „future". In the information-based society, people will need to predict the future based on present. (5) In information society, work will focus on how to choose the right information rather than to provide information. Computers will be playing a great role in people's daily lives and their work. Therefore, information society will inevitably be the phase of social development after industrial society, and today we are living merely a transitional form in between industrial society to information society. And both capitalism and socialism will finally transform to information society.

It can be seen that Naisbitt has based his convergence hypothesis (socialism and capitalism converging) from his two "magical motive forces": scientific determinism and market economy.

1.5 RATIONAL FACTORS IN FUTURISM

Futurism can foresee some general trends of the social development in the process of predicting and designing the future development, which inspires people and possesses some warning significance.

1.5.1.1 THE RELATIONS BETWEEN SCIENCE AND TECHNOLOGY AND SOCIAL DEVELOPMENT

Under the conditions of new scientific revolution, it is significant to fully understand the social role of science and technology and coordinate the progress of science and technology with the development of society. Futurism presents us with useful materials as a reference to solve this problem, which embraces two interrelated aspects.

(1) Futurism reflects a keen awareness on the influence of science and technology on society.

As the outcome of human practice in recognizing and transforming the nature, science and technology can now more rapidly be converted into real productive forces, and consequently becomes a strong driving force for social development. Under the conditions of the new technological revolution, science and technology has became the primary productive force. Although Futurism has not scientifically revealed how science and technology turned to be the primary productive force in the social formation, it is clearly aware of the social value of science and technology, and suggests that social development should be realized through progress of science and technology. That is, 1) New industry structure based on knowledge and information should be the new economic engine, and high-tech industries should be swiftly promoted. With the advance of the new scientific revolution, knowledge and information becomes an important economic resource, and industries using advanced technological developments have become the new economic engine.

For instance, when dividing the process of social development, Bell has made a depiction of the trend of knowledge and information becoming an economic resource, with the belief that the pre-industrial society had directly exchanged with the primitive bare nature, industrial society has communicated with the processed world, while the labor object of the post-industrial society becomes knowledge and information. Then he has elaborated the significant effects of the new industry— with the labor object becoming knowledge and information— on the social development. 2) Measures should be taken to actively meet the challenge of information age through application of intelligence, ways to realize a shift in the economic growth mode —from extensive mode to intensive modes—. The new scientific revolution has made the means of labor symbolized by the labor tools change into the materialized formation on its own. Therefore, it has greatly improved the labor mode in human history. Futurism, however, has evaluated the origin and progress of the intelligent techniques for a significant trend of technological progress and social development. For instance, Toffler has pointed to: "machines in the second wave, most of which can run without any feedback", while " in the Third Wave, intelligent machines are quite different. They have sensors that absorb the information around, detect variation, and then accordingly adjust themselves. They are self-adjustable. The technological progress is revolutionary." 3) The strategies for social development should be centered on progress of science and technology and improving the quality of the labor. Therefore, education should be greatly improved. What restrains the development of the productive forces is cultural quality, production experience and labor skills. And comprehensive quality and all-round skills of laborers could be improved with the advance of science and technology. Science and technology provides more possibilities for the all-round improvement of laborers both physically and mentally. On this issue, the Social History School in France has also recognized the significance of the talent competition among nations in future development. Human quality issue was also noticed by the Club of Rome, emphasis on innovative research was declared in its meetings. It can be seen that Futurism precisely feels the pulse of the times that the new scientific revolution promotes social development.

(2) Futurism has raised the problem of evaluating science and technology

Science and technology is always placed in a certain social system, and in human history,it was always restrained by that social system. Meanwhile, the development of science and technology per se was also a process of progress from relative truth to the absolute truth.

But, the influence that science and technology makes in reality cannot be perfect. Therefore, it is a double-edged sword. As we can see the immense social influence made by science and technology, we should pay closer attention to its negative side as well. On this issue, the pessimistic Ecological School has paid substantial attention to global environmental degradation problems due to the incorrect use of science and technology. This school has advocated that the increasing problems in the spheres like culture, natural value, value of human being should be well handled and need keen attention with the background of rapid development in science and technology. However, even the optimistic Social History School, has not suggested a complete positive stance toward the social effects of science and technology. It has employed the value factor into the assessment of science and technology. As a result, Futurism has raised the problem of coordinating progress of science and technology with social development. This is depicted as follows. 1) A value system should be applied in evaluating the scientific and technological development. In the future, scientific and technological development tends to advance and accelerate without any limitation. Consequently, individuals will not be able to wisely and effectively decide their own fate. Humans should learn how to choose and control the technology available at that point of time, in case that millions of people would be threatened by the negative impact of the technology. For this reason, a yardstick—diversity and humanistic values—should regulate the evaluation on science and technological development. And just on this point, Toffler has emphasized, "The aim to make a regulation which is more humane, foresighted and democratic, overcoming the technological dominance is not the ultimate goal of the Social Futurism School. Our ultimate goal is to place that evolution per se under human conscious control." That is to say, humankind should integrate the measure of truth with the measure of value to evaluate technological progress. 2) Material civilization and spiritual civilization should be in harmony. The social development goes on in a historical process of continuum, so there should be not only great material progress but also great spiritual progress. Only with the combination of the two aspects, can we have a healthy society. Only in this sense, Naisbitt has raised the concept of ,, balance between high tech and high touch". He has suggested that:"High touch is to recognize the life-and-death power of the universe. High touch is pleasantly experiencing and transcending the mass, with a certain spirit higher and bigger." Thus, it becomes necessary for people to learn how to live a humane life. In fact, this implies that science and technology should integrate seeking truth, being good and perfect as a whole. 3) Human development should be the ultimate goal amidst the goals of social development, including progress of science and technology. Either the progress of science and technology or social development should be a human-oriented process, and should take liberty, human's all-round development as its ultimate goal. On this issue, the Club of Rome raised the concept of human-centered development, with the premise that human development should be holistically concerned, an all-round development should be promoted, and "neo-humanitarianism should be established. However, the Social History School put its emphasis on human liberation in their prediction and design of future society. They evaluate human alienation as the outcome of industrialization, and advocate harmonious human development which should be considered as the central aim in the future society,. It has also highlighted the significance of mutual communication. Futurism could not find the core reason behind negative influence of science and technology in human life, nor could it find the real ground behind human alienation. But the problems it has raised concerning the social development is indeed inspiring..

In short, only when the social value of science and technology can be put into full play and the negative effects of it could be avoided, then progress of science and technology and social development could finally be adjusted to co-exist in harmony.

1.5.1.2 HARMONIOUS DEVELOPMENT

Futurism has keenly advocated promoting sustainable development, and efforts to create a harmonious relationship between environment and development.

Natural conditions and ecological environment constitute an important part of the material base for social life. It is another significant subject how to effectively coordinate the human environment with development,and lead a path of sustainable development in future society. The concept of sustainable development originates in the intellectual process of reflection upon the relationship between the environment and development. And in the course of time it has attained a theoretical basis. As for sustainable development, Futurism has provided some significant enlightenment as follows.

(1) Problems should be dealt with a long-term perspective.

In the process of industrialization and modernization, seeking for short-term benefits but neglecting the long-term benefits has increasingly intensified the global contradictions between environment and development. Therefore, the primary demand for a sustainable development is that people should consider and settle those problems with a long-term perspective. The Meadows Group was primarily aware of this significant demand and raised the measure of time concept to settle the relation between global environment and development. The Social History School and the optimists have also seen the disadvantages of seeking benefits with a short-term perspective. For instance, Naisbitt has pointed out, "In the last ten years, the tensions between natural environment and non-renewable resources was also one of the factors that warned us on the risks of settling problems with a short-term perspective. Generally speaking, we have understood more profoundly than ever the long-term impact of our short-term activities. For example, most people can now understand that we have polluted air and water just for the short-term benefits, which will do harm to our life and environment observed from a long-term perspective. Currently, forestry companies in the United States have made plans to plant trees. It is quite obvious that if people just cut trees and do not plant them, our later generations will have no trees available."

(2) It is necessary to view problems from a global perspective.

The process of industrialization and modernization, causes global problems because people have just acted on the basis of their local interest and neglected holistic benefits, particularly overlooking the ecological system. Therefore, sustainable development concept also highlights that people should consider and settle problems with a global view in mind. The Club of Rome has evaluated and underlined a series of negative issues occurring in the process of social development in a "global view". It has applied theories and methods of system dynamics which is also used futurology researches. The Social History School views the occurrence and intensification of the environmental and developmental problems as a significant outcome of globalization, and advocates the significance of global cooperation. In the future, sustainable development could be realized only when local interest and common global interest could be dealt with a global perspective and a global partnership and cooperation mechanism could be established..

(3) For sustainable development, it is necessary to combine the measure of truth and the measure of value. The Social History School and the ecological school shares similar viewpoints on the environment-and-development issue. The main difference is that they focus on different aspects regarding the measure of truth and the measure of value. The Social History School regards technological development as the main means of coordinating environment with development. However, the technology they advocate and support is eco-technology. For instance, Toffler suggests that: "We are living at a time when ecological technological development progresses toward a brand-new stage; that is, we are advancing rapidly towards the super-industry. Only admitting this prerequisite, can we grasp the era we are in. And only accepting this revolutionary prerequisite, can we boldly imagine and predict the future." At the same time, they also attach concern over the measure of value. Naisbitt has argued that the shift from short-term consideration to a long-term consideration reflects the transformation of values. However, the ecological school, particularly the Club of Rome emphasizes factors like culture, value and human quality as the principal measures to coordinate environment with development. It has made a unique definition of "development" on the basis of the "neo-humanism" philosophy. The Club of Rome also admits that technology and its progress is necessary but this should be in a state

of balance. I think with the combination of the above two viewpoints, we can find effective ways of realizing sustainable development at the technological level.

In short, sustainable development could be ultimately realized, by combining short-term and long-term interests, local and global interests, and coordinating environment with development. During this process we should combine the value of scientific progress and the measure of value.

1.5.2 HISTORICAL LIMITATIONS OF FUTURISM

Restrained and influenced by a series of factors, there are several inexplicable contradictions in Futurism. Below, I would like to give some comments on them:

1.5.2.1 EMPIRICAL RESEARCH METHOD

Futurism has laid much emphasis on scientific methodology in predicting and designing the future social development, but their empirical method has some severe deficits.

(1) Futurism bases its theories on limited experience. In the process of predicting and designing the future, Futurism quite absolutely induces general rules from specific things according to limited experience, overlooking the complexity, long-term and integrated characters of social development. Specifically speaking, Bell's assumption of "central-axle" focuses on two points, technology and ownership. He has generalized the conversion of technology, and has applied that finding in social development, while ignoring that technology is just a branch of a social formation. And I can say that social development is restrained and controlled by a series of multi-faceted factors. In Toffler and Naisbitt's analysis of the "newspaper hole", they have established their prediction and design based on the newspaper content, ignoring the related problems in other spheres. If we restrict ourselves with newspaper content we cannot comprehensively reflect the objective process of the social development. In the entire history of social development, the information released in the best newspaper still has certain limitations. If one wants to obtain the in-depth or essential information, he/she should make his/her efforts to do some research, and employ several theoretical assessment methods. As for the model of the Meadows Group, it has divided the complex social system, even the global system into five factors in a quite simple way, ignoring the effects of the other factors. Although its model was established on the basis of system dynamics, it was an idealistic and a simple one. The conclusions drawn from it would inevitably quite limited. As for Khan's Great Transition Hypothesis, he has made a research on social transformations in the history of 400 years, which is a step further than the model of the Meadows Group. However, in the history of the social development, 400 years is also historically transient period. His hypothesis

also seems insufficient to explain the trends of social development in the future.

(2) Based on the empiricism, futurism has made a critique of the deterministic view of Marxist historical materialism. According to Marxism, a social formation is a complex organism, embracing numerous contradictions, like the productive forces and the production relations, the economic base and the superstructure. Amidst them, the productive forces determine the production relations; the economic base determines the superstructure. Futurism has often attacked historical materialism, ignoring the existence of the basic contradictions in contemporary society. If we take Bell for an example: (1) He has totally negated the objectivity of the social structure, and simply observes it as a conceptual map. He has argued: " social structure is not the 'image' of the real society, but the 'reflection' of a conceptual map. A conceptual map singles out special properties from a real world, and follows the common rules to classify and distinguish them. As the method of logical sequence, the conceptual map does not have the distinctions of truth or falseness, but only usefulness or uselessness." As a result, he has negated the objectivity of the social structure. (2) He has misinterpreted the determinism in Marxist historical materialism, labelling it as a single aspect economic determinism although historical materialism advocates interaction and counter action between the economic base and the superstructure of social formation. He has also equated a series of factors like education, profession, politics and religion, on the premise that there is no evidence to prove, which of them was the foremost and primary one. According to him all of them could be classified under interaction force. (3) He has also argued that thoughts have relied on the discovery of the language which could express basic facts to learn and discover nature. Therefore, he has negated the decisive role of human practice which is the main source in the formation and development of knowledge. Toffler has also advocated the same principle and put emphasis on randomness and chance, with the belief that they play a key role in the evolution of human history. For Toffler, it is impossible to clearly define which elements belong to the economic base, and which to the superstructure in a social formation; and all of them could change spontaneously at the same time. Therefore he had explained his stand as follows: "My viewpoint is quite different from Marxists who hold the belief that the alleged superstructure will also influence economic and technological bases. Although they admit there may be such a dynamic role, but the components of superstructure like ideology, law, values and religion are only reflection of the class status, and the class status is fundamentally determined by economy. Consequently, their theory is inevitably some kind of a circular argument. In short, economy and technology are necessary to directly or indirectly dominate the whole system this way or that. This is their viewpoint, which I cannot accept." Most futurists have advocated such arguments against historical materialism.

To put it in a nutshell, the empiricism is essentially a kind of subjectivism namely idealism. Therefore, in the process of predicting and designing of the future, we must combine particularity and universality and at the same time adhere to "observatory objectivity".

1.5.2.2 SCIENTIFIC DETERMINISM OF SOCIAL HISTORICAL VIEW

When interpreting social history, Futurism negates the existence of the basic social contradictions in a society, but extremely exaggerates the social role of science and technology. Although it seems loyal to the scientific determinism, it has finally turned to historical idealism.

(1) Futurism considers technology as the supreme yardstick when dividing social formations. As for the replacement of the social form, the Social History School, has attempted to negate Marxist theory on the social formations which is the core of Marx's historical materialism, and has employed technology as the primary and even as the only yardstick. It divides the social development in human history into three continuous stages without any difference in nature, using capitalism as a reference stage. If we review Bell for an example, he divides the human social development into three stages, namely pre-industrial, industrial and post-industrial society, discarding the basic social contradictions in them and especially the factor of ownership structures in particular. And he has argued that they were in a sequence based on the central-axle of production and their nature differs by the knowledge pattern prevalent in those stages. It can be seen that he has completely negated the distinction between public and private ownership in the primitive society, and classified the primitive, slavery and feudal societies under the pre-industrial society. He has underestimated the essential distinctions between socialist and capitalist societies, and placed them both in the category of industrial society. He has totally ignored the historical certainty of socialism/communism, and claimed the post-industrial society to be the destination of future human society. Apparently, his division lacks a scientific base. Then, he has regarded science and technology as the decisive motive force of social development: "The post-industrial society is organized around knowledge, which aims at the social management and guiding innovation and reform. In turn, it produces new social relations and a new structure. All of these must be politically managed.— as it is supposed to be— knowledge is indispensable to any society. What is different in the post-industrial society is the nature of knowledge itself. And what is of decisive significance to the decision of organization and the guidance to reform is to elevate the theoretical knowledge to a central position." Due to such an assessment, knowledge (science and technology) becomes an independent and dominant force transcending the basic social contradictions in a social formation.. Toffler and Naisbitt have also share that standpoint.

FURURISM

Different from others, Bell "clears up" the basic contradictions of capitalism by the argument that capitalist social structure has changed due to the new scientific revolution. As he had negated that socialism could replace capitalism; the result was the convergence of socialism toward capitalism. But, Toffler, has "adequately" affirmed the identity of two different social formations: capitalism and socialism. But industrial "universality" was established by the second scientific revolution. He used the notion of Third Wave instead of the industrial social wave, and pointed to the Third Wave as the prospect of the social development. He has argued that both capitalism and socialism would die and get merged in the Third Wave, which implies the convergence of capitalism and socialism.

However, when Naisbitt considers the direct influence of science and technology on the social development, although his starting point is to offer a solution to the "challenge" brought by scientific revolution in the economic sphere; he regards privatization as the most effective solution to all existent contradictions between capitalism and socialism. And he considers market socialism as the transitional phase in the socialist development course. As a matter of fact, his information society demands capitalist private ownership as the prospect of human society.

Therefore, the Social History School, based on the scientific determinism and convergence hypothesis, is generally a kind of idealist view on history. In fact, the social development is a natural historical process, as well. None, but the basic social contradictions in a social formation are the essential forces which push forward social development. The genuine mega-trend in social development is that the capitalism will inevitably fall, while the socialism will certainly triumph.

(2) Futurists have argued that science and technology are the decisive factor that detoriated the global environment and development. But they could not see that man-and-nature relationship is always under the restraint of man and man relations in the social formation. Behind environment and development degradation is the complex interest relationship between men and men. Especially, the problem of global environment and development is rather caused by social factors, the unreasonable international order and the world wide division of labor. They have all failed to recognize that greed for pursuing the surplus value predestined that the capitalist countries were inevitably using the strategy of killing the goose that lays the golden eggs. As a result, the environmental problems become a global problem. Observed from the appearance, the relationship between pessimists and the optimists seems like water and fire. However, both share the same theoretical base. They have all viewed science and technology as the decisive force that impacts global environment and development. The reason why opposite assumptions like "zero growth" and "no limits for growth" are raised lay in the purely technological factors stated as follows. (1) Believing that the resources are "limited" is considered as one of the factors that causes this crisis. On this point,

theorists advocating "zero growth" focus on the limits of the earth for growth, assuming that the limited natural resources and space could not support such a vast population, and a fast economic growth and also result in excessive pollution. They suggest that the current growth rate of population and economy should be maintained or even decreased, and strategies of zero or even negative growth should be adopted. But theorists advocating the assumption of "no limits for growth" believe that the natural resources are not a restricting factor for economic growth, instead the primary reasons are aspects like psychology, culture and society which restrict economic growth. For them associating the term "limit" with the term „resources" is not only inappropriate but also obviously wrong, because our knowledge on the scarcity of natural resources is limited. Therefore, the growth is not only possible but also beneficial. (2) Futurists have made different assessments on the role of science and technology. In the eyes of those who advocate "zero growth", science and technology can only delay the coming of the crisis, but could not settle the problem ultimately. If an adjustment cannot be made in the structure and function of science and technology itself, problems will get more and more serious. However, in the eyes of those who stand for "no limits for growth", humankind can find new resources and new usages for the current resources with progress of science and technology. "The most possible solution could be the existing and the knowledge of the future, we and our later generations will be able to get the necessary raw materials. And their prices will be much lower than any time in the past, compared with prices of other things and our total income."

It is obvious that the distinction between them is nothing but the specific technological operation, but in essence they follow the same course and point to culture when analyzing the problem of environment and development. However, the global problem is actually a kind of social problem, and it is caused by the irrational international economic order. It is expounded as follows. (1) Developing countries have become the production places of materials and primary products for developed countries. Excessive exploration intensifies the shortage of the resources and destruction of the environment. An example below is all too revealing. Currently, the developed countries, whose population constitutes 25% of the total world population, consumes 70% of the earth's resources; while the developing countries need to export resources in large scale merely for the payment of their debts. (2) The developing countries becomes a refuse dump. In the process of updating their industries and production structure, Western countries transfer the old "polluting " industries and equipment to the developing world, which are also resource wasting, much more energy consuming and which cause heavy pollution. All these result in expansion of the global problem of environment and development. For instance, in the 1970s, the US investment companies have invested 14.8% of their total investments to the domestic metallurgical and nonferrous metallurgical industrial enterprises, while 3.7% to the overseas enterprises.

A severe leakage accident has occurred in December 1984 in the Indian Bhopal pesticide factory, which was erected in 1969 by an US investment company. The accident has caused 2,800 deaths, and more than 200.000 people were poisoned. (3) But still the developing countries are being criticized as scapegoats by the developed countries in their hegemonic ecological problem discourses.

For instance, the weed remover cast by the US in the Vietnam War had severely destroyed the Vietnam's forest resources; and 20~30 years were needed to restore the coverings. Even more disastrous, the weed remover had changed human genes, which resulted a huge number of disabled people in Vietnam. In this sense, a general discussion about the "global problems" becomes an unavoidable choice to conceal the truth. Of course, in the socialist countries, there are also environmental problems, but they were generally caused by incomplete development concepts or lack of experience.

In short, it is indeed necessary for man to learn how to adjust the relationship between environment and development. All these problems can be completely settled if people could lead a sustainable development road. "However, it is not enough to remain at the level of awareness if the adjustment is to be carried out; it also demands a complete reform in the production modes, which have existed, and the whole social system that coexists with these production modes."

REFERENCES

- Daniel Bell: *The Coming of Post-Industrial Society*. Beijing: Commercial Press, 1986.
- Friedrich Engels: *Nature of Dialectics*. Beijing: People's Publishing House, 1984.
- John Naisbitt: *High Tech and High Touch*. Beijing: Xinhua Press, 2000.
- John Naisbitt: *Megatrends*. Beijing: China Social Science Press, 1984.
- J. L. Simon: *No Limits to Growth*. Chengdu: Sichuan People's Publishing House.1985.
- Alvin Toffler: *Powershift*.
- Alvin Toffler: *The Third Wave*. Beijing: Xinhua Press, 1996.
- Alvin Toffler: *Future Shock*.
- Alvin Toffler: *The Prediction and Prerequisite*. Beijing: International Culture Publishing Company, 1984.

CHAPTER II

NEO-LIBERALISM

1 *Revival of Neo-liberalism in the 1970s*
2 *Basic Ideas and Main Schools of Neo-liberalism*
3 *A General Evaluation of the Neo-liberalism*

CHAPTER TWO

INTRODUCTION

Neo-liberalism, a trend of thought in defense of the capitalist system, emerged in Western economics in the 1930s, when capitalism was shifting from the private monopoly to the state monopoly. Based on the laissez-faire principle, it has emphasized the spontaneous role; market plays in allocating resources on the basis of the private ownership, and opposes governmental intervention in economic activities.

From the 1950s to 1960s, the Keynesianism which has advocated government's intervention in economy turned had become the mainstream in Western economics, while the neo-liberalism was little known then. At the beginning of the 1970s, due to the failure of the government's intervention in economy, Keynesianism was under suspicion and attack. As a result, the Neo-liberalism had revived, and gained an important position in economics. The main schools of the neo-liberalism can be listed as follows: Hayek Neo-liberalism; Modern Monetarism, Freiburg School, Rational Expectation School and the Public Choice Hypothesis.

48 CURRENT GLOBAL IDEAS AND MOVEMENTS CHALLENGING CAPITALISM

2.1 REVIVAL OF NEOLIBERALISM IN THE 1970S

In the 1930s, the whole capitalist society was in a great depression. The classic economics with its laissez-faire principle was under suspicion. Economists and people in all the other fields were eager to find a prescription to save the capitalism. They had reflected upon the classical economics that was featured with unrestrained freedom and the liberal capitalism under the guide of the classical economics. Under such a background, there emerged two different academic camps in economics: the neo-liberalism and the Keynesianism schools. The former had emphasized that laissez faire as the core of its principle, and also highlighted the role of the market, "invisible hand", with the belief that the state or the government intervention in economic activities had to be as little as possible; while the latter, from the perspective of the crisis of the liberal capitalism, emphasized the role of the government's or the state's managing the "visible hand", suggesting that the government should intervene economic activities. Therefore, after the liberal capitalism had shifted to the monopoly capitalism, the dispute between the laissez-faire principle and the state's economic intervention turned out to be the focus in the social economy in the 20th century. It was in the process of this dispute that the neo-liberalism had revived in the 1970s.

2.1.1 NEO-LIBERAL REVIVAL AND ITS SOCIAL BACKGROUND

From the end of the 19th century to the beginning of the 20th century, the liberal capitalism had developed to the monopoly capitalism. The conflict between socialized production and the capitalist private ownership became intensified, with frequent occurrence of economic crises. The great crisis in the whole capitalist world from 1929 to 1933 not only greatly damaged the productive forces but also put an end to the laissez-faire assumption due to the serious crisis. This crisis was not only a significant turning point in the history of the capitalist economic development, but also an important turning point in the history of the bourgeois economics. Most bourgeois economists started to abandon the classical economics based on the laissez-faire principle, and turned to advocate government's intervention in economic and social activities. Among them, the British economist Keynes published his book The *End of Laissez-Faire* as early as in 1926, which shows that he had begun to give up the laissez-faire principle since then. Keynes attempted to testify that only with the aid of the state's adjustment to currency and credit, could unemployment and economic crisis in the capitalist society be diminished. After the end of the crisis in the 1930s, Keynes issued his masterpiece *The General Theory of Employment, Interest, and Money* in 1936, with the guidance of President Roosevelt's New Deal. He formulated systematical theories on employment and a series of proposals on state intervening economy. He completely broke away from the classical economics with his tit-for-tat hypothesis. This reform can be named as "Keynesian Revolution"[1] in the history of economics. Consequently, the combination of the Great Depression, The Roosevelt's New Deal and Keynesian Revolution made the Keynesianism the mainstream thought in Western economic and ideological fields for nearly 30 years after the release of *The General Theory of Employment, Interest, and Money*. And it was increasingly canonized with the economic boom after the World War II, while the economic liberalism was suffering a heavy hit.

On the other side, numerous economic liberalists had still stubbornly insisted on the laissez-faire principle based on economic liberalism. But they were not able to beat the drum for "laissez-faire" as they had done before; they had to admit that the state's intervention in economy was a necessary means for market economy. They began to come up with the novel look of neo-liberalism to obtain the room for survival, and kept a certain dialogue with the Keynesianism in a certain way.

The above statement shows that the neo-liberalism came into being in the settings of the crisis from 1929 to 1933; and with the emergence of Keynesianism. It emerged as a variant of classical economic liberalism in modern times, as well as the opposite of the theory of the state's intervention in the economy of the Keynesianism. Owing to the heavy disaster brought by the Great Crisis in the 1930s and people's reflection upon it, it had unwillingly accepted the suggestion of government's intervention in the economy based on Keynesianism. The efficiency of Keynesianism was obvious. During the World War II, all the countries involved in the war had employed war-time emergency controlling measures; and the government's control over economy turned out to be a significant measure of mobilizing human resources, property and materials. The government intervention tool had left a deep impression on the people and the governors of all involved countries. After the war, either the victors or the loser states were faced with the problem of economic reconstruction. Therefore, Keynesianism had gained a chance to spread wider. For nearly 20 years after the war, the Keynesianism and its paradigm as state's economic intervention had become an "effective medicine" to cure the contradictions of capitalism. When Keynesianism prevailed, the neo-liberalism had survived in the form of a small-scale theoretical exchange circle just like inharmonious music notes criticizing the government. However, later neo-liberalism – just like Keynesianism, — seized the opportunity of revival beginning from the 1960s to the 1970s, when the Keynesianism had become unpopular.

(1) The failure of Keynesianism in practice had become the trigger for the revival of the neo-liberalism. Keynesianism was faced with more and more criticisms after the 1960s, particularly in the 1970s when an economic crisis was

---

1   Stein, Herbert: *Presidential Economics: The Making of Economic Policy From Roosevelt to Clinton*, p. 12-13. Changchun: Jilin People's Press, 1997.

caused by the "government's malfunction" rather than "market malfunction". The Keynesianism seemed to need a self-examination in theory. However, this was an opportunity for neo-liberalism to rise. Before the 1970s, due to policies of the state's economic intervention, the economic development of all countries had revived rapidly, and also growth rates were higher. Therefore, the Keynesian economists had declared that the problems of periodical fluctuations and unemployment that troubled the capitalist economy had already been settled; the mansion of economics had been built. All the work to be done next was to do some small repairs or adjustments.

The Keynesianism has advocated the state's economic intervention because it has believed that the source of capitalist crisis lay in the inadequate demand. And the scant demand was caused by three psychological rules, namely, the psychological consumption orientation had led to inadequate consumption need; the psychological flow preferences and low profit expectations of capital had resulted in insufficient investing need. Therefore, to settle the problem of scant demand and to promote adequate employment, it was necessary for the state to "manage the demand". The state's economic intervention included: expansionary fiscal policies, expansionary income policies and expansionary currency policies, by means of issuing additional currency, and even adopting a policy of appropriate inflation –neglecting some of its defects— to stimulate consumption and trigger investments. Although in theory the Keynesianism had highlighted the alternate use of expansionary and deflationary policies, but in practice the priority was given to the expansionary policies. The implementation of long-term expansionary policies had caused a delay in current surplus production crisis, but had intensified the future surplus production crisis. Thus the new economic crises during, 1969-1970, 1973-1975, and 1980-1982, were featured as stagnation and were also the outcome of expansionary policies. The Keynesianism became inefficient and invalid to tackle the stagnation problem, which led to a dilemma: the expansionary policy had intensified the inflation, while the deflationary policies pushed economic stagnancy. This difficult economic situation led to distrust in Keynesianism. The "government's malfunction" were seen as the result of Keynesianism. Voices were being raised to change the mode of state intervention in economy, namely, to adopt new methods that could directly impact the production, structure, efficiency, and productivity. There were more and more appeals for economic growth.

(2) The reason for the failure of Keynesianism lay in the drawbacks of its theories. When the problems in the policies occurred, the theoretical crisis had also surfaced. Between the end of 1960s and the beginning of the 1970s, the economic liberalism defeated by Keynesianism had sought for self-improvement, and gradually formed its own contemporary complete system. It has started to ascend in the United States under the name "new classic revival"; and directly opposed Keynesianism.

In the 1940s, Philips Curve, a Keynesian analytical tool had provided governments a convenient and a simple mechanism to manipulate the economy. This curve had revealed the stable negative correlation of the variants between unemployment and wages: high unemployment rate with decreased wages, while low unemployment rate with increased wages. To maintain long-term production growth, it had set the disparity between the price and the wage costs as constant; therefore, the variant of wage had equaled that of price. As a result, the relationship between unemployment rate and the inflation rate (price fluctuation rate) was stable when one moved up, the other should go reverse. Under the guidance of this theory, the policy maker could adjust the combination values between unemployment and inflation according to needs when necessary, which had provided a ground for the realization of expansionary policies.

In 1961, John Muth had put forth his "rational expectation hypothesis". In 1967 and 1968, Phelps and Friedman have respectively raised their concept as "natural rate hypothesis", which had greatly enriched the rational expectation hypothesis. According to natural rate hypothesis, there was not a stable relationship between inflation and unemployment as, one up, the other down. What really related to unemployment was not inflation itself, but the unexpected inflation. And only the unexpected inflation rate could impact the unemployment rate. The occurrence of "stagnations" had well proved the correctness of that judgment. This theory had implied that the neo-liberalism had found the drawbacks of Keynesianism, and intensified its systematic criticism on Keynesianism. Later, Lucas' rational expectation economics formally mounted to the historical stage in the 1970s, which gave a fatal hit to the Keynesian economics. Lucas had pointed out that, numerous Keynesian macroeconomic models including Philips Curve were not established on the basis of micro-economics. As a matter of fact, the decision of most macro-economic variants (consumption, investment) mainly relied on the expectation of the economic outcomes. But, the macro-economic models of Keynesians had treated the expectation in an arrogant way with arbitrary choices of variants which seemed to be expectations neglecting the real expectations themselves. Most of the government intervention policies had changed the way in which individuals formed their expectations. But the substitutes applied in the macro-economic models had no solutions or tools to interpret such changes in real expectations. Therefore, these models could not be used to assess and analyze the influences effected by different economic policies. This was the well-known Lucas Criticism. In a certain sense, the Lucas Criticism can be regarded as the neo-liberal attack on the Keynesianism and as a symbol of rising neo-liberalism. If the stagnation in the 1970s was the cause of the failure of Keynesianism in practice, the rise of the neo-liberalism in 1970s had led to the collapse of Keynesianism in theory. Finally, Keynesianism was faced by a real crisis. In the 1980s, the occurrence of global privatization wave and the trend of decreasing the government's economic intervention may be regarded as other symbols of the revival of neo-liberalism.

(3) The economic crisis in 1970s, particularly between the 1973 and 1975, became a significant turning point in the development of the state monopoly capitalism, as well as a turning point in the development of Western economic thoughts. The economic crisis was considered as the outcome of implementing Keynesianism, which provided a real economic basis for the revival of the neo-liberalism.

After the Second World War, three global organizations were established to support the new international economic order on the basis of government intervention policy of Keynesianism, namely, General Agreement on Tariffs and Trade (GATT), International Monetary Fund (IMF) and International Bank for Reconstruction and Development (IBRD). In the post-war era, those brand new international economic coordinating organizations had to a certain degree provided supports to those countries which needed a stronger development. But later it was increasingly difficult for these institutions to push forward further development of the main capitalist countries. The reason had rested in the U.S. dollar-centered Bretton Woods System, which was established after the World War II. This system had adopted the principle of "two hooked, one fixed" (The dollar value was hooked to the gold reserves, and currencies of other countries were hooked to U.S. dollar; and foreign exchange rate system was a fixed one). Consequently, the U.S. economy had such great influence on the others in the world that "when one was booming, all the others were flourishing by, and vice verse." Therefore, the "Triffin Dilemma" had emerged in the international economic field. At the end of the 1960s and the beginning of the 1970s, the U.S. dollar had spread to all over the world without any restriction. And the consecutive balance of payment deficits of the United States had resulted in the increasing decline in gold reserves. All of these had caused U.S. dollar lose its stable foundation, and this effect had pushed "energy resource crisis", especially oil crisis with OPEC countries involved. Finally, it was difficult for the U.S. dollar to maintain its leading position as a currency in the old system, and thus the Bretton Woods System had collapsed. The international financial institutions started to adopt floating exchange rates, which apparently negated the government's intervention in economy.

At the beginning of the post-war years, all the warring countries were faced by economic reconstruction. In 1950s and the 1960s, the Western economies went through two booming decades, and the annual average growth rate had reached as high as 4% to 5%. But the booming economy was based on the cheap oil and raw materials from developing countries. Thus, once any problem occurring in the field of basic resources, Western countries, like being placed on the crater, were threatened by a potential economic crisis at any time. At the beginning of the 1970s, the oil crisis like the prima-cord had worsened the reproduction conditions. Shortage of some important resources and sharp increases in their prices had caused a shift in the economic contradiction: as from sale (demand) to production (supply). With the collapse of the Bretton Woods System, contradictions accumulated in the speedy development of the advanced countries came out markedly. The growth of Western economies had dramatically slowed down. Economic stagnations were wide-spread which were featured as high rate of inflation, high rate of price increases, high rate of employment, and low or negative rate of economic growth. Consequently, international trade and finance were plunged in a great chaos. Take the United States for an example; in the period of stagnation between 1973 and 1982, the annual average growth rate of GDP was 2.4%, unemployment rate was 5.3%, the growth rate of CPI was 9.4%. And, in the crisis between 1979 and 1982, the unemployment rate was as high as 9.7%. At the beginning of the 1970s, there was only a slight rise of the production efficiency; between 1968 and 1973, the annual average increase in efficiency, was 1.3% And after 1973, the growth rates had slowed down markedly; the annual average growth rate between 1974 and 1979, was 0.7% and only 0.2% in 1980. Accordingly, the average profit rates of enterprises tended to decline, and this trend was obvious in the 1970s. Between 1960 and 1979, the average profit rate of U.S. companies was 13.7%, while between 1974 and 1979, the number was merely 9.7%, and in 1980 it had declined to 8.3%. Due to such a decline in profit rates, the bourgeoisie started to push governments for new intervention measures to stop that trend. Since the crisis was caused by general supply, the policy of "demand management" advocated by Keynesianism was naturally attacked and rejected. The neo-liberalism, which was featured in the policy of "supply management", seized that opportunity.

The Keynesianism was out of date. Thus, the neo-liberalism marked with laissez-faire and opposing state economic intervention started to enumerate the drawbacks of the Keynesianism; with an image of new capitalist "redeemer".

2.1.2 THEORETICAL ORIGINS OF NEO-LIBERALISM

The neo-liberalism was the regress of classic economic liberalism in the 20th century. It has inherited the principle of liberalism, and ascended by opposing Keynesianism. In general, the theoretical origin of the neo-liberalism was still classic economic liberalism of Adam Smith, but now his ideas were incorporated into several new thoughts. On the one hand, it employed micro and mathematic methods in analysis; on the other, it applied economic theories to all aspects of social life. It strived to interpret all the historical and real phenomena through its theories and political discourse. Grasping the theoretical origin of the neo-liberalism can be helpful to take a further step in the study and analysis of neo-liberalism and reveal its revival in the 1970s.

2.1.2.1 NATURAL ORDER HYPOTHESIS OF PHYSIOCRACY SCHOOL

It is generally accepted that the traditional economic liberalism was established by M. Quesnay, a French physiocrat, but it was actually set up by Legendre, a French merchant, in the 17th century. Colbert, the French Chancellor of the Exchequer of Louis XIV had met Legendre and raised the question: "What can be the best measure to protect the French commerce?" Legendre had answered, "Laissez faire, Laissez-passer." Boisguillebert, founder of the French political economics, was the first to propose it as an academic term.

The middle of the 17th century was the initial stage of the development of the classic political economics. At that time, the capitalists had not yet completed the primary accumulation. To oppose the fetters that restricted the bourgeois growth, like privileges and monopolies of feudalism, the rising bourgeoisie had raised the slogan of "laissez faire", and advocated "natural order", opposing state intervention in economic activities, and thus attempted to test the everlasting natural law as the dominant factor in economy. State intervention could hinder "natural order" which manifested their will to promote greater development of capitalist economy. The new bourgeois had opposed state intervention in economy, which reflects that they demanded to take the historical stage as a new independent force. Thereafter, the capitalist economy and society had focused on how to establish a "natural order", and the development of human society started to enter a new stage with the backdrop of "liberalism".

In the 1750s, Quesnay, founder of the physiocracy, came to the fore and thoroughly investigated economic liberalism. He comprehensively reviewed economic issues on the basis of "natural order" assumption. Physiocracy had occurred when the social material conditions were quite solidly established. Physiocracy was also the economic origin of economic liberalism.

Its whole theoretical system was established on the basis of the "natural order" assumption. When Dupont de Nemours, the most influential member of the physiocracy, had defined physiocracy, he had clearly pointed out: "physiocracy is nothing other than a theory about natural order." The assumption of "natural order"[2] had originated from natural mythology and natural law philosophy. The physiocracy school had applied them to study economic activities. Quesnay had argued that; "natural order" (he also named it as "natural law") provided "rules for all actual events" and "rules for all human behavior". He had asserted that economics was a supreme science based on behavioral institutions, the "goal" of which lay in "seeking to maintain the expenses of human society re-producible and sustainable, and seeking that expenses realize the highest possible re-production."[3]

---

2   Ji Taoda: *Physiocracy*, p. 33. Beijing: Commercial Press, 1963.
3   Quesnay, F.: *Selected Works of Quesnay's Economics*, p. 245. Beijing: Commercial

Therefore, Quesnay had established the goals for political economics, and focused on revealing the objective economic laws that determined capitalist production and reproduction in order to promote the growth of the national wealth. In fact, he had interpreted the capitalist production as the production of natural form. It is noticeable that the physiocrats called themselves "economists" and distanced themselves from the term of "political economics" since the term "political economics" was employed by mercantilism. Mercantilism had employed this term to emphasize state intervention and management in industrial and trade activities. The purpose of it was to increase national wealth and the amount of gold and silver coins through political-governmental intervention, while the physiocracy had employed the term "economist" to demonstrate that the intervention, restriction and management by government could not make the country rich and strong. On the contrary abandoning state intervention to natural order respecting and considering the nature of economy could prosper the country.

What the economists should do was not to seek for regulating laws for different economic sectors, but protecting that natural laws; natural order and right of liberty should not be not violated, which could lead to the goal of prosperous nation.

After "natural order" assumption was put forth and expounded, the laissez faire thought had become the mainstream in social economy and activities, and had greatly influenced the regulations and implementation of policies. In the first half of the 18th century in Britain, in two different times, people had disputed the laissez faire thought. One had occurred in the beginning of the 18th century. It was about the trade policy against France, centered on whether loosening or strengthening the existing restrictions and controls on trade with France. Which could serve better the interest of Britain? Both the parties in power and opposition were involved in the dispute. The other dispute had emerged in the middle of the 18th century. That was about the internal mechanism of international economic automatic balance, and it went on mainly in the field of economics academia, among scholars and celebrities from Britain, France and Germany. They had debated whether there indeed existed a "natural" mechanism, which made state intervention in economic activities unnecessary. Interestingly, that dispute had ended up with the failure of the laissez faire economic thoughts. It was not until 1776, *An Inquiry into the Nature and Causes of the Wealth of Nations* by Adam Smith was published that the laissez faire economic thought was established on a more solid and complete theoretical base. And till the mid-19th-century, laissez faire economic thought had dominated the economic policies of the British government.

Press, 1979.

2.1.2.2 "ECONOMIC MAN" ASSUMPTION BY ADAM SMITH

The core of Adam's laissez faire economic thought was on natural equilibrium, namely theories like human nature based on self-interest, "economic man", and "invisible hand" in the markets. Till today, the assumption of "economic man" is still the theoretical prerequisite of mainstream economics, particularly of microeconomics. Smith had illustrated specifically the human nature of self-interest in his book *Theory of Moral Sentiments*. In his eyes, the motivations dominating human's behavior were self-love, compassion, desire for freedom, justice, labor habit and exchange tendency. "Self-love" meant "desire of benefits for oneself", namely egoism on the basis of self-interest: And "compassion" represented men's altruism to benefit the public. The two motives in human nature had always accompanied each other. However, according to A. Smith, the contradiction between egoism and altruism should not produce unfavorable outcomes. Actions of egoism should not harm the society; neither should they cause social conflict and chaos. On the contrary, they should lead to the social cooperation and promote social benefits and that was indeed possible. The reason lay in that there is always a mutual restriction and natural balance between human motives; and exchange tendency was an important and indispensable motive of humans.

In a society where there existed labor division and private ownership, exchange was necessary, and the two sides exchanged commodities at their own will. Because everyone was a best judge of his own benefit, when they sought for their own interest driven by selfishness, they had to concern about others' benefits because in this way they also cared for their own benefits. Therefore, exchange would not harm one part but benefit another part. If there was an exchange, it was reciprocal. Thus, exchange tendency turned out to be an intermediate between the two basic motivations of humankinds, egoism and altruism. If we make a further analysis, we would draw the conclusion that division of labor would be finer because the exchange occurred at the will of the two sides and it was mutually beneficial; the finer division of labor would increase the social wealth. Finally, not only the goal of individual's maximized profits could be achieved, but also public interests could be realized at the same time, so that a natural order in human society comes into being with balanced egoism and altruism and harmony of individual interests and public benefits. On this basis, Smith had put forth the notions of "economic man" and "invisible hand" to distinguish a person with both egoistic and altruistic behaviors.

"Economic man" referred to a person who engaged economic activities and followed the universal mode of behavior; the behavior was determined by basic human motivations as: "sole purpose of seeking for profits". The "invisible hand" originated from the human nature of selfishness, such as; seeking for "self-interest" and "individual interest and sensual passion", which could motivate and regulate individuals' activities. This motive force was independent from the control of individual's original will and sentiments. It coordinated individual interest and public benefits, and consequently produced natural balance or natural order in the spheres of ethics, economy, politics and even society. "An invisible hand leads them to distribute life necessities equally to all citizens just as they equally share the land, unconsciously increasing the social benefits, and providing living materials for growing population."[4] This "invisible hand" referred to the instinct and nature of selfishness. With the nature of selfishness, "those, using capital to support industry for the mere purpose of pursuing profits, will naturally make their efforts to maximize the value of the product in the industry, he has invested. In other words, to exchange the largest amount of money or other goods[5]. "On the occasion of planning his own interest," as in many other cases, led by an invisible hand to reach a goal that was no part of his conscious intention. Nor will he harm the society because things occur against his will. By pursuing his own interest, he will promote benefits of the society more effectively than he does when he really intends to."[6] The first invisible hand (self-concern) dominates the "economic man's" behavior, while the second invisible hand (competition process) brings him beneficial results. In the capitalist society, "economic man" is represented by the individuals or the benefit group, while the "invisible hand" is externalized by the supposed "market mechanism". Based on the hypothesis like: natural balance, "economic man" and "invisible hand", Smith coined the terms, like "natural pricing" and free trade, and made a new interpretation on the role of the state. Thus, he was the first to interpret social activities with the laissez-faire principle, and turned out to be the father of various laissez-faire theories of later generations.

After Smith, trends of the laissez-faire thought based on the hypothesis of "economic man" have got enriched and advanced, and numerous theoretical schools came into being, like British Cambridge School, U.S. Institutional School, German historical School, Austrian Marginal and Sweden Lausanne School, etc.

All of them may be regarded as representatives of traditional economic laissez faire. No matter what changes in their analytical methods or in their basic viewpoints compared with the traditional economic laissez-faire; their basic starting points and political tendencies are based on the principles of "laissez faire". Their features display the following two aspects: on the one hand, their research on economic problems is mainly isolated from the capitalist system, which conceals the nature of the capitalist system; on the other hand, the numerical analysis of the internal economic linkage of the capitalism is emphasized, and some scientific conclusions are drawn on the general rules of economy.

---

4   Smith, Adam: *Theory of Moral Sentiments*. p. 230, Beijing: Commercial Press, 1997.
5   Smith, Adam: *An Inquiry into the Nature and Causes of the Wealth of Nations* (Volume 2), p.. 27. Beijing: Commercial Press, 1994.
6   *Ibid.*

2.1.2.3 INHERITING AND INTEGRATING RICARDO AND SMITH

Generally speaking, we can suggest that neo-liberalists had both inherited and integrated Smith and Ricardo's Modern Economic Thought in the conditions of the new economic era. During the period between late 19th century and the early days of the 20th century, the "laissez-faire"; free competition capitalism started to transform towards monopoly capitalism. After Adam Smith had established the principle of "laissez faire", and David Ricardo had further developed it, vulgar economists have developed it a step further, and finally, Marshall transformed it into the New Classic School. The "laissez faire" principle has gone farther and farther away from reality, and vulgar economists have discarded almost any kind of scientific study. Finally, this theory totally turned out to be a tool in defense of the rule of the bourgeoisie.

However, they had to pay attention to the emerging monopoly phenomenon and started to integrate competition and monopoly into their research. Among the scholars, two were the most influential. One was Madam Joan Robinson, British economist, who wrote *The Economics of Imperfect Competition* (1933). The other was Edward Chamberlain, U.S. economist, who wrote *Theory of Monopolistic Competition* (1933). Thus, the traditional concept and analytical methods were negated, which has partly shaken the foundation of the traditional economic laissez faire.

Thus Neo-liberalism was systematically established in the 1930s, when the traditional economic laissez faire policies have collapsed. That was also a time when the Keynesianism rose to serve the monopoly capitalism. Under the pressure of the current reality, the neo-liberalists had to revise their standpoint on the government's intervention; while the traditional economic laissez faire had completely negated that. On the one hand, they admitted that it was necessary for the government to intervene in the economy; on the other hand, they followed the traditional economic laissez-faire principle again in defense of the capitalism, which has entered the monopoly stage. In 1938, the neo-liberalists held an international conference in Paris for the first time, and established the economic creeds of the Neo-liberalism. This conference was known as Lippman Academic Seminar. W. Lippman, an American economist, in his book Free City proposed those principles that not only suited economic laissez faire but also was in favor of the state monopoly capitalism. Thereafter, the development of the Neo-liberalism was generally along Lippman's route, although it is hard to guess the real strength of that influence.

2.2 BASIC IDEAS AND MAIN SCHOOLS OF NEOLIBERALISM

There are many schools of neo-liberalism, and they have manifold political advocates. Based on how much they return to traditional laissez-faire principles and their political ideas, neo-liberalism can be divided into three schools, namely extreme neo-liberalism -the neo-liberalism of Hayek and Modern Monetarism-; mild neo-liberalism -the Freiburg School-, and innovative neo-liberalism -Rational Expectation School, New Property Right School, Public Choice School-. Although there are many schools of Neo-liberalism, and they have different origins, they are all based on Say's law of "production automatically determines demand". Thus their basic ideas share some common features.

Common Features of Neo-liberalism:

(1) They all believe in the spontaneous adjustment of the market and the rationality of laissez-faire market economy. In their view, the capitalist market economy is perfect, and it is able to properly distribute resources. The market, as the intermediate between the consumer and the producer, can transmit the signal from the consumer to the producer, and the competition between producers can not only effectively distribute various resources, but also maintain prices at a suitable level. The market mechanism plays a decisive role in properly distributing production elements. Thus, neo-liberalists adopt the laissez-faire policy to develop the economy coordinately, and they oppose the government economic intervention by Keynesianism.

(2) They praise the advantages of the private enterprise system. Neo-liberalists hold the belief that the private enterprise system offers great advantages, and advocate giving adequate liberty to private economic activities. In their eyes, the adjusting role of the market is based on the private enterprise system, and private ownership is the prerequisite of the competition system, and only the private economy is internally stable, because the driving force of economic development lies in the individual's pursuit for profit, and private ownership can stimulate the individual to be active, innovative and responsible. Only in this way can the pricing mechanism effectively distribute resources in the process of competition, and as well raise the economic efficiency. Therefore, Neo-liberalists claim that sustainable economic development is achievable within the framework of the private ownership, with the belief that private ownership is the perfect system in the human history. Any non-capitalist economic system and private ownership can do nothing but restrict the individual's dynamic functions, which is not good for economic development. And only based on the constant development of the private ownership, can people make their life wealthy and happy.

(3) They oppose government's intervention in the economy. They hold the view that under the state's intervention in economy, the market cannot transmit information effectively, which restricts private economic activities. These results not only decreased economic efficiency but also damage democracy and violate individual rights. They also believe that the state's intervention in economy cannot smooth away the obstacles in economic development, but holds back self-reforms and self-adjustments in the market economy, based on the assumption that only the competition in the "natural order" can bring about a prospered economy. On the other hand, Neo-liberalists do not completely reject the state's intervention in economy, and argue that the intervention should be diminished to some extent. The mode of intervention should be changed, and all possible means should be used to create necessary conditions for the market economy to run successfully.

(4) They advocate market competition, and oppose monopoly. Neo-liberalists believe that monopoly is detrimental to liberty. To give full play to the market, monopoly must be rejected. Thus, it is necessary to create suitable conditions where large economic organizations can run a free competition. However, they equate the trade unions with monopoly economic organizations, and claim that not only the large enterprises but also trade unions are monopoly organizations in the labor market. The trade union with its monopoly status increases the wages to a level which is much higher than that in a free competition state, which would hinder the capitalists from investing. As a result, they have concluded that trade unions are a "very dangerous" monopoly element, and an obstacle in the free market economy, while monopoly capital is of no harm. Since it is impossible to eliminate monopolistic enterprises, it is better to keep the monopoly capital, but suppress the trade unions.

(5) They insist on the sound fiscal discipline in the economy, and oppose the welfare state system and inflation. The alleged sound fiscal discipline refers to budgeting the expenses according to the income: reducing expenses as well as taxes to make both ends meet each other. Reducing the expenses means to cut off the part used for the welfare. Nearly all the schools of Neo-liberalism are against the "welfare" state system. Neo-liberalists believe that the welfare system does no good for free competition, but encourages people to be lazy. However, it is interesting that many capitalist countries actually have adopted the welfare system for economic growth and also to protect private ownership, alleviate class confrontation and conflicts. It is obvious that the Neo-liberal ideas are quite ironic. At the same time, the Neo-liberalists are strongly against inflation, with the belief that it is more harmful than good, on the basis of which they attack the inflationist policies of Keynesianism. However, various schools of Neo-liberalism hold different views on the causes and treatment of inflation.

2.2.1 EXTREME NEO-LIBERALISM

Extreme neo-liberalism refers to the school that strongly advocates restoring the laissez-faire tradition, and opposes government intervention in economic activities. Ideas and policies which this school puts forward have a strong idealistic color.

2.2.1.1 BASIC CONCEPTS OF HAYEK'S NEO-LIBERALISM

Friedrich August von Hayek (1899-1992) was a well-known contemporary liberal economist and philosopher. His thoughts on economics belong to the extreme economic liberalism. He has opposed against all kinds of intervention by the state in economy, and advocated the free market economy under the policy of competitive private currency. Hayek based his study on the method of "value judgments" rather than empirical analysis, and his study has aimed at free market economy under the conditions of private ownership, non-nationalized monetary system and equal opportunity. In his view, a better society must be one that respected and preserved the social system, under the principles and mechanisms described above. The fundamental way to achieve this aim was to get rid of ideological shackles, and idol worships, as well as "loyalty" to those idols either new or old, and instead act according to the "value norms" of his neo-liberalism.

This judging criteria should be the "personal liberty above all else." Thus, it was natural for Hayek to define the aim of economic research in his own way. In his view, researches using the mathematical method to generate numerical values have merely produced abstract results, and could not provide any useful solutions to settle economic problems in practice. Based on the above belief, Hayek made his description of the methodological norms for scientists, scholars and writers. He suggested that they should all be able to think and research independently and opposed to those who had no idea about the significance of their work or the meaning of "liberty". The superiority of economists over natural scientists lay in the fact that economists are politically sensitive, principled and should be independent from rulers. This was the key reason why Hayek has often emphasized that economics should be a science of ideals, and the supposed "ideal science" was just the one which serves private ownership.

Hayek's concepts on neo-liberalism were elaborated mainly in his four works, *The Road to Serfdom*, *The Constitution of Liberty*, and *Studies in Philosophy, Politics and Economics* and *Law, Legislation and Liberty*, which were published respectively in the 1940s, 1960s and 1970s. The four works reflect high praises for the private enterprise system and free market economy, but strongly opposes socialism and planned economy, arguing that the planned economy would finally lead to "slavery". He classified socialism, feudalism and fascism together, and defined them as "extremism". In 1988, he issued his last and most popular book, *The Fatal Conceit: The Errors of Socialism*, to summarize his thoughts opposing Unitarianism, he had pursued all through his life. He was strongly against the economic policies of Keynesianism, arguing that the policy of equally redistributing the income by any organization reflects the unfairness of extremism. Therefore, an ideal and fair social system should be established from the perspective of ethics to maintain private ownership. However, it was interesting that Hayek was awarded the Nobel Prize for Economics in 1974, for his works on the monetary assumption and economic fluctuation hypothesis, and for his in-depth analysis of dependent relationship between economy, society and system. But in fact his works were based on the "balance" order idea which originates from individual liberalism, in line with the laissez-faire advocated ever since Adam Smith. Therefore, Hayek's neo-liberalism actually rose after the 1970s, and he had the chance to popularize his ideas in his initial works.

(1) Hayek has highly praised the market economy based on individualism. In Hayek's view, the principle of the market order is little known, which is reflected by the universally accepted idea that "cooperation is better than competition". In his view, coordination in the "extended order"[7] (free market economy) depended on the ability to adapt to the unknown world, as competition was a process of discovery as well as natural evolution. In this process, humankind unconsciously adapts to the new situation, increases the production efficiency through further competition, and gradually forms market rules. Therefore, the market regulation is not consciously designed by a certain subject, nor is it started by an outer force.

In Hayek's view, the two systems, the private enterprise system based on individual liberty and free market system, has been the best choice for humankind. These systems exist on the prerequisite of the individual's liberty. First, the individual's liberty is essential for liberalism. In Hayek's eyes, a society is made up of free individuals, and the wealth in the society is created by individuals' work. Only if a person is able to opt freely for the means to achieve his goals, could social inventions and creation be guaranteed. Thus, the individual's fate should be in control of his own hands, and the state or others ought not interfere him. However, freedom is not limitless, but restricted with the laws. Furthermore, "only in the era of liberalism, the laws could be consciously developed, and it was one of the greatest achievements in history. The law was not only the protection of liberty, but also the embodiment of liberty."[8] "If a person does not submit to anyone but

---

7　　Hayek: *The Fatal Conceit: The Errors of Socialism*, p. 1, Beijing: China Social Science Press, 2000. "Expansion order" was the core concept that Hayek elaborated in his book *The Fatal Conceit: The Errors of Socialism*; the expression was originally the term "spontaneous order" means the laissez-faire market economy.
8　　Hayek: *The Road to Serfdom*, p. 82. Beijing: China Social Science Press, 1997.

to the laws, then he will be free."⁹ Therefore, all the actions of state must reflect the liberal spirit and the restriction of laws. Secondly, economic liberty could effectively guarantee the efficient distribution of resources. Hayek has argued that economic liberty is the most vital among all the liberties. "The economic liberty must lead human economic activities" It is the prerequisite of other liberties. And "the private ownership is the foremost condition of liberty"; " just because the means of production are in the command of independent individuals; that there is no one having full power to control us and thus we are able to decide what we can do in the name of ourselves."¹⁰ In his opinion, the superiority of private ownership not only lay in the fact that everyone has his freedom to choose his profession but also that it guarantees his political freedom. In Hayek's eyes, the economic liberty could only be realized in the market through competition, as the market mechanism played a good role in meeting the needs of humankind and distributing means of production for a variety of purposes. All of these are determined by the characteristics of the "economic man".

(2) Hayek has emphasized equal opportunity in free competition. The neo-liberalists believe that the production efficiency can be raised through the market mechanism which effectively distributes resources. But this concept is strongly opposed by the welfare economists, who argue that; when "efficiency" was highlighted, equal opportunity will be overlooked.

In Hayek's view, the "social aims" like "common prosperity" and "welfare for all-members" are usually vague. The notion of "welfare" for a nation or an individual only depends on what the yardstick is. The material satisfaction does not equal to "welfare" or "happiness". Hayek is suspicious about the concept of equality in regard to different income levels. He holds the view that income and property cannot be equalized through the market because the market distributes property according to production factors provided by the individual and according to his contribution. Therefore, only through other ways rather than the market, such as administrative and legislative measures, can income and property be equalized. Pursuing equal division of income and property through human efforts would produce those "persons with great powers". Therefore, equalized income and property is based on the premise of another kind of inequality. This inequality will greatly menace efficiency and conflicts the efficiency-oriented character of neo-liberalism. Hayek disapproved strongly of the notion of ‚social justice'. He compared the market to a game in which "there is no point in calling the outcome just or unjust" and argued that "social justice is an empty phrase with no determinable content"; likewise "the results of the individual's efforts are necessarily unpredictable, and the question as to whether the resulting distribution of incomes is just has no meaning." He has regarded any attempt by government

---

9   *Ibid.*
10   *Ibid.*, p. 101.

to redistribute income or capital as an unacceptable intrusion upon individual freedom: "the principle of distributive justice, once introduced, would not be fulfilled until the whole of society was organized in accordance with it." This would produce a kind of society which in all essential respects would be the opposite of a free society.

As a result, Hayek made his definition on "equality", highlighting that equality meant "equal opportunity", where everyone had the opportunity to participate, win and be chosen in market competition and other occasions. The "equal opportunity" is different from "equality of income and property". Its significance lay in the fact that people can have equal chances of competition in the free economy. Consequently, "equal opportunity" actually has the same meaning as free competition, hence the unity between efficiency and equality.

(3) Hayek has negated planned economy. In his eyes, the "fatal arrogance" of planned economy finally would lead to serfdom, and he illustrated his opposition to planned economy from three main aspects: economy, politics and ideology.

First, from the economic perspective, the planned economy will necessarily result in low efficiency because plan restrains the individual's free options, which means the loss of the primary driving force for economic development. Additionally, under the circumstances of modern mass production, the division of labor and social demands becomes increasingly complex. In a pure planned economy, it is impossible to collect and process complex, discrete and fragmented information due to the damaged market mechanism. Consequently, centralized decision-making will fail owing to the lack of adequate information and incorrect judgment, which will result in waste of resources and low efficiency. "Planning and competition can be compatible when planning aims for competition, not against competition."[11] In addition, the planned economy rules out free choices for occupation; instead it provides people with a stable income. This will not only bring low efficiency but also diminish people's expectation for liberty, which will ruin liberty.

Secondly, from the political perspective, planned economy will inevitably produce a huge power center. In Hayek's eyes, the goal of an individual inevitably conflicts with the general goal of a single plan. If a plan policy is applied in democracy, it is necessary to use dictatorship and authority; even if this power is established through democratic means. Hayek argued that socialism required central economic planning and that such planning in turn leads towards totalitarianism. Hayek posited that a central planning authority would have to be endowed with powers that would impact and ultimately control social life, because the knowledge required for central planning an economy is inherently decentralized, and would need

---

11   Hayek: *The Road to Serfdom*, p. 46.

to be brought under control. "Even if the democratic system decides a single task, which inevitably utilizes power that is not under the guidance of principles, it is bound to lead to arbitrary power."[12] In Hayek's view, planning is opposite to democracy, and is also opposite to law. The primary spirit of law is to regulate a set of rules for people's free option and guide their competition. Thus, any law and regulation is universal. Thanks to the extensive use of planning, the law is changed to serve particular purposes of some people to keep a promise "morally". And this fundamentally destroys the principle of law. The planned economy principle has led to unrestrained legislation, and has legalized the most tyrannical governments. Therefore, planning is against law. Meanwhile, Hayek has argued that planned economy has resulted in the controlled targets and means, and produced extreme power. Whoever had the power will have everything under his command. Under the condition of extremism, all economic and social problems will turn out to be political problems. He has argued that the worst people would grasp the power in the process toward extremism.

This is because; those immoral, out of the primitive rush or generally impacted by certain degraded values will form a powerful group leading a large number of people in the same camp with the same aims. They will place their aims above all other aims, break the moral values and do anything to reach what they aimed. In such a condition, the cruelest and the most shameless will have more chance to be a member or even leader as a part of extremist institution.

Thirdly, from the ideological perspective, Hayek has argued that; "ideological nationalization" was bound to result in the "end of truth". Hayek held the assumption that under the conditions of planned economy, the industrial nationalization has advanced in parallel with the ideological nationalization. This is because all must be subject to one supreme goal in an extremist system. To force people to think in an identical and single way, all the propaganda will serve this target so that people will totally accept the uniform norm of values pursued by those in power. In such a situation, it will be impossible to seek for individual and objective truth, while science becomes a defense tool for the officialdom and the ultimate goal of the social sciences would be suppressed, if it is conspicuous or critical against the government, and all this will result in the "end of truth".

(4) He advocated "monetary non-nationalization". Hayek has explored the economic periods/cycles and causes of stagnation on the basis of monetary analysis starting from the economic crisis in the 1930s to the stagnation in the 1970s. He has drawn the conclusion that the cause of the economic crisis in the 1930s was somewhat related to banking system legislation and the trust building deficit of the central banks to some extent. The stagnation in the 1970s was caused by the government's direct intervention in the economy. And the government's

---

12   Hayek: *The Road to Serfdom*, p. 72.

monopoly in monetary distribution and regulation was the main reason for the unstable economy, unemployment and inflation. Therefore, Hayek put forth his proposal of "monetary non-nationalization" as a solution.

Hayek has pointed out that as seen in the history, private banks could also be able to issue currency and that would well work properly. In the past there were times when private banks had enjoyed rights to issue bank bonds and they were accepted and circulated in the market. Thus, the practice of monetary issuance by private banks should be restored. Hayek strongly believed that the government's monopoly on monetary issuance should be abolished and private banks allowed issuing currency. The private banks enjoying that right for issuance should be cautious and consciously control the amount of bank notes in circulation to maintain the currency value and their own credit volumes in order to maintain trust from customers. They should also shoulder the risks for over-issuance. In the competition among private banks, those with bad reputation and who are unable to keep the monetary value stable will be ruled out, while others who are credible and cautious in dealing with the businesses will soundly carry on their operations. This reform would result in the disappearance of inflation, and promote the normal operation of economy, and thus unemployment will be naturally settled in the booming economy.

2.2.1.2 MAIN IDEAS OF MODERN MONETARISM

Modern monetarism, another branch of extreme neo-liberalism, is one of the most popular and influential schools in Western economics. The representative figure of this school is Milton Friedman (1912-), professor at the Chicago University. Rather than a new theoretical system, the modern monetarism is a duplication of traditional monetarism which corresponds to the new development needs of monopoly capitalism.

Primary concepts of modern monetarism are established on the basis of the new free trade hypothesis. This hypothesis was established as a solution for the problem of inflation and unemployment, advocating use of monetary means, particularly by controlling monetary issuance. The epitome of this hypothesis is as follows:

,,(1) Inflation is a monetary phenomenon, caused by over-issuance of currency rather than the abrupt increase of production -although there are several reasons for monetary expansion-. (2) In the current world, the government decides - is able to decide - the amount of currency. (3) There is only one way to solve the problem of inflation, that is: decreasing the currency volume growth rate. (4) The formation of inflation takes time, which should be calculated on annual basis rather than monthly; to cure inflation should also be a long-term task. (5) Side effects will inevitably occur in the process of curing inflation."[13] Modern monetarists have argued that it is necessary to carry out monetary policies on the basis of free market economy to eliminate inflation and the results caused by it.

(1) Modern monetarists generally worship free market economy which should oppose government intervention in the economy as the primary concept of modern monetarism. Modern monetarists hold the view that the capitalist market economy is highly stable and self-adjustable with a sound, balanced growth. The capitalist economy intrinsically features a non-crisis development mode and possesses an internal drive for growth. Hence it is unnecessary for the state to intervene in the economy. Modern monetarists argue that the economic problems, like economic crises caused by surplus production or inflation and structural imbalances, are all accidental phenomena, and these problems are not necessarily related to the internal rules of the capitalist production. L. Yeager, a monetarist, has once said that the disadvantages (inflation, recession and periodical unemployment and disparity between revenues and expenditures) in the capitalist economy were not the characteristics of capitalism; instead he has argued that all these were caused by incorrect monetary policies of the government.

Friedman has insisted on these theoretical principles and advocated the laissez-faire and free competition, asserting that without free market economy, there could be no continuous economic growth. He opposes state intervention in the economy, but has defined the government's sole role as "providing monetary order for competition." "Economic liberty in itself is the aim, and secondly, it is an indispensable means to access political liberty"[14]. Just as Samuelson has pointed out: "Monetarists generally believe that the government should not intervene in the market. In their view, through competition, the market could effectively solve the problems, such as; what and how to produce, and does not need government's visible hand. The government is usually considered to be inefficient, corrupt and hazardous for individual's liberty."[15]

In Friedman's eyes, there is neither a society running totally according to the command principles in reality, nor there is a society going forward completely through cooperation. It is vitally important to combine the two: an economy with command principles could run into difficulty, while the economy with free exchange has the potential to promote prosperity and human liberty. As long as the two sides trade out of their own will with no deceit, "a social functional model is formed through willful exchange" and this is "the unrestrained exchange economy

---

13   Friedman, Milton & Friedman, Rose. *Free to Choose: A Personal Statement*, p. 293-294. Beijing: Commercial Press, 1982.
14   Friedman, Milton: *Capitalism and Freedom*, p. 9. Beijing: Commercial Press, 1986.
15   P. A. Samuelson & Nordhaus W. D.: *Economics* (Volume 1), p. 541. Beijing: China Development Press, 1992.

of private enterprises, namely, what we usually call competitive capitalism."[16] In the book *Free to Choose* co-written with his wife Rose, he included a well-known story, the Genealogy of a Little Pencil, to exemplify how people conducted an unrestrained deal. In the process of making a pencil, thousands of people are involved in the production, from processing the wood, exploiting graphite blocks and copper mineral, to making black lead and copper flake. None of them worked just because they needed pencils for their own use, nor was there anyone ordering them to do so. The reason why they could cooperate well and finally complete the production of the pencil was that the price in the free exchange motivated them to cooperate in their activities. Friedman agreed to the conclusion which Adam Smith drew 200 years ago, "Economic order could come into being as the unconscious results brought by the action of numerous people seeking for their own benefit."[17] He also sang high praise for the role of the invisible hand of the market, and extended its function to all other social fields with the belief that the formation of all social orders, including language, culture and social customs, were pushed forward by means of people's unrestrained exchange and cooperation.

Friedman is against the government's intervention; however, he did not think that the government should do nothing related to the economy, instead, it should intervene in it as little as possible. In his view, the government should be one of the voluntarily cooperative organizations. If people did not choose the government to intervene in some areas, the government should not interfere in them. In his book *An Inquiry into the Nature and Causes of the Wealth of Nations*, Adam Smith had pointed out that the role of the government should be limited in three aspects, like national defense, administration of justice and public affairs. However, Friedman claimed there were few governments with such limited rights in reality as mentioned above. The good examples of them were those, like current Hong Kong of China, Japan in the period of Meiji Reform, Britain in the reign of Queen of Victoria and the United States prior to the 1930s. None of the governments of these countries and areas had employed high custom tariffs, and they had small amount of expenditures for social administration. Their citizens enjoyed absolute liberty. As a result, the countries and areas were prosperous, and people have shared the fruits.

(2) Friedman has advocated controlling monetary issuance and inflation. His assumption on inflation is an important part of his monetary theory -theory of monetary amount-, which adequately reflects his idea on "free trade".

According to his monetary theory, the variation in the amount of monetary issuance is the decisive factor that causes the alterations in price level and economic activity, and the sole cause of inflation. Monetarists hold that inflation is

---

16   Friedman, Milton: *Capitalism and Freedom*, p. 14. Beijing: Commercial Press, 1986.
17   Friedman, Milton & Friedman, Rose: *Free to Choose*, p. 19.

purely a monetary phenomenon anywhere and anytime. Friedman has pointed out, "Fluctuation of particular prices or general price in a short term may be caused by various other factors, while a long-term and constant inflation at anywhere and anytime is a monetary phenomenon. This inflation is caused by the increase of currency surpassing total output."[18] "If the increase of monetary issuance is not faster than that of output, there will be no inflation."[19]

To prove that the monetary over-issuance was the sole cause of inflation, he made an analysis on the factors that are considered to lead to inflation, like monopoly price, government's fiscal budget deficiency and demand for higher wages by trade unions. He drew a conclusion that all of these factors could cause rise of price level, but could not widely keep the price up. They could cause the inflationist fluctuations in a short term rather than a durative inflation in a long term. And these factors merely affect the inflationist pressure by means of influencing the currency provision. Then he exemplified his idea that the expenditures of the government could either be expansive or not. If the government compensated its expenses by means of taxation or issuing bonds, this would not cause inflation because these only impact purchasing power rather than increasing currency. However, if the government's expenditures rely on the currency issuance or expanding credit volume which make the increase rate of currency surpass that of the output in the economy, that would inevitably result in inflation.

In Friedman's eyes, the occurrence of inflation in many countries is attributed to the policy of the state's economic intervention advocated by Keynesianism. This policy has led to the increasing rate of currency faster than that of output. The government's intervention has brought about: (1) abrupt growth in expenditures (2) policy of full employment, and (3) the central bank carrying out incorrect monetary policies. All of these aspects have led to the government's increase in expenditures, which could only be tackled through additional issuance of currency. As a result, it has inevitably led to rising inflation due to the monetary increasing rate surpassing that of output. Thus, Modern monetarists totally attributed the inflation to the implementation of Keynesianism.

(3) Friedman put forward his notion of "natural unemployment rate" opposing the Keynesians' belief that there is involuntary unemployment in the capitalist countries. The notion of "natural unemployment rate" refers to the balanced unemployment rate that is brought about by the leverage of demand and supply in the labor force market and the commodity market without the interference of monetary factor. In Friedman's view, those with professional skills and voluntary

---

18   Liu Dieyuan: *Theory on Anti-inflation – Theory and Practice of Inflation*, p. 55. Guanzhou: Guangdong People's Press, 1992.
19   Hu Daiguang: *Criticism to Inflation Theories of Modern Bourgeois*, p. 54. Beijing: China Fiscal Economic Publishing House, 1982.

to work would sooner or later find their jobs if the measures are taken to improve the labor market, such as enhancing the mobility of labor force, shortening the time of job hunting, providing information for vacant positions and eliminating the monopoly in commodity and labor force markets. However, those who lack professional skills and not demanded by employers will by no means get jobs even if production volume increases.

The natural unemployment is featured in the following aspects: (1) There are only two kinds of unemployment, voluntary and frictional, and there is no involuntary unemployment as the Keynesian put forward. (2) What decided the natural unemployment is not the factor of currency but the actual factors related to the currency, like the legal frame in the labor force market, the degree of competition and monopoly competition, cost of collecting the information on job vacancy and the floating/mobility cost of the labor force. That is to say, the better the labor force market, the faster the vacancy information will be transmitted, thus the more freedom workers will have in order to move between different areas and professions, thus the less external intervention to labor force market, and the lower will be natural unemployment rate. (3) The natural unemployment rate could change with the variations in the population structure, social customs and social system.

What is discussed above is in a situation where "there's no interferential factor of currency". However, how will be unemployment affected, under the condition with the interference of currency, that is, under the circumstance where the administrative policies for expansive demand is conducted which results in the constant increase of monetary issuance? Or what is the relationship between the rate of inflation and unemployment? Modern monetarists hold that the inflation expectations might bring down the unemployment rate a little in a short term. This is because both the employer and the employee will estimate the future price level and its fluctuation rate in the free competition market so that they will calculate some amount of currency wage representing the actual value of wage. However, they both reckon from a different perspective. The employer can be quickly aware of the fall in the actual wages and will raise the amount of labor force; while the employees believe that the increased currency wage represents a higher actual wage, thus they will prefer to be employed, making the number of the layoff workers decrease. Therefore, by this explanation modern monetarists have reasoned why the inflation (the expected inflation) could bring down the number of the unemployed people in the short term. However, the employer thinks that the employee would someday realize that they cannot afford the expected commodities with the higher currency wage they earn, that is to say, they will be aware that their actual wage has gone down. Then, they would change their expectations, decrease the supply of labor force, and ask for higher wages; otherwise, they will not take jobs, resulting with an increase of unemployment. Consequently, monetarists believe that variations in the inflation rate and the unemployed rate as stipulated by the Phillips Curve theory is not correct because inflation cannot eliminate the natural unemployed rate; instead, the inflation co-exists with the unemployment.

Based on the assumption of "natural unemployment rate", Modern monetarists oppose government policies to add more jobs and the Keynesian slogan formulated as "full employment". In their view, employment does not result from the measures the government employs, but it is the result of the general conditions in the human resource market. They believe that if the "monopoly" of the trade union is abolished and workers can "compete freely", the rate of unemployment will decrease. As long as the government kept the pace of currency supply permanently and steadily which will correspond to the economic growth rate, this will surely keep the capitalist economy prosperous and the prices stable, and enable that the unemployment rate remains at the level of natural unemployment rate.

(4) Monetarists advocate the monetary policy of "single rule". Friedman has emphasized the significance of monetary policy with the belief that fiscal policy could work only through the implementation of the monetary policy. He has opposed using interest rates as the indicator of monetary policy, but has advocated the supply of currency as the primary indicator of monetary policies.

Friedman has opposed Keynesians, who had placed the stress on the role of fiscal policies and asserted that the fiscal policies could only work by the monetary means. Friedman took a skeptical attitude on the feasibility of fiscal policy, thus he has tried to prove the validity of his monetary assumption from the opposite perspective. He has pointed out that the government's expenditures are always slow to give its reactions and results, and the time needed to stimulate the economy will be quite long, and it is impossible to adjust the taxation policy swiftly according to the estimated standard owing to the restraints imposed by political factors. Therefore, the feasibility of the fiscal policy is "actually" and "politically" under suspicion. It was the increasing disappointment by fiscal policies that has led to people's trust in the efficacy of the monetary policy.

In Friedman's eyes, nothing but controlling the currency supply could achieve the goals, like control over macro-economic overall demand and supply, filling the inflation deficit and eliminating causes of economic depression and other obstacles to economic growth. He has also admitted the importance of the fiscal policy because it will be helpful to decide the division of macro-economic gross amount between the public sectors and the private sectors, determine the long-term interest rate as well as the consumption rate in the GNP. However, based on his research on currency history of the United States and many other countries, he drew the conclusion that through fiscal policy itself, nothing remarkable was found to impact the situations such as inflation or deflation, high rate of employment or unemployment.

Friedman has opposed using interest rate as the primary indicator of monetary policy because he thought "interest rate had little flexibility on currency demand". The little flexibility of the interest rate on currency demand reveals that the interest rate did not have a quick response to the variations in monetary supply and demand. Thus, it is apparently not appropriate to use interest rate as the indicator of monetary policy. The possible way should be directly "observing the variations in currency volume."

In Friedman's view, currency is not only the substitute of financial properties, but also that of all the other properties including real property. Currency has unique characteristics, and it is a special property like bonds, shares, estate and other durable commodities. Thus, monetary financial regulating departments of the government had limited power to control interest rates; other variables like exchange rate, prices and unemployment rate are not under the direct control of the monetary financial regulating departments. Variations in foreign exchange rates are greatly related to the international market and monetary policies employed by other countries. Prices are not directly related to variations in monetary volume. Additionally, the lag time between the changes in monetary policy to the fluctuation of prices will take long. During this time period, factors like politics, psychology and market conditions are all likely to interfere in prices. Unemployment rate is not purely a monetary problem. Therefore, Friedman believes that the amount of currency is the best and instant indicator or yardstick available for the monetary policy, and has advocated using monetary growth rate as the primary indicator for monetary policy.

Friedman has opposed "the decision-at-opportunity monetary policy" of Keynesianism, with the belief that it could not precisely predict the outcomes of the monetary policy due to the interference of factors like economic information, knowledge and misjudgment. Consequently, it could not successfully adjust the growth rate of currency. He has argued that the policy must be mechanized for the purpose of prediction, and should be simplified so that it can be understood and supported by the public. If a stable growth rate of currency is well established and made known, it will be possible to avoid abrupt changes in the monetary factors. Hence, steady circumstances for the economic development and steady growth in the national economy can be achieved. As a result, it is necessary to leave aside active fiscal policy and all those modeling measures, and let the free market mechanism dominate all, interest rates, unemployment and price level.

2.2.2 MILD LIBERALISM OF FREIBURG SCHOOL

The Freiburg school has the most comprehensive system among the schools of the neo-liberalism. Its social market economic theory and its application in the successful revival of German economy after the War economy has made it the most outstanding school in the camp of neo-liberalism. This school has closely combined its theories with the policies because many members of this school have also held positions in the German governments after the Second World War, and the proposals they have raised were widely adopted by the government. Meanwhile, influenced by the nationalism of the historical school in Germany, the Freiburg school has put more emphasis on liberalism in conformity with Germany's reality, with the attempt to find a way out for economic revival. Therefore, they are generally called the "mild neo-liberalists".

The founder of the Freiburg school was Walter Eucken (1891-1950), father of ordo-liberalism as well as a famous economist. As early as prior to the Second World War, he co-edited and published the neo-liberalist series *Economic Order* with economists and legists, propagating the neo-liberalist theories. When the fascists came into power, they rejected the neo-liberalism of Eucken, father of ordo-liberalism.

After the World War II, Eucken established ordo-liberalism by starting a journal of *Ordo: Annals of Economic and Social Orders*. Ordo comes from Latin, and its original meaning refers to "order". Eucken has interpreted it as "an order that is in conformity with the nature of things", namely a "correct order" that is different from the order of the present society but had something to do with it. This correct order referred to pure variants of economy – "ideal model", which includes two kinds of economy, the centralized economy and the market economy. Members of the ordo-liberalism were mostly from the Freiburg University, and made this university as the base for their activities. Thus, the ordo-liberalism is also known as the Freiburg school. They have advocated limiting the power of the state's intervention in economy, in defense of the free competition and private ownership. Their basic principles – the social market economy – was accepted and written into the party program of Christian Democratic Union of Germany (CDU), and was adopted as the basic policy of government when they came into power.

The Freiburg school has summarized the reform experiences in the Federal Republic of Germany in the period of over ten postwar years, and established the theoretical model of social market economy. Later, the Freiburg school's political ideas have encountered a shift from "limitedly adjusted social market economy" to "wholly adjusted social market economy". The notion of "wholly adjusted social market economy" refers to the realization of being adjusted by the state monopoly capitalism. This new political idea has basically embraced the Keynesian and Eucken's theories as the basis but was developed a step further. Essentially, they have emphasized that the government should do something to formulate political regulations in many fields. This system is what Samuelson calls "the mixed system of the government and the private enterprise".

2.2.2.1 THE THEORY OF "SOCIAL MARKET ECONOMY"

The economic term of "social market economy" was coined by Muller Armack on the basis of Eucken's notion of "ideal model". Afterwards, it was first cited by Adenauer, first premier of the Federal Republic of Germany after the War. He quoted this notion in the preface he wrote for Wilhelm Ropke's book titled as: *Is the German Policy the Right One?* to indicate the economic realities of German government.

Armack has made a concise interpretation of "social market economy". That is, "The social market economy is an economic system that is in conformity with the law of market economy, and it is featured as providing social supplement and social security."[20] His interpretation has revealed the basic target of the "social market economic theory" and means and ways to achieve this target. The term "social" he has highlighted bears two connotations: "fair and reasonable" and "state's intervention"; the former indicates the target, while the latter refers to "ways" to reach the target. Therefore, the "social market economic order" refers to an economic order, in which the state and the laws protect free competition to achieve the target of social fairness and social orderliness. It is "not a laissez-faire market economy, but a market economy under conscious guidance, namely social guidance."[21] His interpretation indicates that the market economy, which the Freiburg school approves, is different from either the state's intervention policies by Keynesianism or the orthodox laissez-faire market economy. It emphasizes that the government should regulate rules for competition, and the regulations formulated by the government will be the basic framework and bottom line for free market economy.

The primary target of the social market economy is to make the "entire nation prosperous". The "prosperity of the entire nation" aims the following three aspects. (1) The social productivity and product output will be greatly raised; resources fully made use of, and will be optimally distributed, so that the output will be maximized at the conditioned cost; (2) The nominal labor wages should be increasingly raised on the basis of highly developed productivity. If the growth rate in the wage level surpasses that of productivity, the principle of price stability will

---

20 Armack: *Investigation on the Social Economy of the Federal Republic of Germany*, p. 17. Beijing: Enterprise Management Press of China, 1984.
21 Ketoff: *The Freiburg School*, p. 65. Beijing: Commercial Press, 1990.

be violated. Therefore, things should be done to control the growth in the wage level so that it should not surpass the level of productivity. (3) The prices should stay stable and at a low level. Without a stable currency, the social market economy will be unhealthy. In real economic activities, if prices move up a little, soon deposit rates will drop down. As a result, a chain-reaction occurs as reduction in investments and production scale; hence the economic growth will be threatened. All of these targets should be centered to serve the consumers. Thus, the primary target of the "social market economy" was defined as a "trinity": integration of the three concrete goals.

The realization of "prosperity of the entire nation" relies on nothing but the market mechanism of free competition. "Free competition" is considered to be the main support for the social market economic system. One of the major representatives of the Freiburg school, Erhard (1897-1977), elected twice as premier of Deutschland, had asserted, "Competition is the most effective means to achieve and maintain prosperity. Nothing but competition could make people as consumers get material benefits from the economic development."[22] This is because the economic development is the prerequisite for civil prosperity; economic progress depends greatly on innovation in a society, and it depends whether people can take the opportunity to strive for development, and depends whether they can be brave enough to take risks for their own fate. Only when all the individuals are active, wise and brave, can the social economy vigorously forge ahead. Whether a person can give full play to his talent depends on his independence and freedom. Conversely, in a society where the economy is under the control of a central power, people will have no independence and freedom. They cannot take their fate in their own hands, but merely try their best to be on the safe side and seek for status quo and they will escape shouldering responsibilities. Consequently, the whole society will lack innovative activities, which will cause a recession in the national economy. Where there is no competition, there will be no progress, and increasingly it will lead to a recession. Hence, the government should cultivate people's consciousness of freedom, promote and encourage them rather than restrain them.

Erhard has highlighted the significance of free competition and opposed the state's intervention. However, unlike the orthodox economic liberalism that completely rejected the state's intervention, he was just against the state's extreme intervention. He cited the example of football match given by Wilhelm Ropke, economist of the Freiburg school, to exemplify the relationship between the economic liberty and the state's intervention. In the social market economy, the government should act as the judge, whose role is to keep the match move on smoothly according to the rules rather than play himself. The responsibilities of the government are to formulate and implement the economic policies, and support the private

---

22　Erhard: *Prosperity Through Competition*, p. 11. Beijing: Commercial Press, 1983.

enterprises with material and the spiritual guidance, rather than directly intervene in economic affairs. However, the private enterprises, like footballers, should be responsible for their businesses. As a judge, the government should do nothing but create necessary conditions and suitable circumstances for the smooth operation of the market economy, through all means within the limits of social market economy. For example, the state should oppose monopoly and implement policy of stable currency, and coordinate the development of the whole national economy. Particularly, the state should effectively invest into such sectors, like highways, post and telecommunication, ports, scientific research and cultural undertakings, those areas which the private capitalists do not like to invest. Only in this way, can the state give the full play to the role of the market economy through regulating necessary rules for the economic operation. Consequently, he has argued that without the state's active intervention, the market economy would be unimaginable.

It was because of the combination of the state's intervention and free competition in the social market economy that neo-liberalists like Erhard has analogized this kind of economic model with an "artificially cultivated plant", to distinguish it from the "wild plant" of the laissez-faire economic model. The road to develop social market economy in the final analysis was based on the market mechanism of free competition as the lead, with the assistance of the state's intervention. The Freiburg school has advocated the implementation of effective macro-monetary policies and policies of all-round welfare state in practice.

2.2.2.2 Competition and monopoly by the Freiburg school

Erhard has argued that the advantages of free competition could motivate people to resist against the monopoly. The reason why monopoly is opposed lay in that it is the opposite side of free competition. The monopoly organizations reject free competition, thus, they exclude free pricing. Consequently, it will be difficult to keep the balance between the supply and demand both in quantity and quality, and the balance of national production and income through market mechanisms. Meanwhile, every monopoly organization will tend to deceive consumers; thus the purpose of the social market economy should be to protect consumers. The essential targets of the two —competition and monopoly- are inconsistent. Furthermore, the monopoly organization harvests exclusively the fruits of technological and economic development, which may result an economic stagnation. If the government policies consciously encourage private monopoly and trade union monopoly, their ill effects will be conspicuously observed in the economic development. Therefore, it is necessary to oppose the monopoly system if the policies of the social market economy will be adhered to.

The Freiburg school has argued that the free competition is the necessary means to realize the economic revival of Germany. However, it is an unavoidable fact that free competition inevitably leads to monopoly. Thus, what the government should do was to learn about the monopoly types and their influences so as to formulate corresponding measures to oppose monopoly organizations. In Erhard's view, there were three variants of monopoly organizations: (1) Dependent companies combining their forces through laws or contracts to eliminate contradictions and fractures among themselves. (2) Large companies in the form of joint-stock companies holding shares of others, so that they assume some part of power in the operation and management of the medium-sized and small-sized enterprises. (3) Powerful large companies with exclusive operations occupying monopoly position in the market. Considering these three kinds of monopoly, Erhard has designed three anti-monopoly strategies to enable free competition. (1) The government should maintain the highest possible competition among companies in case of the occurrence of monopoly. (2) After monopoly comes into being, and competition is partly damaged, the government should try to avoid power abuses by monopoly organizations. (3) Special institutions should be established to supervise the market. Meanwhile, the state should also give some privileges and powers to medium-sized and small-sized enterprises, like special subsidies, preferential taxes and low-interest loan, to promote their development, and restrain the expansion of monopoly power, and finally build looser circumstances for free competition.

2.2.2.3 THE FREIBURG SCHOOL AND THE WORLD ECONOMIC INTEGRATION PATTERN

The Freiburg school has offered an analysis on the international economic theory according to its principal idea of the "social market economy", advocating that international issues could also be solved through free competition to realize prosperity in the global economy.

The Freiburg school has argued that in the international economic sphere, there is an inevitable struggle between liberty and monopoly; the former caused competition, while the latter led to conflict of benefits among the countries and causes wars. With free competition, all the countries could make use of their advantages and get benefits through the international exchange according to their own strengths. From a short-term perspective, countries in the advantageous position would obtain more benefits than those disadvantageous. But from a long-term perspective, the free market economy would as well provide those disadvantageous with opportunities to improve their condition. Conversely, if international monopoly replaces free competition, it is possible that governments of all countries might have a test of power through monopoly strength rather than market mechanism. As a result, it will become unavoidable to turn to military force to settle the international disputes. Therefore, the Freiburg school strongly opposes international monopoly.

Erhard has systematically advocated the idea of economic integration, which turned out to be the ideological base for European Economic Commonwealth (now European Union) in practice. He has argued that policy of international free economy is a part of the social market economy, or part of the entire economic liberty idea; on the other side, economic integration is the application of free economic policy in practice. In the international economic exchange, it is necessary to realize economic liberty, and adhere to the policy of free trade. Based on this idea, Erhard was strongly against "bilateral conventions" with the belief that economic integration either foreign or domestic should follow economic liberalism, and establish organizations like the European Economic Commonwealth. This is the first step to realize economic liberty worldwide.

As for the relationship between economic integration and political integration, Erhard has asserted that it will inevitably meet various obstacles in the process of achieving this theoretical goal, although liberalization of international trade was part of his theory on "social market economy". It needs to go through complex stages of the economic development. Therefore, priority should be given to establish free regional economic order in the process of building the European economic integration. First, efforts should be devoted to the development of economic relations among all countries, rather than political relations, which he considered was more urgent and more important. Otherwise, the European Commonwealth would turn out to be a super-national economic organization under central management. To avoid the occurrence of political integration in the regional cooperation throughout the world, Erhard put forth plans in detail to establish a free regional economic system, which would contain liberties of exchanging commodities, labor and capital.

As for the relationship between economic integration and social stability, Erhard has argued that the nature of the European commonwealth should be an economic cooperation organization forever, on the basis of extensive liberty and competition, rather than a mechanical combination of all members in quantity. Social harmonization could only be realized in the process of economic integration through gradual assimilation of lifestyles of all member countries. This assumption was supported by the foundation of the European Union formally announced on January 1, 1995.

2.2.3 INNOVATIVE NEOLIBERALISM

The innovative neo-liberalism refers to the trends with novel contents in the interpretation of the laissez-faire principle. And this trend has become typical, modern and promising in the 1970s. Although theories of schools of the innovative neo-liberalism were not applied in formulating policies, they have triggered a great influence on people's thinking as well as the paradigms of economic research.

2.2.3.1 Principal Ideas of the Rational Expectation School

The rational expectation school was founded in the United States in the 1970s. Research of this school has focused on the criticism and negation of the orthodox economic theories and policies. This school has not only totally negated the Keynesian economic policies, but also those opposite to the Keynesianism with the belief that those policies were essentially invalid. The rational expectation school adhered to the political strategy of natural economic development, opposing artificially pushing forward the growth of production and employment; they have worshipped free market economy and opposed intervention by the governments.

A historical review of the rational expectation school can be summarized as follows. The ideas of this school have emerged at the beginning of the 1960s. However, it did not arouse people's notice then because it could not yet formulate effective policies and systematic theories to solve the problem of stagnation. John F. Muth, an American economist, was the first to raise the hypothesis of rational expectations in his article "Rational Expectations and the Theory of Price Movements" which was issued in the journal of *Economic Metrology* in July 1961. He has assumed that people had expectations on the future by means of making extensive use of all the information available rather than relying on their memory of inflation in the past. When expectations are in conformity with predictions that are made according to economic theories, they would be rational. With the recession of the U.S. economy and the crisis of the Keynesianism in the 1970s, R. E. Lucas Jr. (1937-), professor of Chicago University, issued a series of papers to criticize the Keynesian economic policies with the rational expectations hypothesis as a weapon. Thereafter, scholars like R. J. Sargent, N. Wallace and R. J. Barro, wrote articles one after another to systematically demonstrate approaches of the rational expectations hypothesis. Finally, the rational expectation school has formed as an independent trend. Scholars and government officials believing in the rational expectations hypothesis have argued against Keynesianism. Due to its foremost influence among non-mainstream economics, combining criticism of Keynesianism with Keynes' criticism of neo-classic economics in the past was also called as "revolution of rational expectations".

The rational expectations hypothesis has partly adopted Friedman's assumption of natural unemployment rate. Based on the assumption of natural unemployment, the rational expectation school has claimed the following: whether the employment rate is higher or lower than the natural rate will depend on the disparity between the actual inflation rate and the expected inflation rate. If the former is higher than the latter, the employment rate will be higher than the natural rate; otherwise, it will be lower than the natural rate. If the two are equal, the employment rate will be equal with the natural rate. The case that the employment rate is higher or lower than the natural rate can only exist in a short period. That is to say, in the long term, even if the producer blindly expanded or shrank production scale due to being misled by the fluctuation of prices, he will still have enough time to adjust his expectations. Once the producers learn about the actual demand in the market, they will rectify their expectations, thus the employment rate will return to the natural rate. Thus, if the government expanded demand or added more jobs through expansive fiscal policy or monetary policy, the employment rate will be higher than the natural rate, and the actual inflation rate will surpass the expected inflation rate. However, once the public adjusted expectations, the government's policy will become invalid. Therefore, the rational expectation school has concluded that the Keynesian employment policy was invalid from a long-term perspective.

The rational expectation school was directly against the Keynesian economics. In their view, the Keynesian economics had reached to a dead end, as Lucas and Sargent have argued in their book *Post-Keynesian Economics*, "the present macro metrological model of the Keynesianism could not provide reliable evidence for the regulation of monetary, fiscal policies or others alike [...]. It could not be expected that minor or even key amendment in those models would give rise to any significant improvement."[23] Thus, this school was certainly against the government's intervention, with the belief that the government's policies were invalid and have advocated returning to the laissez-faire. Economic theories of this school linked the rationality of the economic man with the rigidity or viscosity of the prices, highlighted the significance of expectations to a great extent, and applied the expectation factors into economic models. Therefore, the rational expectation school not only was an opponent of the Keynesianism, but also made a contribution to the analysis and development of economics in the 20th century.

A key event for neo-liberalism winning over Keynesianism was marked as Lucas was awarded with Nobel Prize for Economics in 1995, which also marked the reduction of the government intervention and approval of the "laissez-faire" policy.

The base or prerequisite of Lucas' rational expectations hypothesis offers two aspects: (1) the public can make full use of the limited information available; (2) flexibility of prices and wages. Based on these two prerequisites, he has drawn the following conclusions: (1) The limitation of information is equal for both the public and the government. The government has no superiority over the public in obtaining information. On the contrary, the public's long-standing experience (understanding and mastery of the government's policies) provides it by advantages in obtaining information. Additionally, decision mechanism of the

---

23   Samuelson: *Economics* (12th edition) (I), p. 549. Beijing: Chinese Development Publishing House, 1992.

government is so featured that the government cannot make use of all the information (though it possessed all the information) in the process of regulating policies, while the public has the ability to utilize all the information available. As a result, inevitably "people may swiftly judge the behavior of the policy-maker, so that once the policy-maker adopts a systematic or predictable policy, he cannot deceive anyone."[24] (2) Since both prices and wages are completely or perfectly flexible, it is certain that all the markets including the labor market could get constantly balanced. Thus this indicates that all the unemployment is voluntary. Even in case of a high rate of unemployment, it is just because workers possibly have made mistakes in predicting the economic situation, and have abandoned their present jobs to find better ones. In this case, it is impossible that any policy of the government can change that reality; unemployment rate being equal to the natural rate. Consequently, the market mechanism could totally replace the government's policies, or in short, it is unnecessary at all for the government to intervene in the economy. That will make things worse rather than better. If the government attempts to rectify the policy that has proved to be wrong, change of its policy would lead to confusion in public. As a result, it would distort the economic behavior and cause waste. Meanwhile, the public would learn the lesson from the deceit and loss. To underline these ideas, the rational expectation school has frequently cited such a saying, "You can fool some of the people all the time. You can fool all the people for some time. But you can't fool all the people all the time." The notion of "rational expectations" literally means that people's expectations are rational. This includes three aspects: a precise expectation for a quite long time; expectations are created by fully utilizing all information available, and thirdly expectations produce results which are in conformity with economic theory, models and formulas that expectants employ[25]. To put it simply, rational expectations refer to the ones that are long-standing, rational and in conformity with the outcome.

Based on the hypothesis and conclusion above, the rational expectation school with Lucas as the main representative has drawn the conclusion that the government should choose the laissez-faire policy rather than economic intervention. The rational expectation school has also emphasized that expectations of all economic subjects for the future economic variations are rational.

Thus, as long as the government's policies and their influence came out with regularity, the regularity would soon or later be perceived by economic subjects. The government should abandon short-term policies, but regulate long-term policies to have the market mechanism perfectly play its role with spontaneous adjustment. If this can be done, the public will not take deviated precautions and give

---

24   *Ibid.*, p. 552.
25   Gao Hongye, Wu Yifeng: *Modern Western Economics* (Volume 1). Beijing: Economy and Science Press, 1988.

up rational expectations, hence believe in the government, as a result, the entire economy will progress steadily. Meanwhile, the rational expectation school assumes that the goal of the government's policy could be nothing but to set an optimum price level in order to prevent or diminish inflation, rather than to settle the problems of inflation and unemployment at the same time. They have also argued that everything would progress smoothly on the condition that the government sets a fixed annual rate of currency provision as well as a tax rate that could balance the fiscal budget, and leave the rest to be solved through the market mechanism. The reason is that if the government releases a long-term policy, it will surely relax the public, and avoid a tense situation occurring in the public where "everyone is precautious; guarded for self interests" according to their rational expectations. Such approaches, will promote a healthy economic development.

As a tool of macro analysis, the rational expectation hypothesis actually has developed the notion of "economic man" a step further highlighting that the economic subject would repeat the mistake in the same condition in the process of achieving the optimum goal. It has based itself on the same prerequisites with mainstream macroeconomics and microeconomics. Furthermore, the rational expectation hypothesis is widely employed in the analysis of enterprise stocks, bonds and foreign exchange markets. I think it still needs further maturity as a theoretical hypothesis.

2.2.3.2 SCHOOL OF PUBLIC CHOICE

Public Choice Hypothesis can be dated back to the end of the 19th century, with Knut Wicksell as its founder. However, as an independent complete set of theories, its formation and development can be attributed to scholars like Buchanan and Tullock. As early as in the 1940s, Buchanan and others have started to make researches on public choice. They have set up the public choice association in 1963 and a research center in 1969. In the same year, and started the journal of *Public Choice*. Economist James M. Buchanan has won Nobel Prize in economics for his work on the public choice theory in 1986. He is generally considered to be the founder of this discipline along with Gordon Tullock. Another significant public choice component, the theory of regulatory capture, was developed by Nobel laureate George Stigler, though Stigler is also noted for work in other fields of economics After the 1980s, the public choice school has gradually expanded its influence. However, this influence still remains in the academic level. Unlike other schools, it was unable to effect policy making processes, but a branch of science from the beginning to end.

Through the analysis on the process and structures, particularly focusing on the process of economic policy making, focusing on collective decision or political decision making, their theories involve all aspects of political process, like constitutional development, legislation, administration and judicature. In this sense, Public Choice Hypothesis is a branch of economics in a common sense because it conducts research on the issues of choice. The Public Choice Hypothesis employs economic analysis tools for political research, utilizing economic methods and theories to explore collective decisions and non-market decisions in the spheres of politics. In his collected works *Liberty, Market and the State – Political Economics in the 1980s,* James McGill Buchanan (1919-), one of the primary founders of this school has argued that the difficult situation in the American economy lay in defects of its political system rather than the market system. The U.S governments should abandon the Keynesian political heritage, and find a prescription to cure the political system from the perspective of liberalism.

Buchanan has opposed a standard definition, "economics is the study on how to distribute rare resources amidst all possible options or competitive goals." Based on this definition, the selected behavior and results would be irrelative to the institutional structure and constitutional order. Buchanan rejects „any organic conception of the state as superior in wisdom, to the citizens of this state". In the view of Buchanan, economics should be the science of transactions; "Economists 'should' focus on the research of human activities in special forms. It is these special activities that produce various systems. The particular subject that economists should explore is people's behavior in the market relations. This kind of behavior reflects the tendency of transaction and exchange of goods. They should also make research on various behaviors available in the market relations."[26] "Even if the model [with its rational self-interest assumptions] proves to be useful in explaining an important element of politics, it does not imply that all individuals act in accordance with the behavioral assumption made or that any one individual acts in this way at all times... the theory of collective choice can explain only some undetermined fraction of collective action. However, so long as some part of all individual behavior[...] is, in fact, motivated by utility maximization, and so long as the identification of the individual with the group does not extend to the point of making all individual utility functions identical, an economic-individualist model of political activity should be of some positive worth." "Economics is the study of entire exchange relationships." Thus, Buchanan has challenged the mainstream economics with the attempt to reconstruct theoretical system of economics. Buchanan's work has initiated research on how politicians' self-interest and non-economic forces affect government economic policy. He has criticized Keynesian economics, arguing that the Keynesian economics bestowed politicians with too much freedom, and disabled effective restrain on them. Tolerated by Keynesianism, politicians impose taxes with the excuse of emergency needs arbitrarily. This is because "economists are never clear on the necessary relationship or interaction between basic political structure (constitutions) and economic

---

26   Buchanan, James McGill: *What Should Economists Do?* p. 3. Chengdu: Southwest Fiscal and Economic University Press, 1988.

theories and how this interaction produces political decisions."²⁷ In the eyes of Buchanan, traditional economics has avoided the research on constitutional systems, narrowing their studies, and particularly Keynesian economics has made it difficult to realize effective democratic politics.

Buchanan has established his theories on "economic man's" norm of behavior, and tried to form a yardstick to evaluate both individual behaviors and political decisions. According to this analytical method, the individual is considered as a basic unit of decision and is the only ultimate decision-maker determining collective actions, and those collective actions are made up by numerous independent individuals' actions. The Public Choice Hypothesis is based on the selfish "economic man". Each of those public choices have their respective motivations and desires as background, and perform activities according to their preferences or models in favor of them; seeking for selfish, rational and maximized benefits. Buchanan has refuted "good-evil dualism" approach in politics and economy. He has argued that it would not be right to separate economic viewpoints from political ones because we cannot say that a person is selfish and hideous in the economic market, but pure and noble in the sphere of politics. In fact, motivations commanding a person's political conduct and economic behaviors are essentially consistent, and both are based on self-benefit principle. Either voters or politicians, make public choices based on individualistic cost-profit criterion. Voters always desire to elect those who are supposed to bring them maximized well-being, while politicians, and inevitably opt for decisions that could bring them maximum political advantages. Thus, there is no reason to think that individual's political conduct excludes self-benefit, on the other side it will also be misleading to overrate motivation of political conduct.

Buchanan has employed cost-profit analytical method to make an empirical study on the government conduct in contemporary Western democratic political system, and as a result he proposed a new concept as "failure of governments". In his view, any governmental institution is made up of individuals, who realizes the government conduct and they are unavoidably characterized as "economic man". Therefore, the governments have faults, make mistakes, and seek for benefits for a bureaucratic group without concerning public interests. The distinctions between government departments and private enterprises lay in that the institutional restraint in government departments is much looser than in private enterprises. Individuals in government departments strive for ordinary individual goals, rather than possessing other different motivations. Therefore those in government departments are more likely to seek for maximum individuals' benefits – aggressively- at any cost without any hesitation to violate public interests. This is proved by countless phenomena of corruption and abuse of power related

---

27   Buchanan and Wagner: *Democracy in Deficit*. p. 4-5. Beijing: Beijing Institution of Economics Press, 1988.

to government departments. It will be naive and harmful to see government as sacred, and idealize the government conduct. Once defects emerge in the market some people easily expect the government to intervene, all these approaches intensify the tendency for government intervention. He has argued that under current democratic political system, the government's conduct is usually inconsistent with public and social interests and makes severe impact on socio-economic activities. Too much government intervention in economy inevitably brings about lower service efficiency in the use of social resources compared with the market economy. Therefore, it is necessary to vigorously reduce the government intervention, and give full play to the role of market mechanisms. The government's intervention should always be the secondary choice, unless the deficiencies of the government are markedly less than that of the market, under such conditions a proper governmental intervention can be opted for. As for Buchanan the contemporary modern governments face a failure of political system rather than defects in their market systems; modern society is challenged by this failure.

Thereby, Buchanan has extended the market behavior to the process of political decisions, and systematically formed his theories on public sector and political decision on the basis of "unanimous unity". In his view, the market behavior is mainly based on voluntary agreement and exchanges of goods and labor, which benefited all parties through market transactions.

The political process is also a cooperative means to achieve mutual benefits. Like the market system, the political system can also be viewed as voluntary agreements between citizens. Individuals decide whether to have public choice according to the relative cost of individual or collective actions. The reason why individuals desire to hand over their social powers to the government is that they believe the government will be helpful to create more benefits for them. As a result, people accept a set of rules: the constitution.

Buchanan argues that the outcome of political process is determined by "gaming rules", namely, system in a broad sense. Thus, it is necessary to emphasize the vital significance of institution formation and need for institutional reforms. In his view, it will be of no use persuading politicians on some affairs. This is because things are largely determined by a variety of political institutions and a group of leading politicians. He has asserted that nothing but to put restraints on institutions is the most effective way; only through reforms in the institutional structure, non-idealization of behaviors can be converted. The reform in system structure, such as; to reconstruct democratic politics, particularly to build a political decision-making system that could effectively restrict the governments, and to essentially limit the state intervention is urgently needed. This is the "theory of institutional reform" by the public choice school, which is as well their action creed. When reforming the system, to revise the constitution is the foremost important.

Buchanan has attempted to reconstruct basic rules of constitutions and initiated a new "constitutional movement", to restrict the government's power. James D. Gwartney, professor of Virginia State University, has made a comment on that: "contribution of the public choice school lay in its demonstration that deficiency of the market is not a sufficient excuse to ignore or not to deal with the problems of the government."

2.3 A GENERAL EVALUATION OF NEO-LIBERALISM

Generally speaking, the alleged neo-liberalism is nothing but a trend of thought related to economics carrying the flag of "laissez faire" in defense of the capitalism. It is a modern version of classic economic liberalism. There are many schools of neo-liberalism, and even on some occasions, all other schools except the Keynesianism are classified as neo-liberalism.

I would like to evaluate this school in a dialectical way. In the 1970s, due to the malfunction of Keynesian policy as state's intervention in economy, the neo-liberalism has staged a comeback. It has become a quite influential school in contemporary economics, and impacted the government policies, which have produced some positive outcomes in practice. It has almost become official economics advocated by governments in capitalist countries. However, what neo-liberalism has proposed is not something new. It has just retrieved to the traditional laissez faire of mercantilism, which had protected the benefits of the commercial capitalists in the 17th century. Thus, the neo-liberalism is also known as "neo-conservatism". Below I would like evaluate its characteristics.

(1) The crisis and contradictions of the capitalist economy are determined by the basic contradictions of capitalism, that is, contradiction between the socialization of the production process and private ownership of capital. With the development of social economy, this contradiction fundamentally remains unsolved, and it is extended worldwide with the expansion of capitalism and multinational companies. Therefore, without settling the basic contradiction of the capitalism, it is impossible for either neo-liberalism or Keynesianism to eliminate the capitalist crisis through self-reforms or adjustments in capitalism. In the last decade of the 20th century, the U.S. economy has recorded an orderly growth for more than 100 months, the new mode of U.S economy is also called as "new economy". However, the above fact does not indicate that the basic contradictions of the capitalism has disappeared, it merely demonstrates that the capitalist production relations to some extent are reformed to be more flexible and that reform has provided some room for the development new productive forces. There are predictions that U.S. economy will gradually enter into a recession. It demonstrates that the United States leading science and technological development in the world will have less and less advantages in pushing forward its economic development

despite socialization of science and technology. Therefore, neither Keynesianism nor the neo-liberalism can help downfall of capitalism.

(2) The neo-liberalism and the economic schools formed under the influence of it are essentially still in defense of capitalism, the state monopoly capitalism and even the international monopoly capitalism. As we know, the overt reason why the laissez faire was replaced by state's or the government's intervention was the Great Crisis in the 1930s; its covert reason was the transition of capitalism from liberal to state monopoly capitalism during the end of the 19th century and the beginning of the 20th century. This transition has started to evolve towards international monopoly capitalism with the global expansion of the capital in the 1960s and 1970s. If researchers just put emphasis on the laissez faire but ignore the fact of monopolistic evolution, it will inevitably be insufficient for them to interpret the reality of the capitalist economics. However, during the period between 1930 and 1970 the dominant Keynesian economics has tried every possible means to eliminate the ill effects of the laissez-faire principles in the capitalist countries, and has advised to employ the "visible hand" instead of the "invisible hand". Unfortunately, Keynesian policies have suffered due to stagnation brought about by the energy resource crisis and the crisis in the international financial system. Then the neo-liberalism in defense of capitalist government's states has emerged as the opposite to Keynesianism, giving counsel to capitalist economy which had plunged into the crisis of "governmental malfunction". But, the neo-liberalism did not bring about prosperity for the capitalist countries at all; it was merely an additional choice in the "menu" of the bourgeois government. The modern economy which is featured as globally socialized mass production has already gone beyond the laissez-faire principles. Although neo-liberal trend of thought has exerted a strong force, it could not change the fact of government intervention in the economy.

(3) The neo-liberalism and Keynesianism are not utterly tit for tat, and Keynesianism is not totally incompatible with neo-liberalism. For the same purpose of settling periodical crises of the capitalism, the two are convergent in many aspects. What is "new" in neo-liberalism lies in not only its advocacy of "laissez faire" as the theoretical prerequisite, but also it improves the ideas of classic and neo-classic schools which have emphasized pure "laissez faire" and totally negated the government's intervention in economy. The neo-liberalism advocates that the laissez faire is primary, while the government's control should be secondary. Thus, the government is elevated from the position of simply a "night-watchman" for private property to the position of a "judge" for free competition. In fact, they have acknowledged that the active role by governments is indispensable in the capitalist economic development. Thus, to adapt itself to the rise of neo-liberalism in the 1970s, Keynesianism began to come out in the form of Neoclassical synthesis, and changed its old stance and policies which excluded laissez faire. It

has raised the concept of combing the "visible hand" and "invisible hand", and has attempted to coordinate the conflict between Keynesianism and the neo-liberalism. This tendency also shows that neo-liberalism and Keynesianism are evolving into a new "compound theory" regardless of their different theoretical basis and analytical methods.

(4) The Keynesianism had separated unemployment and crisis from the capitalist system, but established the linkage of curing unemployment and crisis with the development of the monopoly capitalism, which was a brilliant idea. After the malfunction of the Keynesianism, the neo-liberalism attempted to find a new way for further development of monopoly capitalism under the prerequisite of retrieving to the traditional liberalism. This is an overlapping between the neo-liberalism and the Keynesianism. With this identity, the liberalism and the state's intervention are viewed as political means for the economic benefits of the advocator or executor. These two opposite ways are in a unity and mutually dependent. If we look from the perspective of their influence on policies, liberalism and the state's intervention policy are inter-changeable on some occasions. In reality, the governments implement different policies in line with the changing economic situation. I can say that, those two play primary and secondary roles in different spheres of economy; but they are not totally opposite. If economy develops steadily, the liberal policies are more beneficial; in economic fluctuation, the state's intervention can be more effective. Thus, the neo-liberalism and the state's intervention just play a duet: "the less state's intervention, the more market adjustment", and "the more state's intervention, the less market adjustment".

(5) Since its restoration in 1970s, neo-liberalism has turned out to be a hot trend of thought in Western economics, and even tends to be the mainstream economics replacing Keynesian economics and many of its policies was applied in practice. However, it is necessary to underline that the neo-liberalism has indeed made some good achievements in practice, but it was not quite satisfactory. Take the Freiburg school for example; the social market economic model worshipped by this school once had brought about the revival in German economy. However, the economic crisis during 1966 to 1967 had weakened the belief in social market economic policies, and led to the downfall of Erhard (father of German economic miracle) government. In the 1980s, the German government has started to carry out the Keynesian policy of "overall adjustment", on fiscal, monetary and income policies. Thus adjusting the overall demand in national economy they have overcome the economic crisis caused by demand deficit, stimulated the overall demand and realized adequate employment and triggered economic growth again. In the 1990s, Germany has begun to explore a "new German model" owing to the tremendous stress brought by the development of economic globalization.

From the perspective of theoretical development, Keynesians have constantly adjusted their theoretical bugs and policy mistakes, and turned out to be the mainstream economics again. This has occurred in the form of neo-classical synthesis and neo-Keynesian economics, while the neo-liberalism has declined by the "depression" at the end of the 20th century. This "depression" is known as the second crisis of contemporary economic theory in Western economics. Many scholars have started to call neo-liberalism as "utopia", and declared a return to "Keynesian analytical method and policy", with the assumption that in the course of new synthesis, the Keynesian proposals would be in the leading position, and the Keynesianism can again be the policy "leading to prosperity". Although theories and schools are encountering a constant change under the influence of neo-liberal thoughts, it is difficult to hold back the demand of economies. In this sense, the compromise between Keynesianism and the neo-liberalism is quite natural.

(6) We should also notice that the neo-liberalism has originated in the developed capitalist countries; its policies have indeed played an important role in promoting the economic growth and development in capitalist countries. On the one hand, this is partly due to highly developed productive forces and mature economic system in those capitalist countries; on the other hand, this reflects objective rules of the economic development. Thus, we cannot totally negate neo-liberalism, but learn from and take in its scientific and proper elements. Professor Chen Daisun has made a comment on this point: "developed capitalist countries have pushed forward the policy of state's intervention in domestic and even international economic activities, but they demand from developing countries, particularly socialist countries to promote neo-liberal political models and economic policies, demolishing state-owned enterprises and state regulations in economic activities, especially planned management. They demand opening domestic markets to be geared to the world economy which is firmly under the control of developed countries. These policies serve nothing but to the purpose of establishing a neo-colonial economic rule over developing countries." Although there are many differences between the neo-liberalism and Keynesianism, their identity should not be neglected namely, their advocacy and objective as class coordination, which is the "mainstream ideology" in capitalist countries.

REFERENCES:

- James M. Buchanan: *The Capitalism and Liberty*. Beijing: Beijing Institution of Economics Press, 1988.
- R. Coase (etc.): *Property Rights and Institutional Changes*. Shanghai: SDX Joint Publishing Company, 1994.
- Cheng Enfu: Huang Yuncheng. *Criticisms of Zhang Wuchang by 11 Distinguished Professors*. Economics Publishing House of China, 2003.
- Ludwig Erhard: *Prosperity Through Competition*. Beijing: Commercial Press, 1983.
- Milton Friedman & Rose Friedman: *Free to Choose: A Personal Statement*. Beijing: Commercial Press, 1982.
- Milton Friedman: *Capitalism and Freedom*. Beijing: Commercial Press, 1986.
- Friedrich Hayek: *Individualism and Economic Order*. Beijing: Beijing Institution of Economics Press, 1989.
- Friedrich Hayek: *Economy, Science and Politics*. Nanjing: Jiangsu People's Press, 2000.
- Henry Lepage: *Neo-liberal Economics in the United States*. Beijing: Peking University Press, 1985.
- Douglass C. North: *Structure and Change in Economic History*. Shanghai: SDX Joint Publishing Company, 1994.
- Fu Yincai: *Neo-conservatism Economics*. Beijing: Economics Publishing House of China, 1994.
- Gu Yumin and Wu Shanlin: *Conservative Ideology — Neo-liberal Economics*. Beijing: Contemporary Chinese Press, 2002.

CHAPTER III

POST-MODERNISM

1 *Origin and Development of Post-modernism*
2 *Representatives of Postmodernism and Their Basic Ideas*
3 *Rationality and Limitations of Post-modernism*

CHAPTER THREE

INTRODUCTION

Post-modernism has originated in the Western world in the 1960s, and soon turned out to be a dominant and mainstream theory in Western groves of academy. Around the 1980s, post-modernism has reached its peak, but after the 1990s, it has started to decline and disintegrate.

Post-modernism is a general trend of thought that has emerged on the basis of criticism and reflection on Western society, philosophy, science and technology and rationality. The well-known figures of post-modernism are Jacques Derrida, Jean-François Lyotard, Michel Foucault, Richard McKay Rorty, Fredric Jameson and Jürgen Habermas.

94 CURRENT GLOBAL IDEAS AND MOVEMENTS
CHALLENGING CAPITALISM

3.1 ORIGINS AND DEVELOPMENT OF POSTMODERNISM

There is no theory which has emerged without a social background or a theoretical base. From the perspective of its development, a theory goes through a process of birth, maturity and decline; this is no exception for post-modernism.

3.1.1 SOCIAL BACKGROUND OF POST-MODERNISM

Post-modernism was born in Western societies in the 1960s, which was greatly related to the social reality there at that time which can be summarized as follows.

(1) It was set on the background of extreme rapid development in science and technology and rationality, and under the effects of two destructive world wars. It is well known that Western society has established the modern natural science after it went through the medieval "dark" ages. The establishment of modern science had not only overthrown theocracy and restored human rights, but had also advocated the grand slogan and announcement as "knowledge is power" (Francis Bacon). With the leverage of science, Western capitalist society has achieved a rapid development, and pushed science to the extreme. First, the bourgeoisie has set up enormous and rigid industrial mass production systems on the basis of modern science and technology, greedily squeezing surplus value from workers to satisfy their pursuit for profits and getting rich. This has made science and technology and rationality as tools for bourgeois to exploit people and gain private profit, rather than being magic weapons for the society to free from religious rule and step out of the darkness. Secondly, the bourgeois have armed and strengthened themselves with the advanced science and technology to plunder and exploit backward countries in the world. They have illegally obtained cheap production resources and labor forces and squeezed large sums of profit, turning science and technology into plundering tools serving Western colonists.

Western bourgeois have distorted the nature of science and technology, utilizing science and technology to accumulate properties at home and abroad. This not only gave rise to the intensification of various crises and inherent contradictions in capitalist societies, but also worsened the conditions in the colonies and intensified the contest for colonies and world markets. This has eventually resulted in the two inhuman world wars. In these two world wars, there were more than 70 million victims killed by modern weapons and destructive technologies. Even worse, the war and the science were mutually promoted, that is, the wars were armed with science and rationality, which in turn were promoted by the wars. Western countries have intensified armament race, which has pushed forward the application and development of science and rationality. As a result, states have newer machines and most advanced and destructive weapons, with which they have become greedier to snatch, rob and conquer the nature, society and even humankind itself. Consequently, their actions have caused new contradictions and crises, have turned the science and rationality to absurdity, extremeness and distortion, and pushed Western society to a difficult situation.

As we know, science and scientific achievements are created by humankind, and should serve the purpose of better life for them; and rationality is the essential property that distinguishes humankind from animals. However, the history and reality of Western capitalist society reveals that the science and rationality has turned out to be destructive for human beings. Rationality has evolved into a purely instrumental rationality or scientific rationality, and tools for the bourgeois to exploit others' property and increase their own family wealth; humanism and human rights have also become subject to instrumental rationality, hence the status of humankind has shifted. Humans as the subject of rationality and the central object of humanist cause have turned to be the slaves of instrumental rationality and machines; the supreme humanity, human rights and values have become worthless. This turn has removed the living base of Western society who view liberty, rationality and subjectivity as their lives, as well as the base for their values and beliefs, and has pushed them in a vacuum of values, belief and life. This has caused people to take a skeptical attitude when examining modern industry and scientific rationality in Western capitalism.

(2) The political and economic contradictions in the capitalist society have intensified, and people's living conditions have worsened. With the development of industrial civilization, people's material life has greatly improved in the capitalist society. However, this has not changed people's living conditions; on the contrary, behind this rich material life hides severe contradictions and crises. Although there has occurred a qualitative leap in the capitalist production capacity with modern technology and advanced management models, the basic contradictions of the capitalist society has not changed. The contradiction between the capitalist private ownership of means of production and socialized production has become more and more intensified. This has brought more chaos into capitalist social production, giving rise to frequent economic and social crises. An embarrassing scene has emerged: on one side is the poor working class; on the other side are plenty of surplus products being ruined on purpose. In the prerequisite of private ownership, the high mechanization in production and scientific management means that the capitalist production and management turn out to be more enormous, rigid and merciless mechanical system. A man – whether he is an employer, conductor, or employee or producer – becomes a part of this enormous machine. People's life, consumption and ideas are totally merchandized, and are manipulated by advertisements and mass media. Humans have lost their subjectivity and selectivity, and have become a "one-dimensional man" (coined by Herbert Marcuse). Demonstrations and rebellion led by workers and students

frequently occur. Thus, it is ironic that on the one hand people's material life has improved; on the other hand, things get worse. The disparity between the rich and the poor has widened, frequent inflation and economic crises, great loss in human subjectivity and self-dependence, fashion, vulgarization and mechanization have conquered all spheres of life and culture. In capitalist countries, people are mercilessly squeezed under the restriction of the production machine, the state machine and bureaucratic system – either in the production or their private lives; they are pushed into intensified social, political and economic contradictions. Thus, all these bring an all-round alienation in the capitalist society. Just because of this, after Nietzsche's remark as "God is dead", Westerners have claimed, "the author is dead" and "man is dead".

(3) The capitalist society destructs the nature, threatening human's natural home. The achievements of capitalist modernization rely on nothing but the bourgeois' exploitation of the working class, robbery of the backward nations, and random exploitation, plunder and destruction of nature. On the one hand, the capitalist world exploits the nature for materials and wealth, which exhausts the non-renewable resources; on the other hand, the capitalism produces poisonous wastes and gases which threaten the nature, degrades natural circumstances and living environment. Consequently, on the basis of increasingly worsened environment, a series of new disasters have occurred, such as: severe imbalances in ecosystem, polluted air, damaged marine eco-system, forestry system and farming land. Hence, global warming, desertification, ozone holes, floods, debris flows, frequent El Nino occurrences, and polluted water, and disequilibrium between living creatures and microorganisms.

In Marx's terms, nature is the living base that man relies on, and it is human's home as well as human's "inorganic body". The destructed nature and worsening natural environment directly threaten people's living environment and space as well as human itself. Thus, in Western capitalist society, contradictions and crises have not only occurred in the spheres of capitalist politics, economy and social life, but also in the nature, which has caused people's strong dissatisfaction and deep reflection.

In all, in the 1960s, people not only bore material and spirit suffers brought about by the wars, but also the pressure and crises in politics, economy and life as well as the environment, caused by capitalist development. All those problems were believed to have close relations with modernist thoughts, scientific rationality and capitalist greedily pursuit for profits. Post-modernists have relied on all of those facts to rise to the historical stage and constantly developed their critics. Thus, after the loss of spiritual home and natural homeland, Westerners have started to reflect on the capitalist crisis. They were at a loss under those circumstances and have started to criticize capitalism and its ideologies. Post-modernism was born in such a social background. It was established on the basis of criticism and reflection on capitalist social reality, as well as questioning and rebellion against the lopsided thinking modes of Western modernism.

3.1.2 THEORTEICAL BASES OF POSTMODERNISM

As a trend of thought, post-modernism has originated not only in a certain social setting but also on a certain theoretical base.

Post-modernism opposes traditional philosophy and metaphysics criticizing traditional philosophy and its metaphysic thinking model. However, from the perspective of its theoretical origin, the birth of post-modernism is based on nothing but modern philosophy, and it is the integration of concepts borrowed from numerous trends of thoughts, and schools of modern Western philosophy.

(1) Tendency against metaphysics in modern philosophy.

In the history of philosophy, Marx and Comte were strongly against metaphysics and have established the modern philosophy (the path created by Marx will not be introduced here) after Hegel. After Comte, numerous schools and concepts have emerged in modern philosophy. Two categories of thoughts have emerged: humanism and scientism. Their viewpoints were different and even conflicting; however, they were basically identical in their essential content, opposing metaphysics, simply from different perspectives and with distinct models. For example, in scientism, logical positivists have claimed that propositions of metaphysics were "delusional" having no cognitive meaning, while language philosophers of the analytical school have neither acknowledged metaphysical propositions nor assessed them as delusion, but have rounded them, and "suspended" or "bracketed" them. In the humanist trend, Nietzsche and Heidegger were firmly against metaphysics, compared to the schools of scientism. In all, the tendencies against metaphysics in the modern philosophy were reflected as post-modernism.

(2) Wittgenstein's later philosophy of language.

At the end of the 19th century, the analytical philosophy seemed to retreat from traditional philosophy and has simply focused on language, namely, the analysis of grammar and syntax, and has suspended discussions on metaphysics and ontology. However, this has also indicated that a turn in philosophy was occurring. Soon after, this turn can be seen in Wittgenstein's later philosophy. In his view, the source of confusion and disputes in philosophy lay in the misunderstanding of language, and philosophers have expressed what was inexpressible. Thus, philosophy should be an activity to distinguish things. Its essential task is to separate what could be denoted by propositions and language for those unable to be expressed. Thus, Wittgenstein coined his well-known notions like "language games", "meaning" and "language boundary", stressing that language meaning or connotation could not exist without the actual use and language context. Wittgenstein has attempted to break with "mirror of Nature" (Rorty's term), which is also known as "the reflection theory" of traditional philosophy. Thanks to Wittgenstein's emphasis and unique analysis of language, Western philosophy has begun to shift from the study of cognition to language analysis, which was its second turn – "language turn". Just because of this, Wittgenstein's later language philosophy includes elements of "post-modernism", and can be evaluated as the theoretical source of post-modernism. This turn was first brought about by Wittgenstein, which has double meanings, that is, this does not only indicate that Wittgenstein had turned from his former analytical philosophy to his later philosophy of language which was featured as post-modernism, but also demonstrates a turn in the whole system of Western philosophy system because Wittgenstein himself was an important figure of analytical philosophy.

(3) Nietzsche's non-rational and non-moral viewpoints. Nietzsche was a rebel against Western culture. He has attempted not only to overthrow Westerner's belief with the declaration of "God is dead", but also destroyed Western traditional philosophy for thousands of years. He has refuted Platonism. In Nietzsche's view, from Plato to Kant, Western philosophy was in the thinking paradigm of dualism, that is, to match the real world with image schemas created by man's feeling, material, sin or cognition structure. Their thought did not go beyond the dualism, like truth or false, thing-in-itself or derivative, and object or subject. Nietzsche has opposed the traditional thinking mode and concepts that had lasted for thousands of years, and advocated "revaluing" and getting rid of traditional concepts and values. But on the other hand Nietzsche has broken Western philosophy and made Westerners feel hollow; he himself became an advocate of nihilism to a certain extent. Then, Nietzsche has created a superman with powerful will. The highlight of powerful will shows that Nietzsche emphasizes the role of will but devalues rationality. He has proposed a theory of power truth, and opposed rational truth. In his view, whether it is beneficial to "enhance the feeling of power" or whether it is able to "build up the feeling of power", it is the only criteria to measure the truth and distinguish the "good" from "evil". Thus he has manifested his non-rationalism and non-moralism. His opposition to metaphysics, non-rationalism, non-moralism and nihilism has made various influences on contemporary academic research, and his theory has become one of the theoretical sources for post-modernism.

(4) Heidegger's criticism of Western philosophy as well as his assumptions on "Being" and "language".

Like Nietzsche, Heidegger was also strongly against Western philosophy. In Heidegger's eyes, not only Platonism but also theories of Descartes, Newton, Kant, Müller and Marx were part of metaphysics in the history of modern philosophy. They have all followed the tune of Plato's, and were all struggling within the frame of reality and phenomenon, and rationality and non-rationality. Heidegger has argued that Nietzsche's notion of "revaluation" has destroyed traditional concepts and values, but Nietzsche has put ceaseless change of power in the first place. Heidegger says: Nietzsche has actually reversed Plato's notions of Being and "existence", and replaced Plato's "existence" with the powerful will which constantly changes. Therefore, Heidegger thinks that although Nietzsche has broken away from the post-metaphysics of Platonism; on the contrary, he is still a thinker of metaphysics— metaphysics of powerful will, and the last thinker of metaphysics in the camp of Platonism. In all, in Heidegger's eyes, Western philosophy was still progressing within the paradigm of metaphysical thinking mode.

In order to criticize metaphysics, Heidegger, different from Nietzsche, put forward the notions of "Being" and "language". In Heidegger's view, the development of Western philosophy for thousands of years was essentially a process of gradual oblivion of "Being". Heidegger said: "existence, we should "understand", and the nature of "understanding" is the understanding of existence." That is, the understanding of the existence on the basis of previous comprehension, which is human self-understanding and the mode of his existence as well. Heidegger has also proposed that "language is the house of being". In this way, Heidegger has attacked upon Western philosophy but has put emphasis on "Being—understanding—language". He has destructed the metaphysics of traditional philosophy, negated the dualism of conception and reality, and subject and object, which has greatly enlightened theoretical construction of post-modernism and creative practice by contemporary artists.

(5) Impact of hermeneutics on the traditional philosophy.

The hermeneutics has opposed the exploration of noumenon and nature which was explored by traditional philosophy. It has negated center, integrity, cognition and objectivity, and highlighted the subject of interpretation and the meaning that is produced by the interaction between the subject and the object. Thus, hermeneutics negates monism of the traditional philosophy, objectivity of things and definiteness of meaning, and it pushes a shift from monism to pluralism, from definiteness to indefiniteness, and from unity to variety (variety of objectivity).

Additionally, post-modernism was also inspired by Frankfurt school's criticism of modern science, criticism of enlightenment heritage and modern Western industrial civilization; existentialists' emphasis on man's solidity, nothingness and indefiniteness; and also textualism of "all things are texts". Post-modernists have borrowed theoretical sources from different perspectives, such as criticism of modernity, deconstruction of subjectivity and subversion of objectivity.

Tendency of anti-metaphysics in the modern Western philosophy has provided a big context for the establishment of post-modernism; as a result, post-modernism was characterized with anti-metaphysics. Wittgenstein's later philosophy of language possessing features of post-modernism has not only affected Western philosophy to shift towards post-modernism, but also provided an enormous space for post-modernism – language analysis and language games. Nietzsche, Heidegger and hermeneutics have affected Western philosophy with more apparent, heavier and stronger color of post-modernism, and also directly influenced post-modernism with ideas like anti-metaphysics, anti-dualism, anti-rationality, anti-subjectivity, anti-essentialism and logos[1].

3.1.3 ESTABLISHMENT AND DEVELOPMENT OF POSTMODERNISM

3.1.3.1 ESTABLISHMENT AND DEFINITION OF POSTMODERNISM

Post-modernism has gone through a process of establishment and development, which can generally be divided into three stages.

Stages of Post-modernism:

The first stage was during the 1960s and the beginning of the 1970s, when post-modernism was established and initially developed. This was a time when Western society was transforming from industrial society to post-industrial society, and also changes have taken place in the spheres of ideology and culture. For example, at the end of the 1950s, some young French thinkers, like Derrida, Foucault, Lacan and Barthes, began to get tired of existential philosophy, and have turned to follow structuralism with the belief that the world was regular and with rigid hierarchies. However, soon after, scholars like Derrida have started to doubt and criticize structuralism. In 1966, Derrida has delivered his speech: "Structure, Sign, and Play in the Discourse of the Human Sciences" at Hopkins University in the United States; in 1967, he has issued three works, Of *Grammatology, Writing and Difference, and Speech and Phenomena,* which has announced his establishment

---

1   In Greek, logos originally meant "thinking" and "speech", with derivations of "thought", "rule", "concept" and "language". In the Bible, language and noumenon were in unity. Thus, in Western philosophy, it was generally believed logos referred to the essence inside things, including the intension of restoring to truth and origin.

of deconstructionism. Soon after, Foucault and Barthes have joined the group of de-constructionism. They have attacked upon structuralism, de-constructing traditional philosophy.

Derrida's speech "Structure, Sign, and Play in the Discourse of the Human Sciences" has caught Paul de Man's attention and interest. Paul de Man has integrated Derrida's and Foucault's deconstructionism with his theory of literary criticism. He has pushed the research of deconstruction a step further, and also made it increasingly popular among American universities due to his influence in American literature.

The second stage was generally between the end of the 1970s and the middle of the 1980s, during when post-modernism was extensively developed, and has reached its Golden Age. During this period, post-modernists has not only continued to criticize and deconstruct modern society and traditional philosophy, but has also extended their criticisms to all spheres including material life and spiritual life. It was transformed to a cultural trend of thoughts with the purpose of criticizing and deconstructing all that existed, which caught the attention of Western academia. However, with the development of post-modernism and the debates on it going deeper, more and more divaricating occurred, and more and more people were involved in the debates. In 1976, *Boundary*, a journal of theoretical exploration in the United States, sponsored an academic conference with the title of "post-modernity and hermeneutics". In 1978, a national academic group, the Modern Language Association of America hosted an annual forum "issues of post-modernism". In 1984, Utrecht University of Holland held a seminar on post-modernism. Members of the latter two conferences were not only thinkers from the United States and Holland but also authoritative theorists from the other countries of North America and Europe. At that time, there was another attractive event, namely fierce disputes on post-modernism between world-ranked masters, like Habermas, Bell, Lyotard and Derrida. Those conferences and disputes have pushed post-modernism to its golden age, and enriched the connotation of post-modernism. Lyotard said: "Post-modernism is a series of attempt to surpass modernism rather than a special style. On some occasions, this means the 'revival' of artistic style 'abolished' by modernism, while on other occasion, it refers to opposing object art or things including you yourself."[2]

The third stage was around the end of the 1980s and particularly after the 1990s, when post-modernism has declined and disintegrated. During this period, post-modernism began to decline and disintegrate due to its drawbacks. That is, on the one hand, the voice of post-modernism was increasingly trailed off, and turned out to be target that others criticized and reflected on; on the other hand,

---

2   Fokkema, Bertens: *Approaching Post-modernism*. p. 12. Beijing: Beijing University Press, 1991.

new trends of thought came into being, like "post-modern science" (constructive post-modernism) and New Historicism in the course of rectifying the tendency of nothingness and skepticism of post-modernism. Interestingly, when post-modernism began to decline and disintegrate, it caught the attention of the Chinese scholars and became a hot issue.

3.1.3.2 POST-MODERNISM

Whether it was in its golden age or period of descending, "post-modernism" was always a fashionable category frequently quoted by other sciences, and even the prefix "post" has almost become the token of frontier thought and new trends. However, we can make a general definition to the term "post-modernism" after summarizing the interpretation and use of this term by various schools.

Nearly all the post-modernists have argued that it was necessary for post-modernists to learn about modernism first. Modernism represented the social practice of the modern bourgeois in the spheres of culture and ideology. The core of modernism is humanism and rationalism with the advocate of humanity and opposing theology. Modernism has valued rationality with the objective of using it as a tool to overcome all difficulties. In all, modernists have believed that social history was going forward, humanity and morality were improving, and that man would be freed from oppression to liberation; and all of those could be realized on the basis of rationality. Modernists had played a great role in overthrowing theology and feudalism, helping the bourgeois to climb to the historical stage, and realizing Western industrial civilization and modernization. However, it was in the process of industrial civilization and modernization that modernists were also pushed to the extreme, hence rationality has turned out to be a purely instrumental rationality or scientific rationality; humanity and human rights were subjected to instrumental rationality; men have become slaves of instrumental rationality. It was because modernism had become reactionary that post-modernism has emerged. Secondly, it is necessary to learn the relationship between "post" and "modernism". In post-modernists' view, the prefix of "post" primarily means "after", that is, notions of modernism and post-modernism was in subsequence, or post-modernism is an event taking place after modernism. However, post-modernists have also argued that there was a logical relevancy between "post" and "modernism". That is, on the one hand, "post-modern" refers to "non-modern"; it should utterly break from modern theory and cultural practice, modern ideology and artistic style; on the other hand, "post-modern" was also interpreted as "being highly modernized", and that it is the new look and new development of modernization[3]. The co-existence of "breakthrough" and "development" indicates that "post-modernism" is more likely to mean: "after the modernism goes

---

3   Feng Jun (eds): *Speech Excerption on Postmodernism Philosophy*, p. 2-3, Beijing: Commercial Press, 2003.

to the extreme side" or "after the rebellion of modernism"; it means "after" in a sense of "extremes meeting". Therefore, "post-modernism" not only means a sequence between modernism and post-modernism, but also demonstrates the rebellion against and rectification movement against modernism. Just because of this, post-modernists believe that post-modernism is not the end of modernism, but the initial state of modernism; it is a "presence of the future" or "arrival in advance", that is, post-modernism is an "existence" in advance, then it will turn out to be "real".

On the basis of this social background and theoretical sources, post-modernists have believed that post-modernism was a trend of thought that originated from modernism but has rejected it, and there was a successive and rebellious relationship between post-modernism and modernism. To take a further step, post-modernism is also a sort of reflection on and answer to the negative influence brought about by industrial civilization. It is a criticism and deconstruction of exploitation of subjectivity, ossified sensual richness, mechanic integrity, centrality and unity which occurs in the process of modernization, as well as criticism and deconstruction of essentialism, fundamentalism, "metaphysic presence" and "logo centrism". Thus, it was a rectification and rebellion against traditional philosophy and modern society. It was avoidable for post-modernism to "overcorrect", that is, to go to the extreme side in criticism— which has led to skepticism and nihilism.

3.1.4 LYOTARD, DERRIDA, HABERMAS

Based on our previous explanations, it is not difficult to see the theoretical features of post-modernism. It can be summarized as follows.

(1) Opposing logo-centrism and language centrism

Post-modernists have firmly refuted metaphysics with its original meaning, known as "beyond physics". They negate ontology and the view that the world had an ultimate origin and existence of an essence. They also negate concepts like "foundation" and "principle". Post-modernists have pointed out that, traditional philosophy had always assumed that there was an unchangeable essence; what man could do was to discover and learn about it; and human recognition was conducted through language. The traditional philosophy had believed that, language could mirror, express and represent objects. People could also recognize and learn about the world and things through learners' linguistic knowledge on the nature and rules of the world. Derrida has negated this assumption and viewed it as "logo-centrism" and "language centrism". "This assumption emphasizes an innate "presence", which should be deconstructed". Also, in Lyotard's view, this assumption was a sort of "meta-narrative" as well as a "grand narrative", and it should be broken and replaced with "small narratives". Rorty also held the view that there was no neutral permanent and super-historical frame and principle to direct us; people had not, and cannot reach absolute foundation, neither had nor can they obtain absolute truth. Therefore, post-modernists strongly advocate the subversion of metaphysics and ontology as well as de-construction of "logo-centrism" and "language centrism".

(2) Anti-fundamentalism and anti-reductionism

Anti-fundamentalism and anti-reductionism are specific forms of post-modernism when opposing "logo-centrism" and "language centrism". Post-modernism points out that, traditional philosophy had always prescribed a "foundation" for the world and things with the belief that this "foundation" was the ultimate base of the world, from which all things originated and turned back to in the end. The cognition of things in traditional philosophy refers to seek the "foundation" of things as well as reduction of the ultimate essence of things. Post-modernists have called this practice of traditional philosophy as "fundamentalism" and "reductionism", arguing that these notions of "foundation" and "ultimate essence" are a sort of "presence" in metaphysics and a form of logos. Therefore, post-modernists claim that "fundamentalism" and "reductionism" should be destroyed and deconstructed.

(3) Opposing integrity and unity

What "post-modernists" intend to express is a sort of mental state or ideological taste, like "uncertainty", "fuzziness", "elusiveness", "inexpressibility", "non-determinability" and "irreducibility"[4]. Thus, post-modernists negate that the world is an inter-dependent integrity, and that things of the same type have some certain identity, instead they are fragmented and relative. They argue that meaning of things is relative, and relations between things are accidental as well. For example, each work is just a text with no authors or themes. Readers may make various interpretations of it – reading was a sort of misreading. Thus, there is no universality, identity or integrity. Derrida has clearly claimed that meaning is indefinite. For this reason, he coined a new word as "differance" (blended from the words "differ" and "defer") to deconstruct structural meaning, and has eventually destroyed the central identical token. A meaning which was essential and which pointed to an ultimate origin should be broken. Thus Derrida had intended to make the meaning, a continuity of series of signifiers. Lyotard has also appealed, "Let us fight against identical unity, let us be witness of inexpressible things, let us uncompromisingly create various ambiguous differences, and strive for the honors of names."[5]

---

4 *Ibid.*
5 Lyotard, Jean-François: *The Postmodern Condition: A Report on Knowledge*, p. 211, Changsha: Hunan Fine Arts Publishing House.

(4) Opposing any center, seek for differences and uncertainty

Post-modernists have destroyed noumenon, essence, origin, integrity, unity and certainty; as a result, "centrality" does not exist anymore. In their eyes, the existence of centrality means that there is "non-centrality" as well as the existence of dualism, like primary and subsidiary, nature and phenomenon, internality and externality. This also means that nature determines phenomenon, internality dominates externality, and centrality is over non-centrality, that cognition of things is always revealing internality from externality, and centrality from non-centrality. Post-modernists have argued that, this thinking paradigm above is actually a "presence of metaphysics" and "logo-centrism", and they should be criticized and deconstructed. Derrida has remarked that meaning could not be like "presence of metaphysics" diffusing around from the center, but like seeding, spreading meanings of "differance" anywhere. Hassan also said, "post-modernism is of some semantic uncertainty", and the alleged uncertainty was a complex category consisting of the following concepts: fuzziness, discontinuity, heterodoxy, plurality, desultoriness, rebel, perversion and transformation. And only perversion governs many terms of self-counteraction, like anti-creation, dissolution, de-construction, de-centralization, displacement, difference, discontinuity, break, blanking, de-mythologization and discretization, let alone jargons like irony, break and wordlessness. Therefore, post-modernists have emphasized non-centrality, difference and uncertainty, using counterparts of discretization and uncertainty against center and origin.

(5) Opposing rationality and deconstructing modernity

Rationality had close relationship with modernity because modernity refers to concepts about social progress since enlightenment age in Western society, and the most reliable and powerful weapon of enlightenment was "rationality". In other words, it was with the aid of modern science and rationality that the Enlightenment Movement strode forward. The combination of rationality and science has evolved into purely "instrumental rationality". Rationality has destroyed the theology and even all of the feudalism, promoting the development of modern capitalism and bringing about infinite enjoyment and happiness. Meanwhile, rationality has caused a series of negative effects to the modern society and even catastrophes, but people still hoped to solve these problems with rationality with the belief that rationality was a force of liberation. Rationality has become the new object to be worshipped instead of gods. In the view of post-modernists, rationality and scientific rationality has buried the source of slavery and oppression, but set up new forms of slavery and oppression, namely, authority, essence and center. Thus, post-modernists refute all theories of modernity and view the concepts, theories and rationality of modernity as logo-centrism, essentialism and metaphysics, with an attempt to deconstruct them.

(6) Deconstruction of subjectivity

The modernism has turned over mythology and demythologized it, so that humanity and subject could stand up. The actual establishment of subject (rational subject) and subjectivity was one of the greatest achievements of modernity. The establishment of subject and subjectivity indicated to a dualism of subject and object. However, with the rapid development of science and industrial civilization, people live in the noisy circumstances and in the "match packet" that is built of cement and steel, overwhelmed with the desire of material wealth. When people have lost their independence, they strive to endure against the internal and external stress, upsetness, distressed, gloomy, hesitant, lonely, helpless and puzzled.

Post-modernists believe that the existence of subject not only indicates the dualism of "subject and object", but also reflects the drawbacks of modernism. Thus, it is necessary to mercilessly criticize subject and de-construct subjectivity. Post-modernists have pointed out: "First, subject is a fabrication by modernists. Secondly, any attention to subject assumes some philosophy of humanitarianism and post-modernists will not tolerate it. Last, subject spontaneously needs an object, but post-modernists oppose the dualism of subject and object". That is to say, in the eyes of post-modernists, there is no subject at all; even if it exists, it is necessary for modernists to divide the world into halves of "subject and object" rigidly. Therefore, post-modernists have argued that subject was like words written on the sand in a beach, which is likely to be washed away. Thereafter, the linkage between humankind and things are cut off, only to leave things and nothingness. Consequently, men in the world of post-modernism had little emotions or passions due to the loss of subjectivity, initiative and creativity. Just as what Andy Warhol, painter of post-modernism, has said, "I want to be a machine rather than a human being, and I paint pictures like a machine does."[6]

Thus, through de-construction of post-modernism, men in such a condition have nothing but the body, and all the contents inside had been emptied, and they have turned out to be vacuous.

(7) The correspondence theory of truth, practical view of truth and commercialization of knowledge

According to the previous epistemology, cognition was viewed as the conformity of man's internal world with the outside world; the relationship between man and the object was recognizing and being recognized, recasting and being recast, and the dualism of subject and object. Man and the object were equally in the passive place. This epistemology was a mechanic reflection or correspondence

---

6   Wang Yuechuan: *Research of Postmodernist Culture*, p. 241, Beijing: Beijing University Press, 1992.

theory, which is called "Mirror of Nature" by Rorty. However, in the view of post-modernists, there is no innate nature or foundation for people to objectively perceive and master things. They believe that nature and meaning of things only exist in the process of people's reading and interpretation of them. They have replaced correspondence theory of truth with practical theory of truth as well as subjective theory of truth.

Since they have deconstructed noumenon and nature and "Mirror of Nature" has been broken, knowledge accumulated with theory of reflection is naturally negated. In their eyes, knowledge is a sort of commodity. The creator and the user of knowledge are considered the provider and the user of knowledge. This is like the demand-and- supply relationship between the producer and the consumer of goods. Knowledge is not for the sake of knowledge as the ultimate goal, but is produced for sales. Knowledge has lost its "traditional value".

Therefore, post-modernists believe that in the postmodernist society, meta-discourses and their validity are out of date; social contexts of meta-discourse, like purely speculative narrative, liberation narrative as well as heroic sages and recurring liberty are invalid, and they should all be replaced by "small narratives". They also claim that this is now the time of common people, and put stress on the process rather than the results. It is the time when boundaries of various academic paradigms have vanished, and science could do nothing but play games of language. In such an age, people should make efforts to discover the fallacy of the creator with the advocate of heterogeneous criteria.

3.2 REPRESENTATIVES OF POST-MODERNISM

Post-modernism is a big family, amidst which there are numerous schools and scholars. It will be hard to introduce each of them one by one in this chapter. We shall just give a brief introduction on Rorty and his "post-philosophical culture", Derrida's deconstructionism, Lyotard's knowledge legitimatization crisis and Habermas' rescue of modernity.

3.2.1 RORTY AND HIS POST-PHILOSOPHICAL CULTURE

Richard McKay Rorty, an American contemporary well-known neo-practical philosopher, is one of the important figures of post-modernism. Rorty had graduated from the University of Chicago in 1949; in 1956 he got his PhD in philosophy at Yale University. He taught philosophy at the Yale University and the Princeton University as well, as visiting professor in five U.S universities. In 1979, Rorty was elected as President of the Eastern Branch of the American Philosophical Association. His masterpieces are: *Philosophy and the Mirror of Nature* (1979), *Consequences of Pragmatism* (1982), *Habermas and Lyotard on Postmodernity* (1984), Post

108 CURRENT GLOBAL IDEAS AND MOVEMENTS CHALLENGING CAPITALISM

Philosophical Culture (selected papers, 1990).

Different from other post-modernists, Rorty has not only criticized modern philosophy and modern society, but at the same time he has re-constructed them. This reconstruction can be seen from his advocate of "post philosophical culture" on the basis of combination of philosophy with culture. Rorty's post philosophical culture can be depicted as follows.

(1) Criticizing "Philosophy" and advocating "post-philosophical culture"

In order to re-construct "the post philosophical culture", Rorty has first queried the present philosophy. He has pointed out that philosophy at present plays the same role as theology did before Enlightenment and judged all the other spheres including culture. The reason why philosophy has got such a supreme status was that the Enlightenment Movement had overthrown the imperatorial status of theology, and led humankinds into an age of post-theological culture. And philosophy has filled the vacancy left by theology. Rorty has written that this philosophy has aimed at TRUTH, GOOD and RATIONALITY, which is a capitalized philosophy. For Rorty as theology had lost its imperial status and stepped into the stage of post theological culture, the supreme-capitalized- philosophy should as well enter the age of a post-philosophical culture.

Then, what is the "post philosophical culture"? Rorty has argued that in the philosophical culture, "no one or at least no intellectual" believes that there is a yardstick in our mind that reminds us "whether we have contacted with the reality" and "when we have contacted with the truth"; there is no one who is more "rational", "scientific" or "profound" than anyone else. Any kind of culture or some particular parts of it can impossibly be classical in comparison to other cultures; "meta-narratives" do not exist, neither do "Philosophy", "Man" and "Truth"[7].

Therefore, Rorty claims that at present philosophy is only one branch among post- philosophical cultures; philosophy and philosophers are lower-case philosophy and lower-case philosophers. There is no special "problem" to be solved; there is no special "method" available, and there is no special scientific criterion to be followed. Thus, no one can claim that he has unique ways to explain all, and no scientist and scholar should think that their works have "philosophical significance" or "universal significance for humankind". Rorty has added that there are still heroes and philosophers here and there, but the title of "hero" is "only an appreciation to those outstanding men and women who are very good at doing various things". They are honored not because they knew a Secret or achieved somewhat Truth, but because they are those better at "being a person",

---

7   Rorty, Richard: *Post Philosophical Culture*, p. 14, Shanghai: Shanghai Translation Press, 1992.

and philosophers are "intellectuals with wider interests, and always ready to offer their viewpoints to anything hoping that their viewpoints can be related to other things."[8]

In all, Rorty's post-philosophical culture opposes "logo-centrism", "essentialism and ontology".

(2) Opposing to the coherence theory of truth

"What is the truth"? This is a problem of both epistemology and ontology because answers to this question directly involve the ontological standpoint that people hold. Therefore, Rorty has illustrated his viewpoint on truth from his perspective of post-philosophical culture.

First, Rorty has pointed out, "Traditionally, there were diverse opinions on the nature of Truth, just as Plato had said: it was a war between gods and humankinds."[9] Rorty believes, in Philosophy, there were two opinions on Truth: one from "Philosophers" like Plato, who had gone beyond the boundaries of his time and space in pursuit of transcendence; the other opinion was from "Philosophers" like Hobbes and Marx, who were influenced by Galileo's theory, with the belief that things in time and space are dominated by beautiful mathematic rules. They have believed that time and space constituted the entity, and truth was nothing but coherent to the entity. However, just as we have previously stated, Rorty's post-philosophical culture approach opposes "logo-centrism" and ontology; thus, he has made all his efforts to transcend the diversity of all previous philosophies, go above apriorism and empiricism, and oppose Philosophical (capitalized) view of truth.

In Rorty's eyes, truth to be true does not lie in whether it is in accordance with entity; and it is unnecessary for people to ask whether a statement is in conformity with what part of the entity, what makes it true and whether it needs to have moral properties like "should". Neither they need to ask whether it is a "pure opinion" if a statement bears no moral properties like "should". In the age of post-philosophical culture, there is no distinction between first-level truth and second-level truth, or difference between opinion and truth; truth is nothing but common properties of all true statements, like these: "Bacon did not write Shakespeare", "two plus two equals four", "love is better than hate", "*Fable of Paintings* is the best work of Vermeer". From another perspective, truth is of no essence but shows people's attitude toward things, like an approval rather than a certain explanation to things. Therefore, the truth is what we would better believe. Apart from this, it is vain to hope for essence and essential relations between rational cognition, knowledge, thought and the object.

---

8   *Ibid.*, p. 15.
9   *Ibid.*, p. 4.

Rorty has also held that people in the post-modern age have less troubles and annoyance because there is no transcendental entity that people must be conformed with, nor universal criteria or coherence theory of truth. People just needed to treat criteria like pragmatists do; that is to say, viewing criteria as "a temporary supporting point constructed for the purpose of some particular pragmatism.

(3) Science, literature and politics in post-philosophical age

As we have previously stated, for Rorty philosophy is transformed to be cultural supremacy and it has filled the vacancy after the supreme theology is abandoned. In order to prevent such case recurring, that is to say, disciplines related to other spheres might take the place of philosophy and become new supremacy over culture after Philosophy is abandoned. Rorty has made an investigation on three areas, science, culture and politics, which could most possibly gain supremacy over culture. He has drawn the conclusion that it is impossible for these three to gain the new cultural supremacy.

First, as for science, it is generally believed that science is necessarily based on "rationality", which is viewed as "order", or "possesses prescribed criteria for success". Rorty has claimed that according to this interpretation, poets and painters would have no "rationality" because they create poems or paintings based on their inspiration and passions. Their criteria are gradually formed in the process of creation and variation. On the contrary, scientists have criteria and goals in advance. They not only know in advance whether their assumptions are valid or not when predicting on what would happen and what results will be there, but they also are able to predict and control the world with the criteria of scientific theories. Therefore, only natural science is an example in the sense of "rationality".

If "rationality" is understood only in this sense, humanities studies will not be qualified to be rational activities; if humanities studies are as well turned out to be reasonable or rational activities, then "rationality" should have another meaning, which should include some "sober" and "reasonable" things rather than "orderly" things[10]. The notions of "soberness" and "reasonableness" actually integrate a series of moral properties, namely, tolerance and respect. That is to say, when discussing any questions with others, we should be good at listening to others, respect their viewpoints, and communicate with them to get consensus based on persuasion rather than suppression. According to Rorty's interpretation, "rationality" should be "cultivation" and "morality" rather than "order" or "prescribed criteria". In the same way, the distinctions between fact and evaluation, rationality and non-rationality, and natural science and humanities are not that important. Hence in this way, humanities can be evaluated as rational activities.

---

10   *Ibid.*, p. 78.

Therefore, in the eyes of Rorty, the notions of "true" and "reasonable" do not at all mean that thought is in conformity with entity; neither do they mean cognition of some universal common properties. They are moral properties like "reasonability", "cultivation" and "tolerance". When they are mixed with "belief", it makes us to say "believe to be true". On the contrary, the notions of "untrue" and "unreasonable" are not so because they do not conform to entity or object, but because it means others might have a better idea.

Based on the above analysis, Rorty has argued that those scientists are not more objective or rational than others; like in humanities studies. What natural sciences seek is a sort of reasonability or truth of "reasonability" and "cultivation", and it cannot assume a new supremacy over culture.

Second, as for literature, Rorty has made his research from two perspectives: de-constructionist theory and literary criticism.

Rorty has asserted that deconstruction movement can be divided into two kinds: one in broad sense, the other in narrow sense. The former refers to "a movement going beyond literary criticism", namely, de-construction in the spheres like politics, history, law, literature and philosophy. The latter refers to "de-constructionism as a school which pursues literary criticism." When he reviewed the relationship between deconstruction and literature and the growth of de-constructionism, he said: they are mutually influenced and advancing in parallel: on the one hand, literary criticism relies on and makes use of de-constructionism; on the other hand, deconstructionism is a device for literary criticism. Additionally, deconstructionism integrates Paul de Man's literary critical theories and has grown quite influential. Thus, in Rorty's eyes, literary criticism combining with de-constructionist theory cannot not assume supremacy over culture. It can neither be the foundation of other cultures in post-philosophical culture or even that of post-philosophy, nor can it be literature in the sense of Philosophy (capitalized).

Rorty has also reviewed literature-in-itself; literature cannot not gain the new supremacy. Men have three ways to interweave the net of their beliefs: perception, reasoning and metaphor. Perception means that when we see new elements of a thing, we produce new conceptions about it replacing the old ones. Reasoning is defined as the ways we use to deduce new belief that we did not have before on the basis of the previous one. As a result, we have to change the previous one or have to explore a new one. Either perception or reasoning, what they changed are the true value of sentences, not the contents of them. Thus, they do not expand logical space, and still remain closed. However, that is not the case for metaphor. Metaphor highlights that the spheres of language, logical space and possibility are open forever, metaphor opposes and threatens essentialism in the traditional philosophy and rejects the presence of metaphysics. "Metaphor, as it is, is the sound coming from outside the logical space, rather than the experimental activity that filled some part of this space, nor is it a clarification in line with philosophy of logic about this space structure."[11] However, literary language is mainly made up of metaphors. Therefore, Rorty believes that; "we have no reasons to set up an altar for literature like we had worshipped pearlescent logos in the past". Thus, literature like science is impossible to become the foundation of post-philosophical culture.

Thirdly, as for politics, it is generally thought to be a sphere of power, which may seemingly be able to become the foundation of post-philosophical culture. However, Rorty based on his analysis of the relationship between politics and philosophy has also rejected this idea.

It is generally thought that politics needed a theoretical foundation, and that liberty and democracy needed to defend themselves with the support of philosophy. However, based on pragmatics, Rorty has argued that what liberal democracy needed was a philosophical interpretation rather than any philosophical foundation, and politics had nothing to do with philosophy. In his eyes, politics was something practical dealing with social affairs, and it is based on nothing but sociology and history, rather than a permanent support of non-history. What philosophy involves is the discussion on the questions about whether there is humanity and what it is, which apparently has nothing to do with politics. He exemplified that people could discuss abstractly on humanism and responsibility that man should bear; however, that's not the case in politics. This is because when people absolutely discuss what men should be, it is presupposed that there exists a super community, namely, human itself, which must be acknowledged by mankind, but both politics and society are concrete and not abstract. Thus, when it comes to man's responsibility and duties, the discussion is based on nothing but on a concrete community, where man must acknowledge that he himself is one of its members. Therefore, Rorty believes that in political life, politics is always in the first place, compared with philosophy, and philosophy had to adapt to it. When philosophy is in conflict with politics, it is necessary for philosophy to give way to politics. However, Rorty has not totally devalued philosophy. He thought it is possible to separate politics from philosophy, and have political conceptions keep away from issues of humanity and identity, and it is possible to leave issues like humanity and life significance, "to private life". Rorty has clearly demonstrated that politics belongs to public life; and when philosophy enters political realm, it has to be subordinated to politics. Finally, Rorty has concluded that because philosophy can impossibly become a foundation for politics and that politics itself integrates a variety or even opposite viewpoints, it is impossible for a certain culture in the political realm to be the foundation of other cultures, nor could politics itself.

---

11   *Ibid.*, p. 28.

According to the statement above, actually Rorty's post-philosophical culture negates philosophy as a worldview, and confines it into the private sphere. As a result, traditional philosophy is turned into a local issue within the private sphere. He has also assumed an equal relationship between sections, spheres and cultures, which manifest external relationship and have no distinctions like center and edge, and majority and minority. However, when we accept a concept or culture, the judging standard is that the concept or culture is to some extent conform to our beliefs and ideas, rather than being coherent with some entity. It is not difficult to see that Rorty has negated the traditional philosophy and dualism, actually has pushed forward his pragmatism. He was wiser than other pragmatists, because he has not only preserved traditional pragmatism but has also combined pragmatism with frontier issues of modern philosophy, as well as with the modern times.

3.2.2 DERRIDA AND DE-CONSTRUCIONISM

Jacques Derrida, French Contemporary philosopher and founder of Deconstructionism, was born on July 15, 1930, in El-Biar, French Algeria. He had spent his youth in El-Biar, Algeria. After he had finished his bachelor's degree at the age of 19, he went to France for further study. In 1956~1957, he continued his study in Harvard University. From the end of 1960s, he taught in Paris High Normal Institute and later became the director of philosophy department. During this period, he also was a visiting scholar of the Johns Hopkins University and Yale University. He wrote a lot of works, such as *Structure, Sign, and Play in the Discourse of the Human Sciences* (1966), *Speech and Phenomena* (1967), *Of Grammatology* (1967), Writing and Difference (1967), *Dissemination* (1972), *Positions* (1972), *The Work of Mourning* (1974), and *Margins of Philosophy* (1982).

Derrida has initiated a change in structuralism when it was in its peak, and turned to de-constructionism. What Derrida has de-constructed and overturned mainly was traditional philosophy, namely, dualism, essentialism, logo-centrism and presence of metaphysics. Below we shall review his de-constructionism.

(1) Analysis of language, opposing "logo-centrism" and "presence of metaphysics" According to traditional philosophy, it was generally thought that language could express, depict and reflect objects, and people could as well get to learn the object from the linguistic expression of the knower. Consequently, language was considered the thing utterly coherent in origin with the real world and the experience, and language was equivalent of "logos". "Logos", with its origin from Greek, means "language" or "definition". It refers to the essence that exists inside the world or things.

Post-modernists like Derrida have argued that viewpoint of traditional philosophy in fact implies a prerequisite: presetting internal and essential things, or logos, in the world. They are considered the origin or center of all things. In Derrida's view, this was "logo-centrism" or a "presence of metaphysics".

In the eyes of deconstructionists, like Derrida, there is no fixed, pre-existing and essential property. All is changeable and indefinite. Meaning only exists in the process of the interpreter's interpretation. Thus, Derrida has pointed out, thing-in-itself and presence do not exist at all, and concepts like "logo-centrism" and "presence of metaphysics" must be de-constructed.

(2) Destroying centrism and dualism, dual structure and hierarchical structure

According to "logos" and "presence of metaphysics" in traditional philosophy, everything and even the world has internally an essential center, and language is considered to be expression as well as the epitome of this center. Hence Derrida has pointed out, if people insist on observing and knowing things by the approach of "logo-centrism" and "presence of metaphysics", it inevitably will lead to the dualism. And this assumes that there is a distinction of dual structure, like spirit and material, life and death, entity and fiction, center and non-center, essence and non-essence, and internality and externality in the world and things. Amidst them, the former is believed to be the center and source, while the latter is marginal and derivative, which moves around the former. It was also believed that knowledge would be inevitably featured in dualism and rigid hierarchical order, like truth and fallacy, profoundness and shallowness, authority and ordinariness, and classics and later interpretation. In the view of Derrida, this was because "the idea was restricted in the source [...] namely, people had always attempted to find a real origin, all this follows is nothing but a repetition [...] exactly influenced by the same powerful myth, the syndrome of which can be seen in the dialogue of Plato's [...] To view Plato as the source of this concept is to turn again to duality which is heavily marked with the rational discourse of logic centrism – speech/writing, presence/absence, and source/its complement."[12]

Therefore, Derrida was firmly determined to overturn previous notions like hierarchy, structure, depth, center and origin, and has put them all onto the same level, and brought the relationship among the elements and bi-polarized hierarchy into the scope of "free play". Derrida warned as well that it is useless returning to seek source or origin, or attempting to escape from "complementary logic". Otherwise, the shackles in thoughts and deeds caused by traditional logo-centrism will still remain.

(3) Opposing linguistic-centrism, removing the mansions of metaphysics

For Derrida, in traditional linguistic views of philosophers, like Plato, Aristotle

---

12   Christopher Norris: *Derrida*, p. 32. Beijing: Kunlun Publishing House, 1999.

and Saussure, language and writing, speaking and writing used to be in opposition to each other. They had argued that speech and speaking were superior to writing because they were direct and live. When speaking or uttering, the speaker and the listener were both present. The speaker could be aware what he/she spoke or thought, and could manage his speech to be in conformity with his thought. On the other hand, the listener could grasp better what the speaker meant according to the situation. On the contrary, writing and written language were merely the recurrences of speaking and oral language. They were a kind of substitutions when speaking was impossible. Once thought was recorded in words on paper, a gap or disparity occurs between the writer because of indirectness and it is impossible for its meaning to be totally self-evident. Thus, in the view of traditional grammar, oral language was granted a positive value of self-evident truth with its homologues (presence, origin and meaning), while writing was put in the opposite side: as a supplementary or affiliated token. That is, "the nature of language was speaking rather than writing; writing was merely a derivative of the speech."[13] Derrida has evaluated that as "linguistic centrism".

In Derrida's eyes, it was a prejudice that writing was viewed as an obstacle for the speaker to approach to the self-presented meaning, and held back the speaker to reach the truth; and this unique prejudice in the written texts of these thinkers should be much suspected. Derrida said, as a matter of fact, speech was not in conflict with writing, and it produces, to some extent, indefinite and a repeated meaning. From the perspective of traditional linguistics, writing and words were viewed as pure tools to record speech or utterance, so that when the speaker was not present, his speech could as well be repeated and spread. However, the repetition and spread of words were actually those of speech and utterance. The reason was that words were recordings of the utterance, in terms of any utterance or any oral expression, they were all signifiers, despite that it would be repeated in words next time or what the speaker and the re-teller would think. Thus, not only writing and words but also utterance and even the whole language system were repeatable. However, the repetitiousness and indefiniteness of utterance were merely veiled by speech/ words for a long time.

Derrida held that in this case, speech does not bear authority, priority and centrality to written words. Hence the original dualisms, like center/margin, definiteness/indefiniteness, presence/absence, were deconstructed. Derrida also believed that speech and words were equal and complementary: words and writing recorded speech; speech was complementary for words and writing, neither of the two can be neglected.

However, it is necessary to emphasize that Derrida did not intend to break one center to establish another. That is to say, that he has destroyed speech center

---

13 Feng Jun (eds): *Speech Excerption on Postmodernism Philosophy*, p. 9.

without any intention to set up a writing center instead of speech center. This is because for the Derrida reconstruction of a center is nothing but only an adjustment or "reform" within logo-centrism, which will still be dualism. Derrida would not tolerate that. Derrida did not intend to establish any center. Following the line of deconstructing language centrism, Derrida further continued to abandon dualisms, like phenomenon/ nature, material/motion, necessity/contingency, and symbol/metaphor. Then, he queried the notions of value, rationality, origin and laws; finally he reached the mansion of metaphysics itself, breaking the center of presence/absence.

In all, Derrida has deconstructed all Western philosophies since ancient Greece. He negated logo-centrism, presence of existence, de-constructed subject and hierarchies opposed any kind of dualism, and emphasized flatness and fragment. He believed that reading was misleading. His de-constructionism had skipped to an extreme side: nihilism and skepticism.

3.2.3 LYOTARD AND CRISIS OF KNOWLEDGE

Jean-François Lyotard was a French contemporary philosopher and one of the representatives of post-modernists. He had graduated from French Higher Normal School in 1950, and earned a Ph. D in Paris University. He was a teacher at his early age, and taught at the philosophy department in Paris University 8. His works include: *Phenomenology* (1954), *Discourse Image* (1974), *Libidinal Economics* (1975), *The Postmodern Condition* (1979) and *Justice* (1980).

Lyotard is different from other post-modernists, like Derrida, directly criticizing nature, origin, law, rationality, logo-centrism and linguistic centrism. Neither did he choose to construct a postmodern theory based on philosophy and culture, like Rorty. He blazed a new trail: shifted from criticizing ontology and delved in research of knowledge legitimacy and intellectuals' status. He has intended to achieve his goal of "decentralization", and oppose identity, integrity and meta-discourse.

3.2.3.1 LYOTARD AND HIS ANALYSIS ON TRADITIONAL KNOWLEDGE SYSTEM

Since Lyotard has demonstrated his viewpoint through research of changes in knowledge, he had to analyze the traditional knowledge system. He has pointed out that there are two kinds of knowledge in the knowledge system: narrative and scientific.

He has defined the narrative knowledge as knowledge whose expression depended on narrative forms – "Narratives are the prototype that traditional knowledge

POST-MODERNISM

had advocated"[14]. It was featured in the following aspects: when the narrator told a story, he had always introduced his own experience that of his forefathers and of his forefather's father. The narrator, listener and the hero of the story could play different roles: sometimes the three were one. The ultimate purpose of telling the stories time and again was to make what was passed down into infallible laws and to make people bear them in mind forever, so that people would know why the social system was legitimate and how to behave in line with the standards that was prescribed by the society itself. In short, "Narrative can determine the establishment of "legitimate standards", or demonstrate how to apply them in life. Therefore, the role that these narratives had played the role for instructing people what to say and what to do by means of the narrative culture. Why these narratives were legitimate lay in that they sounded plausible and self-regenerative"[15].

But, scientific knowledge is different from narrative knowledge, but it could not get rid of "entanglement" by narrative knowledge. Scientific knowledge requires the narrator to provide evidence, and illustrate all that was real of the signified. The listener, however, should clearly express agreement or disagreement. Compared with narrative knowledge, scientific knowledge is not directly associated with social norms. It is indicative, that is, it denotes an object, and makes a judgment about the object according to what is true. However, scientific knowledge has also its own problems that are difficult to tackle, and it is just these problems that put scientific knowledge in a dilemma. That is to say, scientific knowledge has no way to show people the truth of its own, "Unless it turns to the other kind of knowledge— narrative knowledge— from the perspectives of science, however, narrative knowledge is not considered as real knowledge at all."[16] For scientists, this is undoubtedly a dilemma that they cannot get escape.

3.2.3.2 IN POST-MODERNITY, KNOWLEDGE BECOMES MERCHANDIZED

Lyotard held the belief that in the post-modern society knowledge is not what it used to be in a traditional sense, and its connotation and criteria has changed.

In the postmodern society it is necessary for knowledge to transform in bulk into consultative information, and through various media, into data that could be operated and applied. And all those knowledge that could not be transformed fall into disuse. This undoubtedly means that all knowledge should be converted into computer language or digital language, and only this kind of knowledge can be considered as knowledge. As we all know, one of the most remarkable characteristics of digital or computer language is that it is editable, inter-textual, movable,

---

14   Lyotard: *The Postmodern Condition*: A Report on Knowledge. p. 77.
15   *Ibid.*, p. 82-83.
16   *Ibid.*, p. 101.

can be copied, pasted and transmitted. Thus, knowledge that must be computerized, just like commodities, can be manufactured, copied, transferred, sold and updated. Thus, on the one hand, the creator, possessor and user of knowledge has to master computer knowledge and its operation; on the other hand, the relationship between provider and user of knowledge is just like supply-and-demand relationship between the provider and consumer of commodities. Knowledge would be produced for the sake of sales in the future. This shows that in the eyes of Lyotard, knowledge that had produced legitimate standards and instructed people how to narrate is not accepted in post-modern society, while knowledge in post-modernity was a kind of commodity, and could be changed into digital, technical and operational data. Thus, it is not only learning and understanding, or a set of directive statement, but also a skill, ability and understanding, including concepts like "how to operate", "how to survive" and "how to understand"; "therefore, knowledge is kind of capability." Lyotard has argued that exertion of this ability has gone far beyond knowledge and practice to obtain the truth; it could be extended to the assessment and applying criteria on the efficiency of technological qualification, justification and happiness of ethics and wisdom, and pleasure to hearing and sight. It could be used to understand things, make a judgment, and make assessment and conversion.

3.2.3.3 PURSUIT FOR KNOWLEDGE IS TO SEEK FOR DIFFERENCE AND INDEFINITENESS

Based on the analysis above, Lyotard believes that knowledge is acquired through antinomy reasoning, unlike the previous ways. Through antimony reasoning, what the current knowledge and science seek for is "exactly 'infiniteness' other than consensus. Lyotard has argued that, the alleged uncertainty is directly the outcome of applying antimony reasoning; it must include conflictive and half-heroic competitions, and "antimony logic does not focus on reaching a consensus but internally destroying the basic frame that the previous 'standard science' had established."[17] In other words, Lyotard held the belief that in post-modern society, there was no universal standard in between discourses and knowledge, "it is unnecessary for us to establish steady language combinations, even if we establish them, they might be featured as incommunicability."[18] Thus, "knowledge-in-itself is not supposed to be the supreme goal of knowledge any longer; knowledge has lost its 'traditional value'"[19], "meta-knowledge" (Lyotard's term), the original knowledge based on ontology about law, nature and origin, and "old education via mental training or individual delving to obtain knowledge have been obsolete, and have faded away."[20]

---

17   *Ibid.*, p. 21.
18   Qin Xiqing: "Crisis of Meta-narration and Graves of Intellects: Criticisms to Lyotard's Theory on Intellects". *Foreign Social Science*, 1996(2).
19   Lyotard, Jean-François: *The Postmodern Condition: A Report on Knowledge*. p. 36.
20   *Ibid.*, p. 35.

Lyotard also believed that from the beginning of the 19th century, "self-erosion" has occurred inside science; with the rapid development of science, the crisis of science has increasingly intensified. These crises are summarized as follows: identical systems have begun to disintegrate, the boundary of the whole net has started to break, thus science was restored to liberty, "science is playing its own games, and it has no power to legislate for other language games", because other games have their own rules. The society is made of games, and the social subject is restricted in these game rules. This situation is just like what Wittgenstein thought about language: language is like an ancient capital city. In this city, there are crisscross streets and plazas, and houses, old and new, next to each other. Outside the city, lay the new area with straight and wide streets and identical houses. And the city ceaselessly expands outward. Therefore, Lyotard pointed out that there can be no meta-language, legitimate criteria or universal rules in the post-modern society. "The issue we are facing is to use legitimatization as the original source to de-construct legitimate activity", but "if we make a further exploration for de-construction and extend it to a larger scope, we start to get access to post-modern society: science can only play its own language game."[21]

By his analysis on the changes of connotation, criteria and acquisition of knowledge in post-modern society, Lyotard has announced that, meta-language was obsolete, the social context of meta-narrative, like heroes and sages, rescue and liberation, great victories, all these are scattered in the swarms of stars of the post-modern knowledge. People do not believe in the great "motivator", great "theme" any longer; they just use "small narrative", with the belief that postmodern world was a world of "common people".

3.2.3.4 CRISIS OF KNOWLEDGE LEGITIMATIZATION AND RETREAT OF UNIVERSAL SUBJECT

In Lyotard's opinion, since "meta-knowledge" did not exist any longer and large narratives have disintegrated, problems of knowledge legitimatization and intellectuals' status has become prominent.

The notion of legitimatization, in Lyotard's view, is "that a legislator is authorized to issue laws and makes it a series of regulations. This process is called legitimatization."[22] However, just as demonstrated above, today things are different from what they were in the past. Knowledge in the post-modern time is not what it was in modern age. Language has disintegrated, and consensus knowledge, regulations and rules are discarded. Knowledge has not only become digits but also broken into pieces that could not be integrated any longer and there is no consensus in between them. And the supposed knowledge system and national knowledge are nothing but assembling those pieces of knowledge that bore no

---

21   *Ibid.*, p. 126.
22   *Ibid.*, p. 46.

consensus and cannot be universally accepted. This means it is impossible that there is another kind of knowledge which can be labeled as principles or norms to standardize other knowledge or people. Neither is there a group of people who had some kind of knowledge and thus could make principles or norms to standardize other people's knowledge. Therefore, Lyotard has concluded that legitimatization had disappeared or lost.

Meta-language and meta-narratives are disintegrated and the knowledge unity is broken into independent language games; as a result, the previous universal subject has abruptly vanished: "the social subject itself also has merged in various language games."[23] Lyotard also held that supposing there were intellectuals in the postmodern society, they would be different from the traditional ones, who were intellectuals or subjects in a general sense, while the intellectual in the postmodern society is a concrete one. Directly in this sense, Lyotard has drawn his conclusion, "there ought not to be 'intellectuals' anymore."

In all, it seems that Lyotard is only talking about conversion of meaning, standard and validity of knowledge; in fact, he has disintegrated the universal validity and legitimate norms of knowledge. Through turning knowledge into pieces, heterogeneity, digitalization and games, he intended to achieve the goals of de-constructing meta-discourses, universal narratives, identity, integrity, ontology and oppose legitimacy, and finally overturn traditional philosophy and de-construct modernity.

3.2.4 HABERMAS AND RESCUE FOR MODERNITY

Jürgen Habermas is a German contemporary philosopher and sociologist, as well as one of the representatives of second generation of Frankfurt school. From 1945 to 1949, he had studied philosophy, history, psychology, German literature and economics, in the universities of Göttingen (1949/1950), Zürich (1950/1951), and Bonn (1951–1954), and earned a doctorate in philosophy in 1954. From 1956 on, he worked as an assistant of Theodor Adorno at the Institute for Social Research at the Johann Wolfgang Goethe University, Frankfurt. Later he became a professor of philosophy sociology at the University of Heidelberg and Frankfurt University in 1962. His main works include: *Knowledge and Human Interests* (1968); *Technology and Science as Ideology* (1968); *The Re-construction of Historical Materialism* (1976); *The Theory of Communicative Action* (1981); *The Philosophical Discourse of Modernity* (1985); *The New Conservatism* (1989).

Habermas has a paradox identity. He has joined post-modern trend with the identity of "non-post-modernist". It is necessary to make some explanation on his identities: is he a "post-modernist", or a "non-post-modernist" in the camp of

---

23   *Ibid.*

post-modernists, or a postmodernist who is against post-modernism. It is well-known that Habermas has firmly opposed post-modernism with the belief that modernity was not completed; thus, it is impossible for post-modernity to occur. He has joined the post-modernist trend with the identity of opposing post-modernism. Therefore, rigidly speaking, Habermas cannot be seen as a post-modernist. However, any discussion on post-modernism, whether it is for or against post-modernism, can't go around Habermas. And any debate on post-modernism inevitably should involve his criticism on post-modernism. Without Habermas, any introductions and discussions on post-modernism are neither brilliant nor profound. This is the reason why he has a paradox identity: a postmodernist as well as a non-postmodernist.

3.2.4.1 HABERMAS, MODERNITY AND RATIONALITY

First, Habermas has illustrated his concept of "rationality". After since the Enlightenment Movement, science has played loudly the song of triumph after destroying omniscient-and-omnipotent God, and freed people from the exclusive rule of God or Pope, removing the authoritativeness of people's life. However, science has established a new authoritativeness based on rationality. Thus, rationality has become pure "scientific rationality", "instrumental rationality", turning out to be norms of all things as well as the judge of right and wrong. Science and rationality has become a double-edge sword: on the one hand, it liberates productive forces, pushes forward social development, enlightens people's wisdom, and bestows people with power and liberty; on the other hand, it becomes a tool of damaging human living sphere, massacring people and disordering social politics and economics. It has brought people substantial material wealth, but it has produced mechanic orders for the society, and has increasingly hollowed people's spiritual life, disordering people's spirit and values, making people poor in spirit and chaotic in values. This double-edged sword, science and rationality, has moved farther and farther to its opposite. Furthermore, a divide has come into being between science and rationality. With privileges in its hand, science attempts to become the only legitimate body of knowledge, while all the other kinds of knowledge are devalued to expressions of knowledge. Therefore, Habermas has drawn the conclusion that something is indeed wrong with science and modernity.

Habermas has also argued that facing the crazy expansion of rationality and the problem of modernity in itself, philosophers have started to criticize this situation, with the intension of putting things right.

Marcuse and Adorno, key figures of the Frankfurt school, have argued that all the contradictions and crises of the capitalist society lay in economics and science. Therefore, they have negated science, rationality and all of the advances in the industrial society. On the contrary, deconstructionists, like Derrida, have taken different measures. They have shifted from action and truth-oriented "macro-narratives" to culture, with the attempt to counteract the extreme effect of rationality, opposed science and metaphysics of traditional philosophy by means of changing linguistic structure and conducting cultural criticism. However, Habermas does not agree with the negative attitude of Marcuse and Adorno who have negated all, nor does he agree with Derrida's practice in deconstructing culture instead of criticizing reality. Habermas believes that the reason why errors occur in science and rationality in the capitalist society and cause deviations in modernity lay in the administrative institution that is getting increasingly bureaucratic and secondly the defense system of culture and ideology brought by institutions, rather than science and technology. In his opinion, it is necessary to reform the capitalist superstructure. Only in this way, could people break away from the capitalist cultural and ideological system, and build new human relations and rationality.

For Habermas, life is in variety of forms with the co-existence of kinds of integrities. Amidst these integrities, there existed differences as well as frictions, but they could adapt and adjust each other by themselves. This is also true for philosophy, values and beliefs. Philosophy can be transformed to deal with rationality in all aspects; but rationality is one of human life forms, which is interactive with social life. Although rationality is misused and distorted time and again, it would still tenaciously raise its voice in every proper communication.

Therefore, Habermas held the view that though errors have occurred in Western philosophical view on rationality since ancient Greece, and philosophers had been going along an irreversible path of self-negation and self-counteraction, they had not gone so far that they were incurable. And this situation has required post-modernism to take kinds of actions, such as criticizing modernity, totally overturning subjectivity, integrity, identity and originality, eliminating deep meanings behind language, and counteracting nature behind phenomenon. But has replaced them with non-center, non-subject, non-integrity, non-nature and non-origin. From another perspective, the Enlightenment Movement has weakened traditional religious rule. But it is unknown whether the Enlightenment Movement could effectively find a counterpart for itself or not form consensus on rationality. How could it be said that the Enlightenment Movement had completed its mission of liberation? How could it be said modernity has been over?

3.2.4.2 HABERMAS HIGHLIGHTING COMMUNICATION AND CONSENSUS TO ESTABLISH "NEW RATIONALITY"

Just as previously demonstrated, due to the errors of science and rationality, traditional metaphysics has taken the leading position, while post-modernists like Derrida have totally negated rationality, metaphysics, order, generality, universality, consensus, ontology, origin and nature. Habermas has criticized modernity in a way that is different from post-modernists in essence. More specifically, on the one hand, Habermas has argued that modernity was not over, neither can the post-modernity possibly occur; on the other hand, he highlights rationality, consensus, generality and universality, and has committed himself to establish a set of new rationality. He firmly believes that "a self-evident species must rely on language communication and cooperation to survive, and rational activities necessarily depend on rationality." As a result, "In legitimate advocate, no matter how implicative the way we are compelled to adjust ourselves, or no matter how many times we are restrained in the communication, it is necessary for the covert rationality to be always unswerving."[24]

Habermas has started his research from "interest". Interest is related with cognition, and it is the inter-media between the subject and the object. Various interests cause the subject to choose different objects, producing categories of knowledge. In Habermas' assumption, humankinds had three basic kinds of interests: (1) the existence of substance, namely, technology of material reproduction of existing substance; (2) the interpretation of situational meaning and mutual understanding and communication between people; (3) the social factors that hold back people's communication and the effort to overcome them to win human liberty and liberation. Those three interests respectively bring three basic categories of knowledge, namely, science, metaphysics and theories of criticism. His division of knowledge in parallels actually reflects his intension to oppose the dominant position as "neutral values of science". He puts emphasis on the latter two, metaphysics and theories of criticism, and has focused his research on communication and understanding between people to reach consensus. It can be seen that Habermas' "new rationality" is actually a process of seeking meanings, as well as reaching a general consensus by means of communication and a criticize those factors that hold back communication.

Consensus in Habermas' term refers to norms, rules, generality, universality, meanings of things and nature of things behind the phenomenon. Therefore, emphasis Habermas put on consensus not only refutes the viewpoints of those, like Derrida, Lyotard and Foucault, who have utterly de-constructed ontology: anti-center, anti-nature and anti-rationality, but also against their epistemology on "the author being dead", "reading being misreading", which was difference-oriented relativism – and even skepticism. His position has inevitably caused the opposition and retort of post-modernists, giving rise to disputes in the history of the contemporary Western philosophy, which were most attractive, speculative, wonderful and exciting. These disputes were between Habermas and Bell, Habermas and Lyotard, and Habermas and Derrida.

24　　Habermas, Jürgen: *Horizons of Modernity*, p. 19. Shanghai: Shanghai People's Press, 1997.

124 CURRENT GLOBAL IDEAS AND MOVEMENTS CHALLENGING CAPITALISM

3.2.4.3 DISPUTES BETWEEN HABERMAS AND LYOTARD AS WELL AS DERRIDA

The dispute between Habermas and Lyotard was around "consensus". Just as previously demonstrated, in Lyotard's eyes, "modernity" meant some meta-discourse, macro-narrative, and sciences, like spiritual dialectics, meaning hermeneutics, rationality or liberation of the action subject and creation of wealth, which depended on meta-discourse and macro-narrative to be legitimatized. However, "post-modernity" is suspicious about meta-discourses and have de-constructed macro-narratives. Lyotard has also argued that "legitimacy" in the postmodern time was under the control of pragmatism and it was a pure technological operation. The legitimatized knowledge must be convertible into codes or operative knowledge, rather than like in Habermas' view: knowledge exists in the consensus through discussion. In order to show that they firmly oppose "consensus", universality and generality, post-modernists, like Lyotard and Foucault, have never used the word "we" in their works. Foucault has declared that he did not like to address in the tone "we know there is a better way; let's find it together."

However, in Habermas' eyes, when we are making a criticism, first we must have a stand. We must also have a yardstick to judge right or wrong, which could get away from "a criticism of self-denotation". Without this prerequisite and criteria, it would be meaningless to talk about suspicions on meta-discourses and deconstruction of macro-narratives. Habermas has reiterated that the starting point of his new rationality is: life form, values and belief system, which are always in the form of pluralistic unity; although co-existence of diversity might produce frication, the differences would not automatically lead to irreconcilability, but they could still reach a consensus by means of communication. This actually means that any knowledge and science had their own principles, prerequisites and standards. Otherwise, if everyone had his own thought and each had his own standard, it will be impossible for any communication to happen. In that case, would criticism target at the imaginary enemy, and turn out to be a Don Quixote–style fight? How could knowledge and science be universally acknowledged and accepted?

The dispute between Habermas and Derrida was different from that between Habermas and Lyotard. It was around whether the distinction between philosophy and literary criticism could be blurred? However, Habermas did not change his viewpoint; that is to say, he insisted that modernity was not over.

Derrida believed all languages were featured in sign; in other words, all languages had first emerged as a sign. Therefore, all writings – whether it was literary or philosophical – were texts consisting of signs. That is to say, in Derrida's eyes, philosophy was as well rhetorical and narrative rather than texts to reveal nature of things. The basic content of the philosophical text could also be obtained through literary criticism. Thus Derrida breaks the barrier between philosophical discourse and literary criticism, removing the boundary between them. Consequently, reading a philosophical work was like enjoying a literary work, the meaning of which totally came from the reader's understanding and interpretation of it. This view negates the existence of the author, central idea and consensus.

Habermas has bravely opposed what deconstructionists, like Derrida did – blurring the distinction between philosophical discourse and literary criticism – actually negating consensus and philosophy. He held the view that languages had various functions and forms. Apart from literary criticism and poetic language, there were also daily life language, philosophical discourse and other special forms like literature, arts, science and moral. They all play different roles. However, in Derrida's view, poetic language covers all fields, which negates all the other functions of the language, the independent status of all the other discourses and the complex relationship between them. Habermas has seriously pointed out that Derrida's de-constructionist philosophy was retrogressing in thought, which would lead to a dead end. If it got out of such a situation, it should go back to modernity, which was established in the Enlightenment Movement. It is obvious that Habermas has preserved space and position for philosophical discourse. He insisted on its relative independence, and defended the distinction between philosophy and the other subjects. And he held the view that it was impossible for the coming of post-modernity because modernity was not over yet.

3.3 RATIONALITY AND LIMITATIONS OF POST-MODERNISM

It is not difficult to see from the previous demonstration that post-modernism was like a strong wind, pushing out the roots of traditional philosophy, which was viewed as "broken broom", and it was discarded in the wild field; like a sharp sword, post-modernism directly thrust at capitalism, exposing the demerits of the capitalism in culture. However, it is just with this powerful destruction and merciless disclosure that post-modernism has gone to the other extreme side – nihilism.

3.3.1 RATIONALITY OF POST-MODERNISM

The emergence of post-modernism not only relies on certain social background, but also a certain theoretical ground. Post-modernism reflects social reality in theory. Therefore, it did not deviate from the track of human social civilization, nor did it exist outside Western philosophy. Just as its occurrence, its existence necessarily has its own reasonability.

First, post-modernists have adhered to philosophical criticism. Marxists hold the view that philosophy is a learning of "reminiscence". Philosophy is neither established knowledge, nor a ready-made conclusion, nor explanation of examples, nor dull regulations. It requires criticism and creativity, as well as constant query and reflection on life-world and theory. It leads people to opening self-reflection and self-criticizing in all the spheres of social life forever. Therefore, criticism or critical spirit is its indispensable feature. It is the large flag of critical spirit that post-modernists have raised to mercilessly and "cruelly" de-construct all the previous things and all different from them. Those included philosophical ontology, "dualism" of traditional philosophy, thinking modes of metaphysics, and social modernization, modernity, negative effects of science and technology – of course with no exception they have borrowed some viewpoints of Marxist philosophy. When it comes to the drawbacks of post-modernism, post-modernists have gone a bit far and even to the extreme side in philosophical criticism.

Second, post-modernists have paid attention to the real life. Marx has once remarked that philosophy was the essence of spirit. Marxists have always emphasized that philosophy must be related to reality and keep up with times. This is because philosophy needs to take in nutrition from social reality, obtain inspiration in the analysis and critics of reality, and reflect on itself. And the criticism of philosophy also requires that it should directly face real life. Just as previously stated, post-modernism originated from people's criticism on the capitalism and critically observing human conditions in the Western social modernization. It also came from theories that were established in the course of people's criticism. That is to say, post-modernism was established on the basis of reflection on the capitalist destiny, merits and demerits of modernization. And it was also the outcome in reflecting whether rationalism and enlightenment spirit was true or not, which were viewed as theoretical foundations of capitalist modernization. Therefore, post-modernism is not only the necessary outcome of capitalist culture, but also the inevitable result of the movement of contradictions inside the capitalist society. Post-modernism has some significance in reality.

Third, post-modernists have criticized the thinking modes of metaphysics and opposed the modernist view of the world. Marxists hold the view that metaphysics on the one hand adheres to ossified "dichotomy" or "dualism"; on the other hand, due to the incompatibility of the two parts, it goes to the extreme side – either approving all or totally disapproving. Consequently, once a concept is advocated by metaphysics, it is absolutely objective, just and right; and considered as absolute truth; existence subsuming all, thus it is "unique" and permanent. Post-modernists believe that it was under such influence of metaphysical thinking modes that Westerners have deviated in the understanding of modernization, modernity and the role of science. That is to say, Westerners have always understood the society and its development from the perspectives of "dualism" and "absolute truth". As a result, intolerant negative effects have come out. The criticism of post-modernists shook the foundation of metaphysics that came into being accompanied by modern science – which opened the door of Western modern society and created wealth that piled like hills; science itself was the wealth that Westerners took pride in. Post-modernists have also shaken the traditional concept that is rooted in people's mind.

Fourth, post-modernists have put stress on what modernists have ignored and all that happened after and outside modernity, such as indefiniteness, heterogeneity, disorder and flattening. But they have repelled all that modernity has focused on, like principles, integrity, definiteness, authority, identity and rules. It should be said that post-modernists have focused on the principal problems and hit the nail on the head of modernists, which was a deep theoretical reflection on the development of Western philosophy. This strike was helpful for Western philosophy as an attempt to jump out of the restrictions of traditional philosophy, and advance toward another direction[25].

Fifth, post-modernists have criticized the capitalist social reality, queried and anatomized scientific rationality and industrial civilization, which have double practical significance. The first is that post-modernism has disclosed the basic contradictions and crises of the capitalist society, unveiling its disguise and nature. This cannot only trigger capitalism directly face its own malpractice, but also be helpful to see clearly its genuine appearance. The second is that post-modernists have disclosed problems and symptoms occurring in the capitalist modernization, have pointed out mistaken industrial concepts, which has undoubtedly enlightening and warning significance for those countries that are stepping from pre-industrial modernization to modernization. It is also likely to help them transcend the capitalist —"Caudine Forks" mentioned by Marx — modernization. That is to say, it is possible to avoid sufferings of capitalism but utilize its modernization fruits to achieve their goal of modernization.

3.3.2 ERRORS OF POST-MODERNISM

Just as previously stated, post-modernists have "righted wrongs" of the traditional philosophy and the capitalist reality; in other words they have "overcorrected" them. It was due to this "overcorrection" that post-modernism inevitably has some limitations.

The first is of skepticism and nihilism. Metaphysics emphasizes identity and integrity, but blurs their internal differences. As a result, identity and integrity form a "castle" that is ossified, closed and lifeless, like "atoms" and "monads" in the

---

25   Feng Jun (eds): *Speech Excerption on Postmodernism Philosophy*, p. 24. Beijing: Commercial Press, 2003.

traditional philosophy. "Atom" and "monad" are closed, undividable and self-origin-and-cause. There is no window for anything else to get access to it ("Atom" and "monad" are also believed as "origin" by the traditional philosophy, as well as paragon of "fundamentalism"). Metaphysics also puts much attention to nature of things, foundation, as well as the "subject-object" and "phenomenon- nature", "dualisms", but considers nature and foundation to be absolute and abstract, like "monad" as the "origin" of all things they originated and reverted hither; the "subject-object" and "phenomenon-nature" "dualisms" are ossified and patterned, turning out to be two "opposite" poles. It can be seen that the errors of metaphysics do not lie in its acknowledgement of identity, integrity; nature of things, foundation and "dichotomy", but that it makes them abstract, ossified and closed. Post-modernists have attempted to chisel a window in the closed "castle" of metaphysics, but ruined it completely, turning it into pieces of rubble. They have advocated pieces, differences and varieties instead of identity and integrity of metaphysics, emphasized anti-nature, anti-foundation and nihilism instead of nature foundation and "dichotomy", but deconstructing and ruining all things, with the belief that "man cannot step into the same river once at a time." Consequently, while post-modernists revived the world, which was ossified and solidified by metaphysics, they made it broken and vacuous. The concepts, like "the author is dead", "man is dead", "anything goes" and "existence means difference", became the main theme of post-modernism. People were at a loss at the empty rubble-like world, and almost turned out to be nihility. Thus, post-modernism as well went to another extreme.

Second, post-modernists were against rationality, counteracting subjectivity. From the Enlightenment Movement, rationality advanced ahead by leaps and bounds; especially in the 20th century, scientific rationality strode forward. It brought about social modernization as well as adequate fine materials to people; meanwhile, it produced worst effects mainly in the form of seriously damaged environment as well as nearly total loss of human subjectivity. Post-modernists attributed all these to rationality, especially the ill expansion of scientific rationality and the control of metaphysical thinking modes. Then, they have advocated counteracting subject and opposing rationality. Derrida has declared, "Outside texts, nothing else exists." All was nothing but games, and "the rules of games are replaced by games themselves." Rorty has pointed out, "rationality" did not refer to concepts that people usually regarded as "orderly" or "possessing the preset norms for success", but indicated to be "conscious" and "reasonable"; it was a kind of "morality". Such nihilist attitudes as "baseless", "segmentary", "man-being-dead" and "anything going" inevitably led to conclusions like "loss of rationality" and "death of subject".

Actually, there is nothing wrong with rationality itself, neither can it be counteracted. This is because only man has rationality, and people still rely on subject to rectify rational errors with rationality and restore man's subjectivity. J. Marsh has once remarked when commenting on post-modernists' criticism of rationality, "I am willing to share the discontent of the capitalist system, their wishes of transcending the system to reach a new realm, their disillusionment from egoism, positivism, instrumentalism and rationalism, their troubles about modern social abnormal state. [...] Like post-modernists, I will push forward the movement of intelligence, culture and politics, rather than revert or adhere to the contemporary capitalism."[26] But "can rational criticism be made without the rational method?" Thus, the question is how to return to the essential properties of man being a man, how to make rationality soundly and orderly – both to man and nature – develop and play its role, rather than go to the extreme side in a metaphysical style. Therefore, it ought to be said that post-modernism made a correct diagnosis of Western society, but unfortunately made wrong prescriptions.

The third is the relativism of post-modernists. The foremost important and effective strategy of post-modernists deconstructing the traditional philosophy is that they have mixed philosophy with literature, blurred the boundaries between them, and treated philosophy as a text for people to read. Furthermore, post-modernists have also held the view that reading was a misreading. Therefore, everyone could interpret what was different from others and on his own (this time from the next time). Post-modernists have as well destroyed all criteria with the advocate of "anything going" (term of Feyerabend). As a result, post-modernism inevitably went toward relativism. In fact, just as Habermas believes, there was consensus, rules and norms, and philosophical language was different from other languages. We also believe that though philosophy cannot stay in the ivory tower of abstract thinking; neither can it take extreme pride in possessing logic concepts and self-evident meaning; but philosophy has its own academic norms and its own concept system. Particularly, since the ancient time, philosophy has taken the responsibility of revealing nature of things and seeking consensus. Scholars, like Lyotard and Foucault were "greatly afraid of being plunged into meta-narrative of a certain 'subject', they undoubtedly belong to the culture of the subject of its generation, but they have avoided the word 'we' from their mouth, in case of being identified with the subject."[27] However, how ridiculous and miserable it was.

Fourth, post-modernism has limited the critics and deconstruction in the scope of knowledge. Post-modernists attributed series of social problems caused by modernity (rigidly speaking, it is Western social modernization.) to concepts of modernity or metaphysical thinking mode that was inherited for thousands of years. In fact, they have simply equaled a real social problem with a conceptual or philosophical problem or a thinking mode. Then, post-modernists have "madly"

---

26   Marsh, J.: Escaping Strategy: Self-referencing Paradox of Postmodern Rational Criticism, from Wang Yuhe: Complicated Games: *Research of Postmodernist Trends of Thought*, p. 24. Beijing: Social Sciences Academic Press, 1998.

27   Sheng Ning: *Humanistic Puzzle and Reflection*, p. 256. Beijing: SDX Joint Publishing Company, 1997.

criticized and deconstructed the traditional philosophy and metaphysical thinking mode. After Nietzsche overturned God and Foucault toppled "the author" and "man", they have overthrown everything with the advocate of "anything going" and treating everything including life as merely playing games. Post-modernists have treated the whole social life and thought about the contemporary society just from the perspective of knowledge. Thus, post-modernism was nothing but to express their attitude toward contemporary society from the angle of knowledge. This wore down post-modernism after a riot of emotion, and it has started to disintegrate and decline.

Fifth, post-modernists have opposed metaphysics but were still restrained within the framework of metaphysics. In order to avoid following the old road of the traditional philosophy, post-modernists had no choice but to deconstruct all things. However, when they opposed and de-constructed metaphysics and the traditional philosophy, they could not keep away from metaphysics. This was because on the one hand, they deconstructed major concepts of the traditional philosophy, such as truth, values, origin and presence; on the other hand, they kept and borrowed other concepts of the traditional philosophy. They counteracted and deconstructed concepts of the traditional philosophy, like "foundation", "logos", "integrity", "nature" and "dualism", subverting those like gradation, structure and authority and interpreting meaning with indefiniteness, while they highly praised notions of non-foundation, non-nature, margin, fragments and anti-rationality with the regard of them as new "sages", establishing new definiteness and authority with "indefiniteness of meaning" and non-center to construct "post-modernism". Therefore, post-modernism is nothing but the metaphysics opposite to traditional philosophy in the place of traditional philosophical metaphysics, going to the extreme side and turning out to be the metaphysics that is against metaphysics. After Rorty saw that, Derrida was attempting to escape from the trap of traditional metaphysics, he pointed out Derrida had no choice but to be a metaphysician in defense of himself, "because apart from being disguised itself inside beings, existence has never had a "meaning", neither has it been speculated or uttered like this. And 'difference', in a queer sense, is more 'ancient' than the ontological term of "difference" or existent truth. This unfathomable chess board has no support or depth; existence involves the games that are played on this chess board."[28] Apparently, this means that behind the existence, there is still a "root" more profound as well as an "origin" more mysterious and elusive. This is indefinite abstract "nothingness". Stubborn with the abstract "nothingness", Derrida had nothing to do but return to metaphysics that he deconstructed. Thus, to blindly criticize and deconstruct all, post-modernists regarded criticism and deconstruction of the traditional philosophy as the goal itself, and were never ready to say "construction". Finally, they could not stand but to set a trap and

---

28   Derrida, Jacques: Margins of Philosophy, cited from Wang Yuechuan. *Postmodernist Cultural Research*, p. 225.

unconsciously weave a "cage" for themselves. As a result, it was inevitable for post-modernism to decline.

Nevertheless, post-modernism is useful as a reference and deserves to be thought in depth for countries which are under modernization and stepping towards industrial civilization. Just as David Griffin wrote in the preface of his book of Chinese edition Postmodern Science: The Re-enchantment of Science: "My starting point of consideration is: China can avoid the destructive influence brought by modernization by means of learning about the mistakes that Western world has made. To do so, China actually is a country of 'post-modernization.'"[29]

REFERENCES

- David Griffin: *Postmodern Science: The Re-enchantment of Science*. Beijing: Central Compilation & Translation Press, 1995.
- Zhang Guoqing: *Center and Margins — Outline of Trend of Post-modernism*. Beijing: Chinese Social Sciences Press, 1998.
- Feng Jun (eds): *Speech Excerption of Post-modernism Philosophy*. Beijing: Commercial Press, 2003.
- Jean-François Lyotard: *The Postmodern Condition: A Report on Knowledge*. Changsha: Hunan Fine Arts Publishing House, 1996.
- Sheng Ning: *Humanistic Puzzle and Reflection — Criticism of Western Post-modernism*. Beijing: SDX Joint Publishing Company, 1997.
- Richard Rorty: *Post Philosophical Culture*. Shanghai: Shanghai Translation Press, 1992.
- Wang Yuechuan: *Postmodernist Culture Research*. Beijing: Peking University Press, 1992.

---

29   David Griffin: *Postmodern Science: The Re-enchantment of Science*, p. 13. Beijing: Central Compilation & Translation Press, 1995.

CHAPTER IV

POST-COLONIALISM

1 *Rise of Post-colonialism*
2 *Main Contents of Post-colonialism*
3 *General Evaluation of Post-colonialism*

CHAPTER FOUR

INTRODUCTION

In the contemporary Western social theories, the three terms: post-colonialism, post-colonial theory and post-colonial criticisms are equivalents. The notion of post-colonialism can be understood from three aspects: (1) It is employed to refer to nation states and to the native people there that used to be colonies of other countries and they are now are independent, like post-colonial countries and post-colonial intellectuals; (2) to denote the reflection, criticism and research on historical facts and results of Western cultural colonization, like post-colonial theory and post-colonial critical approach; (3) to mean global state of politics, economy and culture, such as post-colonial world and post-colonial time. In short, as a theoretical critical discourse and social trend of thoughts, what post-colonialism targets and reflects are the historical facts on European colonialism and results it had produced. It is based on the crisscross study of sciences, such as philosophy, history, literature, anthropology, psychology and culturology. It extensively involves culture and imperialism, colonial discourse and Westerners' recurrence of Eastern culture, globalization and national cultural identity, issues of races, classes and sex relationships, and reviews the global relations after the cold war.

Post-colonialism originated at the end of 1970s, with Said's book of *Orientalism* as the milestone. It was at the end of 1980s and the beginning of 1990s that post-colonialism turned out to be a wide influential social trend of thought. With the prominence of cultural issues in social life, post-colonial research on cultural relations of West and East caught more and more attention. A series of theoretical forums on post-colonialism were held one after another in European and American countries. There were various journals focusing on the study and criticism of post-colonial culture. Some universities started teaching courses on post-colonial literature, criticism and theory. Post-colonialism increasingly became a unique cultural research mode, and effected extensive social influence.

CURRENT GLOBAL IDEAS AND MOVEMENTS CHALLENGING CAPITALISM

4.1 RISE OF POST-COLONIALISM

Just as other social thoughts, the rise of post-colonialism was not rootless, but based on particular social historical settings. To put it in a nutshell, it was set in the colonization of East by West and the results it brought about. Post-colonial stage has been over for a long time, but it does not mean that colonial history has completely vanished in ideological sphere and social customs. On the contrary, it still plays a role in people's life. Therefore, post-colonialism is not only a "historical" research, but also a significant research on "reality". Post-colonialism borrows from various theories, but generally speaking, these theories belong to critical approach. Based on the existent literary research and text research, Post-colonialism is generally featured as cultural study. And cultural study itself has become the vital part of the contemporary social theories.

4.1.1 HISTORICAL SOCIAL BACKGROUNDS

To put it briefly, historical social backgrounds for the rise of Post-colonialism can be summarized as follows: intensified relations between Western and Eastern countries after the World War II; intellectuals of Eastern blood and life experience have gained access to Western groves of academe; revival of nationalism after the cold war; reminiscence of ethnic cultural independence of the developing countries in the age of economic globalization.

4.1.1.1 RELATIONS BETWEEN WESTERN AND EASTERN COUNTRIES AFTER THE WORLD WAR II

After the end of the World War II, many colonies in Asia, Africa and Latin America gained political independence one after another, and the traditional empires have disintegrated. However, imperialism did not immediately come to an end, neither did it utterly become the "past", but has still remained foremost powerful force in economy, politics and military. Traditionally, people still associate such countries as Algeria and India with France and Britain. For example, residents from pre-colonies, like Muslim, African countries and West Indian Federation, are now living in their former European suzerain countries. Some Westerners have always insisted that they are defenders of modern civilization and take the responsibility to lead the world. They constantly impose their concepts of law and justice upon the world, and tend to interfere with internal affairs of other countries under the pretext of liberty and human rights. Meanwhile, the newly independent countries and regions may also encounter various difficulties, frustrations and mistakes in their economic and social development. Consequently, these facts have inevitably reinforced some Westerners' belief that the ex-colonial states seemingly could not go without the guidance of their former suzerains, and they even desire to restore colonization. Particularly, the United States often interferes with the Third World, launching wars, plotting coups and overtly toppling regimes, from assassination to financially supporting "anti-government troops". There are frequently opposing voices in the United States, but the necessity and validity of the American intervention is often distorted and exaggerated by the government, decision makers, military, think bank, news media and academia. Theories defending the global expansion of the United States have remained almost without change generation after generation. In such settings, how to look upon the colonial and post-colonial world have turned out to be a vitally important theoretical issue under discussion. Post-colonialism was the direct outcome of such theoretical discussion.

4.1.1.2 INTELLECTUALS WITH ORIENTAL BLOOD AND LIFE EXPERIENCE ENTERING WESTERN ACADEMIA

There are varieties of cultures in the world. They contain different and even opposite values. The applicability of them varies in a particular area, ethnic group or community. Therefore, it is improper to evaluate them simply with high-low or superior-inferior norms; let alone we cannot use the values formed in Western Enlightenment period as the only true norm. This common knowledge actually was not accepted by Western academia until the middle of the 20th century. Recently the distinction between Western and Eastern cultures are not simply regarded as the opposition between tradition and modernity any more, but are acknowledged as the co-existence of multiculturalism. Particularly in the migrant attracting poly-ethnic states like the United States, more and more people have begun to admit the co-existence of multiculturalism, and pay attention to the survival of the ethnic groups. Accordingly, subjects studying social marginal groups like minorities have become increasingly hot, and migrants have successfully assumed positions in universities and research institutes. These new subjects -from the stand of marginal and weak groups-, have started to criticize the mainstream social culture. Intellectuals born in the marginal groups and with the low-class life experience naturally had the priority to have a say in the criticism. Those with Eastern origins and once lived in the ex-colonial states started to enter the academia of the United States and gained higher positions in the research of the relationship between East and West.

For example, Edward Said (1935-2003), a founding figure in post-colonial theory, was born in Jerusalem (then the British Mandate of Palestine). He had his early education in Jerusalem and Cairo, and had later immigrated to Lebanon with his parents, drifting in the European countries. In 1957, he went to the United States to further his study, and won his bachelor in Princeton University, and his master's and doctoral degree in Harvard University. Later on, he taught for a long time in the University of Columbia, and was a member of editing committee and counselor of famous journals like *Critical Inquiry and Boundary*. Gayatri Chakravorty Spivak was born, in Calcutta, India, 24 February 1942, to a middle class family. She received an undergraduate degree in English at the University of Calcutta (1959), graduated with first class honors. After this, she completed her Master's degree in English from Cornell University, and then pursued her Ph.D. while teaching at the University of Iowa. Currently, she is professor of English and Cultures Research Department of the University of Pittsburgh. Homi K Bhabha was born into a merchant family from Mumbai, India. He received his early education in India, and later immigrated to England to further his study under the guidance of Terry Eagleton, a theorist of Western Marxism. Shifting from the research on marginal to central cultures and strived in the long journey of studies, Bhabha was appointed visiting professor at the University of Chicago in 1994, and guest professor at the Harvard University in 2000. Those scholars with special experiences have made researches on post-colonialism from a unique perspective, employed distinctive methods and which have produced rather strong repercussions in post-colonial countries.

4.1.1.3 RE-EMERGING NATIONALISM AFTER THE COLD WAR

In the colonial period, the rulers had carved up land boundaries at random, either forcibly joining different tribes together, or separating groups with same cultural origin. In the course of opposing the colonial oppression, the colonized people have united and fought against the colonization. When the colonialists were driven away, the liberated people in the ex-colonial states have faced the problem of identifying themselves, and it was necessary for them to negotiate on the conditions to establish nation states. Such cases could be seen in Africa and areas of the Middle East. In the confrontation period between two rival camps under the leadership of Soviet Union and the United States, ideological conflict had assumed a leading place, while ethnic contradictions in the nation states were in the secondary place. But with the end of the cold war in the 1990s, ideological conflict retreated to the back stage, and the configuration of the world politics encountered a re-integration. The contradictions in the nation states stood out, giving rise to the separation of some nation states, which was in the form of conflicting ethnic areas. And movements seeking for national homogeneity turned out to be bloody wars. Solutions for all these problems required further studies on colonial history and the relationship between current nation states, ethnic cultures and former colonial traditions and identity establishment for ethnic cultures. The reason why post-colonialism aroused extensive attention, to some extent, lay in its involvement with those problems in advance, and the increasing significance of those problems have pushed forward the study of post-colonialism a step further.

4.1.1.4 PURSUING FOR THE INDEPENDENCE OF NATIONAL CULTURES IN THE ERA OF ECONOMIC GLOBALIZATION

Since the 1990s, all the countries in the world have faced the tendency of economic globalization. As the outcome further development in global production and communication, economic globalization is undoubtedly a progressive process in promoting further formation of the world market, allocating natural resources, funds and labor force worldwide. It reflects the objective demand of the social development and represents an irretrievable historical tendency. With the development of economic globalization, differences between nation states are reflected primarily through culture. Economic globalization certainly has more than economic significance. While Western advanced countries transmit science and technology and knowledge of economic management to the rest of the world, they also spread capitalist values and ideology of the European centralism with the attempt to globalize Western culture. Therefore, it turns out to be an urgent problem for the developing countries to maintain independence of their own cultures in the process of economic globalization, and preserve national characteristics in the communication between Western and Eastern cultures. Based on those questions, post-colonialists have oriented their theoretical thinking at a more practical research goal, which has urgent significance.

4.1.2 THEORTEICAL SOURCES

Theories of post-colonialism mainly come from critical discourses of African colonialism, Marxists' nation-state approaches, Gramsci's cultural hegemony and Foucault's discourse of power. Additionally, Derrida's deconstructionism, psychoanalysis works by Freud and Lacan have also provided vital theoretical resources and methods.

4.1.2.1 CRITICAL DISCOURSES OF AFRICAN POST-COLONIALISM

Theories on post-colonialism originate from critical discourses rising in the African continent in the 1920s. And the critical discourses on colonialism which had emerged with the national liberation movements. In the process of opposing Western colonial rule and pursuing national independence, the African native intellectuals had strongly criticized Western "assimilation" policy to awaken the African national consciousness defending the dignity of African aboriginal culture. Among them, the most noticeable and frequently commented by post-colonial theorists are Aimé Césaire, Frantz Fanon, Chinua Achebe.

In his poem at a book length of *Notebook of a Return to My Native Land* issued at the end of 1930s, Césaire had advocated identifying the tradition black culture. In his book *Discourse on Colonialism*, he has revealed the internal relationship between

Western civilization and colonialism, and has concluded that colonial rule has materialized humankind. An emphasis on identifying black cultural tradition meant the awareness of being a black man, and admitting the fact to maintain his fate, history and culture as a black man. He has made a careful research on how colonialism had uncivilized the colonized and degraded their personality. Primarily, he has linked the proletarian revolution with the liberation of the colonies. However, later he thought that racial and colonial problems should be put in the first place in the analysis of the current world, which has affected later theorists of postcolonialism. Césaire's thought has made great influence on scholars like Fanon.

In his books, like *Black Skin, White Masks*, *The Wretched of the Earth and Toward the African Revolution*, Fanon has revealed the interaction of psychological factor and political factor, demonstrating that colonialism had not only influenced society but also individuals, resulting in the separation of blacks from themselves. His thought has focused on the study of psychological analysis, pointing to the fact that the influence of suzerains had penetrated into the minds of the colonial people and that it was mirrored in their novels. He has dialectically commented on the native intellectuals' defense of national culture emphasizing that national culture does not mean customs. In his eyes, to strive for national culture is to fight for national liberation. It is only with the people's struggle that the African blacks could gain their idiosyncrasy. Said has remarked, "Fanon was the first theorist to oppose imperialism, and he has asserted that the orthodox nationalism was walking along the road paved by imperialism, which seemingly transfers the authority to the national bourgeois, but actually imperialism was expanding its hegemony. Therefore, simply telling stories of a nation is duplicating, extending and serving new imperialism."[1]

Achebe wrote texts about colonial peoples' lives from the perspective of Africa in his novel *Things Fall Apart* which was published in 1958. He has criticized in a striking language the viewpoints that Westerners took for granted, advocated that the African writers had right to express their own thoughts in the English language. In his later works, like African Writers Series and *An Image of Africa: Racism in Conrad's "Heart of Darkness"*, he disclosed that the concept of universality that Western literary critics put forth actually had the connotations of Western nations, appealing that the concept of universality should be rejected by the African literature.

On the one hand, he has emphasized the particularity of national cultures, and insisted that Africa should be Africa itself, and it was necessary for the African to take in nutrition from its own cultural sources rather than regard Western cultures as universal; on the other hand, he warned that it would not be right under any

---

1 Edward Said: *Culture and Imperialism*, p. 390. Beijing: SDX Joint Publishing Company, 2003.

circumstance to turn utterly to the past; this would net help to resist the colonialists' distorting the tradition of national culture. The African critical discourse on colonialism was first to interpret colonialism from the perspective of culture and emphasize the construction of national culture, but later this trend has shifted to courageously transcending nationalism and has paid precious efforts to provide ideological guide and theoretical base for post-colonialism.

4.1.2.2 MARXIST NATION-STATE THEORY

Most theorists of post-colonialism have studied Marxism. Some of them even believe in Marxism. In his works the *British Rule in India and the Future Results of British Rule in India*, Marx had condemned the British colonialists who have destroyed the whole social structure of India, "cut ties with its old traditions and all the history of its past."[2] "Compared with all the catastrophes the Hindustanis have suffered, the one brought by the British colonialism undoubtedly belong to another sort in nature, which is much more severe"[3]. Marx had pointed out that, the British would complete a double mission in Hindu: one is destructive, namely eliminate the old Asian-style society; the other is reconstruction; that is, to make a material base for Western-style society in Asia. Thus, Marx had made a dialectical analysis on India under the colonial rule of Britain: "Hindu did not have a golden time before it was colonized, and the Britain acted as an unconscious tool in the history". Post-colonialist theorists like Said have sung high praise for the first judgment made by Marx, but they were discontented with his second statement, asserting that Marx as well could not avoid the restrictions of European centralism. No matter how they evaluated Marx, positive or negative, it was impossible for them to overlook Marx's critical thinking on the history of colonialism.

In the eyes of colonial theorists, no interpretation on imperialism is more careful and thorough than Lenin's classic work *Imperialism, the Highest Stage of Capitalism* up till now. Lenin had asserted that there was no rudimental conflict between nationalities. It was only in the modern time that the bourgeois and the proletariat have formed the two basic classes, producing two conflictive views on nationalities and national policies – the bourgeois nationalism and the proletarian internationalism. In the rising stage of capitalism, the bourgeois nationalism was progressive opposing feudalism and national oppression; but in the imperialist stage, it turned out to be national egoism, big-power chauvinism and colonial imperialism. But the nationalism of the oppressed nationalities was characterized as anti-imperialist, anti-colonialist and anti-racial. Lenin had emphasized that the proletarian cause and the liberation struggle of the oppressed nationalities were inseparable; the proletarian class in the world should unite with the oppressed

---

2   Marx/Engels *Collected Works, Second edition, Vol. 1,* p. 762. Beijing: People's Press, 1995.
3   *Ibid.,* p. 761.

people and the oppressed nationalities, to fight against imperialism together. The Russian October Revolution with the guidance of theories of Marxism and Leninism had opened a new path to establish independent nation states in the imperialist stage, fundamentally influencing, inspiring and pushing forward national liberation movements in the Third World.

In the course of confrontation between the two camps under the leadership of Soviet Union and the United States respectively, some theorists on post-colonialism usually avoided mentioning that they have adapted Marxist thoughts on national liberation and nation states, due to their precautions against Soviet hegemonism and difficulties in distinguishing Marxism and Soviet foreign policies. After the cold war, more and more theorists of post-colonialism have begun to speak up frankly on the practical significance of Marxism, and attempted to interpret some of Marx's thoughts from the perspective of post-colonialism. Consequently, Marxism has been increasingly influential on the study of post-colonialism.

4.1.2.3 GRAMSCI'S THOUGHT ON CULTURAL HEGEMONY

Post-colonialists focus their research on culture, which is undoubtedly under the direct influence of Gramsci, great thinker and Marxist party leader in Italy. As an important representative of Western Marxism, Gramsci had spent arduous efforts to reveal why socialist revolution could not achieve success in Western Europe. In his view, the socialism was not a natural and spontaneous process, but should be realized and grasped through the active participation of the working class and through their liberation struggles. Thus, it was vitally necessary to awaken the ideological awareness and class consciousness of the working class. Therefore, Gramsci had put forth the important notion of cultural hegemony. The notion of cultural hegemony means that under the capitalist rule, capitalist control in the sphere of culture occupies a vital position. And the capitalist overall control over culture and ideology is realized through consciously seek for an identity as ruler and ruled; rather than by external coercive means. Gramsci has argued that the bourgeois maintain their rule in two ways: one is coercive state apparatus like army, police and court; the other is non-coercive means like school, family, church and media. The latter factors impose the ruler's thought, norm of values and life style as the only reasonable and legitimate institution, impelling the ruled to consciously identify with the ruler. Consequently, the ruled loses the consciousness of being socially oppressed; they get used to humility and obedience, completely turning out to be the ruler's vassals.

Gramsci had argued that the role of ideology and culture in the ruling structure will increasingly get intensified with the advance of human history. And the conflict between economic and political benefits is usually reflected through cultural and ideological contradictions. In modern capitalist society, if hegemony cannot be established in culture, ethics and then politics, it cannot be established in the economical sphere. Based on this idea, Gramsci held the assumption the proletariat in order to succeed in their revolutionary movement in Western Europe, must go through a long period of complex struggles, analyzing and revealing the discourses and ideological logic of the bourgeois, how they maintain their rule through ideology and culture. Proletariat should reveal the truth of capitalist non-coercive means of rule, thus proletariat could take a critical attitude towards the social reality, and assume the hegemony for itself.

Gramsci has discussed the significance of cultural struggles between the ruling class and the ruled class, and the bourgeois and the proletariat. He has also focused on the cultural struggle inside the nation states. Theorists of post-colonialism have extended Gramsci's thoughts of cultural hegemony to their analysis on the world colonialism, and have asserted that cultural hegemony was dominant through the whole process of colonialism. In the post-colonial time, cultural control and hegemony is still an important form of imperialism. It is vitally important that the colonists should take over the cultural hegemony from imperialist powers. E.Said has remarked, "Gramsci has pointed to the dominant form of cultural hegemony. And his notion of hegemony is indispensable for understanding cultural life of Western industrialization. It is the hegemony or cultural hegemony that has bestowed imperialist orientalism with permanent endurance and power."[4] The term "subaltern" in the masterpiece written by Spivak — *Can the Subaltern Speak?* — was also quoted from Gramsci. This term, apart from bearing the meaning of "subordination" and "inferiority", denotes specifically the community of being oppressed and exploited without self-consciousness. We can say that the basic research mode of theorists on post-colonialism analyzing imperialist cultural hegemony is primarily based on Gramsci's thought of cultural hegemony.

4.1.2.4 FOUCAULT'S POWER OF DISCOURSE ASSUMPTION

Post-colonialism has also borrowed a lot from Foucault's assumption on power of discourse. In his works like the *Archaeology of Knowledge*, Foucault had declared that there is no objective knowledge; production, transition and consumption of knowledge are always miscellaneous with power. The power in Foucault's works implies social position, political power, economic benefits, and sorts of those factors constituting settings, main body or atmosphere of knowledge production. All of those are inter-woven into a net, severely restricted and even determined the nature and the use of knowledge. Foucault, through examining the issues like mechanism, strategy and function of power in social operation, he has provided post-colonialist thinkers methods for analyzing the structure of colonial rule. In the late 1970s, Foucault has directly studied post-colonial issues, analyzed nation states, distinguished personal identity issues and multinational economic issues.

---

4   Edward Said: *Orientalism*, p. 9-10. Beijing: SDX Joint Publishing Company.

In the Age of Enlightenment, intellectuals had hoped and believed that it was possible to absolutely distinguish truth from falseness, science from pseudo-science and knowledge from politics, which has given rise to an extreme idea: absolute science or its absolutization. On the basis of his researches on public establishments in modern society, like prisons, asylums, schools and mass media, Foucault has pointed out, that if we concede that the function of knowledge is to enable humankind to understand actual life, and that it orients our places in the society and determine our development direction, then we have to admit that knowledge is always miscellaneous with society, politics and power. Pure truth is non-existent, and purposes of all knowledge lay in corroborating the legitimacy of ruling structures. Therefore, intellectuals with critical spirit should query all preset self-evident prerequisites with the aid of the research in their own sphere, shook the bases of thinking modes and behavior that people are used to, we should de-familiarize the alleged "order of things" which are always considered unalterable and reasonable, re-examine the current social norms and check out their demerits, holes and non-humanness. On the basis of Foucault's above concepts, theorists of post-colonialism have criticized the colonialists viewing themselves as token of truth and as God's envoy, arguing that all the discourses of the colonialists were nothing but defenses for their ruling legitimacy.

Foucault has argued that the language as a social system had existed prior to individuals, and individual's expression of himself should be based on a particular language system; the expression of individuals could not be understood by others unless expressed in a particular language system. Therefore, we should not overestimate individual's independency and creativity. On the contrary individual must construct his/her identity with the help of language. However, it is impossible for language to have permanent meanings. Additionally, meanings of words do not match the outer world one to one. Any utterance had a fictional part in it, and fiction could make up reality. Foucault's thoughts have provided a basis for Said's book titled, Orientalism.

Edward Said pointed out, "The discourse concepts Foucault has researched in his books *The Archaeology of Knowledge* and *Discipline and Punish* are very useful for us to establish the identity of *Orientalism*."[5] The book Orientalism focuses on: how orientalism as a special way of expression controls the study of an individual orientalist; how Western colonialists preset and fabricate a conceptual frame in term of East and West on the basis of orientalism, then construct East and West with this frame, and finally build the real world of East and West in line with their original figment. Post-colonialism theorists have learned from, applied and exerted Foucault's analytical methods of power of discourse in their studies on cultural identity of Eastern nations, and have debated on the role that language played in cultural construction and interpretation of identifying constructive culture.

---

5   *Ibid.*, p.4.

4.1.3 BASIC FEATURES OF POST-MODERNISM

On the basis of analysis and study of specific texts, contemporary post-colonialists have reviewed the economical, political and cultural relationships and differences between East and West. They have tried their best to transcend traditional thoughts of nationalism. Hence their theoretical views have differentiated from the thoughts of early anti-colonialism.

4.1.3.1 RE-UNDERSTANDING THE CULTURAL RELATIONSHIP BETWEEN EAST AND WEST

Western academia has always focused their study on economic and political spheres. Some thinkers with reflective and critical spirit were also aware of the control, exploitation and robbery of West over East in the colonial time, and they have showed mercy and concern on the oppression of Eastern nations. However, as to the cultural relationship between East and West in those colonial ages, their viewpoints were pretty identical; they have claimed that: "before the invasion of Western colonialists, Eastern nations were in an uncivilized, primitive and backward status; it was Westerners that had brought brightness and civilization to East, and even led them into the history of civilization." Insomuch, as it were, the rise of post-colonialism has initiated a breakthrough in the conventional knowledge of the cultural relationship between East and West in Western academia. It has focused its research on the cultural colonialism of West over East all through history, dissected and criticized cultural imperialism, and finally set up a new viewpoint on the relationship between East and West, especially on the cultural relationship.

As for cultural imperialism, there are two opposite viewpoints: one emphasizes the primary place of economic control arguing that the purpose of cultural control is to dominate economy; the other puts stress on cultural control with the assumption that the aim of economic control was to dominate the culture. Post-colonialism has swayed between the above two viewpoints and tried to reveal that the economic, political and military policies of Western colonialists have directly influenced their study on literature, culture and history. However, any cultural principle that seems aloof and non-political greatly relies on the process that West had colonized East, and had involved the process of colonial history in a complex form. Consequently, contemporary theorists have not limited their study on the cultural relationship on the basis of politics, economy and culture, but they have extensively discussed their complicated and subtle relations. As a result, their research was multi-dimensional.

4.1.3.2 RESEARCH METHOD OF TEXTUAL ANALYSIS

The study of post-colonialism on cultural relations between East and West is mainly based on textual analysis. The notion of text is understood far beyond what is conventionally known as works. It includes all written data, as well as all those, like products and works, involving human activities and values. The reason why they are called text lay in the following two aspects: on the one hand, to emphasize their self-sufficiency, believing that internal structure of a text is independent, and that the analysis on their meaning could be independent without considering the author's social status and writing aim; on the other hand, post-colonialism opts to emphasize the relationship between texts and the specific context of the social politics because they believe that their meaning is attached and subordinate to social politics.

Based on various files, written data and literature of Western suzerains in the colonial ages, like government documents, investigation reports, explorers' diaries, novels and poems, post-colonial theorists have extensively explored the internal relationship between disciplines, like linguistics, lexicology, history, biology, political economics and literature, and cultural imperialism. They have discussed evolution, adjustments and modulations in cultural imperialism, including the changes between the stage of colonialism and the transformation period from colonialism to post-colonialism. They have made documentary research on the complicated relationships between individual authors or theorists and cultural imperialism. Attention was paid to the historical complexities and details of post-colonial study. They have treated cultural imperialism, cultural and historical phenomena as things true to life and internally related them with the real activities of humans, rather than reasoning them logically or considering them as inevitable historical outcomes externalizing individuals' thoughts and emotions.

In textual research, post-colonial theorists have focused on the change of Eastern image in the eyes of cultural imperialists. This image was exhibited in museums, narrated by missionaries, and theorized in humanities studies like anthropology. Post-colonialist theorists have revealed how East opposite to West had been fabricated, how it was distorted and how it was imposed to Westerners and Easterners. Their studies have enabled people to realize that East in a sense of geography is an objective existence, while East in the literary meaning relies mainly on the construction of man's brain. They have argued that the colonialists have studied the relationship between East and West in a paradigm of dualism, hence criticism of colonialism should reject this false paradigm, and the relationship between regions, nations or states should be viewed from a multi-dimensional and dynamic aspect.

4.1.3.3 ATTEMPTS TO TRANSCEND THEORY OF NATIONALISM

The purpose of post-colonialism in theory is different from that of nationalism. The nationalism, as it was, argues that Western intellectuals should pursue and support independence of the colonies and criticize Western cultural colonization from the standpoint of colonized nations, emphasizing on the excellent traditions and positive values of native cultures. But the original post-colonial theorists were all of Eastern blood, and have more or less lived in East, but their research of post-colonialism was done in the universities of Western countries, like the United States; their works were written in idiomatic English, and their intended readers were Westerners. Their original intention was to reconstruct the relationship between marginal and central cultures in Western cultural world. They did not intend to defend the nationalism of Eastern countries.

Fundamentally, the theoretical theme of post-colonialism was to examine the formation of the conflict between cultures of East and West, seeking a possibility to alleviate that contradiction. The post-colonial theorists have attempted to disclose Western colonists distorted Eastern cultural tradition with emphasis on the significance of equal dialogue, seeking common ground while reserving differences, and sought peaceful co-existence in the sphere of culture. By the same purpose, they have reflected on the limitations of cultural nationalism. In a nutshell, the post-colonialism has hoped to face the future, establish national culture in the constructive identifying, and build a national culture in communication.

4.2 MAIN CONTENTS OF POST-COLONIALISM

In his book *Orientalism* published in 1978, Said has opened the curtain of post-colonialism, revealing the colonialism and its cultural colonization over East. Said has focused on the history and current status of the Middle East, while Spivak and Bhabha have focused on the British colonial rule over India. The arguments among post-colonialists has included the following: how colonists' culture had influenced the colonies; how Eastern nations was regarded as evil and savage colonists, formed their own cultural identities; whether two nations having much cultural differences could share common reasoning and cognitive modes; whether science can stay neutral in ideological struggles; whether some cultures could be superior to others in a multi-cultural country; what languages should be used in schools; and which literary works should be read by the youth.

4.2.1 CRITICS ON ORIENTALISM

In Orientalism, Said made a critical analysis of how the Europeans depicted East and their contemporary fate. He has summarized three connotations of orientalism in a logic sequence, revealing the internal correlation between overt oriental studies and covert orientalism and exploring geographical and political background of oriental studies.

4.2.1.1 ORIENTAL STUDIES AND ORIENTALISM

In the book *Orientalism*, Said has illustrated the notion of orientalism from three aspects.

First, as an academic research category, orientalism covers a variety of spheres related to the Orient, from documentary translation to studies of numismatics, anthropology, archaeology, sociology, history, literature and culturology, including Asian and African civilizations that are known since ancient times up to now. Orientalists refer to those who are engaged in teaching, research and writing on Oriental issues. They may be anthropologists, sociologists, historians or linguists, who discuss concrete or general problems. What they do involves oriental studies.

Second, as a paradigm, orientalism is based on the dualism of West and East. That is, rationality, advance, civilization and superiority of the West, while irrationality, backwardness, savage and inferiority of the East; West being constantly progressive and East eternally remaining unchanged; West self-defining, East unable to self-define; West as the subject, while East the object; West as universality, while East particularity. The distinctions between East and West are widely accepted by Westerners, like poets, novelists, philosophers, politicians, economists and administrators. Based on those differences, they have formulated theories on customs, psychology, characters and fate of the Eastern people.

Third, as a mechanism to deal with East, orientalism has made several statements concerning East, evaluated and determined Eastern affairs. On this basis, theories are postulated, policies are defined and applied to rule Eastern colonies. In this sense, orientalism is "a mechanism that West uses to control, design and govern East."[6] Said has called oriental studies orientalism at this level.

In Said's eyes, the three connotations of oriental studies constitute an integrated hierarchy: orientalism as a mechanism to deal with East at the first level, which relies on the study as a thinking mode at the second level, while this thinking mode depends on academic research category at the third level. Oriental studies have gone through a long period of evolution, shifted from "an academic discipline" to "a thinking mode", then to "a systematic theory". According to Said, orientalism had emerged at the beginning of the 14th century, but did not possess above three dimensions until the 18th century. That is to say, until the late 18th century, oriental studies had transformed to orientalism. It was only when oriental studies had developed into a higher stage orientalism had assumed its full properties.

4.2.1.2 OVERT ORIENTALISM VERSUS COVERT ORIENTALISM

Whether it is a discipline, a thinking mode or a systematic theory, orientalism was formed and established in a long period of accumulation. In Said's view, it seems that knowledge on the East had encountered a constant change with the development of this discipline. However, people's impression on East, like indolence, immobility and continuity, has remained intact. Therefore, he put forth two concepts: "overt orientalism" and "covert orientalism".

In the 19th century, orientalists had started to conceptualize their impression on the East as an unbroken continuity, such as dictatorship, perverseness, inaccurateness and indolence. Western readers had started to know East just through these discourses. In Western readers' view, these discourses were believed to reflect the status of Eastern society objectively. By means of them, readers could "accurately and completely understand" East. Even if they were the latest textual materials, they were also interpreted in the frame of those established discourses. Said has discovered that in the 19th century, numerous academic and literary works without any exception had contained more and more explicit discourses, circumstantial and transparent. On this basis, Said has categorized the conceptual distinctions among Western writers and thinkers in the 19th century as overt differences. Most of the distinctions were featured as personal style differences and on forms of writing, and there were no differences in the essence of their knowledge. All of them had increasingly strived to prove, strengthen and deepen the inequality between East and West.

---

6   *Ibid.*

Said has also put forth the conception of "covert orientalism" with the purpose of illustrating that orientalists' prejudices were not based only on their political stand, but mainly on orientalism, the cultural mechanism, itself. After analysis of works by numerous writers and thinkers, Said has discovered that even personages with humanist orientation consciously or unconsciously had adopted the thinking mode of orientalism. They have treated East from a commanding position, and always thought that East was to be helped and needed care. Said had even made such a comment: "Every European, no matter what opinion he held about East, finally turns out to be a racialist, an imperialist and an utterly ethnocentralist."[7] On this point, it might be apt to use covert oriental studies instead of covert orientalism: the overt studies of East were constantly in change, while the covert orientalism has remained invariable.

In Said's eyes, as an institutionalized and systematic discipline, orientalism has focused on three aspects, namely, oriental studies, orientalists and Western readers. Orientalism has regarded East as biological specimens to be anatomized, students to be cultivated, suspected to be tried and even criminals to be recast, fixing East that was different from Western world into the one to be controlled. Orientalism had depicted the East as an object to be studied and judged, as a thing to be rescued and looked after, or to be restricted and punished, or other kinds of similar images. Additionally, the images of East were always fixed and unchangeable. To orientalists, to comprehend orientalism meant to understand East and to have some knowledge on East meant to rule over it and exert power over it. Orientalism has a particular research scope, a special mode of statement and a specific operational mode, all of which constituted an all-around mechanism. It restricted Westerners' perspectives, manner and viewpoints on East, and made them believe their superiority in rationality and culture, as well as in racial evolution, as a result this belief has enhanced their self-imagination.

According to Said's analysis, the reason why orientalism had prevailed for long was that it tried to answer the questions of Western culture itself. From the beginning to the end, orientalism had treated East as "another party", the opposite and marginal side of West. This was similar to Westerner's study on heterogeneous part in their society. As a result, it was natural for orientalists to link their study with some negative factors in both Western and Eastern societies, such as criminals, lunatics and the poor. It is not difficult to understand that the evolution of orientalism was closely related to the internal conversion of Western society. As a result, "West is everywhere, in West, out of West, in the social economic and cultural structures, as well as in people's mind."[8] In a nutshell, under the scope of orientalism, East as a particularity constantly served as a foil to the universality of West; the marginal existence of East played foil to the central position of West.

---

7 *Ibid.*, p. 260.
8 Ashis Nandy: *The Intimate Enemy: Loss and Recovery of Self under Colonialism*, p. xii, New Delhi: Oxford University Press, 1983.

The orientalism had not only believed that East existed for West, but also took it for granted that East was frozen in a particular time and space forever. In Said's view, "Orientalism made such great achievements in depicting that in all stages, Eastern culture, politics and history were just considered as a passive response to West. West was the active initiator, while East was a passive responder. West was the witness and judger of the behaviors of Easterners."[9] As a result, the distinction between East and West has ran to the extreme side, East goes increasingly far away from West, the disparity between them opening wider and wider, and the gulf between them deepening. Thus, West was limited in the room of self-imagination, while East was confined by the fabrication about East by orientalism, leading to two opposite worlds. East turned out to be more "eastern", while West more "western", this image holding back equal dialogues between them.

4.2.1.3 GEOGRAPHICAL AND POLITICAL SETTINGS OF ORIENTALISM

As an academic research branch, orientalism had no direct relationship with political power; neither did it directly present the conspiracy of Western imperialism toppling East. However, as the actual reflection of culture and politics, it was impossible for orientalism to totally get away from colonial ideological frame. It has inevitably interacted with Western colonization over East through all measures. In other words, any text of orientalism was not superficial and formal expression of the Western cultural hegemony. However, behind a single text or in the contexts, there indeed hid the schemes of West to manipulate and even annex East. Said's research has demonstrated that the rise of modern orientalism was surprisingly in parallel with Western countries, like Britain and France, snatching plenty of colonies.

First, the rise of oriental research itself implied the contrast of force balance between East and West. Since the end of the 18th century, works about East in West outnumbered those by Eastern writers on West. Correspondingly, Easterners' travel westward was by no means on a par with Westerners' moving eastward. East was always hot destination for Western military, missionary groups, merchants, science and archaeology to explore. Besides, people traveling to Europe from East of Islam in 19th and 20th century have greatly outnumbered the European travelers moving eastward.

Second, orientalism has got rapid progress in research and contents closely parallel with the period of European speedy expansion. Between 1815 and 1914, the area that the Europeans' directly controlled has expanded from 35% of the earth's surface to around 85%. All the continents in the earth were trampled by the colonists, with Africa and Asia in particular. During this period, the most powerful colonial empires were Britain and France, and orientalism was at its

---

9   Said: *Orientalism*, p. 142.

peak. From the early 19th century to the end of the Second World War, the two countries have always dominated Orient and orientalism; from the beginning of the Second World War, the United States gradually has taken the leading place in this field, and treated East the same way as Britain and France did.

Said disclosed that in orientalism, Asia was always considered to be an alien territory far away, silent and strange, where Islam was regarded as the wild and intractable opponent of European Christianity. To control East, first it was necessary to understand it, then invade, occupy and finally recast it through scholars, soldiers and judges. Therefore, modern orientalists believed that they "were heroes who rescued East from what they thought: "silent, isolated and unearthly;" "because they pushed East into modernity, orientalists gained the capital to boost their methods and stand. They felt they were worldly creators, generating a new world just like God creating the old world."[10] The more Western colonists wanted to save Eastern from the alleged darkness, darker the Eastern image was painted. The darker the Eastern image, the more urgent they felt to rescue East. The two complement each other, jointly formulating the history of colonialism.

The book *Orientalism* has initiated a new theoretical method. For example, Bhabha pointed out in his book *Criticisms to Post-colonialism* (1992) that Orientalism has started the post-colonial academic discipline. Spivak has also praised the book. However, there were also many fierce criticisms on Orientalism after it was published. For example, in the book *Orientalism and Its Problems*, Dennis Porter has pointed out that Said has put insufficient attention to the varieties in colonial discourses; particularly he has neglected the difference between British orientalism and French orientalism, neither did he sufficiently explained the internal contradictions of the imperial culture. In her paper *New Method in the Study of New English Literature*, Diana Blyden (1989) has commented that Said has focused on colonial discourse, but neglected national resistance in the colonies, therefore, he has unconsciously raised the role colonial discourse had played. In his book *Inside Theory: Class, Nation and Literature* (1992), Ahmad put forth five points to criticize Said. He has argued that Said's book was preserved in thought and style; actually it was a new presentation of Western attempt for overrunning the rest of the world.

No matter if praised or criticized, the influence of *Orientalism* was great. This book has revealed the basic points that were disputed among post-colonial theorists. In subjects, like comparative literature, anthropology, sociology, regional study and political science, Said's thought has aroused much interest. Said's thoughts itself was also increasingly developed in this book. In *Orientalism*, Said took in a lot from anthropology, history and regional study, mainly focusing on the Middle East and targeting his criticism on the old colonial countries, like Britain and France. Later, in his book Culture and Imperialism, Said has attempted to expand

---

10   *Ibid.*, p. 157-8.

his viewpoints on *Orientalism*, to make a universal description of the relationship between Western suzerains and their overseas dominions. He has quoted a lot from works of European writers about Africa, India, some part of Far East, Australia and the Caribbean area. He has argued that those known as African and Indian writers' are a part of the European scheme to rule the faraway regions and nations. Said has developed his research by means of exploring particular literary works, starting from those well-known writers, like Daniel Defoe, Joseph Conrad and Rudyard Kipling, and then he turned to those who were generally thought not to be directly involved with the imperial problems. He has revealed that their works were also affected by orientalism thus he has attempted to disclose the relations between culture and imperialism. He has argued that those writers were not mechanically driven by ideology, class or economic benefits, but it was noticeable that they did live in their own society, and were influenced by their history and experience.

Developing the viewpoints in *Orientalism*, Said held the view that in our age, direct control was nearly over; imperialism continues to exist in politics, ideology, economics, specific social activities and common culture. Compared with *Orientalism*, this book put more stress on colonial resistance, and held an optimistic attitude toward the realization of a harmonious relationship between Orient and West on the basis of mutual acknowledgement and respect.

4.2.2 CULTURAL IDENTITY IN ORIENTAL NATIONS

Said has revealed basic features and operational modes of orientalism, setting up a milestone in post-colonial study and his thought was constantly enriched. Post-colonial theorists, like Spivak and Homi Bhabha, have focused their research on the cultural identity of oriental nations, examining how colonists distorted cultural traditions in the colonized nations, how the colonized fought against them, and what cultural identity a particular oriental group has.

4.2.2.1 CONNOTATIONS OF CULTURAL IDENTITY

Identity means "a strong feeling of belonging to a particular group, race" or "who someone is". Cultural identity, involves three aspects: role orientation, self identification and others' acknowledgement. In human society, it is necessary for an individual, a group or a nation to know its position in the actual life when it makes its choice about where it would go. Thus, it requires people to establish their roles and positions. During this course, there are three stages: one expresses his identity in action or in words; one identifies it by himself; others acknowledged it. The three supplement each other, constituting actual, specific cultural identity. On the basis of the three stages, post-colonial theorists have focused their research on the cultural identity of the oriental nations.

Said has disclosed that colonists have negated that the oriental nations were able to understand, interpret and express themselves. In colonial discourses, East was phrased as a rigid thing that depended on West to explore itself, and even relies on West to provide knowledge about West and East. The colonial rulers have insisted that without the vitalization of West, East will be indolent forever. The relationship between colonial rulers and Eastern people was: the former wrote about the latter, and the latter was written by the former; the former observed and studied the latter in a commanding position, while the latter accepted its self character in a passive way. Consequently, colonists spoke on behalf of the colonized, and have written the history of the colonies.

In fact, Fanon has disclosed that colonists have distorted, dissected and ruined the cultural tradition of the colonies in an abnormal logic. They were always depicting the history of the colonies in a dark mess with the belief that it was the living fossil remaining at the beginning of human evolution. They have obscured, suppressed and turned a blind eye to it, or viewed it as irrational thing. They have demanded colonists acknowledged their existence, but refused to admit East had a complete humanity. In the eyes of colonialism, the colonized were always considered inferior and uncultivated primitives.

The colonial rulers have not only interpreted East in their way, but also encouraged Eastern people to understand and interpret the reality in a Western way. They were imposed to view Western values as the only acceptable norms; the road West had followed was the only right one in human history. They have imposed the belief that West represents the human "modernity", while East was in the "traditional" belt. East had no choice but to follow the Western road.

The result that the colonists distorted the cultural identity of Eastern nations has finally pushed Easterns to consciously acknowledge that distortion. In opposing colonial oppression, some of the oriental nations needed to learn from and take in some of Western thoughts. However, orientalism itself was a part of Western thoughts. As a result, some of the oriental tenets were accepted unconsciously or distortedly. Thus, the oriental nations have more or less acknowledged their images distorted by the colonists. For example, some oriental nations understood themselves in the frame of dualism, regarding their self-development as abandoning tradition. The outlook they imagined principally came from Western constructed reality. Therefore, Said pointed has out, "Modern East indeed participates in orientalizing itself."[11]

Establishment of cultural identity always depends on the relations between itself and others. If a nation was not acknowledged or distorted by other nations, its role orientation would be twisted; it would exist in a false and deformed manner.

---

11   *Ibid.*, p. 418.

The post-colonial theorists have argued that the deformation was striking in African blacks. For ages, the white society has designed a deformation for the blacks, in which some blacks had no power to resist but only have to accept. As a result, they have internalized this image, turning out to be self-deformed and self-twisted. This deformation has become the most powerful means for colonial oppression. Cultural identity is an intricate problem. Fanon has always paid his attention to the colonized, while Said since his early works has completely focused on the colonizing. In his book *The Other Question*, Bhabha has put forth his idea that the relationship between the colonized and the colonizing was much more complicated and subtle than they were aware of, and it was fully determined by political atmosphere. In the colonial discourse, the colonized were either savages or obedient servants, either mysterious primitive single-headed inferior animals or worldly adept liars. In Bhabha's eyes, the colonial discourse was not always continuous, copious, fluent and highly consistent with what the book Orientalism has suggested, but that discourse was full of contradictions and worries.

Spivak has noticed that the colonial relationship between West and East was heterogeneously co-existent and vagrant, rather than totally different or conflictive. East, as "other" to West, was not so much an integral totality without differences; East had multi-boundaries in it. In the book *The 'Rani of Sirmur'* (1985), Spivak has emphasized that India cannot represent other areas in East; and varieties in the history of the oppressed should be respected. In colonists' eyes, some oriental nations were much closer to what the European fabricated. Therefore, deformation of cultural identity in colonial oppressed nations has encountered some differences, and it requires a more careful analysis.

4.2.2.2 DISTORTION AND RECONSTRUCTION OF CULTURAL IDENTITY IN ORIENTAL NATIONS

Post-colonial theorists have put an important stress on Western colonial culture effect in the spheres of language, translation and literature. They have also emphasized that it was vitally important to choose and use a language in establishment of one's natural and social identity. Using a language was accepting a kind of thought, and the process of writing in a certain language meant that one was gradually assimilated by this foreign language. In some African colonial schools, a yardstick to judge whether a student was progressive or not, was how well he/she had mastered the language of the suzerain. People in colonies built their identities using the language and culture of the colonists, and it was impossible for them to form their unique ideology. However, in the view of the colonists, even though natives in the colonies have entered schools of the whites to receive education, it is impossible for them to become civilized. Thus, due to the colonial culture and language, the colonized nations were in aphasic state, which has blurred their cultural identity.

Spivak has pointed out, "If language is considered as a process of constructing meaning, translation politics itself is an important subject."[12] When a translator re-worded a language into another, he/she restated one culture into another. Thus, the translator mediates between languages and cultures. The translator's knowledge of the foreign language and culture, the relationship between them and native cultural values determine their choice of source texts and ideological conveyance. Additionally, translation was opted according to the problems to be settled in the translator's settings; successful translation depended on whether the rendered text could be understood related to the background where the translator lived. Therefore, translation was inevitably a process of naturalization. Post-colonial theorists have argued that cultural translation of the colonized by the colonists reflect political and cultural values of the colonists themselves. The culture they restated in the target text was always presented with an alien marginal sight. The colonized have established their identity with the aid of this sight, which inevitably produces a twisted image.

In literature, colonial fictions and poems depicted the struggles and victories of the colonists, to maintain their authority. Novels about the colonial world were nothing but adventures of the colonists and the whites. Though there were aborigines in their stories, they served as a foil to Westerners. Their presence in the stories was nothing but helped to shape the heroic image of the colonists. To put it in a nutshell, what the colonial literature has presented was such a panorama: through all adventures and legends, Westerners have ceaselessly presented the history and beliefs of their own, and repeatedly claimed that they were the invincible in the world. When the colonized have read those narrations, they would be inevitably impacted by the values implied in them, which would make them feel inferior. Boehmer, a post-colonial theorist, has pointed out that "literary texts could help maintain colonial imagination, strengthening a colonial world that had already been closed."[13]

In his book *Culture and Imperialism* (1993), Said has focused his research on Western fictions from the 19th century to the 20th century. He has concluded that fictions were vitally important in the formation of imperialist attitude, offered a frame of reference and life experience. For example, *Robinson Crusoe*, the stereotype of realistic novel, did not accidentally tell a story that a European man built a territory of his own in a faraway isle out of Europe. As a matter of fact, realistic novels have defended social acknowledgement of overseas expansion. Contradictions among empires were certainly around occupying lands. However, all the problems could be seen in those fictions, like who had once owned the land? Who had the right to settle down in this land? Who had managed it? Who had taken it back?

---

12   Spivak: *Translation Politics*, Xu Baoqiang (eds). Language and Translated Politics, p. 277. Beijing: Chinese Social Sciences Press, 2001.
13   Boehmer: *Colonial and Postcolonial Literature*, p. 50. Shenyang: Liaoning Educational Press, 1998.

And who was formulating a plan for it? Disputes sometimes even were determined by those stories. Therefore, the core of those fictions was that the colonial adventurers and novelists told stories of those faraway countries. Those stories were also the norms the colonized applied to establish their identities and historical existence. Narrating or preventing others from narrating is vitally important for the formation of culture or concepts of imperialism.

It was undoubtedly a historical fact that the tendency of colonization in the sphere of language, translation and literature had distorted, dissected and ruined the cultural tradition of colonized nations, and fundamentally has twisted the colonized's recognition on their own images. However, during this course, the colonists were not utterly voiceless. The struggle between cultural colonization and anti-colonization has never ceased. Where there was deformation, there was also a resistance; where there was ruin, there was a reconstruction. Dirlik, a post-colonial critic, has pointed out, in the contemporary sense, "post" meant a style of presentation, an analytical or reading mode, or a strategy of reading a colonial text or event. It is vitally significant to subversively re-read or re-write European historical or fictional texts. In his early research, Said, as well as Bhabha, have paid much attention to the analysis of colonial discourse. However, Spivak has focused on the study of various anti-discourses, analyzing all efforts that people in the colonies had made to maintain and re-construct cultural identity of their own.

In the early struggles against colonialism, the colonized insisted that though a nation was oppressed for long, its national characters were deeply buried in the source of their culture, and its original features could be restored intact. The robbery of the colonists could not make it deformed.

African native writers have created a series of novels narrating on "roots", depicting their primitive forefathers and exploring national traditions, to re-construct their national culture that was ruined by the colonial rulers. To uphold national traditions and narrative modes, some Africans have advocated that African thoughts should be "re-Africanized". Additionally, some native writers have collected folk songs and chants to prove that the local cultures had a long history and rich sources. They have as well put forth that their cultures had a deep structure that was not intelligible to the colonizers. On the basis of this, some post-colonial theorists held the assumption that all the literary works of the Third World were national fables. That is to say, whether the Third World literature was narrating individual stories or national events, it was with no exception metaphoric, symbolizing the sufferings of the national culture and promoting national resistance and struggle. For example, in the Third World literature, the heroes/heroines have repeatedly mentioned the names of their countries as well as the collective noun "we": what should we do? How should we do? What shouldn't we do? How should we do it better than other nations?

158 CURRENT GLOBAL IDEAS AND MOVEMENTS CHALLENGING CAPITALISM

Post-colonial theorists have argued that it was significant to define national cultural identity as shared common culture, history and ancestry in the struggle of seeking national independence. According to this definition, cultural identity reflects common historical experience and culture mode, which can provide a nation with a stable and continuous meaning structure, and it can impart an identical imagination to the ethnic culture that was dissected by the colonizers. However, the post-colonial theorists did not stop there, but made a further query on post-colonial states, whether the construction of ethnic cultural identity was just to explore things that were destroyed and masked by the colonists, or was it just to restore the continuity that was cut by them.

Take language for example, in the post-colonial theorists' opinion, it was impossible for languages of the oriental nations to turn back to the pre-colonial state. English was once the language of the colonists', and it is now the media for the United States to establish global culture hegemony. Could the post-colonial states refuse using English because of this? As a matter of fact, English is widely used in numerous post-colonial countries. Take India for example, the English-speaking population is around 20 million. English co-existed with local languages, and they were mutually penetrative. Post-colonial theorists have believed that English had already turned out to be a blended language. In Africa, people speak English and write in English, which is sufficient to prove that English is no longer a foreign language, but it has become a nationalized language. Ahmad, a post-colonial theorist, held the view that it was not only ridiculous but also meaningless to take away English from East, just like to reject railways. The important thing was using native expressions to reform English when necessary, mixing the rhythmic sense that was featured in national characteristics into English and transforming English, which was originally an alien language, into a national language. Spivak, targeting the "School of Roots" which seeks a pure primitive identity, in his book *The Post-Colonial Critic* (1990) he has argued that this attitude actually white-washes the history of colonists' violence. She has emphasized that the word "India" was the historical outcome of colonization.

For post-colonial states, negotiation, imitation and blending were feasible ways to construct national culture identity. In the process of unconsciously misreading the discourse of ex-suzerains, it is likely to produce a series of similar and innovative variance, de-construct and weaken the colonists' discourse. Spivak has proposed that stress should be put on texts of the colonial time in order to reveal the logic antinomy of the colonists and deconstruct their preset universality in their discourse; meanwhile post-colonial theorists could not simply produce an antihistorical discourse, but should examine far old and newer cultural relations between East and West in the colonial ages, and reconstruct cultural identity of oriental nations. In her paper *Three Woman's Texts and a Critique of Imperialism* (1985), Spivak wrote the racial characteristics that were unnoticeable in the ideological

POST-COLONIALISM 159

frame, on the basis of an analysis on small people, minor plots and marginalized parent themes. However, these characteristics have played an important role in feminist psalmody texts. In her view, compared with "excursive" "unruly" informal attack, direct discourse against hegemony is more likely to be counteracted and misappropriated. Therefore, she suggested measures should be taken to "negotiate" with Western cultural mechanism, text, values, theories and practice, rather than blindly refusing them. However, she primarily took a critical attitude toward those mechanisms and practice.

Homi Bhabha has pointed out that the colonists and the colonized shared the languages, but the latter cannot independently imagine their identity. In the post-colonial age, cultural identity of a national state could exist in a blended form[14]. In the view of Homi Bhabha, cultural construction of the post-colonial states generally needs to go through three stages: First, they imitate the colonists' culture; second, they assimilate it with local culture to transform it essentially; finally, they openly turn against it, and thus re-shape the colonists' culture with their national culture.

Post-colonial theorists have suggested that cultural identity has its own sources as well as its development history; it has gone through constant change, rather than remaining permanently in a past state. Cultural identity belongs to the past as well as to the present. The establishment of national identity in the post-colonial states was not, and impossible, to go back to its pre-colonial state. The tradition of the national culture is to be interpreted, and this interpretation could not exclude the colonial history. On the contrary, reconstructing national cultural identity can only be based taking into account the historical confrontation between Eastern and Western cultures. Therefore, construction of ethnic cultural identity should include two dimensions: similarity and continuity; secondly disparity and fracture. The former provides people tradition and roots, while the latter reminds people to ceaselessly transcend themselves when reconstructing national culture. The post-colonial theorists held the view that the notions of reversing the history reversed by the colonialists and restoring the cultural tradition cut by them should only be developed in the sense of rhetoric, instead of going to the extreme side.

4.2.2.3 DIASPORAS AND THE IDENTITY OF THE WOMEN IN THE THIRD WORLD

In their research on cultural identity of Eastern nations, post-colonial theorists have paid special attention to issues like descendants of an ethnic group which now lives in a scattered status in many parts of the world and also identity of women in the Third World.

14　Homi Bhabha.: The Other Question: The Stereotype and Colonial Discourse, *Screen* Vol. 24, p. 20.

Term Diaspora means that descendants of an ethnic people scattered in many parts of the world due to external reasons or by their own choice. The overseas Diasporas live in the local host social cultural structure, but they still keep their original community in mind, and create their own spiritual orientation in their imagination. They have turned out to be "imaginary communities". In the view of post-colonial theorists, the black Diasporas caused by Western colonists were "imaginary communities".

In colonial time, the blacks were forced to leave their homeland, and were scattered in overseas countries. Their descendants have remained unknown and humble. That is to say, the black Diasporas were always regarded as minor groups, being observed by blind eyes or neglected. They had neither independent identity nor any right to express themselves. The black Diasporas have fought against this attitude only to show that they were no different from whites. However, post-colonial theorists held the view that it was useful to establish a positive image for the blacks, but in fact, blacks still regard the culture and values of the whites as universal things, and this idea blurs the particularity of the blacks. By the effect of assimilation, they overlook the distinction of the blacks in the aspects like class and sex. As a result, this has triggered a conceptual formation of "homogeneous black groups". It was with this concept that the bureaucratic elites in post-colonial states restrain the variety in black peoples' life.

Post-colonial theorists believe that the ethnic culture does not mean folk culture; it is neither an abstract genuine nature of a nation, as populist nationalists have argued. In this sense, the question of "where in?" is different from that of "where from?" The search for cultural identity does not mean to return to the source of national culture. Identity is always a kind of "production", and it is an endless process. Additionally, for those people belonging to a race or living in different regions, or belonging to different classes and ages, nationality has different meanings for them. It was through reflection on their fate that the blacks have reconstructed their cultural identity. Post-colonial theorists have emphasized that this was a multi-dimensional construction process, and they have tried to demonstrate the complexity and variety of the blacks' culture during and after colonial ages.

Post-colonial theorists have noticed the sex difference in the colonial discourse from the very beginning. Said has pointed out that this feature has encouraged a unique masculine viewpoint of the world. And orientalism has paid special attention to the research results of male orientalists. In fact, males have built orientalism from their demanding perspective. Thus, East was always presented with the image that was passive, sexy, silent and ignoble. As for the role women have played in orientalism, some post-colonial critics held different views from Said. Helen Callaway put forth her views in her book *Gender, Culture and Empire: European Women in Colonial Nigeria* (1987) with an attempt to restore Western women's role in the imperial affairs, hoping that women would play their role in producing colonial texts. There were also some post-colonial theorists holding the view that women's discourse was different from men's. In her book *Imperial Eyes: Travel Writing and Transculturation* (1992), Mary Louise Pratt has emphasized that traveling themes and forms women concerned in non-Western world were entirely different from men.

To demonstrate the miscellany of colonial discourse and post-colonial discourse, Spivak has focused on women (gender) as a unique stereotype in her researches. In her writings like *Three Woman's Texts and a Critique of Imperialism* (1985), *Imperialism and Sexual Difference* (1985) and *Displacement and the Discourse of Woman* (1983), she made an analysis on woman's situation in the Third World, demonstrating that under the oppression of paternalism, racialism and capitalism, women have completely lost their subjectivity, and they were unable to express themselves, but have become objects and empty tokens. In their research, post-colonial theorists have revealed that in the eyes of colonial rulers, women's status in the society was similar to that of the colonists, namely, in a subordinate marginal position. For example, in some colonial fictions, the colonists were frequently depicted as extremely delicate females. Consequently, it was natural for feminism to focus on colonialism, and study of gender orientation was naturally done in post-colonialist context, giving rise to the emergence of "post-colonial feminism".

Apart from Spivak's criticism, Bell Hooks' book; *Revolutionary Black Women: Making Ourselves Subject*, Chandra Talpade Mohanty's essay *Under Western Eyes: Feminist Scholarship and Colonial Discourses* and Ketu Katrak's *Decolonizing Culture: Toward a Theory for Post-colonial Women's Texts* have all focused on the research of feminism from a post-colonial perspective, discussing how the Third World women constructed their unique identity. Compared with men in the Third World, women were suffering shackle of paternalism. However, compared with women in the First World, the Third World women also suffer oppression of colonial culture. Post-colonial critics have considered Third World women and women generally as a homogeneous group. As a result, they have overlooked the complex situation of the Third World women. As a matter of fact, they have used the model of white women to represent images of women in the Third World. Post-colonial theorists have as well studied the cultural identities of the whites and their descendants who have immigrated from suzerains into colonies in the colonial ages. After the end of colonial rule, those who had a cultural superiority in the colonial time, generally clashed with the local cultures. They were far away from their national culture, but found hard to merge and be accepted by the local culture. Thus, the white descendants in post-colonial states also have problems of identity. In the view of post-colonial theorists, such problems were all remnants of colonialism; and needed careful study.

4.2.3 VALUE ORIENTATION AS ANTI-NATURALISM

Criticism on cultural imperialism and research on cultural identity of the oriental nations both are related with actual politics, and we think they reflect a value orientation as anti-naturalism.

4.2.3.1 REJECTING THE ETHNICIST VIEW OF NATIONALISM

After it was published, Said's book, *Orientalism* has evoked a resounding repercussion in East, particularly in the Islam and Arab world. One viewpoint was that orientalism was the metaphor or miniature of West. Actually it reflected how West viewed East. West was the enemy of the Arab and Islam world, and even all the non-Western nations. However, another view held that West as a robber and its orientalism trend were offensive to Islam and Arab world and Islam itself was perfect. Apparently, these two views commonly agree that Orientalism was written as a defense of Islam and Arab world.

Said has remarked that all those views above have totally overlooked his criticism on naturalism. As a regional division, East and West certainly had their definite denotations, but thereby they could not be considered to possess unchangeable natures. As a matter of fact, the conception of East and West was largely a mixture based on experience and imagination. As for conception of orient prevailing in England, France and the United States, it does not only depict East, but also controls and confronted by that concept.

Said added, he wrote *Orientalism* with the attempt to demonstrate that identity was of no meaning for isolated individuals. Identity comes into being always in comparison, or construction of identity relies on comparison with others. For instance, if there is no ugliness; there is no beauty, and vice versa. Similarly, establishment of any culture cannot go without the existence of other cultures. Additionally, this comparison was a process, which was interpretative, dynamic and innovative, rather than a static or objective one. When a cultural identity is established in comparison with others, it is based on the knowledge of other cultural identities. Thus, any society in any stage constantly interprets and re-interprets their "others". This process is not only related to knowledge and culture, but also to politics and economics in a large part, which is also interwoven with contest of power, hegemony and anti-hegemony.

Thereby, Said was extremely against the practice of classifying West and East in an opposition to each other because criticizing orientalism with this approach could severely harm oriental image, Said has also refused to worship a "genuine East", and he took a critical attitude against ultra-nationalism which blindly sought permanent nature, chauvinism and fundamentalism. In Said's view, the mistake of Islamic fundamentalism lay in that it regarded "the original Islamic doctrine" as a non-historical category with the belief that it ought not to be critically explored. Therefore, it rejected this exploration. Said also held severely critical attitude toward smug nationalists, who had no critical awareness, with the belief that extreme emphasis on unique features of nations and civilization was likely to sink into narrow regionalism and obscure localism. For instance, cultural nationalists usually put tradition on the top of modernity, reversing the dualism between tradition and modernity on the basis of native orientation. And as a result, they have argued that for the Third World, tradition was superior to modernity, on this basis they advocate an obscure stand of cultural nationalism. Said has extremely opposed extreme nationalism and militarism, with the advocate that only through peaceful dialogue could sufferings that were caused by endless wars between Arab and Judah be alleviated.

Post-colonial theorists have negated the nationalist view of essentialism, but they did not intend to totally deny the difference between national cultures. They held the assumption that the reason why it is impossible to have a rational dialogue or communication between cultures primarily lay in that both the conflicting parties hold the view of an essentialism and either-or self identity; the possible solution to eliminate instead of intensifying conflict is to establish a concept possessing dynamic multiple identities and illustrate the correlation between cultural identity and context. Said opposes orientalism, because it treats multiple dynamic complex human reality from a perspective of essentialism and has no critical awareness. Orientalism implies that there is a permanent East, as well as an invariable West, in opposition to East. If the genuine norm is considered as absolute, this approach will inevitably cause severe crisis of values and national confrontation.

In his book of Culture and Imperialism, Said has divided the Eastern national resistance into two stages: nationalists opposing imperialism and post-nationalists fighting against imperialism. He pointed out that nationalists' opposing imperial culture was based on the dualism between East and West; on the other hand to fight against imperialism means that people of nation states oppose Westerners and Western culture; national liberation was to restore pure national identity and national culture, rule out all those related to West, so that they could build an Egyptians' Egypt, Africans' Africa and Indians' India. The question was to see that hegemony does not only come from imperialist culture, but also exists in national culture. Therefore, it is necessary to turn to post-nationalism. The notion of post-nationalism, which post-colonialists currently study includes: researching those values of nationalism as counter-discourse, possibility of nationalism converting to state ideology and thus being utilized by the new native oppressors which they evaluate as covert or transformed existence of colonial structure.

4.2.3.2 ETHNIC CULTURAL AWARENESS

In the opinion of post-colonial theorists, heterogeneous co-existence was largely caused by imperialism and colonialism. However, it will be inappropriate to define anti-colonialism as returning to the isolated status of pre-colonialism. As a matter of fact, it is impossible to have cultural genuineness and language purity. Basic components of national identity, like language and customs, in fact have merged with "others". Consequently, integration was unavoidable to develop and people have constructed their identity in a specific historical context and circumstances.

It is necessary to treat the relationship between East and West in a proper way. In the view of post-colonial theorists, differences between East and West did not reflect a permanent order, but a historical experience. The end or decline of them might be just round the corner. There were varieties of cultures. The cultures and civilizations are mutually associated and dependent; any attempt to polarize or simplify them will be doomed to failure.

Post-colonial theorists have pointed out that, neither West nor East was a homogeneous integration. They have revealed that the subject's position was multiple, drifting and confusing, and have argued that there is no identical Third World. The alleged Third World was also internally heterogeneous. For example, in Africa, the colonists' invasion has resulted in the co-existence of capitalism and tribe society. In China and India, people could see another extreme phenomenon of capitalism blending with the Asian production mode. Apparently, the common experiences such as being colonized, exploited and oppressed do not make these countries homogeneous. Therefore, people should pay attention to distinctions of social economic systems, cultural traditions and historical experiences in the countries of the Third World.

Post-colonial theorists have emphasized that it is necessary to keep a sober attitude toward the disparity between East and West, as well as conflicts among different nation states. The disparities exist, but it ought not to be regarded as an unchangeable thing. Difference brings obstacles, but people should not think that it is impossible to communicate among the nations. The existence of dissimilarity does not mean hostility or confrontation. The study, discussion and description of disparity should just seek common ground while reserving existing differences and co-exist peacefully. In all, the purpose of knowing the divergence should be to initiate an equal dialogue rather than make new confrontations, to seek consensus of values instead of intensifying conflict of values.

Post-colonialism does not only advocate identity politics, but also emphasizes humanistic politics, respecting politics of cultural divergence and politics of advocating individual rights to seek overall consensus. The first is to respect individual's unique identity despite of their gender or race; the second is to esteem the life styles of members of the weak groups, like women, minorities and migrants. Said thought, "On the one hand, it is necessary to strive for the right of representing themselves and show their national spirit and characteristics; on the other hand, their national spirit should be combined with practice with broader goal. [...] This practice is nothing but liberation, which must properly deal with the relationships between classes or different groups."[15] That is to say, post-colonialism is not only against Western cultural colonization over East, but also criticized oppression itself. Thus, post-colonialism opposes not only the oppression from outside the nation, but also internal oppression. It adjusts its critic and strategies against oppressions coming from different sources. Post-colonialism does not limit itself in disclosing and resisting Western cultural imperialism any more, but had more complex critical values, directly or indirectly relates itself with various survival struggles in the real society.

Spivak's "strategic essentialism" typically reflects the value orientation of neo-cosmopolitanism. She emphasizes that the task of post-colonialism is not to defend some universal subject or history of the "Third World". Spivak has declared her primary identity as a Marxist, feminist, deconstruction critic and member of an Indian-blood minority. When answering the question on the role her Indian roots played in colonial criticism, Spivak explained, "I seldom write books about 'India', but I am quite pleased to see that India is highlighted with the quotation mark because India for those like me is not a place where my national identity was really established. It is always a man-made structure. When mentioning 'India', it makes me feel about talking of 'Europe'. For instance, when it comes to some features of Europe, one apparently makes this response to the United States." [16] Her explanation was explicit. That is to say, to an Indian, "India", as a place, is of no significance; it makes sense only when it is used as the opposite side that people make a corresponding response to.

---

15   Bruce Robbins: American Intellectuals and Middle East Politics: An Interview with Edward Said, *Social Text* 19-20 (1988), p. 52.
16   Sarah Harasym (ed.): *The Postcolonial Critic Spivak*, p. 38-p39, New York: Routledge, 1990.

4.3 GENERAL EVALUATION OF POST-COLONIALISM

As of today, it is unable to give a final evaluation on post-colonialism. On the one hand, post-colonial theory and criticism are still being enriched; on the other hand, the significance and role of post-colonial theories in reality depend on how people interpret, understand and apply them. How to interpret, understand and apply them determines the significance of post-colonialism in reality. Therefore, the current evaluation and understanding of post-colonialism are temporary, and would be adjusted and bettered as time passes.

THEORETICAL ESSENCE OF POST-COLONIALISM

Strictly speaking, post-colonialism is not a "systematic theory", because it does not have an identical creed, nor does it have a definite plan, and the viewpoint of different post-colonial theorists are mostly conflicting. What combines them together is their common research themes and cultural identity.

Post-colonialism is the practice and extension of post-modernism. Post-modernists have criticized Western mega narratives produced since the Enlightenment Age, and advocated to notice the voice, community and ideas that were long oppressed, suspended and even forgotten, to re-comprehend the relationship between center and margin inside Western society and pay attention to the marginal existence. The basic thought train of post-colonial theory is based on the center-margin structure when interpreting the relations between West and East. Thus it can be evaluated as a practice of post-modernism. Post-modernism has focused to self-reflect on Western culture, while post-colonialism focuses to explore global culture. Post-modernism is tinged with theoretical color all through its setup, while post-colonialism has disclosed cultural hegemony of the imperialism, and criticizes Western mainstream culture penetrating, controlling and deforming Eastern countries, which bears a political significance in reality.

Most of the post-colonial theorists have double identity. They are both renowned professors in Western universities and descendants of post-colonial states. Due to their double identity, post-colonialism has demonstrated a unique perspective: continuity of Eastern ideological tradition as well as Western ideological perspective. Therefore, it has provided a new research frame from a global perspective. However, this is just one side of the problem. Seen from another perspective, post-colonial theorists were rootless: on the one hand, there is always a gap between intellectuals with oriental blood and Western cultural traditions; on the other hand, they write in pure English, and are neither close nor distant to Eastern cultures. To some extent, they are always spiritual drifters. Partly due to this, post-colonialism has double effect: In West, it regards itself as the spokesman of East; In East, it is regarded as the representative of Western culture and ideology. Post-colonialism increasingly arouses wide notice with this double effect.

As a matter of fact, post-colonialism is an academic discourse as well as a trend of thought that originated and rose in Western society; having features of oriental culture and its historical settings. In terms of the double identity of post-colonial theorists, the occurrence of post-colonialism itself was the outcome of the historical fact of Western colonialism. As for the problems, like cultural colonization and re-occurrence of identity, cultural communication and penetration, and limitations of localism and global view, all these are greatly related with the colonial history. In this sense, it can be said that post-colonialism is nothing but criticism of the colonial history and its outcomes. Additionally, we can say that post-colonialism has generally pointed to problems rather than provide a definite feasible solution.

SOCIAL IMPACTS OF POST-COLONIALISM

Post-colonialism has two positive effects. First, it is helpful for West to re-evaluate its colonial history. In West, there are always some scholars defending the crimes colonists made, with the argument that colonialism had its historical rationality, and played an important role in promoting oriental nations to get away from their traditions and advancing toward modernization. There are also some who are always criticizing oriental affairs in a demanding position, negating the specific conditions of the oriental nations and their culture with the yardstick of Western values. The colonial theorists' critical analysis on cultural colonization was helpful for West to understand the spiritual and cultural hurts it brought to the oriental nations, make in-depth reflection upon the crime Westerners made during political and economic and cultural expansion toward East, abandon their regular practice of intervening oriental affairs. They should not regard themselves as infallible, but should treat East equally, correctly view the oriental history and reality, and strengthen cultural communication between East and West, rather than aiming cultural penetration.

Second, it was helpful for the oriental world to re-think about the East-West relations. In East, some people are habitually vigilant against colonialism. They take antagonistic attitude due to their alertness for colonial history. However, there are still some who view Westerners as pioneers on the road of modernization. They hold a convergence attitude, regarding Western values as universal norms. These two attitudes are virtually based on dualism. The only difference is that the former views East and West as the opposite sides in the same space, while the latter treat the two as two successive stages in the same temporal series. As for cultural identity, post-colonialism takes a constructive attitude, and opposes both regarding West as center and conservatism that adheres to native traditional culture. This is helpful for oriental nations to understand their cultural tradition. It has a great significance in the post-cold war era. Because with the speedy development of global economy, there is more communication and interaction among different nations, cultures and states. It is impossible and inconceivable to identify national cultures in a pure still absolute way. Post-colonial theorists' research in this sphere offers some enlightenment for oriental nations to understand and construct multiple and flexible cultural identities.

The drawbacks of post-colonialism lie in the following:

First, though most of the post-colonial theorists were descendants of oriental nations and had the experience of living in Eastern countries, they have accumulated their theories and realized their academic activities basically in Western countries, like the United States. They do not really know the history and realities of the oriental nations. Additionally, their research is based on Westerners' experience, western understanding and imagination about East. As a result, post-colonialism stays at the level of academic research, and also lacks thoroughness.

Second, since influenced by post-modernism, works of post-colonial theorists are hard to understand. And their strategies for constructing cultural identity are obscure and likely to produce misunderstandings. Additionally, most of them have great ambitions. It is notable that they have unconsciously neglected and under-estimated the researches made by the scholars of oriental nations with their outcomes about Western colonial culture.

Third, Marxists hold the view that economy is prior to and determines politics and culture. They apply this in the analysis of the relationship between social history and nation states. Theorists of post-colonialism also discuss the relationship between cultural colonization and economy, politics and military expansion, but they are unconsciously trapped in cultural determinism. Consequently, it is unaccountable for them why West had colonized East, rather than the opposite case, why Western culture is still quite penetrative, and why numerous talents in post-colonial states still immigrate into their ex-suzerains. With this approach, post-colonialism emphasizes the criticism to Euro-centralism from the cultural perspective, which distracts people's attention from global hegemony in politics and economics.

REFERENCES

- Xu Baoqiang (eds): *Language and Translated Politics*. Beijing: Chinese Social Sciences Press, 2001.
- Xu Baoqiang (eds): *Decolonization and Nationalism*. Beijing: Chinese Social Sciences Press, 2004.
- Gu Bin: Study of "Other". Beijing: Peking University Press, 1997.
- Elleke Boehmer: *Colonial and Post-colonial Literature*. Shenyang: Liaoning Educational Press, 1998.
- Arif Dirlik. Post-revolutionary Atmosphere. Beijing: Chinese Social Sciences Press, 1999.
- Luo Gang (ed): *Post-colonial Cultural Theory*. Beijing: Chinese Social Sciences Press, 2001.
- B.J. Moore-Gilbert: *Post-colonial Theory*. Nanjing: Nanjing University Press, 2001.
- Edward Said: *Orientalism*. Beijing: SDX Joint Publishing Company, 2003.
- Edward Said: *Culture and Imperialism*. Beijing: SDX Joint Publishing Company, 2003.
- John Tomlinson: *Cultural Imperialism*. Shanghai: Shanghai People's Press, 1999.

CHAPTER V

ANALYTICAL MARXISM

1 *Historical Background of Analytical Marxism*
2 *General Features of Analytical Marxism*
3 *Cohen, Roemer, Wright*
4 *Evaluation of Analytical Marxism*

CHAPTER FIVE

INTRODUCTION

After structural Marxism of Louis Althusser, Analytical Marxism became another representative trend of Marxist thoughts and has begun to rise in the 1970s in the Western countries (mainly the United Kingdom and the United States). Representatives of this trend were primarily professors in the universities in United Kingdom and the United States, such as G. A. Cohen (formerly Visiting Quain Professor of Jurisprudence, University College London and Chichele Professor of Social and Political Theory, All Souls College, Oxford), John Roemer (Elizabeth S. and A. Varick Stout Professor of Political Science and Economics at Yale University), Jon Elster (Professor of Political Science at the University of Chicago) and E. O. Wright (Professor of Sociology of the University of Wisconsin). The main representatives of analytical Marxism have based themselves on the method of contemporary Western analytical philosophy and methodological individualism of social sciences; they have allegedly strived to re-construct "both scientific and revolutionary Marxism" to provide a reasonable solution to various problems existing in the contemporary capitalist society.

5.1 HISTORICAL BACKGROUND OF ANALYTICAL MARXISM

The emergence of analytical Marxism in the United Kingdom and the United States in the 1970s was not fortuitous, but had deep socio- historical reasons.

First, the birth of analytical Marxism was the outcome and evolution of social contradictions in contemporary capitalism that had intensified with the development of new scientific and technological revolution. After the World War II, the new scientific revolution has swiftly developed, and the productive forces in the Western advanced capitalist countries were greatly improved. The living conditions of working people were as well improved to some extent. However, the basic contradictions of capitalism remained to exist. After the 1970s, the whole capitalist world was trapped into an economic "stagnation", with the coexistence of continuous high rate of unemployment, high rate of inflation and low economic growth. The worst economic crisis and social crisis after the World War II had occurred. These crises have made some left intellectuals turn their eyes to Marxism with the purpose to give a theoretical explanation to the reason why the socialism will replace capitalism.

As for the emergence of analytical Marxism, Cohen, one of the founders, gave such a remark: "In my opinion, presently there are three problems which should come into the notice of those who are engaged in the study of traditional Marxism. These are the design, correctness and strategy of fighting against and overthrowing capitalism. The first question is: what do we want? More specifically, why do we want such a kind of socialism? What on earth is wrong with the capitalism? What on earth is right with the socialism? The third question is: how can we realize socialism? Currently, working class in the advanced capitalist states is no longer what it used to be, or no longer what it was thought to be. What does this fact mean in practice?"[1] Most analytical Marxists conducted their research and made their achievements on the basis of the three questions raised by Cohen. Therefore, as it were, the emergence of analytical Marxism in the last analysis was a respond to the basic contradictions of the contemporary capitalist society. They wanted to give a better explanation on the reasons for the perishing of capitalism and victory of socialism.

Why did the analytical Marxists turn to Marxism? Roemer, another founder of analytical Marxism, wrote in the preface of the book Analytical Marxism he had compiled: "This is because in our age, socialism records a checkered victory. It is dubious to assert that the capitalism is inevitably to wane. This is undoubtedly a great challenge to Marxism that had arisen from the circumstances in the 19th

---

1 Cohen, G.A.: *History, Labour, and Freedom*, p. 12. Oxford: Oxford University Press, 1988.

century. There are four responses to this challenge: the first is to retreat to defense Marxist concepts in a Jewish classic style in order to seek an interpretation in accordance with the history. The second is to deny those things that seem to be historical facts. The third is to refute Marxism as something principally wrong. The fourth is to acknowledge that Marxism was a social science in the 19th century. Thus, according to modern criteria, it is apparently rough and some details of it are inaccurate, and even some primary concepts of it are wrong. However, it is quite convincing when interpreting some historical stages and events. Thus, we feel that there must be a reasonable core in it that needs to be clarified and demonstrated. One should not throw away a good tool because of its malfunction on some occasions, particularly when there is not found a better one."[2] From Roemer's reply it can be inferred that analytical Marxists held the view that Marxism that had arisen in the circumstances of the 19th century is still the best theory at present in understanding social history, although according to norms of modern social sciences, it seems rough and possesses some details which are inaccurate, and even its some primary concepts are wrong. What analytical Marxists have strived to do was to re-construct the traditional Marxism into a rigid modern social science, and then use that re-constructed Marxism in the analysis of capitalism and socialism in reality.

Second, the emergence of analytical Marxism is the outcome of long-term struggle of the left intellectuals and masses in the United Kingdom and the United States. After the victory of October Revolution of Soviet Union, several trends of Western Marxism rose, which were opposite to the Russian orthodox Marxism in the Western capitalist countries. They were: Neo-Hegelian Marxism with Lukács (Hungary) and Korsch (Germany) as its representatives at the beginning of the 1920s, Freudian-Marxism occurring in Germany with the prominent members as Reich, Fromm and Marcuse at the end of 1920s and the beginning of the 1930s, Existentialist Marxism emerging in France with its initiators like Merleau-Ponty and Sartre at the beginning of the 1950s, Neo-positivistic Marxism rising in Italy at the end of 1950s, represented by Della Volpe and Colletti, and Structural Marxism originating in France in the middle of the 1960s with its founder Louis Althusser. Though these trends of thoughts have much disagreement on some issues, they all share common features as following: 1. They have interpreted, complemented and revised Marxism using Western philosophies, and put forth new varieties of interpretations different from the orthodox Marxism in the Soviet Union; 2. They made an in-depth criticism of demerits of the Western capitalist system and bureaucratic unitary system of the Soviet Union based on their knowledge of Marxism; 3. They have explored ways of liberation for the proletariat and masses of working people in the Western countries. On the one hand, these trends of thoughts have opposed the existing capitalism; on the other hand, they

---

2 Roemer, H. E.: *Analytical Marxism*, p. 1-2. Cambridge: Cambridge University Press, 1986.

have criticized the socialism pattern of the Soviet Union. Consequently, neither could they get support from bourgeois parties of the Western countries, nor could they get assistance from Communist Parties which were under the influence of the Soviet Union at that time in the Western countries. Additionally, due to their own drawbacks, they were basically limited in the scope of academic research for a long time, and had only limited social influence. However, after the occurrence of successive academic upheavals in Western European countries, they were worshipped as ideological weapons by rebellious young students in the middle and later part of the 1960s. It was until then that they arouse wide attention in the society. However, with the failure of students' rebellion, those trends of thoughts have also suffered much blow, and began to decline in the 1970s.

Before the 1970s, Western Marxism was always centered in the "Latin area", namely Germany, France and Italy, while in Britain and the United States there were no influential trends of Western Marxism. It was just because of this that the occurrence of analytical Marxism in Britain and the United States can be evaluated as a great geographical shift in the studies of Western Marxism. The reason why trends of Marxism have appeared so late in Britain and the United States lay in the world political situation that had formed after the World War II. For a long time after the war, Marxism was always regarded as devil and phantom ideology in the U.S. due to the intensifying conflict between the United States and Soviet Union. Especially when McCarthyism ran amuck, democratic and progressive intellectuals were always persecuted, let alone Marxists. Britain was an old-brand bourgeois state, and has closely followed the United States in politics after the war. It has followed an all-round rejecting attitude towards Marxism. Britain and the United States had strictly suppressed Marxism by political means until the 1960s. In the struggle for civil rights and against Vietnam War, some intellectuals in the United States have gradually started turning to Marxism and have deeply criticized traditional theories and ideologies with an attempt to understand and interpret the social phenomena in the United States. In the 1970s, this practice has swiftly spread in the American university campuses. Young students have showed a strong interest in Marxism. U.S Universities have started to acknowledge that Marxism was a legitimate research sphere, and opened courses on Marxism one after another. All those have provided a prerequisite for the occurrence of analytical Marxism in the United States. The rising of analytical Marxism in Britain was related to the criticism of British traditional culture appearing in radical left journals launched by the New Left in the 1960s in Britain. Among them, the foremost influential was the *New Left Review*, which has started in the beginning of the 1960s. On the one hand, it deliberately got in touch with publishing houses to translate and publish works of those like Marx, Engels, Lenin, Mao Zedong and Trotsky; on the other hand, it has actively introduced works and ideas of those Western Marxists, like Lukács, Gramsci, Horkheimer, Marcuse, Della Volpe and Althusser. As a result, it has evoked an upsurge in studying Marxism in Britain.

Third, the emergence of analytical Marxism was closely related to traditional analytical philosophy and methodological individualism of social sciences prevailing in the United Kingdom and the United States. Analytical philosophy was a leading trend of philosophy in the United Kingdom and the United States in the 1930s. Britain is generally considered the cradle of analytical philosophy at the beginning of the 20th century in the Western philosophical field. Bertrand Russell's book *On Denoting* is regarded as the symbol of the birth of analytical philosophy. Though there are different schools of analytical philosophy with various viewpoints, they all attributed philosophical problems to language with the belief that confusion of philosophy lay in abusing or misusing language. Then philosophical contents came down to either logical analyses of scientific language or semantic analyses of daily language. In the view of analytical philosophers, philosophy is not a theory but an activity. The task of philosophy is not to discover and raise new propositions but to elucidate ideas and classify the existing propositions. That analytical Marxism which was born in Britain and America was closely related to the tradition of analytical philosophy that prevailed for long time in the two countries. This was because analytical Marxists have generally argued that Marx's works as well as those popular works on Marxism gave people an impression of insufficient conceptual explicitness and logic rigidity. As for Althusser's *Reading 'Capital'*, Cohen has remarked, "I find that *Reading 'Capital'* is quite vague. Logical positivism as well as its decisive affirmation about the preciseness of rational activity has never been popular in Paris, which may be a matter to be regretted. [...] Althusser's vague expressions would bring misfortune to Marxists in Britain where explicitness is a rigid tradition. In Britain, people generally do not accept a theoretical statement which is abstruse."[3] In the view of analytical Marxists, if Marxism should be a scientific revolutionary theory, it is necessary to reconstruct it with the methods of analytical philosophy. And emergence of Analytical Marxism has started from the analysis and clarification of basic concepts and theories of Marxist historical materialism. Methodological individualism prevailing in the Western social sciences also had a great influence on the emergence of analytical Marxism. According to the advocates of methodological individualism, all interpretation of social phenomena must finally be categorized as individual matters. Most analytical Marxists held the view that Marx's historical materialism was merely a macro interpretation on social history. That is to say, Marxism has interpreted the social historical phenomena simply through reasoning class, productive forces and production relations, economic foundation and super-structure or things alike. This interpretation was insufficient because it is unable to explain why the sure events had not happened as predicted in this macro interpretation. Therefore, it was necessary to make a supplementary micro analysis in addition to the macro description of traditional Marxism applying methodological individualism. It is generally accepted that the mark of the emergence of analytical

---

[3] Cohen, G.A.: *Karl Marx's Theory of History: A Defense*, p. X. Oxford: Oxford University Press, 1978.

Marxism was Cohen's *Karl Marx's Theory of History: A Defense* published in 1978. During the decade that followed, scholars like Cohen, Roemer, Elster and Wright, published more than 20 works on analytical Marxism one after another and over a hundred papers. Among them, the foremost renowned works are: Cohen's *Karl Marx's Theory of History: A Defense*, *History, Labour, and Freedom*, Roemer's *Analytical Foundations of Marxian Economic Theory*, *A General Theory of Exploitation and Class*, and *Free to Lose: An Introduction to Marxian Economic Philosophy*, Elster's *Making Sense of Marx*, and Wright's *Class, Crisis and Government and Class*. From 1985, Analytical Marxists have begun to release the "Marxism and Social Theoretical Research Series" to present their research achievements, and have published over ten works and collections of theses.

The emergence of analytical Marxism has aroused a wide attention in Western academia. Marxists, non-Marxists or anti-Marxists, all released works or papers, either in praise or depreciation, and also a bitter debate against analytical Marxism had occurred. Additionally, analytical Marxists also held different views, and they as well argued fiercely among themselves. As it were, from the middle of the 1970s, another upsurge of Marxism study based on analytical Marxism lines was rising in the Western countries.

5.2 GENERAL FEATURES OF ANALYTICAL MARXISM

A trend of thought usually establishes itself from the very beginning through what it opposes, and finally builds its own definite features. So is that with Analytical Marxism. Primarily, Analytical Marxists have established their own standpoints through opposing some advocates and methods of traditional Marxism. Their ideological consensus mainly lay in what they commonly oppose.

The traditional Marxism mentioned by analytical Marxists primarily refers to the viewpoints and theories of Marx himself. However, in terms of how to evaluate the viewpoints of Marxism, they share more or less the same views on some issues. For example, most of them are against Marx's theory of labor value; however, as for many other problems, like historical materialism, they usually disagree with each other, and some are even opposite to each other. Thus, the general features of analytical Marxism cannot be based on the issue if it agreed or disagreed with Marxism.

Seen from the works of analytical Marxists, they have claimed time and again that what they pursued was to reconstruct the Marxist theories both in a scientific and revolutionary way. The scientific theory, as they define, has two meanings: one is that this theory conforms to the norms of analytical philosophy in the 20th century, namely, it is a theory with explicit conception and precise reasoning; the other is that this theory not only contains a macro description of social history but also includes a micro analysis of it. Their revolutionary theory refers to that it serves human emancipation. Starting from the definition they give to the scientific and revolutionary theory, analytical Marxists have argued that although the basic theory of traditional Marxism is still very vigorous, it has three problems: first, implicit conception and loose reasoning; second, having merely a macro view on social history, but insufficient in micro analysis of it; third, some of its conceptions are either outdated or incorrect. They claim that if Marxism should be turned out to be a scientific and revolutionary theory, it is necessary to reconstruct, rectify and supplement it with the analytical method. However, there is much disagreement among analytical Marxists on the issue which theories are outdated, which are wrong and which needed to be revised or supplemented. As a result, analytical Marxism is generally featured as the reconstruction of Marxism with the analytical method and those analytical methods applied in its reconstruction.

What is the analytical method that analytical Marxists called for? Seen from their explanation to this problem, the so-called analytical method refers to not only the method of analytical philosophy to make a statement more explicit and precise but also to the methodological individualism in the social sciences of Western non-Marxism. It is generally accepted that the analytical method that analytical Marxists have used primarily originates from these three methods: first, logic of analytical philosophy and approach of language analysis, which were formulated by philosophies of positivism and post-positivism prevailing in English-speaking countries in the 20th century; second, analytical method of Western economics, started by David Ricardo, and then was endowed with rigid mathematic formulation by Neo-classical economics that was established by Walras and Marshall; third, various methods of describing choice, behavior and strategy, which had originated from Neo-classical economics, and then developed together with Neo-classical economics, which are also known as "decision theory", "game theory" and "rational choice theory" in a more general sense. Analytical Marxists have argued that it was feasible to paraphrase Marx's ideas applying analytical method that was established in non-Marxist philosophy and social sciences because those methods could make Marx's ideas more explicit, precise and convincing to prevent misunderstandings. This is the reason why it was called "analytical" Marxism.

To summarize it, analytical Marxism has two features as follows:

First, it advocates the method of analytical philosophy and opposes dialectics. Analytical Marxists have claimed that many concepts were implicitly stated in traditional Marxism but with loose reasoning. If Marxism is to be a scientific revolutionary theory, it is necessary to reconstruct Marx's ideas using analytical philosophical method. With this approach Cohen has directly pointed out in his masterpiece *Karl Marx's Theory of History: A Defense*, "This book is in defense of historical materialism, supporting its argumentation and introducing this theory in a more attractive way. I am restricted by two aspects in presenting this theory: one is what Marx wrote; the other is the criteria of explicitness and preciseness of analytical philosophy of the 20th century. I am aiming at establishing a well-grounded historical theory, which is basically in agreement with Marx's statement in terms of this aspect. Of course, I hope that Marx could acknowledge that this historical theory is a reasonable explicit paraphrase of his ideas, which is not an excessive desire. Marx was an inexhaustible creative thinker. He raised rich thoughts in many fields. But he had neither any time, nor had planned, nor possessed a quiet study to sort out all of those ideas. It is not an excessive requirement to provide a more accurate statement than his expressions in terms of his principal ideas."[4] This passage shows the reason why Cohen has defended historical materialism. In his view, due to the restriction of all factors, Marx had just expressed his ideas about historical materialism vaguely when he lived, and his statement does not meet the criteria of explicitness and preciseness of analytical philosophy of the 20th century. In Cohen's view, a theory cannot be considered scientific unless it fulfills the norms of analytical philosophy. Marx's statement about historical materialism is to a great extent in pre-analytical stage. Therefore, it cannot be considered as a science in a rigid sense. Since they have paid every effort to reproduce a scientific Marxist theory as they have aimed, every important analytical Marxist emphasizes that the most important aim in their theoretical work is explicitness and preciseness. Thus, it is not surprising that analytical Marxism primarily came from analytical philosophy because the latter was usually featured as seeking explicit definitions.

Based on the reconstruction of scientific Marxism as they define it, analytical Marxists have extremely emphasized precise interpretation of basic concepts. In the works of analytical Marxists, one can see their painstaking efforts to demonstrate concepts, like productive forces, economic structure, exploitation, class structure, fetishism, economic foundation and superstructure and state. However, there is no such demonstration in traditional Marxism. Their way of practice makes one feel that this conceptual elaboration is abstract and they pay much attention to details. However, analytical Marxists claim that any theory could not become a scientific one without a thorough clarification of basic concepts. Besides this delicate elaboration of concepts, they have persisted in systematically and rigidly expounding the logical relationships between Marx's theories. Analytical Marxists have argued that loose reasoning absolutely causes problems in theoretical discussions. This point of view explains from one aspect the reason why analytical Marxists prefer to use formal logic and mathematical models, and why they usually exemplify meanings of a certain theory and test whether it is true or not with artificial suppositious examples.

Starting from their method of analytical philosophy, analytical Marxists have all

---

4   *Ibid.*, p. 1.

opposed dialectics which traditional Marxism adheres to. In their view, Marxism does not have unique and reliable methods, opposing to traditional Marxists who claimed that it does have a method and called it dialectics. However, analytical Marxists have argued that the term "dialectical" does not always have a definite meaning in practice, and it can never be definite when it is used as a method opposite to analytical method. Thus, dialectics can only be trusted under the condition of vagueness. In their eyes, it is both wrong and harmful to think that dialectics constitutes a reliable reasoning mode and that dialectics is superior to formal logic from the perspective of demonstrating social theories. They have argued that the practice of regarding contradiction as the basic concept of interpretation blurs up the distinction between correct and incorrect reasoning modes. The influence from Hegelianism weakens the grasp of Marxism, and some false argumentations may divert the theoretical dispute, which results abundant incidents of intricate chaos, which can only hinder the development of Marxism.

Second, they have advocated methodological individualism, and opposed methodological holism. Analytical Marxists have argued that any theory cannot remain at the level of macro description of things and phenomena if to be a scientific one in the modern sense. They have claimed that it is one thing to know that salt is a compound of sodium and chlorine, but it is another thing to know how they combine and why they can form salt. The prediction that capitalism was bound to collapse and necessarily be replaced by socialism does not explain how individual's behavior would produce such a result. But only individual's behavior can produce this result because any outcome is the product of man's behavior in the final analysis. It is in such a sense that analytical Marxists holds the view that the obscurity of traditional Marxism is similar to that of pre-modern chemistry because both of them fail to describe the unity at a macro level as the permutation and combination of its most basic constituents. Elster, another founder of analytical Marxism, has pointed to it more clearly "traditional Marxism makes a holistic description and explanation of the social phenomena, but it is insufficient from the perspective of theoretical norms possessed by modern sciences". ..."It will cause various problems just to explain collective behaviors simply with the benefit of a group. Take this question for example: Why can such a collective behavior not occur even if it is of great advantage to members of a group? Explanation at the individual level should be constructed in line with the enlightening principles as follows: The first assumption is that behavior is based on both rationality and selfishness; if this does not work, it can be assumed at least to be reasonable; but when it also fails, it can be assumed that it is irrational for an individual to take part in a collective action. Finally, the hazard of an immature reductionism will always be remaining in our minds. Compared to the interpretation that can be currently applied at the individual level, collective behavior is too complicated, as it were."[5] This shows that in Elster's view, it is insufficient to reason the interest

---

5   Elster, John: *Making Sense of Marxism*, p. 359. Cambridge: Cambridge University

of groups and interpret historical phenomena merely at the macro level of social history. This is because the macro description is unable to explain why things that are predicted to occur according this macro interpretation do actually not occur. Thus, it is necessary to supplement the macro description of traditional Marxism with microanalysis from the perspective of individuals. It is just due to this that analytical Marxists refuse to accept such a viewpoint as describing social forms and classes as unity of behavior occurring in line with the laws, thereby rather prefer functional description of individual's behavior that constitute them. Analytical Marxists who possess an extreme attitude even put forth a view that any satisfactory and sufficient interpretation must be traced back to the social phenomenon that totally embodies individual's features.

Based on the idea that only individuals could act, analytical Marxists regard the individual as a vitally important analytical unit with the belief that all interpretations of social sciences should be able to restitute (at least restorable in principle) to feasible explanation of individual behavior. In their view, any satisfactory interpretation of social events must all elucidate why those individuals involved in those events choose that action. Their concept is called methodological individualism of rational choices, which interprets the trends in macro phenomena or processes from two aspects: analytical elements as parts of a unity and secondly micro mechanisms as the foundation of the general transformation process. In the eyes of analytical Marxists, all social phenomena should be ultimately explained through individual features, like formation of men's motivation, values, emotion, capability, insight and knowledge.

Starting from methodological individualism, Analytical Marxists oppose the viewpoint of describing social relations and classes with methodological holism and deny that they have their own development laws. In their opinion, methodological holism attributes individual characteristics to the existence of various collectives and bestows the latter with priority in interpreting their constituents. However, ideas originate from individual's mind, and behavior is merely individual's capability. Thus, to interpret social behaviors, both Marxism and other social theories should logically proceed from individuals. The general behavior in the last analysis is merely representation and function of individual behaviors being its component. Not all analytical Marxists absolutely agree with methodological individualism. Some analytical Marxists, like Levine, Sobel and Wright, have questioned the scientific value of methodological individualism. In their view, interpretation of macro phenomena cannot always be validated based on making suppositions on individuals. And on some occasions, individual's different variety of characteristics can produce the same macro process. However, they approve the role of micro interpretation in explaining macro phenomena, and have continued the efforts to explain macro events based on suppositions on individuals though they

---

Press, 1995.

have doubts to employ methodological individualism as an interpreting principle.

Analytical Marxists generally exaggerate the methods mentioned above. In their view, the approval of those methods reflects nothing but the agreement to rationality itself. Therefore, they oppose any deviation that can weaken those norms which enable explicit statements and rigid argumentations and believe that resisting analytical reasoning is nothing but representation of irrational obscurantism. Consequently, in the works of analytical Marxists, the exploring object is always Marxism rather than analytical methods, but these methods are applied to explore Marxism. Through the analysis of Marxism, analytical Marxists discard numerous propositions of traditional Marxism. But they claim to keep the core ideas of traditional Marxism as well as its value orientation though they rule out many propositions of traditional Marxism. They also argue that through rigid review by their analytical methods, the concepts deserving to be preserved become more convincing than before, while those to be discarded cannot be advocated any longer from a rational aspect .

Based on the ideas above, analytical Marxists also oppose the idea that Marxists can only use a unique method that is different from those applied by other social scientists. In their view, what makes Marxism unique are its several concepts related to social historical development rather than its method. If the emphasis is put on the application of a unique method, it means that Marxists have chosen to separate themselves from the useful methods that other social scientists developed. As a result, this attitude will hinder the rectification of false theories and development of right ones. Therefore, analytical Marxists boldly employ various methods that are developed by contemporary social sciences, such as game theory, linear programming theory, structural equation model and logical programming. One of the reasons why traditional Marxists oppose to those methods is that they view them as an outcome of bourgeois social sciences. But analytical Marxists hold that the relationship between the bourgeois social sciences and the capitalist society is intricate; and the research fruits of the bourgeois social sciences are not always for the capitalist system, or in other words, they do not intend to prove that other economic systems do not work. For this reason, some analytical Marxists discard the notion of "bourgeois social sciences" with the belief that it will harm to the efforts of establishing scientific Marxism.

5.3 COHEN, ROEMER, WRIGHT

Compared with previous Western Marxist thoughts, analytical Marxism covers a wider range of research. The former schools have limited their research in the sphere of philosophy, or studied Marxism from a philosophical perspective; the latter, however, involves economics, politics and issues of sociology, like exploitation, class, social justice and social morality, apart from philosophical issues, especially some issues of historical materialism, like motive forces and laws of historical development.

Due to their wider scope, analytical Marxists have a different attitude towards theories of traditional Marxism. Some of them prefer to apply analytical methods in defense of some propositions of traditional Marxism, while others put emphasis on the application of analytical method to rectify and supplement traditional Marxism. The major research achievements they have made on Marxism are: Cohen's demonstration on historical development proposition and primary proposition on historical materialism, Roemer's general theory about exploitation- the non-labor value theory, and Wright's theory on class structure in contemporary capitalist society.

5.3.1 COHEN AND HIS DEVELOPMENT THEORY

Among analytical Marxists, Cohen is generally acknowledged as one of the founders and the most influential representatives of analytical Marxism. He was born into a Jewish communist family in Montreal, Canada in 1941. He got his BA in McGill in 1961, and then he went to the University of Oxford, London for his MA degree. From 1963 to 1985, he taught in London University. He was appointed as assistant, lecturer and associate professor. During this time, he was visiting assistant professor in McGill University of Canada, and Princeton University, the U. S. from 1965 to 1975. By 1985, he was appointed to be professor and researcher of politics and philosophy at All Souls College, Oxford. Cohen is well-known as an enthusiastic strong researcher. And he has two masterpieces: *Karl Marx's Theory of History: A Defense* published in 1978 and *History, Labour, and Freedom* in 1988.

As one of the founders and the most influential representatives of analytical Marxism, Cohen's status lies in that he was the first to defend Marx's historical materialism with the method of analytical philosophy. In his famous work *Karl Marx's Theory of History: A Defense*, Cohen had declared, "What I want to defend is an old-patterned historical materialism, a traditional concept. According to this theory, history is fundamentally the development of human productive forces, and changes in social forms either promote or hinder this development."[6] In his

---

6   Cohen, G. A. , *Karl Marx's Theory of History: A Defense*, p. X.

works, Cohen has employed analytical philosophical methods to clarify a series of basic concepts of historical materialism, like productive forces, production relations, production mode, economic foundation and superstructure and defended some basic principles of historical materialism in a unique way.

Cohen's efforts in defense of basic principles of historical materialism are mainly represented by the two propositions he has raised and demonstrated: development proposition and primary proposition. The development theory is about the internal trend in the development of productive forces from the aspects like human rationality and intellectuality and environment that cannot meet the needs of humankinds. His primary proposition, using the method of functional interpretation, elucidates the primary role that productive forces and production relations play in expounding relationships, such as relations between productive forces and production relations, and relations between economic foundation and superstructure.

5.3.1.1 THE DEVELOPMENT PROPOSITION

Development proposition, one of the most important propositions of Cohen, explains that the constant development of productive forces goes through the whole history. The reason why Cohen raised and demonstrated this proposition is that this proposition was in his view the foremost basic proposition in Marx's historical materialism; however, it was seldom rigidly elucidated in the works of Marx himself as well as later Marxists.

Why are productive forces likely to ceaselessly develop? In terms of this question, Cohen has argued from three aspects. First, the historical circumstances people lived in are short of living materials. In such a circumstance, without human efforts, the nature cannot provide rich living materials to human beings. This means that what humankinds need is seldom totally provided by nature, no matter what stage in historical development. Though men had paid enormous efforts for centuries, till now they cannot overcome the state of insufficient living materials, or they cannot accumulate enough living materials. Under the conditions of current nature and the level of productive forces men could reach, most of them cannot meet their needs unless they devote their energy to the work that is more or less tiresome. Second, men possess intelligence and other capabilities of inventing technology and tools to discover new resources and develop the productive forces. Third, men have an adequate rationality to take the opportunity to use their capability to settle the problem of insufficient materials in their work. To be specific, "those rational men who know how to satisfy their indispensable needs will be likely to grasp and utilize these means to meet their necessities. In terms of this, men, to some extent, are of course rational, which is a perpetual aspect."[7] To

---

7   *Ibid.*, p. 152.

put it in a nutshell, men would not miss the chance frequently occurring in front of them to develop productive forces, because they are rational when faced with the hard natural environment. The development of productive forces will settle the problem of inadequate living material supply, because humankind is a rational creature, which has a strong motivation to overcome it. Thus, productive forces have a tendency of advancing, which will go through all human history.

To make his development proposition precisely understood, Cohen illuminated it further from three aspects as follows.

First, the development tendency of productive forces is self-disciplined. "It is independent from social structures, and just rooted in those essential material facts, like human nature and the situation he is in."[8] Cohen emphasizes in his explanation that what he employed to support his argument was all non-social material facts that have nothing to do with a particular social structure. Those non-social material facts are: the general fact that the humankind is able to give up temporary benefits to pursue more comprehensive needs, and Cohen has proposed a concrete case that in the year 1250 the productive resources available in Europe had made most of the European people engage in agricultural work. Cohen has pointed out that it is undeniable that the development of the productive forces was unachievable in some special circumstances due to some non-social material factors. For example, it had occurred on those occasions, like destruction caused by an great earthquake, exhaustion of the energy that was necessary for the development of productive forces, or may be the deficit of some special resources that was unimportant previously but had become necessary at a later time for the further development of productive forces (for example some special metals). Additionally, there can potentially be such an occasion that things that were then needed cannot be produced under any previous production relations. For example, today an enormous irrigation system is badly needed by present productive forces. Common features of those potential factors that hinder or have hindered the development of productive forces, under every condition, have nothing to do with the social structure men live in. If the hindrance of such a non-social structure is quite commonplace, then the assumption of constant development of productive forces will be inappropriate. But Cohen has assumed at the very beginning that such cases were not prevalent. To put it brief, Cohen's argument strategy to point to non-social factors was to establish his idea: the trend of normal development of productive forces, which might –in some occasions- fail to occur. But the failure does not lie in non-social factors.

Aiming at Cohen's argumentation, some scholars have questioned or criticized that the development of productive forces cannot be separated from the development of the production relations; and have argued that Cohen's development

---

8   Cohen, G. A.: *History, Labour, and Freedom*, p. 84.

proposition can only be feasible with the assumption that production relations are assumed to be always conducive to the further development of productive forces. As a result, they have asserted that the essential reason for the development of productive forces lie in the existence of conducive production relations. Against that critic, Cohen has asserted that development of productive forces is surely inseparable from supportive production relations, but he added that the supportive production relations are only the external condition for productive forces, rather than being the internal source reason for the tendency of development of productive forces. Thus, for Cohen the conclusion that the source reason for the development of productive forces is the existence of supportive production relations cannot not be deduced from the proposition that the development of productive forces can only be possible unless conducive production relations exist. He exemplified it with the tendency of a baby's self-disciplined growth, which she/he internally has, rather than being externally determined by its parents. But, the conclusion that she/he could grow owing to its tendency of self-disciplined growth cannot be drawn from above sentence and also cannot be drawn that she/he did not need care from its parents. The self-disciplined growth of productive forces is similar to the baby's growth. For Cohen, the source reason for this tendency does not lie in production relations, but in those non-social factors related to human features, like human rationality, creativity and tolerance for deficiency. But, we cannot draw the conclusion from Cohen's above statement that the development of productive forces can occur without the support of social relations. The development of productive forces can only be promoted by conducive production relations, which does not contradict with the statement that the self-disciplined development of productive forces are determined by non-social factors that are related to human features. On the contrary, it is the self-disciplined development of productive forces that enables the conducive production relations being prevalent or chosen. In all, I think Marx advocates that the development of productive forces can be achievable by conducive production relations, which do not deny the self-disciplined development of productive forces.

Second, for Cohen the source reason for the development of productive forces is that people wanted to solve the problem of deficiency by means of improving productive forces. Cohen pointed out that man was a rational and creative creature when faced with the problem of deficiency; he managed to tackle the problem of deficiency by improving productive forces. However, Cohen has as well mentioned that the purpose of utilizing more advanced productive forces is to alleviate men's labor burden. That is to say, individual laborers or their cooperative/collective groups take pains to improve their techniques and means of production to ease their labor process. But this idea evaluates general production progress as the result of rational efforts paid by a specific class. As a result, this idea naturally eliminates Cohen's self-disciplined development feature of the development of productive forces. Consequently, in its broad meaning the production progress can be evaluated as the result of the accumulation of numerous efforts; and the tendency of development of the productive forces can be linked with the rationality of a specific class. Hence the loss of its self-disciplined feature. For this reason, Cohen has argued that rational producers' adoption of advanced productive forces to ease their labor process is a specific reason for the development of the productive forces rather than being the source reason. The specific reason for the development of productive forces could be either easing the labor process or serving other purposes. For example, if a self-dependent free peasant used a more advanced plow, as it were, he does it just to reduce his necessary labor he has to devote; however, if a capitalist utilizes a more advanced producing facility or a method, it could be said that he does so to maintain or increase his profits, rather than relieve anyone from his burden of work. Fundamentally, I can say that the reason why productive forces are further developed is that its progress alleviates the shortage of living materials. When the specific cause for productive force development works, so does naturally its source reason. For instance, the dominance of capitalist production in some historical stage lies in that it made great contribution to overcome deficiency, despite the wide difference between that outcome and the motives of the capitalists who have improved the productive forces.

In his book *Karl Marx's Theory of History: A Defense*, Cohen has admitted that he inconsiderately claimed that as long as scarcity existed, people tended to seize any existing opportunity to develop productive forces because if they did not do so, they would be irrational. This view is also problematic. As a matter of fact, even if such an innovation was achievable, rationality cannot be always in agreement with innovation or improvement. The ruling class which firmly controls the production process sometimes may have adequate reasons to prevent production innovation, and introduction of innovation sometimes can lead to non- beneficial results. Therefore, as it were, introduction of innovation can be irrational on some occasions.

However, Cohen added even if men acknowledged these matters, they still could insist because: first, this innovation is sometimes rational, so it is adopted; second, due to rationality and inertia, the achieved innovations hardly disappear unless they are replaced by a more advanced technology. Men do not always pay attention to production improvement and seize the opportunities for improvement, but when they actually succeed in such an improvement, they will not indiscreetly abandon it. Consequently, the result is that production improvement is a tendency in every society, even if this tendency had not become evident in every stage of human history.

Third, the tendency of productive forces' development is universal. It goes through human history as a whole. To take a further step, it runs through every society that suffers deficiency in the history. During a long and stable period of time, even if it was under the condition of scarcity, a society can lack the internal drive (namely caused by other factors rather than social interaction) in terms of production progress. If circumstances are not always detrimental in all societies, progress can occur somewhere, and the progress achievements can be maintained. Thus, Cohen came to the conclusion that there is a universal tendency of progress, which is inclined to be a progress of the world as a whole, although not every social structure has such a tendency. The universal trend of progress is discussed here in a sense of elements. That is to say, no matter what happened anywhere in any part of the earth, progress continues in the world as a whole. However, an advanced society is likely to establish hegemony over laggards through conquering or other means. When this gives rise to the convergence of the two, progress occurs in the bigger society as a whole, even if the progress is only represented by the advanced part in that unity. Finally, this progress is probably embraced by that bigger unity. This progress may be caused by internal factors of that society, or when there are no such internal factors, this society will consequently be pulled into the progressive track by those that internally engender such a trend.

In Cohen's view, universality related to the development of productive forces unnecessarily means that in every society productive forces go from inferior to superior levels. On the contrary, there can be a "torch-relay" mode of progress: in an ex-leading society, when its productive forces reach a stable development level, it will retreat for the growth of another society it has previously influenced. The latter, however, would further push the productive forces forward. The advanced torch holder much probably gives the leading place to the ex-laggards. It is not necessary for the laggards to copy all the stages of those societies they had imitated. The torch is relayed to a new holder partly because the former advanced countries or regions are inclined to close themselves in the economic structure that was once advanced: this is the cost of their leadership.

5.3.1.2 PRIMARY PROPOSITION

Primary proposition was the other significant proposition Cohen has raised. This theory was critical in interpreting the relation between productive forces and production relations, relations between economic base and superstructure. In Cohen's view, Marx's statements on superstructure and economic base, productive forces and production relations include two propositions: 1- The superstructure plays the role of maintaining and supporting the economic base, while production relations restrain the development of the productive forces. 2- Features of superstructure should be understood through considering the economic base, namely, considering the character of the production relations, while the character of the production relations should be explained by the nature of productive forces. In his eyes, these two propositions from Marx's seem to be paradox. This is because the former statement could not deduce the latter, and vice versa. To settle this problem, Cohen has put forth his approach of functional interpretation and believed that only this interpretation can eliminate the apparent contradiction between the two propositions and make Cohen's primary proposition tenable. He has commented: "no other method can prove the primary role that productive forces play in interpreting economic structure in correspondence with the great control of the latter over the former, or prove the primary role of economic structure when interpreting superstructure in agreement with the restriction of the latter on the former."[9]

What is functional interpretation? Cohen elucidated it with two examples: (1) Birds have hollow bones because they are conducive to flying; (2) Shoe factories manufacture in large scale because mass production brings higher economic profits. He pointed out that in these two examples birds' hollow bones should be explained from the perspective that hollow bones are favorable to fly, and mass production in shoe factories should be understood from the angle that it could bring economic profits. These two ways of understanding is what he called functional interpretation. To make people precisely master this functional interpretation, he rigidly defined it with an approach from the analytical philosophy. He said supposing E was the cause, and F was its effect; we would make a functional interpretation of it with E having such an effect. It is not right to interpret the occurrence of E caused by F because we interpret the prior cause with the effect afterwards. Consequently, functional interpretation was in disagreement with cause-effect interpretation. It was also wrong to explain the occurrence of E lay in that it caused the occurrence of F because when E caused F, E had already happened. Thus, the fact that it caused F could not be employed to interpret the occurrence of it. The only selectable interpretation was: the occurrence of E lay in that it could cause F; in other words, the occurrence of E was due to such a matter, namely, Event E could lead to Event F. It could be stated with marks (E→F) →E. In Cohen's view, this functional interpretation was not in disagreement with cause-effect interpretation, and it was just a specific form of the latter.

Cohen thus demonstrated the relationship between productive forces and production relations based on his functional approach: "the reason why current production relations are dominant lies in that they promote the development of productive forces; the existing productive forces determine what production relations to match with it, and the suitable production relations will become dominant . In other words, if K-type production relations are prevailing, then judging from existing productive forces, the K-type production relations are in agreement with the development of productive forces. This is the norm of interpretation in a normal state."[10] Cohen thought that in his explanation there are three pro-

---

9   *Ibid.*, p. 13.
10 *Ibid.*

positions: (1) Level of productive forces explain why any particular production relations rather than others will push forward productive forces; (2) Prevalence of the production relations that push forward productive force development lie in that they promote the productive forces' development; (3) Development level of productive forces demonstrate the nature of production relations. The third proposition can be reasoned from the former two. Cohen emphasized that among the three only the third proposition, which integrated the former two, can bestow the primary role productive forces play in interpreting production relations, while Proposition One and Proposition Two cannot independently establish Proposition Three. Proposition One does not bestow the primary role to productive forces in the interpretation of production relations because it does not involve which production relations would actually be prevalent. Neither can Proposition Two bestow the primary role to productive forces development because without Proposition One, from Proposition Two, it comes to the conclusion that it is the dominant ideology rather than the development level of productive forces that determines what kind of production relations will push forward further development of productive forces.

Cohen goes so far as to make a further explanation about how Proposition Three can be derived from Proposition One and Proposition Two. He pointed out: in Proposition One, the development level of productive forces explained why K-type production relations currently raises this level; Proposition Two reveals the fact that those production relations are likely to raise productive forces and it explains why it was such type production relations that are prevailing; by eliminating the overlapping parts of the two propositions, Proposition Three, namely, "K-type production relations raising development level of productive forces", and then Cohen puts together the rest part of the two, which was blended from the proposition of "development level of productive force interprets" in Proposition One and "prevalence of such production relations ". Hence the proposition of "development level of productive force determines the prevalence of some specific production relations" was generated. In Cohen's view, Proposition Three proves the restriction of production relations on the development of productive forces, because P3 includes part of Proposition Two that the dominance of any production relation lies in that " it further develops productive forces"; P3 also proves the primary role of productive forces in determining production relations because it contains part of the Proposition One as: "the development level of productive force determines" why some particular production relations will promote productive force development.

Cohen also made a further demonstration on the primary role of productive forces in Proposition Three. He pointed out, "the evidence that economic structure promotes the development of productive forces does not weaken the primary role of the productive forces; this is because productive forces choose an economic structure according to what elements of economic structure will push forward productive force."[11] That is to say, although production relations have the function of pushing forward productive forces, the realization of them relies on what productive forces choose, i.e., choose for their development needs. In other words, which production relations could promote the development of productive force did not depend on the production relations themselves, but on the development level of productive forces. Cohen has also felt it was apparently a little far-fetched to evaluate the determinative role of productive forces over production relations just as the choice that the former makes to choose the latter. This is because choice is usually understood something bilateral. For example, "If high technology is incompatible with slavery, slavery is also in disagreement with high technology."[12] Thus, if the determinative role of productive forces is made reasonable, it was necessary to add something to it. This thing was the development proposition that was previously mentioned above— "the development of productive force runs constantly through the entire history." According to the development proposition, productive forces tend to be ceaselessly going forward, which will turn the original harmony between productive force and production relations into disharmony. This disharmony/contradiction will not last for long. Consequently, productive forces will make a new choice of production relations. Therefore, it is always the productive forces which choose production relations rather than vice versa. In Cohen's view, the problem of productive forces determining production relations is basically settled in this way. His demonstration on economic base determining superstructure is generally similar to that of the determinative role of productive forces upon production relations.

5.3.2 ROEMER: GENERAL THEORY OF EXPLOITATION

Compared to Cohen who chose to defend traditional Marxism with analytical philosophy, Roemer, another founder and main figure of analytical Marxism, devoted himself to modifying traditional Marxism. In Roemer's view, there is nothing sacred and unchangeable in traditional Marxist principles although they are widely accepted. For this reason, he set about to rectify theories he deemed to be outdated or wrong, with the attempt of rebuilding traditional Marxism into a systematic theory of rigid logicality and revolutionary nature.

Roemer was born in the United States in 1945. In 1966, he graduated from the Mathematic Department of Harvard University with excellent achievements, and finished his B.A. degree there. After graduation, he worked as a math teacher in a middle school for some time, and then went to the University of California for his further study, where he gained his PhD in economics in 1974. Afterwards, he worked at the economics faculty at the University of California, Davis, for years.

---

11 Cohen: *Karl Marx's Theory of History: A Defense*, p. 161.
12 *Ibid.*

In September 2000, he became professor of Political Science and Economics at Yale University. Roemer's research interest was broad, involving Marxist economics, optimal economics, microeconomics and issues of fair distribution. His masterpieces are: *Analytical Foundations of Marxian Economic Theory* (1981), *A General Theory of Exploitation and Class* (1982), *Free to Lose: An Introduction to Marxian Economic Philosophy* (1988). In these three works, Roemer applied analytical method and game theory of Neo-classic economics in modifying traditional Marxist theories on exploitation and class. He put forth many new viewpoints, among which the foremost influential was his general theory on exploitation.

5.3.2.1 TECHNICAL DEFINITION ON EXPLOITATION CONCEPT

Exploitation is an important concept of Marxism. Analytical Marxists, with Roemer as representative, made an in-depth discussion and reinterpretation of it. As for this, they remarked, "the revival and reinterpretation of the exploitation concept are indeed a significant achievement of analytical Marxists."[13]

Why is there exploitation in capitalist economy? Marx gave his explanation to this question with his labor theory of value. According to Marx's labor theory of value, the value of the worker's labor power that goes into the labor market as a commodity is determined by the socially necessary labor time to reproduce it. The worker's wage is merely the monetary form of the value of labor power. The exploitation of the laborer by the capitalist does not occur in the circulation domain of the economy, namely, in the labor power market because here the capitalist pays the worker the wage according to the value of labor power, but exploitation occurs in the production domain. This is because when the laborer sells his/her labor power to the capitalist, he will work under the control of the capitalist, and the value of the product produced by the worker is higher than the wage the capitalist paid him. Therefore, the capitalist gains the surplus value created by the worker that is higher than the value of his labor power. In this way, the worker is exploited. As some Western economists do, Analytical Marxists as well believe that the labor theory of value is problematic. Among them, Elster has argued that the labor theory on value of power is unable to explain why some products without any cost of labor power can also be exchanged at a set ration which can be widely seen in a completely robotic capitalist economic system. Roemer said, "Actually, Marx's labor theory of value is supply-oriented. In this theory, prices are considered to be utterly decided by their cost of labor, while emphasis on the significance of commodities that satisfy people's desire, needs or welfare in deciding prices is demand-centered. A correct theory of market price must include the two aspects: supply and demand."[14]

---

13   Mayer, T. F.: *Analytical Marxism*, p. 80. California: Sage, 1994.
14   Roemer J.E.: *Free to Lose: An Introduction to Marxian Economic Philosophy*, p. 55. Beijing: Economic Science Press, 2003.

But different from the Western economists, Analytical Marxists hold the view that the notion of capitalist exploitation Marx had raised exists in capitalist society but labor theory of value he used as the basis of his theory is not tenable. The problem is to provide a new theoretical foundation for this exploitation as well as reveal exploitation in other societies too. On the basis of this consideration Roemer put forth his technical definition of the concept of exploitation.

What is exploitation? In Roemer's view, the concept of "exploitation" in English in Marx's works has two meanings, either "non-technical" or "technical". The alleged "non-technical" connotation referred to the concept of exploitation is used in daily expression. For example, it is possible to mean to treat someone unequally. "Technical" connotation refers to the meaning of exploitation in scientific terms. In Roemer's words, "in the current economic circumstances, some persons cannot gain their necessary consuming items unless they have to do a labor that takes more than socially necessary labor time, while others could reach their consuming items with less than socially necessary labor time. As it were, exploitation will exist."[15] In other words, if the goods one could buy with his income (wages, profits and other individual incomes) contains less labor than he devoted in his production activity, he is exploited; vice versa, then he exploits others.

By applying the analytical method of Neo-classical economics, Roemer's technical definition of exploitation concept is as well based on the prerequisite of the existence of market economy, substitution of capital and labor or optimal choices by rational persons. The market economy here refers to commodity-exchange economy; substitution of capital and labor means that in the production the same amount of products, people can opt for labor-intensive modes which consist of less capital and more labor, or choose another alternative capital-intensive mode that contains more capital and less labor. Optimal choice by rational persons means that human beings are rational, and they can rationally choose certain criteria to maximize their economic benefits. In Roemer's view, if there is inequality of scarcity and inequality in distribution of capital in market economy, some members' labor time will be more than the socially necessary labor time, while others' labor time would be less than the socially necessary labor time. As a result, there will be exploitation of the former by the latter.

Starting from his definition of exploitation, Roemer elucidated the mechanism of capitalist exploitation. In his view, under the condition of capitalist market economy, what economic actors pursue is their maximum economic benefit, but how to realize their economic benefit is determined by the property they own. Capitalists hire workers to produce because they occupied production means and materials. Hired workers can bring capitalists maximum economic profit. The employees sell their labor power because they do not occupy any production materials, and

---

15   *Ibid.*, p. 23.

selling their labor power is the necessary means for them to gain the maximum economic benefit. Since the value of labor in the consumption commodities the workers buy with their wages is less than the value of labor they devote in the production activity, they are exploited by capitalists. Since the value of labor in the commodity the capitalists can buy with their profits is more than the value of labor they spend in their production activity, they exploit the workers. In Roemer's view, exploitation is inevitable to occur in the capitalist market economy, the source of which is the unequal distribution of wealth.

This technical definition of exploitation Roemer put forth mainly serves the purpose of demonstrating that the source of the capitalist exploitation is unequal wealth rather than the labor market. This shows that it is also possible to explain the capitalist exploitation without the labor theory of value. To take a further step to illuminate this problem, Roemer has raised the hypothesis of two independent economic models: labor market and credit market.

(1) An economy only with a labor market: Suppose there are 300 members producing and consuming grain in this economic model. Each of them would consume two units of grain in a month. There are two kinds of techniques to produce grain: capital-intensive method (one unit of grain plus five days of labor would produce two units of grain, namely, the net income is one unit grain), and labor-intensive method (labor of ten days could produce one unit of grain without input of any grain). Among the 300 members, ten people each possess 30 units of grain as their capital; the other 290 have nothing but their labor power. There exists a labor market, and the average wage rate is one unit of grain for every ten days' work, but the socially necessary labor time is 15 days.

In this economy, ten people each with a property of 30 units of grain can hire 150 proletarians to work for 10 days. During this period, each of the proletarians is supposed to produce 4 units of grain using the 2 units of grain with the capital-intensive method. Two units of grain from the four are used to compensate the input of the seed, one unit is used to pay the workers' wages, and the one unit left is the profit of the property owner. In this way, each of the property owners investing 30 units of grain makes a profit of 15 units of grain. The profit rate is 50 percent a month. The 150 proletarians each sell their labor power and are paid one unit of grain as their wages, and this time they have to undertake a further work to produce another unit of grain for ten days using labor-intensive method, so as to earn their living for two units of grain a month. Consequently, they work 20 days altogether a month. Another 140 proletarians are engaged in utterly independent production using labor-intensive method. Though they are not employed by those ten property owners, they also had to work 20 days to produce 2 units of grain they needed in a month. Roemer has pointed out that exploitation in this labor market economy is quite apparent. No matter whether the 290 proletarians sell their labor power or not, they are exploited. This is because they work 20 days a month, but the socially necessary labor time was 15 days. Obviously, the ten property owners were exploiters because they are not involved in any laboring process, but make a profit of 15 units of grain.

(2) An economy only with a credit market: Now he supposes other conditions but above parameters remain unchanged, but labor market is substituted by a credit market. In this economy, the ten property owners lend their grain as credit instead of hiring workers; the 290 proletarians can use either labor-intensive technique without any need of grain, or capital-intensive technique with the grain they borrow from the property owners (but in this case they have to pay a credit interest to the property owners). The ten property owners lend 2 units of grain to 150proletarians total 300 units of grain, and the average interest rate is 50 percent for a month. The 150 proletarians each undertake the capital-intensive labor for ten days with the borrowed 2 units of grain and produce 4 units of grain. Among the 4 units of grain, 2 units are used to pay the basic value of the credit they borrowed, one unit of grain is used to pay back the interest, and one unit is left for his own consumption. Thus, each property owner had lent 30 units of grain, and profited 15 units of grain. The profit rate was 50 per cent a month. After these 150 proletarians get one unit of grain, they have to work ten days longer using labor-intensive technique to get another one unit of grain they needed in a month. However, the other group of 140 proletarians work 20 days using the labor-intensive technique, and produce two units of grain they needed. Exploitation is also evident in this credit market economy. These ten property owners are obviously exploiters because none of them participate in any labor, make a profit of 15 units of grain. The 290 proletarians, however, are exploited whether they borrow from the property owners or not. This is because they have worked 20 days a month, while the socially necessary labor time is 15 days.

In Roemer's view, the two economic models mentioned above prove that exploitation in credit market economy is in correspondence with that in labor market economy. As the ten employers of labor power, the ten grain-lenders are not involved in any labor and get 15 units of grain. However, the 150 labor-power sellers, and the 150 grain-borrowers cannot get the two units of grain unless they work for 20 days. For the other group of 140 proletarians, the result is the same in two economic models. Seen from the two economic models, the credit market economy is homologous with the labor market economy. Therefore, we can conclude that capitalist exploitation continues to exist without labor market economy. The existence of capitalist exploitation is related to nothing but initially unequal distribution of production materials, and has nothing to do with the existence of labor market.

5.3.2.2 THE CORRESPONDENCE BETWEEN WEALTH, CLASS AND EXPLOITATION

After technically defining the concept of exploitation, Roemer takes a further step to put forward his two correspondence principles between wealth, class and exploitation, namely, "correspondence principle between class and wealth" and "correspondence principle between class and exploitation".

Roemer's two principles are also deducted by the analytical method of Neo-classic economics. Roemer has asserted that economic actors are all pursuing their maximal benefit under the circumstances of market economy, and they make an optimal choice according to the wealth they possess. They can choose to hire others to work for themselves, or sell others their labor power, or work for themselves. People cannot survive unless they choose at least one of the three ways, and there is no one who can manage to sell his labor and hire others to work at the same time. Thus, the choices of the economic actors will result in five types of social groups, namely, five classes. They are: pure capitalist (or landlord) class that hires labor power; half capitalist class that both hires labor power and works for itself; independent handicraftsman (or middle peasants) class that works for itself; half proletariat (or poor peasants) that both sells labor power and works for themselves; working class (or employed peasant) that only sells their labor power . Based on the clarification of the relations between wealth and class status above, Roemer has put forth his two "correspondence principles" between wealth, class and exploitation.

The first is "class-wealth correspondence principle". This principle holds that if all the production parties are ranked in a scale from the richest to the poorest, they will be in such a sequence: pure capitalist (or landlord) class, half capitalist class, independent handicraftsman (or middle peasant) class, half proletariat (or poor peasant) and working class (or employed peasant). The wealth condition of the production parties determines their class status.

The second is "class-exploitation correspondence principle". This principle holds that on the condition that one is a capitalist or a half-capitalist, one belongs to the exploiting class; as long as he is a half-proletariat or proletariat, he belongs to the exploited class. The independent handicraftsman can be of the exploiting or the exploited, or neither, which is decided by his wealth.

Roemer's two principles seem to be simple, but analytical Marxists believe that these two principles demonstrate a kind of relationship between categories of traditional Marxism. This kind of relationship in Marx's early works is merely a kind of simple hypothesis. Due to this hypothesis, Roemer's principles are not surprising. However, it is an excellent fruit because it reveals a kind of internal mechanism. That is, it is in accordance with the wealth people possess and because of the optimal choices they make; they form different classes in the market economy. This mechanism shows why things inevitably advance towards a direction which we feel by our intuitions. Analytical Marxists have argued that the view of above explanation has "apparently objective features of all genuine sciences". This is because it is rigidly demonstrated by the logic what is usually taken granted for.

5.3.2.3 EXPLOITATION THEORY OF "WITHDRAWAL GAME"

Roemer believes that Marx's theory on exploitation has principally illuminated exploitation in the economic system on the basis of voluntary exchange, namely, capitalist exploitation. But Roemer has targeted to establish a general theory of exploitation that transcended all specific forms of exploitation. For this reason, he has established a theory on exploitation known as "withdrawal game".

To elucidate his "withdrawal game" exploitation theory, Roemer assumes a game system in social economy. In this economic system, any group can participate in the game, or withdraw from it. The alleged "withdrawal game" exploitation theory means that if a group "withdraws" from an economic system with the per capita titular property and undertakes independent production, and the income of its members records a small increase, then members of this group are the exploited ones in the original economic system. If the income of its members has a marginal small decrease, they have been an exploiting group in the original economic system.

With his "withdrawal game" exploitation theory, Roemer has also made an analysis of three kinds of exploitation — feudal exploitation, capitalist exploitation and socialist exploitation. Feudal exploitation: In the feudal economy, the property people possess is mainly in the form of land. If the tenant group withdraws from the feudal economy with its per capita titular land and its members live a better life, this discloses that they have been the exploited in the feudal economy. If the landlord group takes its per capita titular land away from the feudal economy and its members live a worse life, this reveals they have been exploiters in the feudal economy. Capitalist exploitation: In capitalist economy, the property that people possess is mainly transferable/mobile production materials, like land, facilities and factory buildings. If the working group takes away its per capita titular property and withdraws from the capitalist economy and after the withdrawal if its members can live a better life, then they have been the exploited in the capitalist economy. In socialist exploitation: In socialist economy, production means are publicly owned, people's main property is non-transferable skills. Roemer said, "After the transferable property is equally divided, if a group withdraws with its per capita social non-transferable property and is able to improve its fate, then this group is exploited in socialism. Though it is impossible to re-distribute this kind of technology, or at least to meet a hard nut to crack, this calculation can be established with a little of experience."[16]

5.3.2.4 SOCIAL NECESSARY EXPLOITATION

According to Marxist theories, exploitation will be ultimately eliminated with the development of human society. That is to say, existence of exploitation is a historical necessity in a certain period. In Roemer's term, the exploitation as a historical necessity is called "social necessary exploitation". What makes a kind of exploitation a "socially necessary exploitation"? In Roemer's view, when the attempt of eliminating exploitation will do harm to the exploited rather than be beneficial to them, this kind of exploitation is a socially necessary exploitation. Exploitation can turn out to be socially necessary exploitation under two different circumstances. One is when elimination of certain exploitation will do a great damage to the economic prompting mechanism, and will worsen the condition of the producers in a short term; this kind of exploitation is socially necessary exploitation. The other is that when the elimination of any exploitation will cost a further development of technology or other productive forces, this kind of exploitation will also be a socially necessary exploitation. For example, in the early capitalist society, the capitalist exploitation still prompted the development of productive forces and technological innovation. At that time, if the working group withdrew from the society with per capita production materials and undertook independent production, their production would soon lag behind the capitalist production, neither would their life improve for better. Thus, the early capitalist production had improved productive forces as well as workers' life; this kind of exploitation was socially necessary exploitation. He has argued that in the socialist society, the existing exploitation caused by disparity of labor skills is also a socially necessary exploitation.

Roemer's concept of socially necessary exploitation emphasizes that eliminating exploitation is not a problem of a determination or morality. However, evaluating a kind of exploitation as socially necessary exploitation does not mean admiration of it or taking utterly negative attitude towards it, on the contrary, proper measures should be taken to eliminate it as soon and painless as possible.

---

16   Roemer, J. E.: *Analytical Marxism*, p. 109. Cambridge: Cambridge University Press, 1986.

5.3.3 WRIGHT AND NEW SOCIAL CLASSES

Erik Olin Wright is also an influential representative of analytical Marxism. Wright was born in 1947, in Berkeley, California. In 1964, he went to the Harvard University to study sociology, and gained his B. A. in 1968. After graduation, he spent two years at the Oxford University for his research. In 1971, he continued his study for PhD on sociology in the University of California, and completed his doctoral dissertation on *Class Structure and Income Inequality*. Wright is now a professor of sociology at University of Wisconsin-Madison. His masterpiece is the book titled *Class* published in 1985. Among analytical Marxists, Wright is the most influential figure in the research of social classes in capitalism due to his important contributions.

In the view of traditional Marxists, social structure in the capitalist society is predicted to be bipolarized with the further development of capitalism. One pole will be the increase of the exploited proletarians, while the other the decrease in the number of exploiting capitalists. However, with the changes of science and technology and industrial structure after the World War Two, an intermediate middle group with an increasing population has occurred in modern capitalist countries. They neither belong to pure proletariat nor are they pure capitalists, with numerous managers and senior technicians belonging to this group. This new phenomena challenge the class theory of traditional Marxism. "The history of the past hundred years has made lots of Marxists believe the notion that the prediction as deepening tendency of class bipolarization in the capitalist society was incorrect. [...] Among the wage earners a large group of technicians and experts with higher incomes have been formed plus a managerial stratum with high bonuses and wages have emerged. These kinds of changes have markedly eroded the simple bipolarized structure."[17] Wright has put forth two theories to make a new elaboration on this problem which will be presented as follows.

5.3.3.1 CONTEMPORARY CAPITALIST CLASS STRUCTURE BASED ON THREE EXPLOITATION FORMS

As for the relationship between exploitation and class, Wright has incorporated Roemer's viewpoints on property, exploitation and class. He has also argued that property inequality is the basis for the existence of exploitation and the class divisions. However, he made a further demonstration of what is property and forms of exploitation caused by property in his definition. In Wright's view, the source of exploitation lies in the inequality of property distribution. Property is not only represented in the form of ownership of production means, but also of labor power, organization and skills. In the modern capitalist society, unequal distribution of property is mainly represented in the unequal property of production means,

---

17   Wright, E. O.: *Class*, p. 8-9. London: New Life Bookstore, 1985.

but also of organization and skills. In accordance with the latter two unequal distributions of property, there are two exploitation relations and class structures caused by them in the capitalist society. He divides people in the capitalist society into two groups and 12 strata based on the unequal distribution of the three kinds of property.

The first group is holders of production means property. It consists of three types of people: (1) capitalists who possess adequate capital and employed workers to work for them, while they do not work; (2) employers with sufficient capital, both hiring workers to work and themselves also working (3) proprietor in possession of enough capital, engaged in the production as sales activity and not hiring workers. The second group is a larger group which holds non-production type means of ownership. There are nine sub-groups among them: (1) specialist managers who possess more skill property and organizational property; (2) specialist managers who have more skill property and less organizational property; (3) non-specialist administrators who hold more skill property but no organizational property; (4) intermediate skilled managers owning less skill property and more organizational property; (5) intermediate skill administrators who have less skill property and less organizational property; (6) intermediate skill workers who have less skill property but no organization property; (7) unskilled managers with no skills but more organizational property; (8) unskilled administrators with no skill property but less organizational property; (9) proletarians possessing neither skill property nor organization property.

Wright believes that the class structure of the capitalist society is constituted with the three exploiting forms that interwove the two groups and 12 strata of people. In this hierarchy, the most important is the division between holders of production means ownership and the second large group those with non-production means property. The former can be further divided in accordance with the amount of their production means property. Wright opposes to the idea which confuses or relates the status of those owners of organizational property and skill property with the status of the owners of production means. He has argued that the exploitation of these groups should be evaluated differently and the former group should be classified as owners of non-production means; and they form nine strata.

Wright also conducted a survey of class structures in the United States and Sweden on the basis of his theoretical framework on the capitalist class structure. He has revealed the remarkable differences between these 2 countries. (See table 5-1).

202 CURRENT GLOBAL IDEAS AND MOVEMENTS CHALLENGING CAPITALISM

Holders of production material property	Holders of non-production material property (employed laborers)		
1) Capitalist	4) Specialist manager	7) Intermediate skilled manager	10) Unskilled manager
U.S. 1.8% Sweden 0.7%	U.S. 3.9% Sweden 4.4%	U.S. 6.2% Sweden 4.0%	U.S. 2.3% Sweden 2.5%
2) Employer	5) Specialist administrator	8) Intermediate skilled administrator	11) Unskilled administrator
U.S. 6.0% Sweden 4.8%	U.S. 3.7% Sweden 3.8%	U.S. 6.8% Sweden 3.2%	U.S. 6.9% Sweden 3.1%
3) Proprietor	6) Non-administrative specialist	9) Intermediate skilled worker	12) Proletariat
U.S. 6.9% Sweden 5.4%	U.S. 3.4% Sweden 6.8%	U.S. 3.9% Sweden 4.4%	U.S. 39.9% Sweden 43.5%

TABLE 5-1: Class Structure and Personnel Distribution in the Capitalist Society of the U.S. and Sweden[18]

5.3.3.2 "INTERMEDIATE STRATUM" THEORY

Wright's analysis on the class structure in modern capitalism is intended to demonstrate that there is no tendency of bipolarization. He has then pointed out that the ten "intermediate stratums" between the capitalist and the proletariat is the key to understand the whole class structure of the capitalism. He defined "intermediate stratum" from two aspects: from one perspective they exploit others, while from the second perspective they are exploited. Take non-managing specialists as an example, they are exploited by capitalists because they have no capital, but they exploit others because they possess skill property. Another example is unskilled managers. They are exploited by capitalists because they possess no capital, but they exploit others because of their possession of organizational property. The "intermediate stratums" are in a contradictory position due to their double identity, being both exploiter and the exploited.

---

18   Personnel did not include the unemployed, like household women, prisoners. Data from: Wright: *Class*, p. 195.

In Wright's view, the contradictory position of the "intermediate stratums" is significant for the historical transformation. This is because, it is impossible for any social revolution to eliminate exploitation in all forms, but in a certain step only a specific one. Therefore, the majority who will benefit from social revolution is not those suffering the worst exploitation in the society, but might be those in the contradictory positions. He exemplified that with the revolution against feudal exploitation, pointing out that in this revolution the major beneficiaries were not the exploited serfs but the bourgeoisie, namely, the class in the contradictory position in the feudal society.

Wright put forth the theory of "intermediate stratums" with the attempt to demonstrate that the main opponent against the bourgeoisie was not the exploited proletariat but the "intermediate stratums" that are both the exploiters and the exploited who possess organizational and skill property. In addition, the substitution of the capitalist society is not socialist society but the state socialism which will be similar to Soviet Union, which integrated organizational property exploitation and skill property exploitation. According to this logic, for the dominant bureaucratic class in the state socialist society, the major opponent is not the working class but the specialist stratum which possesses a contradictory class position, and the latter will become the exploiting class in socialist society.

5.4 EVALUATION OF ANALYTICAL MARXISM

Analytical Marxism has both its positive and negative aspects as the other trends of Western Marxist thoughts. Therefore, it cannot be affirmed or totally negated, thus it is necessary to take an objective and critical attitude toward it.

Its positive aspects lie in: (1) Its occurrence has pushed forward the spread of Marxism in the Western countries, especially in the United States and Britain, strengthening the influence of Marxism in the Western academia. For a long time, Marxism in the Western countries, particularly in the United States and Britain, was attacked by the ruling class. As a result, its spread and development were under numerous kinds of restriction. In Britain and the United States, it was difficult for Marxism to have a foothold in the academia and be discussed in the academy. The occurrence of analytical Marxism, to some extent, has changed this situation. Representatives of analytical Marxism are mostly professors in the well-known universities in Britain and the United States. Their works have made a great impact in the academia. We may say that its occurrence has raised the position of Marxism and widened its influence to some degree in the academia and universities of Great Britain and the United States. (2) Its analysis and elucidation of some basic concepts and principles of Marxism are not entirely unreasonable, although it has partly deepened the Marxist research. Analytical Marxists have emphasized that Marxism cannot be convincing unless it has clear concepts and logical demonstration. For this reason, they have clarified and illustrated some basic concepts and principles of Marxism with methods of modern analytical philosophy and social sciences, and achieved important results, with Cohen in particular. In his book Karl Marx's Theory of History: A Defense, Cohen has contributed to clarify and demonstrate some basic concepts of historical materialism, like productive forces, production relations, production mode, economic base, superstructure and social formations, clearing up the confusion in many aspects and making historical materialism more scientific. (3) They have discussed the new situation and problems in the current capitalist society, making a profound disclosure and criticism of the irrational parts in the capitalist system. Analytical Marxism is not purely an academic Marxism. It has paid attention to the new changes occurring in present capitalism, and put forth many new theories directly pointing to these latest changes, like Roemer's correspondence theory between class and exploitation and Wright's theory on the capitalist class structure. Though these theories are problematic in one way or another, analytical Marxism has a definite choice of values – it opposes capitalism and advocates socialism. Therefore, their works have revealed various demerits of the existing capitalism from different dimensions, and raised new proposals about how to replace capitalism with socialism. This is undoubtedly significant for the world socialist movement when it had evolved towards an ebb in the 1970s.

Its negative aspects lie in that some of its basic propositions are incorrect, and a number of its specific conclusions are quite unreasonable. As for the basic stand, an obvious mistake of Analytical Marxism is its methodology which opposes dialectics. It is well known that dialectical thinking method is one of the most important methods in Marxism, which Marx and Engels have repeated many times in their works. The dialectic thinking method naturally does not lessen the clarity of theory; on the contrary, if appropriately used it can make the expression of a theory more precise and clear. The most convincing case is that Marx applied the method of dialectic logic in his work Capital. Due to their stand against dialectics, and choice of formal logic Analytical Marxism has a deadly weak point that it can only make a static analysis on social structures and history, but it is unable to elucidate the movement, changes and developments in the society. Another obvious mistake of Analytical Marxism is its advocacy of methodological individualism. Many Analytical Marxists have also underlined that to employ microanalysis to supplement Marxism is inappropriate in principle, but still employed it in their research. To be frank, methodological individualism starts from the isolated individual, to be more specific, from the unchanged and abstract nature of individuals to interpret and demonstrate the changes in social history. The abstract nature of individuals they propose is quite controversial: humans are rational, selfish, unwilling to suffer etc. Marxism firmly opposes interpreting historical changes with an unchanged and abstract human nature. This is not only because this approach is unable to explain the historical changes scientifically, but also because it will ultimately give rise to the conclusion that the capitalism should exist forever. Several conclusions by Analytical Marxists are unreasonable, particularly their negation of Marx's labor theory of value.

Analytical Marxism is currently still in development, and its members are actively continuing valuable researches in their own fields, with new achievements continuously coming out. It is necessary to continue studying their researches, absorbing their positive fruits and criticizing their wrong viewpoints. This will help to deepen our research, raise the research standard of Marxism globally.

REFERENCES

- G. A. Cohen: *Karl Marx's Theory of History: A Defense*. Oxford: Oxford University Press, 1978.
- G. A. Cohen: *History, Labour, and Freedom*. Oxford: Oxford University Press, 1988.
- John Elster. *Making Sense of Marxism*. Cambridge: Cambridge University Press, 1995.
- T. F. Mayer: *Analytical Marxism*. California: SAGE, 1994.
- Marcus Roberts: *Analytical Marxism*. London: Verso, 1996.
- John. E. Roemer: *Analytical Foundations of Marxian Economic Theory*. Cambridge: Cambridge University Press, 1981.
- John. E. Roemer: *A General Theory of Exploitation and Class*. Boston: Harvard University Press, 1982.
- John. E. Roemer: *Free to Lose: An Introduction to Marxian Economic Philosophy*. Beijing: Beijing Economic Science Press, 2003.
- John. E. Roemer: *Analytical Marxism*. Cambridge: Cambridge University Press, 1986.
- Yu Wenlie: *Marxism of Analytical School*. Chongqing: Chongqing Press, 1993.
- Erik Olin Wright: *Class*. London: Verso, 1996.

CHAPTER VI

ECO-SOCIALISM

1 *Rise and Development of Eco-socialism*
2 *Basic Advocates of Eco-socialism*
3 *Evaluation of the Eco-socialism*

CHAPTER SIX

INTRODUCTION

Eco-socialism came into being within the Green movement in the 1970s, and turned out to be an attractive component of left-wing thoughts in the 1990s. It is another interaction of new kind of social movements with socialist ideology. This socialist trend of thought bears the influence of Marxism, establishes the necessary connections between overcoming eco-crisis and socialist aims, and embodies a profound understanding of socialism in contemporary world. It offers a series of theories for the future society that are based on the establishment of keeping ecological balance and a harmonious human-and-nature relationship to meet new needs of human beings. It attempts to find a new access to eco-socialism. This trend of thought is highly regarded by some left wing theorists and evaluated as the hope of socialism in the 21st century.

CURRENT GLOBAL IDEAS AND MOVEMENTS CHALLENGING CAPITALISM

6.1 RISE AND DEVELOPMENT OF ECO-SOCIALISM

It was not fortuitous that eco-socialism came into being and has recorded a rapid progress. It has emerged as a reflection to in-depth social and historical reasons under definite theoretical settings. In the contemporary capitalist society, contradictions between mankind and nature, as well as the global ecological crisis increasingly intensify. This was the social source for the rise of eco-socialism. With the rise of Green movement in the 1970s, more and more people were discontented and frustrated with the existing capitalism. They were eager to seek a way to tackle the ecological problems radically. This was the direct cause for the rise of eco-socialist thoughts. This trend of thought has integrated Marx's theory on human-nature relationship, ecology, system theory, futurology, and theories of Frankfurt School.

6.1.1 BACKGROUNDS OF ECO-SOCIALISM

The rise and development of eco-socialism was initiated under the social background of contemporary capitalism, intensified human-and-nature contradictions, which has led to global eco-crisis, on the other hand it has considered the socialist model of Soviet Union and East Europe which was unable to offer an alternative to global eco-crisis, and it was directly affected by the rise of Green movement in the 1970s. Therefore, it is necessary to explore the social and historical backgrounds of eco-socialism within the trend of contemporary world as a whole.

6.1.1.1 CAPITALISM AND GLOBAL ECO-CRISIS

The evolution of contradictions in contemporary capitalism cause increasingly severe global ecological problems and crises, directly threatening human survival and development. Eco-socialism was another reflection of the contradictions in the evolution of the contemporary capitalism.

Basic contradictions of the capitalism have undergone a new change with the rapid economic development. Previously, these contradictions have manifested themselves as follows: contradiction between organized/planned production in an individual enterprise and the anarchic production in the whole economy, secondly the contradiction between the endless expansive tendency in capitalist production and relatively decreasing demand by the working people due to their disbursement deficit. When these contradictions intensified it was inevitable to cause an economic crisis. But recently capitalist basic contradictions have attained new and more complex expressions in the settings of full development of modern social productive forces, rapid economic globalization and deeper modernization in the world. Among those new, the contradiction between the tendency of limitless expansion of capitalist production and limited natural resources has increasingly become prominent. Based on their powerful economies and advanced science and technology, several capitalist countries control the major resources in the world. Their predatory exploitation of world resources leads to the worsened global ecological environment.

On the one hand, the capitalist rapacious exploitation of world natural resources results in the shortage and extinction of numerous irreproducible natural resources. The advanced capitalist countries with 26 percent of the world population not only consume more than 75 percent of the world energy and over 80 percent of the resources, but also enjoy the advantage of high resource consumption. They rapaciously exploit natural resources of the developing countries to preserve the natural resources in their own countries. Hence, humans face intensified shortage of resources. On the other hand, expansion of the capitalist mode of production to the whole globe, gives rise to the ecological imbalances and polluted environment. The ecological imbalance manifests itself mainly in the form of greenhouse effect, soil erosion, desertification of land and species extinction. Environmental pollution mainly includes water pollution, air pollution, solid waste pollution, pesticide and other industrial chemicals pollution. As for air pollution, industrial exhaust emission in the advanced capitalist countries covers 2/3 of the world's total. Wastes, like waste gas, waste water, scrap, dust, noise, electric wave, waste heat, radiation and heavy metal severely threatens human survival and health. In order to alleviate the domestic tensions, the developed countries move industries with high consumption and high pollution to the developing countries, and pour their industrial waste materials into the land of the poor countries, which do great harm to health, giving rise to worsened ecological environment in the undeveloped countries and regions. Taking advantage of technology, resources and markets, the advanced countries plunder global resources and move their pollutions abroad. As a result, they not only cause severe unbalanced development between the South and the North, but also produce a series of ecological crises, in form of global resource exhaustion, environmental pollution and ecological destruction.

From the 1930s to the 1960s, severe environmental accidents have occurred widely in the advanced countries, such as water pollution in Japan's, the pollution of Rhein River in continental Europe, air pollution in London and photochemical smog in the U.S. In the 1970s, there were also great events, like energy crises successively happening in the developed countries, Seveso chemical pollution in Italy and Three Mile Island nuclear-power plant accident in the U.S. To settle the problems, like shortage of domestic resources, unemployment, inflation, economic stagnation and environmental pollution, the developed capitalist countries have strengthened adjustments in their economic structure, expanded global resource distribution, and swiftly pushed forward the capitalist mode of production to the whole world. With the worldwide development of the capitalist system, a series of global problems have occurred one after another, which have seriously impacted the fate of humankind. Among them, the foremost prominent was the severe unbalance between human and nature. Just as Alvin Toffler remarked, "It is not an exaggeration that there has never been a civilization that was able to create such an apparatus which can not only destroy a city but also ruin the whole earth."[1] After the World War II, the capitalist countries have begun to utilize scientific achievements better, have self-adjusted and self-improved themselves to a great extent within the limits of the capitalist system, have adopted some of the successful socialist experiences. As a result, these practices have partly alleviated domestic class contradictions and social contradictions in the advanced capitalist countries. However, this self-adjustment by capitalism was done at the cost of predatory exploitation of global natural resources and environmental destruction. Generally on the global scope, the majority was pushed to poverty and the wealthy minority has increased their wealth.

As the ecological crisis became increasingly severe, this important social problem has become the focus of global attention, causing people to think on and seek ways to settle it. Thus eco-socialism was just the reflection to that contradiction between the capitalist social system and ecological environment which has attempted to develop an in-depth thought on ecological crisis. In the view of Pepper, a renowned eco-socialist, "the internal logic of capitalism pursuing for maximum profits causes social injustice and ecological unbalance; the global ecological crisis cannot be settled unless capitalism is eliminated and the problem of social injustice is tackled."

6.1.1.2 SOVIET UNION AND EAST EUROPEAN CASE

In the view of eco-socialists, only socialism can fundamentally solve the ecological crisis; only socialism can solve the basic contradictions of capitalist society. However, the socialist mode of Soviet Union and East Europe had also severe ecological problems, and it could not avoid the threat of ecological crisis. It was unable to carry out the historical mission of eliminating capitalism and settling global ecological crisis. This was another important historical setting for the occurrence of eco-socialism.

First, on the relationship between human and nature, the socialist mode of Soviet Union and East Europe has not done well during the historical process of building socialism. For a period of time that practice has indeed greatly changed the historical process in the world, and also pushed forward the social progress in those countries. However, they have preserved their unique mode for a too long time unable to reform it when it had become necessary; as a result, they have

---

1   Toffler, Alvin: *The Third Wave*, p. 128

met various troubles in economy and politics, and they were quite unsuccessful on handling the relationship between development and ecological environment. Consequently, this practice has caused a lot of serious problems. We cannot deny that the socialist countries, like former Soviet Union and those in East Europe had more urgent social and political needs such as economic modernization with industrialization as the core; we should see their different conditions compared with the advanced countries. It was a reality that socialism was mostly established in poorer, less developed countries; in fact vast areas of Soviet Union had lacked any basic industry. It was inevitable for them to face first the issue of development for survival. This issue had become the most prominent task during their long confrontation with the capitalist powers. However, they have neglected the relationship between human and nature and almost all socialist countries have longed and forced a rapid industrialization, while its long term conditions were unquestioned. Thus, severe ecological problems have emerged in practice. They were also financially insufficient and were unable to deal with these problems in time. In the middle of the 1970s, the former Soviet Union has started to face regional environmental problems, like water pollution. But due to financial insufficiency, it could not effectively treat environmental pollution, such as in Middle Asia, Lake Baikal, and the Baltic Sea. In 1986, the Chernobyl Nuclear Power Plant accident has shocked the world. Also in Poland, the government has led an aggressive industrialization strategy giving priority to the heavy industry for years, which has given rise to extremely severe ecological environmental problems. Rapid industrialization has severely polluted drinking water sources, and one quarter of the farming land was no longer fit for agricultural production owing to being overworked. Meanwhile, this ecological environmental problem has aroused great attention by the international society.

Second, the demerits of the socialist mode of Soviet Union and East Europe and their negligence on the ecological issues has triggered those political activists who held different political viewpoints, who have started to criticize socialist governments basing themselves on the environmental problems. During the 1980s, countries like Czechoslovakia, Poland and Romania has become the foremost severely polluted countries in Europe. And in 1980, some Polish intellectuals and scientists have established the "Polish Ecological Club", disclosing the conditions of environmental pollution in Poland, criticizing the development of economy and science which has led to ecological unbalance, and started to organize citizens' protests opposing the destruction of environment. It was the first green organization in the Soviet Union and East European socialist countries. In 1981, the dissident Polish Solidarity Trade Union has established a "Human and Environment Committee", and attempted to combine ecological issues with political opposition. By the 1988, Poland was the first country in East Europe where a green party was established. The "Green Movements" under the leadership of those ecological environmental groups were apparently featured as opposing against the traditional socialist system, and have played some roles in the system transformation in these countries. Thus some observers or those involved have even considered and equaled "Green movement" as a part of "Peaceful Evolution Strategy" from socialism to capitalism.

Third, the closed and isolated socialist development mode in the Soviet Union and East Europe was unable to transcend the contemporary capitalist system, so it was impossible for those countries to shoulder the important task of settling the ecological crisis. They have attempted to construct a second parallel market opposite to capitalism, and this closed socialist system has not led an isolated relationship between domestic economic development and the economic development abroad, but also led an economic development with high costs which exploited higher degree of resources. These practices have aroused some people's doubts on the socialist mode led by Soviet Union and East Europe, and some of them have gone so far as to negate socialism itself. Besides, among the early eco-socialists, most were thinkers who have escaped from East European socialist countries.

6.1.1.3 THE RISE OF "GREEN MOVEMENT" IN THE 1970S

The rise of "Green movement" in the West during 70ies has directly triggered eco-socialism to come into being. To grasp the direct reason for the formation of eco-socialism, it is necessary to review the new social movements and the Green movement in particular.

Opposition and protests against ecological destruction and environmental pollution in Western countries has a long history. In 1953, American scholar K. E. Boulding has raised the concept of "ecological revolution". In the 1960s, new social movements have emerged due to the occurrence of new crises in contemporary capitalism; including the anti-war movement, anti-nuclear movement, peace movement, civil rights movement, Green movement and feminist movements. Among those new social movements, Western public has mostly supported and was interested in the Green movement, rendering the ecological problem as a social problem directly threatening human future, thus this movement has gained a substantial political significance. In essence, the Green movement was a mass movement in which the public protested against the capitalist system aiming to prevent an ecological catastrophe and preserve human living circumstances. Led by the Green Movement, people took the streets, demanding radical measures to treat and control environmental pollution; renowned professors have written articles to condemn negative behaviors, plunder of natural resources and destruction of ecological balance; scientists with foresight have continuously disclosed those accidents that have severely polluted the environment. In the 1980s, the Green Movement has spread through all capitalist countries, and has become an important part of Western new social movements.

The Green Movement has directly criticized the capitalist system in terms of its anti-human and anti-nature character, which reflect the discontent, doubt and disappointment of the masses from all classes and united those who are most concerned on the ecological problem. They have pinned their hopes in a new socialist society. Hence the occurrence of eco-socialism. With the development of the Green movement, different political trends have put forth varieties of green approaches. Under those circumstances, ecological socialism has started to develop ideas on the source of ecological crisis, and has revealed that the ecological crisis was caused by the capitalist system; the essential way of averting the ecological crisis could be nothing other than ways through a new type of socialism, namely eco-socialism.

The eco-socialism has definitely claimed itself to be "Red and Green" with the advocacy of settling the ecological problem and it has turned out to be a foremost influential theory and made greatest social impact on the Green Movement.

6.1.2 THEORTEICAL SOURCES OF ECO-SOCIALISM

There are three main aspects in the development and shaping of the eco-socialist thoughts: (1) Marx's theory on human-and-nature relationship; (2) the contemporary ecology theory, system theory and futurology; (3) theories of Frankfurt School of Western Marxism.

6.1.2.1 MARXIST THEORY ON HUMAN-AND-NATURE RELATIONS

Many eco-socialists have started their research on the ecological problem basing themselves on Marx's theory criticizing the relationship between human and nature. They were more or less influenced by Marx's thoughts, especially his early works in *Economic and Philosophical Manuscripts* written in 1844.

Eco-socialists have inherited and adopted Marx's theory from the following aspects:

First, they have applied the method mentioned by Marx's as "human scale" when approaching the problem areas in the relationship between human and nature. Different from common concept raised by ecologists, eco-socialists have adhered to Marx's thoughts based on human centralism, namely, to the idea that humankind should not abandon "human scale" when settling ecological crisis and they have elevated eco-socialist ideas to the level of world-view. Reiner Grundmann has argued that Marx, different from previous philosophers, as early as in his early works – his *Economic and Philosophical Manuscript of 1844*, had clearly pointed out the idea that the "human society is a well-integrated unity as human and nature", and he had emphasized that it was necessary to pay attention to human world as well as the existing world. In the existing world, the nature has "priority", but this nature is not primarily the ecological nature, instead, it is an "anthropological nature". And in the existing world, the nature and the society mutually restrain each other and mutually penetrate each other. Through practice, humankind not only remolds the natural existence, but also merges itself with the natural existence, bestowing the natural existence with a new scale – sociality. Thus, a dialectic approach on relationship between human and nature is the very prerequisite to construct eco-socialist theory.

Second, eco-socialists have inherited Marx's approach when exploring problems; thus associating social problems with natural problems. In his work *Capital*, Marx had made an in-depth analysis of the capitalist society – economy – nature and linked environmental problems with the social contradictions in his era. He had argued that "domination" of humankind over nature was not the "cause" of the ecological problem. This ecological problem was caused by nothing but the "certain" way humankind treats nature. Therefore, it was necessary to explore this problem by combining the natural problem with the basic contradictions of capitalism. In his work *Critique of the Gotha Program* of the Social Democratic Party, Marx had taken a further step to manifest that the capitalist system was the source reason for the ecological crisis; the ecological destruction was the inherent logic of capitalism, and the way of solving this problem was to break and transcend this logic and replace it with socialism.

Third, they have inherited Marx's thought that technological progress on the whole may promote the natural liberation of humankind, and it could also promote the emancipation of human society. In Marx's approach, the domination of humankind over nature did not mean "ruling", namely, not the alleged conquer and destruction, but refers to human's collective and conscious control over the relationships between human himself and nature. The development of science and technology and the improvement of social productive forces could help people grasp the necessity of nature more deeply, and they could have more free time to engage in creative activities and achieve liberty in a genuine sense. In terms of social relations, the future society will overcome the capitalist private ownership and thus people will freely shape the relationship between man and nature. The actual realization of human emancipation and historical unity of human and nature are two basic aspects of future socialist society.

However, in the view of eco-socialists, Marx's ecological thoughts were still inadequate and unsystematic. Marx had sufficiently demonstrated the contradiction between human and nature in the capitalist society as early as a hundred years ago, but the capitalist productivity was not so advanced at that time; exploitation of natural resources was still limited, and the contradiction between human and nature was not so deep yet.

6.1.2.2 ECOLOGY THEORY, SYSTEM THEORY AND FUTUROLOGY

The occurrence and prevalence of the ecology theory, system theory and futurology in the contemporary Western society has provided significant enlightenment to the birth of eco-socialism, which has expanded its theoretical space.

Ecology is a science that studies the relationship/interaction between living organisms and the natural environment. Since early times, humankind had started to pay attention to the relationship between living organisms (including humankind itself) and their natural environment. For example, in ancient China, the concepts of "unity of heaven and man" and "Dao follows the law of nature" had initially expounded how to deal with the relationship between man and nature in an appropriate way. With the development of modern large industry, the environmental protection and ecological balance has begun to arouse scientists' attention. In 1866, Ernst Haeckel, German zoologist, was the first to raise the concept of "zoology", which meant the study of living environment of organisms. At the beginning of the 20th century, ecology has become an independent science. In the view of Howard T. Odum, a contemporary zoologist, ecology is a science that studies the relationship between individual or groups of living organisms and their environment, and constitutes a systematic theory focusing on the structure and function of the ecological system. In the 1960s, "ecology" has started to become a popular word in the Western society. When analyzing problems, Ecology stresses combining human life and its natural environment taking them as a whole. Thus, it has provided an important theoretical method for the rise of eco-socialism. On this basis, eco-socialism has focused on the integration of ecology and socialism, and formed an independent school of ecological thoughts.

The rise of eco-socialist theory was also related to the development of system theory. Particularly, it combines ecology and system science. Ludwig von Bertalanffy, founder of system theory, has argued that a system is an organic unity embodying a certain structure and specific functions which is composed of interactive and interdependent elements. Generally, a system has the features of entirety, associability, purpose, environmental adaptability and hierarchy. In 1935, Sir Arthur George Tansley, British botanist and one of the founders of the British Ecological Society, and editor of the Journal of Ecology for twenty years, has put forth the concept of "ecosystem". He has assumed that organisms were interdependent and interactive with natural environment, forming an organic natural system. With the rapid development of science and technology after the World War II, countries in the world have increasingly become an inseparable and interdependent unity. Due to the intensification of the ecological crisis, the human ecology theory and system theory turned out to be an important method to grasp the ecological crisis. In such settings, the concept of system was adopted and has become a "new political principle" in the Green movement in the 1970s.

Greens have viewed the whole nature as a big system, namely, ecological system, consisting of indefinite interdependent and ever-growing sub-systems. Ecological system constitutes an inseparable unity, and humankind is only a part of it. This new concept has triggered the formation of Western environmentalism. The environmentalists have demanded that nature should be the center of the ecological system; people should follow the law of nature and bestow nature with ethics and morality. One the one hand, this green approach on the human-and-nature relationship has enlightened eco-socialists when exploring on the sources of ecological crisis from the angle of ecological system. On the other hand, it has promoted eco-socialists to re-think on the criterion which should be used.

Futurology was as well one of the main sources of eco-socialist theory in the 1970s.

First, futurology has initially started researches on the contemporary global problems threatening human survival, and emphasized the global and universal character of the ecological crisis. Among them, a series of research reports, like Limit to Growth by the "Club of Rome", is a well known example. The research report of the "Club of Rome" has applied quantitative analytical means in the research of human disasters, highlighting the priority of nature and warning against ecological crisis. People should pay attention to the global problems that threaten human survival, and joint efforts should be made by all countries to settle the ecological problem. This analysis has offered a profound enlightenment to eco-socialists.

Second, futurology has advocated adjustments in technological development to settle the new problems arising in the capitalist modernization. In his book *Small Is Beautiful: Economics As If People Mattered*, Ernst F. Schumacher, an optimistic futurologist, has proposed small-scale technology and production and advocated reforming capitalism by avoiding its high centralization and concentration in the modern industrial production. He has argued that people should not place their life goal as endlessly obtaining commodities, but should seek a balance between demand and consumption to establish "stable economy". His thoughts have enlightened, Ben Agger, a renowned eco-socialist, who pointed out, "By means of radicalizing Schumacher's viewpoint, we can grasp the social political significance of small-scale technology."[2]

6.1.1.3 THEORIES OF FRANKFURT SCHOOL

The occurrence of ecological socialism was also closely associated with the theories of Frankfurt School. The latter has played a great role in enriching the former theoretically. Eco-socialism has adopted and inherited theories from Frankfurt School in the following four aspects.

---

2 Agger, Ben: *Western Marxism: An Introduction*, p. 500. Beijing: Renmin University of China Press, 1991.

First, the discussion of Frankfurt School about the relationship between human and nature has a vital influence on the emergence of eco-socialism. Among Western Marxism schools, Frankfurt School has noticed the environmental problem at an early time and has linked the analysis of ecological crisis with the criticism of capitalism. Just in 60ies, Marcuse, main representative of this school, has shown a keen awareness on the relationship between ecological problem and the capitalist system. In his book *An Essay on Liberation* (1969), he has argued that the contemporary capitalism was suppressing man as well as nature at the same time, giving rise to the alienation of man as well as that of nature; ecological crisis is not a purely natural and scientific issue; in essence, it reflects the integration of political crisis and economic crisis of capitalism and structural crisis of human instinct. In his work *Counter Revolution and Revolt* (1977), Marcuse has proposed the hypothesis of "liberation of nature" with the assumption that "Liberation of nature is the means for human liberation", and "if we discover the liberating force of nature and the important role it plays in building a free society this awareness will be a new force to push forward social transformation."[3] On the other hand, Frankfurt School has put stress on the research of Marx's ecological thought. Works by other representatives of Frankfurt School, like Max Horkheimer & Theodor Adorno's *Dialect of Enlightenment* (1947), Alfred Schmidt's *The Concept of Nature in Marx* (1971), have focused on the research of Marx's ecological thoughts. These scholars have spent great efforts to criticize the phenomenon of "alienation from nature" in contemporary capitalism basing their ideas on the alienation approach Marx had argued in his work; *Economic and Philosophical Manuscripts of 1844* .It is generally accepted that Marx has reviewed that approach in his later works. They have argued that men's rule over men is based on men's rule over nature, and human emancipation could be achieved on the prerequisite of his liberation from nature. In the existing society, the relationship between man and nature is in the state of alienation. By scientific progress and utilizing technical means, humankind makes nature an object to be conquered and plundered, which leads to severe ecological crisis. However, in the future society with liberty, a new relationship between man and nature will come into being, so that ecological crisis can be avoided. These ideas have made an important influence on the occurrence of eco-socialism.

Second, eco-socialism has generally inherited Frankfurt School's perception of nature. In terms of man-and-nature relationship and on the question which of the two was "pre-existent", Frankfurt School has argued that nature was a social category, and nature at any stage of social development was always related to man and was determined by society. Meanwhile, man and nature were not opposite but unitary. It is not valid to interpret nature without man's social labor and all the practice of humankind. Thus, nature embodies a social historical character.

---

3   Marcuse, Herbert: *Counter Revolution and Revolt, see Industrial Society and New Left*, p. 127. Beijing: Commercial Press, 1982.

Third, eco-socialism has also absorbed the "theory of alienation" established by Frankfurt School. Frankfurt School criticizes that the capitalism suppresses and alienates humanity, and distorts the relationship between man and nature. Marcuse has emphasized that the alienated nature of man becomes the tool of rulers, and thus is subjected to the real rationality of capitalism. Therefore, the ecological problem is fundamentally the problem of the capitalist system, which causes the environmental pollution. Eco-socialists have also adopted this view. They advocate the practice of combining ecological problems with the capitalist system. For example, in his books, *The Domination of Nature* (1972) and *The Limits of Satisfaction* (1976), Tyson E. Lewis, Marcuse's student, has applied the "theory of alienation" to the analysis and criticism of capitalist alienation reflected in the phenomenon of consumption, and argued that consumption alienation is a primary cause for the occurrence of ecological crisis.

Fourth, Frankfurt School has highlighted the liberation of nature and human liberation. They have also pointed out that the harmonious development of man and nature is the basic characteristic of the socialism. In Marcuse's view, the liberation of nature is the prerequisite and means of human liberation; the liberation of nature involves liberation in two dimensions: liberation of human nature (namely, human rationality and instinct) and that of the outside nature (human living circumstances). The liberation of nature is the actual foundation for human liberation. It is impossible for humankind to realize human liberation unless human rationality and instinct and natural environment are liberated. Therefore, on the basis of reality, the first thing to do is to seek ways of liberating human nature. Eco-socialists have not only inherited this idea, but also paid attention to real circumstances, making efforts to explore socialist solutions to settle the ecological problem in reality.

6.1.3 DEVELOPMENT STAGES OF ECO-SOCIALISM

Eco-socialism has first appeared in the 1970s, and turned out to be an attractive trend of social thoughts in the 1990s. To this day, it has gone through approximately three stages.

6.1.3.1 THE RISE OF ECO-SOCIALIST "GREEN MOVEMENT" IN 1970S

While Green movement developed vigorously, eco-socialism was still quite weak in this movement with little influence and less important position, like a red spot among green leaves". At that time, eco-socialist position could hardly be distinguished in the Green Movement. However, at the moment when the Green Movement took a mature shape, some Marxists with ecological awareness have started to think on the political direction of the Green Movement and attempted to clarify their distinct positions. They advocated combining the protection of ecological environment with the realization of socialism, and made important contributions to the Green movement both in theory and practice.

The French theorist André Gorz started to explore the relationship between ecological movement and political struggle at an early time. In his works, like *Ecology and Freedom* (1977), he has criticized the contemporary capitalism from the perspective of ecology, with the advocacy that it is necessary for ecological movement to become a part of a wide-ranging struggle, and that it should not be regarded as the purpose in itself. The ecological crisis of capitalism can be settled either by means of democratic socialist model or through the dictatorial capitalist model. He has argued that it is utterly possible to establish an eco-socialist society which will be technically based on democracy and non-centralization and this society should promote individual independence and cooperate with nature. Second, some Marxists have joined the Green movement in practice. Among them, the most prominent figures were those former neo-Marxists from Eastern Europe like Rudolph Bahro and Adam Schaff. They were organizers of ecological movement since the very commencement of Green movement. They have joined the Green parties one after another and also participated in the debates on human survival initiated by the "Club of Rome", they have also advocated the convergence of "Green" (ecological movement) and "Red" (socialist movement) political forces, establishing an alliance against capitalism.

During this period, eco-socialism did not come to the fore and was still under the great influence of Frankfurt School; neither did it separate from the Green Movement. With the failure of "New Left" movement in the 1960s, people have showed more interest in Green Movement than socialism. Thus, during this period, eco-socialism remained weak and could not form its systematic theories yet. It has successfully criticized ecological crisis as well as the results caused by it, but was insufficient in depicting the configuration of the future new society; that is to say, it was adequate in "deconstruction" but inadequate in construction.

6.1.3.2 THE 1980S – "CONVERGENCE OF RED AND GREEN"

The Green Movement has reached its peak in the 1980s. Green parties in many countries have increased their votes and gained electoral victories one after another. Green parties not only won seats in national parliaments in Britain, Germany and France, but have also entered the European Parliament. The Green movement have begun to spread to North America, Asia and Oceania, and established new parties in these regions. With the growth and expansion of the Green Movement, also theoretical features of eco-socialism have started to shape and become prominent; more and more "green" theories were added to the content of "red" theories.

222 CURRENT GLOBAL IDEAS AND MOVEMENTS CHALLENGING CAPITALISM

Above turning point in the development of eco-socialism was marked by Ben Agger's book *Western Marxism: An Introduction* published in 1979. In his book, he declared the emergence of eco-Marxism, and also introduced William Leiss, who was less-known ecological Marxist at that time; Ben Agger has praised him and his work *The Domination of Nature* and *The Limits of Satisfaction*. William Leiss has attracted a wide attention among left forces in the West. They have clearly advocated reviewing green theories with a Marxist approach and combined Marxism with ecology. Thus in 80ies, eco-socialism has rapidly developed, and turned out to be a quite influential and radical school as a part of ecological movement. Under their influence, a group of European scholars have joined eco-socialism, and helped to form a powerful theoretical core. During this period, were many new works were published, like Ashton's *Green Dream: Red Reality* (1985), Murray Bookchin's *Towards an Ecological Society* (1980) and *The Modern Crisis* (1986), William Harvey's *The Limits to Capital* (1982) and Pepper's *The Roots of Modern Environmentalism* (1984).

The achievements by eco-socialists in this period can be summarized as follows: first, they have emphasized sticking to Marxism and developing it, and declared themselves as "Marxists" in public. Leiss has attached importance to the succession of Marxist theory of alienation and focused on criticizing the alienation phenomenon in capitalist consumption, arguing that alienation by consumption is a principal cause for ecological crisis. He has argued that the spark of social revolution will appear in the sphere of consumption rather than in the sphere of the production. However, Agger and Bookchin have laid more stress on the theory of capitalist crisis; the crisis of the contemporary capitalism is an "ecological crisis". They have attempted to "supplement" Marxist theory with the notion of ecologic crisis and started to construct the ecological socialist model. They have raised clear positions in the spheres of economy, politics, social life and ideology from an eco-socialist approach. As for economy, they have suggested a "stable economy", namely, zero-growth economy, which will replace the current sole pursuit of economic growth in quantity by the pursuit of improvement in life quality. As to politics, eco-socialism should realize decentralization and non-bureaucratization. Decentralization not only refers to small-scale production, but also means that political power should exercised by smaller groups. In terms of social life, eco-socialism should aim a thorough elimination of alienation and enable humans' all-round development and establish the conditions for an unprecedented freedom. In regard to ideology, eco-socialism has advocated combining Marxism with reality and thus forms a brand-new ideology.

All these achievements have explicitly shown that ecological socialism had become a socialist school different from other schools in the Green movement in terms of political ideology, aims and political, economic and social programs. The eco-socialist theory had gradually progressed towards maturity. At the same time, ecological socialism has influenced other schools in the Green movement; eco-socialist analysis on capitalist ecological crisis with Marxist analytical method has gained a prestige to a certain extent. In this period, the Green movement was vividly appeared as a watermelon – "green" from the outside and "red" in the inside: "green" appearance wrapped by "red" contents.

6.1.3.3 THE 1990S – A PERIOD OF INDEPENDENT ECO-SOCIALIST DEVELOPMENT

In the 1990s, ecological socialism entered a new stage of independent development which was quite different from the previous two stages either in its theoretical structure or actual effect.

In the 1990s, the independent development of eco-socialism was directly related to the abrupt changes occurring in the Soviet Union and Eastern European socialist trend, as well as the situation of socialist movement after those great events. From the perspective of reality, on the one hand, the abrupt demise of Soviet Union and socialist countries in East Europe has caused arrogance in capitalist ideology which has claimed the "end of socialism"; also some people have lost their faith in socialism. Could socialism still shoulder the historical responsibility of replacing capitalism? Resisting left theorists have vigorously started to discuss and explore the issues and future of socialism. That period has enabled a free debate atmosphere in which ecological socialism–by its focus on the ecological circumstances- has aroused much attention because of increasingly worsening global ecological crisis and causing worries among wide masses of people and ecological socialism has offered a unique understanding of socialism which attracted a great sympathy. Under those circumstances ecological socialism seemed to have a bright prospect. On the other hand, I can relate its development with the previous decade (80ies) in which Western socialism had inclined to be "greened".

At the beginning of the 1970s, when the Green movement has emerged, it could not receive great attention of other socialist schools and forces like communist parties and social democratic socialist parties, but was regarded as a fashionable fantasy. But in the 1980s, the Green movement has rapidly developed and at the same time political winds in Europe blew from the right, while left forces were quite frustrated. In such circumstances, some communist parties and social democratic socialist parties in Europe have adopted the policy of alignment with the Green parties. For example, the Italian Communist Party has advocated that the communists, social democrats, greens and ecological movement should unite to form a coalition. Communist parties in some countries have advocated direct alliance with Green party, for example Dutch Communist Party has tried to ally with Radical Party, Pacifist Social Party and the Evangelical People's Party to fight the election in 1989 with a common party list. In a local election in Belgium in 1985, Social Democratic Party formed a coalition with Ecological Party, forming the local municipal government, which set a precedent for "Red" and "Green" to jointly come into power. "Greening" of Western socialists (greening of "Red") has objectively raised the status of ecological socialism.

Luciana Castellina, Italian socialist theorist has evaluated this new development, in her paper *Why Must "Red" Be "Green"* which was presented in the forum named as "Socialism on the Eve of 21st Century. She has argued that; "the new relation between "red" and "green" "undoubtedly represents a new stage in the development Marxism on the eve of new century." She has even suggested that it was necessary to regard "red" as "green" because it could bestow socialism with brand-new contents and properties.

6.2 BASIC IDEAS OF ECO-SOCIALISM

Eco-socialists claim that their theories are based on Marxism and socialism guided by the human ecology theory and system theory. They advocate re-examining the relationship between man and nature and the relationship between the ecological problem and the capitalist system with a Marxist approach, seeking practical schemes and ways of realizing eco-socialism and construct a new socialist society in which human society and nature will have a harmonious development.

6.2.1 UNITY OF MAN AND NATURE

In the Green movement, there are two dominant views about nature: one is based on ecological centralism which lay emphasis on the idea that humankind should live in conformance with nature, and pay "respect" to nature; all human activities should follow the law of nature because nature has pre-existed human existence; therefore, nature is superior to humankind; the other view bases itself on technological centralism; humankind is the master of nature, and should, and utterly can, lead nature because humankind is in a supernatural position; thus, humankind is superior to nature.

Eco-socialists criticize both those two views in the Green movement, and argue that when settling the ecological crisis and reviewing the relationship between man and nature, it will not be appropriate to discard "the human scale", and neglect the harmony between man and nature.

First, human and nature share the same natural and social properties. Some early eco-socialists have initially followed the view of ecological centralism, emphasizing "priority of nature". But, since after 90ies, eco-socialists argue that it is undeniable that nature was prior to biological existence of humankind and humankind indeed relies on nature to survive, and humankind is a part of nature. However, nature is of no significance unless it co-exists with humankind and unless they interact upon each other. Nature has no independent value without human existence. Nature could not have a practical meaning until being discovered and explored by human. Through human practical activities, nature obtains its social property. As a result, nature is part of society, and a social-historical category in essence.

Second, in this mutual interaction, man and nature progress toward unity. Eco-socialists assume that the ecological problem is not a natural issue but a social one. The main reason lies in the truth that man and nature co-exist in unity which is formed through human practice. In Grundmann's view, human living conditions are featured by the fact that human has to live in and depend on nature. On the other side, humankind rebuilds nature through technological means for its aims. Technology is an intermediary-medium- through which humans conduct their exchanges with nature. On the one hand, society is not opposite to nature, and it is part of nature, and nature is a socialized (humanized) nature. On the other hand, society and nature are interactive. Nature restricts and changes society; in return, society as well rebuilds nature; in turn the transformed nature impacts the social progress. With these repeated movements, man and nature increasingly progress toward unity in the development of history.

Third, humankind occupies a special status in nature, which is marked by the domination of man over nature. In Grundmann's view, this is the starting point to explore natural and ecological problems. Why is the nature beautiful? Why should the nature be "balanced"? This is because humankind bestows nature with a definition. Environmentalism brings the "human scale" into the natural system, bestowing nature with ethics as well as with value. As a result, it gives rise to the separation of man from nature as well as separation of subject from object. Eco-socialism not only points to the methodological mistakes in ecological centralist approach, but also establishes man's special status in the relation between man and nature. All solutions for the natural problem should be related to human benefits. Therefore, humankinds can be aware of the fact that the world that they create could be much better than the one that nature offers. Through human creation, humankind is necessarily able to build a "second nature" besides the primary-original- nature and those two could form a unity of opposites. The more human beings transform the first nature into the second nature, the more likely that they can become masters of their fate.

Fourth, man and nature should be in harmony and unity. Eco-socialists assume that according to the historical unity of man and nature, the reason for the occurrence of modern ecological crisis does not lie in the priority of nature, but in the lack of human domination and control over nature. In other words, the current mode of human ruling over nature leads to a severe contradiction between men and nature. And human domination over nature should be different from human mastery over nature. This domination over nature requires "humane occupation" of nature, that is to say, "to rebuild the nature into such an environment which will be in conformity with human essence"; it also requires "rebuilding the nature in line with the law of beauty" and requires that human should establish a harmony between man and nature. This harmony is established through human labor. Due to the social and historical factors, the capitalist mode of production causes alienation of labor, which severely intensifies the contradiction between man and nature. The only solution to solve this contradiction is to combine human domination over nature and adjust the man-and-nature relationships with the communist approach. The communist society is the society which is able to give full play for human associations to realize itself. It has the ability to jointly co-ordinate not only the human social life, but also nature. The actual realization of human emancipation and the historical unity of man and nature are, just as Marx pointed out, two basic aspects of future socialist society. Self-awareness and comprehensive understanding on the dialectic relationship between man and nature will inevitably result in the establishment of a new socialist society, namely, a new green socialist society, which realizes an advanced harmonious unity between man and nature. Although there is a narrow consensus among eco-socialists in the understanding of socialism, and their comprehension is different from Marxist interpretation, they all approve the Marxist view that socialism is a superior social formation to capitalism, and it transcends the existing capitalism, and it will be an ecological society where humankind and nature are in harmony.

To put it in a nutshell, eco-socialists emphasize that when people consciously grasp and put into practice the historical unity of man and nature with "human scale", they will more and more see that the contemporary ecological problem is not a natural issue, but a social one. To settle the problem of environmental pollution is not a purely natural process, but a social process, and it is the solution to a social problem.

6.2.2 GORZ, LEISS, PEPPER AND ECOLOGICAL CRISIS

Eco-socialism undertakes an important theoretical mission by adhering to criticize the capitalist system, it profoundly explains the social source of the ecological crisis and reveals that the capitalist mode of production inevitability causes ecological crisis. The early eco-socialism was greatly influenced by ecological centralism when exploring the causes of ecological crisis and targeted industrial system as its critic object. Later they have directed their criticism against contemporary capitalist system.

6.2.2.1 ECOLOGICAL CRISIS AND CAPITALIST MODE OF PRODUCTION

When exploring the causes of the ecological crisis, the Green movement and its theories generally attribute it to science and technology, industrialization or human selfishness, also to Christianity and traditional concepts like sin and to the "prevalent" advocate which values humans as the master of nature. Eco-socialists advocate that people should have a profound understanding of ecological crisis through the superficial contradiction between men and nature. They argue that the modern environmental problem is not merely caused by man's backward traditional concepts or industrialism. The basic cause is still the capitalist system. This is well revealed in their works, like in Leiss' "hypothesis of alienated consumption", in Gorz's "assumption of ecological crisis" and in Yvon Quiniou's "theory of productive forces". These works from different angles argue that the ecological crisis is the inevitable outcome of the capitalist mode of production. On the other hand, Pepper and Grundmann have argued that it would be most appropriate to explore the relationship between capitalism and ecological crisis on the basis of Marx's relevant works. Generally, ecological socialism discloses the relationship between capitalism and ecological crisis from two aspects.

First, ecological crisis is the inevitable outcome of the endless pursuit of maximum profit in capitalism. On the one hand, eco-socialists argue that it is the capitalist overproduction and overconsumption that leads to the ecological crisis. This is because the aim and motive of capitalist production are to seek maximum surplus value. This production aim determines that the capitalists take a hostile attitude towards nature, and consider the nature as an object they can plunder and make profit of. Thus, when capitalists strengthen exploitation of man by capital, they as well reinforce the exploitation of the nature by capital. In his book The Domination of Nature, Leiss emphasizes that the internal drive of ceaseless expansion of capital pushes the capitalists forward to continuously enlarge the production scale to meet the cumulative aggregate demand in endlessly expanding commodity markets. When average profit margin decreases, capitalists will use techniques to over-plunder and over-exploit natural resources in order to guarantee the realization of their profit; that is, "the capitalist system ceaselessly swallows the natural foundation which it owes its survival" Exclusively targeting maximum profits, capitalist production results in an anarchy of social production, as well as overproduction, overconsumption and waste of natural resources, consequently giving rise to human alienation and destruction of ecological balance and occurrence of ecological crisis. Leiss' viewpoints have made great influence on ecological socialism. The U.S. scholar, Victor Walls has also suggested that: "the current severe global ecological problem is utterly caused by the capitalist countries' excessive production and consumption, Western advanced countries in particular."[4] German scholar, Jacob Moneta, has emphasized that "there are two pillars in capitalist mode of production, namely, to produce for the sake of surplus value and excessive consumption," and "the essential solution to global ecological problem is to restrict capitalist countries' production and their consumption, but this is something they cannot achieve and will not do."[5]

On the other hand, ecological problem is the outcome of the capitalist mode of production at the cost of environment to maintain profits. Capitalism tries to decrease the cost of enterprises as much as possible but does not care how much costs society will suffer. This mode of production does its uttermost to "externalize the costs"; that is, to enforce the society undertake the ill effect of destructed environment. This determines that it is impossible for capitalists to protect the environment and sacrifice their profits. In the view of eco-socialists, intensified market competition requires enterprises to try their best to cut down production costs. As a result, they would transfer production costs to the society —outside of the enterprises— and also to future generations as much as possible. Although the enterprises invest to cure pollution under some conditions, there are two prerequisites for them to do that: 1) future cumulative growth of profits 2) curing environment should help to raise enterprise profits.

In terms of this, Gorz put forth his view that in capitalism a contradiction between economic rationality and ecological rationality exists. Economic rationality refers to pursuing maximum profits with maximum production efficiency, consumption and demand. Ecological rationality means to have a better life with less labor and consumption, and to achieve maximum ecological profit. However, these two rationalities are incompatible under the capitalist system. The purpose and motivation of the capitalist production is to pursue maximum profits. Today's capitalism is unceasingly pushing environmental protection into framework of the capitalist system and becoming eager to develop ecological business. Capitalists go so far as to develop ecological business with high profit, and adopt different capital-intensive techniques to produce recycling industrial products in accordance with the new environmental standards. However this, essentially, merely extends the economic rationality of capital, which can never change the general tendency of the capitalist system and it may go so far as to bring forth Fascism of ecological technology. Pepper has argued that the capitalist mode of production endlessly pursues profit; as a result, it is impossible to achieve the alleged sustainable development in capitalism and also green capitalism has no feasibility. This is because producers pursue maximum profits for their own interests; consequently, it is impossible for them to conduct their production and business management

---

4 Excerpted from Chen Xueming (compiled): *Tendency of Marxism Abroad after Abrupt Change of Soviet Union and Eastern Europe*, p. 396. Beijing: Renmin University of China Press, 2000.
5 *Ibid.*

from the perspective and interest of public and they cannot care long-term benefits. Pepper has opposed placing man-and-nature contradiction above the social contradictions in capitalist society, or treating the two contradictions as equally important. He has also argued that the internal logic of capitalism seeking for maximum profit leads to ecological crisis. The capitalist production mode determines not only interpersonal relationships (exploited and exploiter) but also the relationship between humankind and nature (the capitalism plundering nature). Thus, in the view of eco-socialists, to completely transform "human-nature" relationship of capitalism and avoid capitalism destructing ecological system, it is necessary to change people's thoughts and the capitalist ideology, and above all, change the capitalist mode of production and its economic relations.

Second, the ecological crisis is the unavoidable outcome of globalization of the capitalism. Eco-socialists emphasize that occurrence of the ecological crisis is a sharp exposure of capitalist crisis, such an exposure is unparalleled in history, and is the result of the spread of capitalism all over the world. Since the nature of the capitalism is to pursue the maximum profits, it ceaselessly needs to expand its markets. Through global allocation of resources, capitalism makes full use of its advantages in economy and technology to exploit global resources, which are limited and scarce; all these resources are vital for the future of humans. David Harvey points out that the capitalist production "aims endless appreciation of capital value, without any consideration on its political, economic, geographical and ecological results it brings forth at all."[6] With the global expansion capitalism, capitalism promotes ecological imperialism; that is to say, it "ecologically plunders" developing countries and exports ecological crisis to them, which directly leads to worsened global environment and threats to human survival and development.

In the view of eco-socialists, also in the past, the developed capitalist countries have continually ecologically plundered the backward countries for centuries and sought for narrow self interests. There are two kinds of robbery: direct and indirect.

Direct plunder is defined as the one that the advanced countries move, high-consumption, high-pollution and labor-intensive industries to the developing countries; they go so far as to view those countries as refuse dumps and directly plunder their land, labor and natural resources . The existence of developed countries is based on the "backwardness" of those developing countries, and the modern ecological cities in developed countries owe their existence to numerous polluted cities in developing countries. The environmental quality enjoyed in those cities is an unjust privilege, which is robbed from developing countries. Pepper points out that "environmental quality is closely related to whether the wealth of a society is

---

6   Harvey, David: *The Condition of Post-modernity*, p. 180. Oxford: Basil Blackwell Press, 1990.

sufficient or insufficient. Environmental quality in Western countries has become admired object by the whole world, but this is the result of plundering the countries of Third World, they maintain and improve their own environment through ecological plunder."[7]

Indirect plunder is realized through "structural violence". The U.S. scholar, Robert Heilbroner, points out that the capital's internationalization is an inevitable trend due to the internal contradictions of capitalism. The capital originating from advanced countries forces developing countries to formulate political, social and economic policies and exerts "structural violence" upon peasants under the term "transformation" or "industrialization". As a result, plenty of public land in rural areas is privatized and is pulled into capitalist world markets. Peasants in order to survive with their small land left are forced to over-farm the land, leading to sterility and even desertification of the agricultural land. Meanwhile, under the condition of open market policies, advanced countries have gained a dominant in the markets of agrarian products with their technological and market advantages, which in turn forces developing countries to strengthen predatory exploitation on the decreased farming land in order to "reduce the cost of farm products". This indirect plunder by capitalism abruptly worsens the environment in developing countries. They are forced to sacrifice the environment and resources of their own countries to survive. Therefore, the ecological problems of the developing countries are as well caused by the capitalist mode of production.

Thus eco-socialists have revealed the internal relationship between the capitalist system and ecological crisis, correctly illustrated the cause for the contemporary global ecological crisis as the internal contradiction of the capitalist mode of production. Eco-socialist theory is based on these core ideas.

6.2.2.2 CRISIS OF THE CONTEMPORARY CAPITALIST SOCIETY

Eco-socialists, have to some degree, grasped new phenomena, changes and contradictions in the contemporary capitalist society. They have argued that the ecological contradiction has turned out to be the primary contradiction in the contemporary capitalist society, ecological crisis has become the principal contradiction, and ecological crisis is currently the new expression of the capitalist crisis.

How to evaluate the new changes and contradictions in the contemporary capitalism? Eco-socialists generally agree that Marx's theory on internal contradictions of capitalism is still valid because these internal contradictions are still there. However, with the development of Western industrial society, things did not occur as Marx had predicted namely capitalism does not inevitably collapse owing to the economic crisis. But on the other side ecological crisis is increasingly menacing human survival and development. With the advocacy of facing reality,

---

7   Pepper, David: *Eco-socialism: from Deep Ecology to Social Justice.* p. 95.

eco-socialists have made a new analysis on the capitalist crisis taking their starting point as the anarchy in the capitalist production which brings about destruction and crisis of natural environment and natural balance.

In their view, the ecological problem has become the main contradiction of the contemporary capitalist society. When exploring the contemporary capitalism, people should not only see the inherent contradictions of capitalism revealed by Marx, but also perceive the new changes and trends; such as further human alienation and intensified contradiction between man and nature. In Leiss' view, the modern capitalist production causes two big social problems: "overproduction" and "overconsumption". Overproduction is the result of the capitalist production aim, while overconsumption is caused by human alienation caused by capitalism. They promote each other, leading to human alienation and alienated man-and-nature relationship. As a result, they turn out to be the unsolvable social contradiction in contemporary capitalism.

They also hold the view that the ecological crisis has become the main crisis of the contemporary capitalism instead of economic crisis. In Leiss' view, there are two new features in contemporary capitalism different from early capitalism. One is that the capitalists manipulate consumption and make people generate an imposed or false demand, which creates "overproduction". It manifests itself as: the motive of pursuing profit, blindly pushing forward technologies growing to a larger and larger scale, more and more demand for energy resources, increasing centralization in production and population, and more and more professional functions or jobs . The other feature is that capitalists do their best to distort the nature of peoples' demand in order to postpone economic crisis, enticing people to consider pursuit for blind consumption as a genuine satisfaction. which results in "overconsumption". It manifests itself as people measuring the degree of their happiness according to how much they consume. Consequently, this kind of manipulated demand hurts and damages the limits of nature. This consumption becomes an important means to maintain and increase profit margin and exert social control over people. There are not only inherent contradictions of capitalist production, but also there are deep contradictions in the interaction between production mode and the whole ecological system. In Agger's view, "Ecological Marxism embraces two kinds of analytical concepts: on the one hand, the driving force in capitalism which expands the capitalist commodity production sphere results in increasing scarcity of resources and causes environmental problems, like air pollution. Ecological Marxism, on the other hand, attempts to evaluate the contemporary ruling style in the society – under this new rule humans are sensibly subject to alienated consumption of commodities, and it attempts to eliminate the mediation of dictatorship and the burden of alienated labor." That is to say, it is necessary to change the whole social system to fundamentally settle the ecological crisis.

They have also drawn a further conclusion that the contemporary capitalism postpones the occurrence of economic crisis by means of high production and high consumption, just to prolong the life of the capitalism. However, the economic crisis cannot be postponed, but converts to an ecological crisis. Agger points out, "The historical changes has invalidated Marxist theory of crisis which originally focuses to the sphere of capitalist industrial production. Today, the development tendency of capitalist crisis has moved to the sphere of consumption; that is to say, ecological crisis has replaced economic crisis." The ecological crisis fuels "the driving forces for social transformation to solve the crisis/contradiction occurring in the interaction between human demands and commodities. This new trend is determined by the limited ecological system."[8] In his view, some "Marxists insist and put their emphasis on production crisis; and fail to see that the crisis has moved to the sphere of consumption, and they are also unable to perceive that in contemporary capitalism the economic crisis is replaced by the ecological crisis." Some eco-socialists have even argued that ecological crisis is a supply crisis that occurs under the new historical conditions of industrial prosperity and material richness in the advanced capitalist countries. The natural resource system has already become insufficient to bear the capitalist mode of production and this reality ruins all the hopes of people in the advanced capitalist society. Eco-socialism attempts to explore the possibility of meeting their demands, re-construct their values and desires, re-evaluate means of satisfaction and re-construct human attitude towards nature and seeks for a new understanding on qualities of a happy human life.

In all, eco-socialism emphasizes that the internal contradictions of the capitalist mode of production is the essential cause for the ecological crisis. Thus, the struggle for settling ecological crisis should be combined with the struggle against international capitalism. It is on this point that eco-socialists differ from the Green movement. In eco-socialists' view, capitalism has initially promoted productive forces; however, today it holds back the non-alienated rational development of productive forces; therefore, it should be replaced by socialism.

6.2.3 GREEN SOCIETY: ESSENTIAL FEATURE OF SOCIALISM

Based on the criticism of contemporary capitalism, eco-socialism points out that people cannot fundamentally settle the ecological crisis, and rescue human survival without abolishing the capitalist system. Thus a combination of ecological principle and the socialism is necessary to transcend the modes of the contemporary capitalism and existing real socialism, and construct a new socialist mode with the harmony of man and nature. Its great difference compared with the traditional socialist theory lies in the emphasis that socialism should, and must

---

8   Agger, Ben: *Western Marxism: An Introduction*, p. 420.

be a green society, and the realization of the green society inevitably relies on socialism. Therefore, ecological socialism bestows socialism with new theoretical contents, and it also enriches ecology theory with revolutionary spirit.

6.2.3.1 ECO-SOCIALISM AND GREEN SOCIETY

Ecological socialism emphasizes that it is necessary to "re-define" socialism, and illustrates why the future society should be a green society from the two perspectives: in theory and reality.

From the theoretical perspective, they hold the view that the prerequisite of designing future society is based on the correct understanding of Marx's theory on man-and-nature relationship. According to this theory, a totally new harmonious relationship between man and nature will come into being in the future society, where human emancipation in material and spiritual life will be fully realized; meanwhile it will be a green society in accordance with ecological principle. The alleged new relationship between man and nature means that humankind is the center of the world, and men "dominate" of nature. The term "dominate" here contains meanings of "planning", "management" and "recovery". It implies that humankind will use rationality to properly develop production in arrangement with natural resources from the starting point of social and public benefits and to meet the needs of all humans' overall and free development. The socialist society will be one in which harmonious development between man and society, man and egoism, and man and nature is realized. Thus the green society should be part of the connotations of socialism.

From the perspective of reality, they emphasize that the future socialism is a green society, which is different either from the green society that the contemporary environmentalists pursue who have departed away from materialism, and also different from "ecological modernization" pursued by contemporary capitalist rulers. The contemporary environmentalists also aim to construct a green society. However, in this society, nature is the tutor of humankind; environment is prior to all; in the man-nature relationship, nature will hold the central position; all human actions should conform to nature and the natural laws. In terms of this, Pepper has pointed out that "eco-socialism is a kind of human-centralism (of course it is not the one in the sense of the capitalist technology-centralism) and humanism. It opposes biological moralism and natural mysticism, as well as other ideological-theoretical systems that may lead to anti-humanism. Eco-socialism highlights the importance of human spirit and non-material communication between humankind and other natural objects. Humankind is not naturally an object to pollute the nature, neither humankind is not born into arrogance, greed, aggression, competitiveness, brutality and cruelty; if we say humankind is degraded with such "guilt", this is not a hereditary or "sinful" outcome, but all these are caused by the existing social system."⁹ In his view, green socialist society will greatly alter the man-nature contradiction; and a fundamental change will as well occur in people's ideology; human development will be all-round and decent. The green socialist society is also different from the alleged ecological modernization of existing capitalism. With the development of Green movement critics, the traditional capitalist ideology as well puts stress on ecological awareness, and seeks solutions to the ecological problem. However, this capitalist green reform is still established on the basis of theories like that humankind dominates nature, and human is the master of nature; nature is the object that humankind should conquer and plunder; thus the contradictory human-nature relationship remains. Just as Gorz has remarked, capitalism has no way to overcome its internal contradiction; it is impossible that ecological rationality can replace economic rationality; as a result, the green society is unachievable for capitalism.

Specifically, the green society that the ecological socialism has constructed has three dimensions. First, this society overcomes the contradiction between man and nature. In this society, the man-nature contradiction under the capitalist condition will be settled together with the men and men (social) contradiction. Destruction of natural environment does not exist anymore; even if it may occur accidentally, it can be solved soon. Second, this is a conditioned green society. It appreciates or nurtures moral awareness towards natural environment and biological species but ultimately serves humankind and maintains the benefits of human society. Third, this is a green society where material and social human emancipation are both fully realized harmonious with ecological principle. With the development of science and technology and improvement of social productive forces, it is possible for people to better understand and control natural necessities; although compulsory labor still remains, people will have more free time to spend for creative activities. As for social relationships, by transcending the capitalist private ownership, people can independently deal with the man-nature relationship, and alleviate the destruction of natural environment to the lowest degree.

6.2.3.2 ECO-SOCIALISM AND ECOLOGICAL MODERNIZATION

In the view of eco-socialists, there are merely two approaches to solve the ecological crisis in modern Europe. One is the capitalist ecological approach. It advocates solving the ecological problem within the framework of the existing system, partially reforming several parts of the social system and improving technology to fit the ecological environmental needs. The other is the approach of ecological socialism. It advocates abolishing capitalism replacing it by new ecological socialism based on the harmonious man-nature relationship. Eco-socialists emphasize that there are no other ways to liberate humankind except the realization of eco-socialism, and certainly ecological reform by capitalism will not work. In their

---

9   Pepper, David: *Eco-socialism: from Deep Ecology to Social Justice*, p. 232.

view, the new mode of eco-socialism will also transcend the traditional industrialism. The industrialism means what humankinds had formed in the historical process of industrialization and life of industrial society, like mindset, cherishing material values, economic growth, and technological progress with the worship of economic rationality being superior to all the others. Transcending traditional industrialism and realizing ecological modernization by socialist approach, namely, "ecological re-construction" is an important content of ecological socialism.

The alleged socialist "ecological reconstruction" aims to reform the industrial social system with ecological modernization and completely re-establish the production process, exchange and consumption relations in line with social ecological standards. Eco-socialists hold the belief that the economic norm as maximum profit must be subject to the social ecological norm, which is the core of socialist ecological modernization as well as the unique feature of eco-socialism different from previous socialist modes. In Gorz's opinion, the spotlight of ecological modernization will enable people to understand the socialism with fresh eyes. The contemporary socialism must answer the questions of how to coordinate economic development and social development with ecological development. In the view of eco-socialists, realizing socialist ecological modernization should start to combine three aspects, namely, to integrate economic, social and ecological developments in unity.

First, they have reviewed economic rationality. Ecological socialists hold the view that the capitalist economic logic of maximum profit not only results overall waste in economy and causes ecological crisis, but also leads to social bi-polarization. Socialism aiming to replace capitalism should follow the principle in line with ecological requirement of "less production with better outcomes" instead of maximum profit. In Gorz's view, socialist ecological modernization is realized on the basis of overcoming the contradiction between the capitalist society pursuing maximum profit and environmental destruction. This socialism should adhere to economic efficiency, but economic rationality should comply with the social ecological rationality as much as possible in order to achieve the aim of ecological rationality together with economic growth and development. The alleged ecological rationality means that an adequate production mode should be selected and adequate measures should be taken to meet the material needs of humans, which consume as less as possible natural resources, and which improve the use value and durability of commodities. It aims at establishing a society where people can have a better life with less labor and consumption. This is the new ecological modernization with the new rationality. It starts from a novel production pattern and guarantees economic rationality on the basis of ecological rationality, that is to say, aims to prevent overall economic waste, alienation of labor and destruction of ecological environment and evaluates the economic benefit as a whole system. In Gorz's view, this essentially involves the transformation of the whole production paradigm. In accordance with the new principle of ecological rationality, "less production with better outcome", it is necessary to restrict economic rationality and the range of commercial exchanges, and economic rationality should be subordinated or comply with non-quantitative development goals such as social, cultural and development of individual freedom. Economic rationality should also serve the purpose of motivating creative labor as well as human spiritual life.

Second, they emphasize social rationality. When establishing their theories on future ecological modernization, eco-socialists hold the view that further refinement of social rationalities, like democracy and legislation, are the basic means of realizing socialist ecological modernization. Some eco-socialists point out that the future society will be based on rigid contract systems. That is to say, rigid contracts and regulations will not only be formulated in the spheres of economy and politics, but they will also regulate the relations between man and nature, these contracts will enable proper utilization and protection of nature. However, contracts in the ecological sphere will be different from those in the economic and political spheres. They will not only regulate the relations between our generation and nature but also regulate our relations with the future human. This is a potential contract, transcending time and space. This is because, if the last generation destroys the ecological environment, it will be impossible for the next generation to survive. Construction of this new social rationality relies on nothing but socialism[10].

Third, they have refined the concept of ecological rationality. Socialism with ecological modernization opposes traditional concepts, like intemperately pursuing high consumption and equaling consumption with satisfaction or happiness. They advocate the monistic view of leisure labor; namely, labor is the intermediate to establish a harmonious relationship between man and nature. Sound ecological rationality requires people to seek happiness, content and meaning from labor, or in other words, paying attention to raise life quality. They lay emphasis not only on material life, but also on spiritual life, men should learn how to gain happiness from creative labor and transcend alienated labor, in order to achieve the unity of ecological rationality and economic rationality. Gorz has attempted to demonstrate that ecological rationality, economic rationality and social rationality are in a unity. But to have a sound ecological rationality, it is inevitable to involve and satisfy each's needs, as well as the liberation and liberty for each. This is the only way for humankind to achieve emancipation.

---

10 Excerpted from Chen Xueming (compiled): *Tendency of Marxism Abroad after Abrupt Change of Soviet Union and Eastern Europe*, p. 396. Beijing: Renmin University of China Press, 2000.

6.2.3.3 ECO-SOCIALISM AND ALL-ROUND SOCIETAL DEVELOPMENT

In the eyes of eco-socialists, the contemporary capitalism is a society of an all-round alienation, suppression and deformation. It is necessary to replace it with a new sound society. The socialist mode of the former Soviet Union and East Europe is nothing but a variant of advanced industrial society, where there are also problems of democracy, alienation and unbalanced ecological environment. Therefore, it is vitally important to construct the future society by a comprehensive perspective. If we redefine socialism from the ecological angle, and lead an economic development in conformity with social and ecological development, the development mode of the future socialist society will no more be that mode we are acquainted with, but will be a society that actually has a harmonious relationship between individuals and society, human and itself, and man and nature.

As for economy, eco-socialists propose to replace the current "market economy" with "the social ecological economy" to establish an economic system that is featured in protecting nature and using natural resources rationally by considering later generations. This economic system has the principle of "less production with better outcome" in line with social ecological standard as the principal lever for economic development, which considers humans' long-term benefits, benefits of the later generations and the overall revival and development of humanity. In the view of eco-socialists, when people evaluate whether an economic system or activity is effective and reasonable, they should not only consider whether it serves the majority in the society and/or its direct economic profits/benefits, but the most important thing is to consider the social benefits and its environmental costs.

In terms of economic system, eco-socialists advocate overcoming the capitalist private ownership, and establishing socialist ownership. Pepper emphasizes that; social ownership means the producers re-possess means of social production in the form of associated ownership, namely control the man-nature relationship collectively, independently and consciously. This can enable that social production actually realized in conformity with benefits of the majority, and protect their long-term benefits, especially ecological benefits. This is also an essential precondition to guarantee green economic development.

As for economic system, early eco-socialists have focused their attention on the production mechanism, which should be featured as being small scale, decentralized, low pollution or non-pollution, and motivating people's intelligence. In this way, social production could meet the needs of humans without destroying ecological system, creating a harmonious relationship between man and nature. In the 1990s, eco-socialists pointed out that it is impractical to have that economic mode with small scales and decentralized due to economic globalization and growing bipolarization between South and North. They began to think that it is groundless to advise developing countries zero economic growth in the situation where the world economy is severely bipolarizing between South and North. Therefore, they have accepted a proper economic growth which should aim to meet the needs of humans (rather than profit) and such proper growth should not contradict with natural environment. The socialist green economy should grow with the increase of people's demands. This growth should be rational. And it should be a planned growth aiming to satisfy equal demand of everyone, but it does not mean and should not go to high centralization of economy. Eco-socialists believe that there is a third way apart from market economy and centrally planned economy. Arguing against traditional socialist ideas, Grundmann has claimed that it is impractical to wipe out market, currency and international exchange and advocated implementing ecologically planned economy, combining planning with market, and properly integrating centralization with decentralization, and promoting interaction between the central government and the local government. This new economic mode highlights the function of state planning and its regulatory role in economic life, but does not discard individuals' autonomy and liberty in production and does not reject modern economic mechanisms like market. Like Gorz, he also accepts economic role of the market combined with social management of the state in the future socialist society. The government's economic tasks should be administrative management, planning and coordinating; that is to say, government should utilize plan mechanisms and management functions it should act in accordance with human rationality when using natural resources and guide production in a proper and planned way. Consequently, governments will help people to consume sufficient materials and meet their various demands, and finally aim to free them from the restriction of economic rationality. The Third Way thinker Lawrence Wilder also advocates limited economic rationality compromising by market logic which in turn will also aims to accord with socialist aims and regulations, and limited economic rationality means that all the economic activities that are dominated by economic rationality should serve socialized individuals and comply with human liberty.

As for politics, eco-socialists propose a new type of democratic political system combining bottom-to-up with up-to-bottom effects, decentralization with integration, regionalization with internationalization based on the unity of economy, politics and environment. Firstly, they hold the view that it is not right to totally negate modern democratic politics, but necessary to reform it. In his book *Capitalism, Socialism and Ecology*, Wilder points out that socialism does not mean abolishing the economic system and administrative management system, but limiting them in real human life, so as to coordinate them with autonomous social and individual life. This democracy should neither mean government by specialists nor should it be autocratic, democracy should essentially mean integrating individual and collective benefits. It should serve human development enjoying all-round liberty through bottom-to-up and up-bottom democratic autonomy and participation patterns. Additionally, they highlight the universality of political democracy. In the 1970s or the 1980s, the eco-socialists have adopted the principle of grass-root democracy from the Green movement, with the aim of decentralization and non-bureaucracy in the political process, to achieve grass-root democracy such as workers' autonomy. But in the 1990s, eco-socialists thought this principle seems impractical and helpless in settling the ecological problem. Because all the ecological problems had turned out to be global issues, the political, economic and ecological problems in the contemporary society are impossible to be settled at the grass-root level. They could rather be settled at the regional, state and even international levels. Some eco-socialists have advocated replacing "European Union" with "European Ecological Commonwealth"; using ecological distribution zone instead of national state; establishing a world government to protect nature, and establishing an "international organization" and leave aside forefathers' endless conflicts, overcome ideological differences, and transcend the conflict between Occident and Orient. Additionally, they have to a degree acknowledged the necessary role of the state or similar organizations undertaking functions in economic and social management. Though the future ideal society will be democratic and decentralized, it should not be totally dispersive and totally based on local autonomy. In this new political structure, grass-root democracy and participation are important; but the state will play certain roles in managing social life for quite a long time in future too[11].

As for the social culture, eco-socialists have advocated to establish a new life style with the purpose of all-round human development leading to human liberty. In their view, everyone should enjoy rights enabling liberty, equality, sound health and self-determination. Only socialism can realize these rights because socialism can enable people to consciously unite and voluntarily cooperate in the social sphere, socialism can give full play to their abilities and creativity. In this new social life style, people can freely opt for their working time. Labor will become a free and an independent activity. Everyone can share joy and self-realization in the labor and tap all his potentialities. They can adequately feel the significance of life and joy of work.

---

11   Gorz, André: *Ecology as Politics*, p. 15. London, 1980.

6.2.4 INTELLECTUALS AND SOCIALISM

The question how to realize socialism is another important aspect studied by eco-socialists. In their view, the realization of eco-socialism will rely on class struggle and collective action, and the working class is the principal force of this change, while the leading force should be mature intellectuals who possess revolutionary enthusiasm, ecological awareness and certain practical skills.

6.2.4.1 REVOLUTION AND INTELLECTUALS

Ecological socialists have basically adopted the viewpoint of "Frankfurt School" on the historical position and political attitude of the working class, they hold the view that the contemporary working class has been "assimilated" by the capitalist consumption society, and lost their revolutionary, critical, oppositional spirits. Who will on earth shoulder the historical responsibility of being the gravedigger of capitalism? In the 1970s or the 1980s, ecological socialists thought that only those who had never been harmed by the capitalist alienated consumption and were highly concerned about the future of socialism could undertake the leadership for future social revolution. This kind of people were among the members of the "intermediate class", including medium and small bourgeois, intellectuals and young students. In the 1990s, with the abrupt changes occurring in the Soviet Union and East European socialist countries and the intermediate class turning right, some ecological socialists have raised a new idea that it would not be right to predict which class will be the leading force in the revolution. This leading force should prove itself in the real struggle, and be decided by subjective and objective factors in the revolutionary practice. In ordinary times some social classes or strata might be inactive or seem weak, but they could develop an extremely powerful revolutionary strength whence their revolutionary passion is awakened. As a result, they could become the leading force of the revolution. Generally speaking, they incline to the view that the leading power to realize ecological socialism will be intellectuals with "ecological awareness" and who voluntarily devote themselves to the ecological cause, concerned with the socialist future and able to master Marxist methods.

6.2.4.2 THE WORKING CLASS AND THE SOCIAL CHANGE

In the 1980s, eco-socialists have started to pay more attention to the role of the working class and trade unions in social change. Although working class lacks "ecological awareness", they directly conduct productive labor, have direct contact with nature, and suffer from severe environmental pollution during their work and private life. Thus, they have an enormous revolutionary potential, and can be the mainstay of the future social change. Scholars, like Pepper in Britain and Gorz in France, claim that the working class should not be excluded from the revolution. Meanwhile, it is necessary to unite the working class, medium and petty bourgeoisie and intellectuals; it is imperative to combine various new social movements, like ecological movement, feminist movement, civil rights movement and peace movement, with the workers' movement; it is also important to join the anti-capitalist movements in the advanced countries and anti-ecological anti-imperialist movements in the developing countries, so as to form a global force to fight against the capitalist system and launch a global revolution against "ecological imperialism – international capitalism".

6.2.4.3 "NON-VIOLENT" STRATEGY AND SOCIAL CHANGE

The early eco-socialists were greatly influenced by the theory of "non-violence" advocated by Green movement. But in the 1980s, eco-socialists have emphasized that "non-violence" is nothing but a kind of struggle strategy and if it is considered as an absolute sacred ideology, it will only cause unnecessary loss in the struggle against the capitalist system, because the reactionary class will not abandon using reactionary violence just for the sake of people's non-use of it. In Pepper's view, "Under the current conditions when bourgeoisie still has the control of the state machinery, it is impossible to overthrow and eliminate capitalism. Therefore, the first thing to do is to take over the state, and re-build it into an apparatus serving the public. It is necessary to limit the means to achieve this goal in two lines: "raise the revolutionary consciousness of the masses by education and employ the method of demonstrating the problems in their real lives. It is also vitally important to bear in mind that the any struggle aiming to "manage the capitalist production mode" can never settle the ecological crisis fundamentally"[12].

6.3 EVALUATION OF ECO-SOCIALISM

Studying eco-socialist thoughts enables us to understand several trends in contemporary capitalism and also offer us some new ideas for future socialism. Though ecological socialism has not formed a complete set of systematic theories, its sharp criticism against contemporary capitalist production bears positive significance and is a valuable contribution for us in our socialist cause and exploration.

6.3.1 THEORETICAL ACHEIVEMENTS OF SOCIALISM

Eco-socialism is both a left wing trend of thought in the contemporary Western society as well as a new socialist thought. It has emerged due to problems caused by modern capitalism in the ranks of the Green movement. It aims uniting ecological movements with socialist movements and combining ecological theory with Marxist theories. It has a clear stand point that opposes capitalism and advocates socialism.

---

12   Pepper., David: *Eco-socialism: from Deep Ecology to Social Justice.* p. 232.

In terms of theory, eco-socialists, under the influence of Marxism, apply Marx's theory of man-nature relationship when analyzing the ecological crisis in contemporary capitalism and depict the new outlook of the future socialism. Compared with other green viewpoints, eco-socialism not only bears a significant revolutionary and progressive character, but has also achieved some breakthroughs in theory.

First, eco-socialists apply the Marxist theory on man-nature relationship, reinforcing the holistic criticism of capitalism. Specifically, from the angle of man and nature, they reinforce the holistic criticism of the capitalist mode of production from the angle of man and nature relationship, and have raised some new valuable viewpoints and theoretical epitomes. In the era when man-nature issue turns out to be a hot topic in theory in the contemporary world, eco-socialists have emphasized grasping the ecological problem with Marxist approach and advocated "human scale", which should be highly evaluated. In the analysis of the ecological problem, the notion of "human scale" is a Marxist approach and expounds that it will not be proper to simply put men in opposition against nature and separate them, but evaluate them as a unity, linking nature with man, and nature with social problems. This distinct feature of ecological socialism is its superiority compared with various environmentalist and green viewpoints. Through studying ecological problems, eco-socialists have grasped that capitalism severely destructs man and nature, and have revealed the crimes of capitalist society.

Eco-socialists have also correctly evaluated the nature of ecological crisis that is closely related with the internal logic of capitalism pursuing maximum profits. Under the conditions of production aiming at profit, predatory exploitation of natural resources and anarchy of production is an inevitable result. Capitalism not only owes an enormous ecological debt in its past development, but still causes ecological crises and generating new ecological problems and threatens human survival. The ecological crisis is the inevitable outcome of the capitalist mode of production. As it is, the social and historical analysis made by eco-socialists on the ecological problem is profound.

The eco-socialism discloses that the capitalism not only realizes its rule over man but also rules science and technology and at the same time rules over the nature. And its rule over man is based on its dominance over the nature. These new ideas demonstrate its unique features, compared with other socialist schools. The Soviet mode of socialism widely applied in Russia and Eastern Europe has put stress on social revolution, while democratic socialism which is widely accepted in modern advanced capitalist states advocates social reform. On the other side ecological socialism suggests natural revolution, namely, that the realization of socialism should not only based on social revolution, but is also on natural revolution, or in other words, liberation of nature. In Leiss' view, the intensified capitalist control over nature does not eliminate or weaken the rule over human, but strengthens the rule over human. As it is, bringing the criticism of man-nature relationship into the scope of capitalism critic and combining its problems with the capitalist system are the unique features of the eco-socialist theory.

Eco-socialism theoreticians demonstrate the new changes in contemporary capitalism: on the one hand, the capitalist mode of production strengthens its control over nature, expanding humanized nature; on the other hand, the capitalist production mode intensifies the enslavement of people. As a result, the living environment is increasingly shrinking. With the globalization of capitalist development in the current era, the capitalist system has matured itself in terms of governing the society which brings about a strong trend of integration. As Frankfurt School has pointed out, among the capitalist powers, ideological integration, integration of technological rule, mass culture and integration of psychological oppressive mechanisms deepen. Above all, the most important is the integration of capitalist production. It attempts to maintain and raise profit margins and control the society and nature by means of alienated consumption and manipulates individuals' leisure time and consumption. Thus, in their view, man-nature relationship is unable to be coordinated under the capitalist mode of production. This viewpoint reflects an important real aspect of contemporary capitalism, and inspires us in our efforts to enrich socialism theories.

Eco-socialists also link the real manifestations of the current capitalism with the global ecological problem, and take a further step to reveal the internal linkage between the capitalist production and the destruction of the global environment. By the 1990s, eco-socialists have strongly focused on ecological problems and have revealed the enormous debt the North owes the South, and raised the critics that this was the outcome of capitalism plundering and exploiting the underdeveloped or developing countries. Besides previous modes of plundering, like the commodity export and capital export, the new mode can be defined as ecological plunder, or "ecological imperialist" plunder. Just as Pepper has commented; "Quality of environment is closely related to whether the material wealth of a society is rich or short. It is just through plundering the Third World countries they have maintained and improved their environment and thus Western capitalist countries have turned out to be the stars admired by the whole world. Some newly established green areas in the developed world are nothing but such privileged islands."[13]

Eco-socialists have also raised the idea that a spiritual decline and spiritual poverty haunt in the Western industrialized society, an important aim for eco-socialism to solve this problem. People can completely transcend the capitalist value orientation with the eco-socialist value orientation with the aid of eco-socialist theory.

---

13   Ibid., p. 96.

CURRENT GLOBAL IDEAS AND MOVEMENTS CHALLENGING CAPITALISM

The capitalist value orientation is based on the belief that social life is inherently a competition for survival, massive blind consumption growth could lead a limitless growth in economic sphere, the universe is a mechanical system and humankind is also a kind of machine. These concepts render men to lose themselves in the process of work and occupation, vulgar enjoyment and limitless pursuit of consumption, which results single-dimensional man as sharply criticized by Marcuse. Eco-socialists argue that it is necessary to change concepts of life: from material needs and demands to spiritual ones, from pursuit of numerous living articles to elevate life quality, from a hedonistic style life enjoyment to physical and mental health and harmonious relationship with nature. These ideas have indeed deepened the holistic criticism of the capitalism.

Second, in accordance with the new changes in the contemporary international situation, particularly after the 1990s, eco-socialists have made a new exploration and analysis on socialist prospects and its development in the future, and raised some valuable theoretical questions to be discussed.

The important theoretical contribution of eco-socialism lies in its demonstration on the internal linkage between social development and ecological problem and placing the problem as an indispensable component of socialism. In the history of the socialist theoretical development, Marx and Engels were the first among modern thinkers to criticize the capitalist view on social development and its destructive effect on environment and have argued that it was necessary to holistically grasp social development and the development of natural ecological system. Ecological socialism has inherited those Marxist thoughts, and has enriched the views on social development, such as raising harmonious relationships between man and nature, between social development and natural system, thus have established a new socialist theory with ecological socialist foundation, which provides us new scopes in our current theoretical and practical exploration of socialism.

Analyzing and facing the capitalist changes and adjustments in the 1970s, especially the socialist setback in the 1990s, ecological socialism has put a special emphasis on the relationship between socialism and ecological problem and reviewed the content of socialist aims and cause from the perspective of man-nature relationship, which is of great theoretical significance. Different from traditional socialism based on the social transformation of ownership relations, its theory aims several interrelated tasks; eliminating the capitalist ownership to liberate the society, eliminating the capitalist alienated labor and alienated life style to emancipate humankind, realizing the harmonious man-nature relationship to liberate the nature and establish a fair green society. It has enriched development concept which includes three lines as economic, social and ecological development, thus has contributed to socialist theory. This contribution is of great value for those in opposition in capitalist countries and also those socialists who are still in power and explore to enrich their socialist development practice.

6.3.2 DRAWBACKS IND WORLD VIEW AND STRATEGY

Eco-socialism as a left-wing trend of thought has also obvious historical limitations although its positive significance in theory is obvious and undeniable.

First, ecological socialism has failed to correctly employ Marx's theory on man-nature relationship in its theory. And there are also several theoretical inconsistencies and paradoxes in its holistic criticism of capitalism and understanding of socialism. Though eco-socialism expands the content of socialism to the level of man-nature relation, it views the ecological problem as the core, and replaces the theory of "economic crisis" with the theory of "ecological crisis", and consequently departs away from the basic contradiction of capitalist society and bases itself on the man-nature contradiction, discoloring the class contradictions in the capitalist society. In Agger's view, the shift from economic crisis to ecological crisis is caused by the changes in social history. This is because in the new era of capitalism "the driving force which can push social reform is rooted in the process of interaction between human needs and commodity; today the fate of this process is rather determined by the limited ecological system." Thus, eco-socialists pin their hopes of realizing socialism on the "enlightenment of peoples' thoughts". They hold the view that with the improvement of man-nature relationship, human natures like arrogance, greed, pugnacity, competition, barbarism and cruelty will be cultivated and transformed to modesty, peace, kindness, solidarity and rationality in the future eco-socialist society. Apparently, I can suggest that the realization of an ideal society relying on the enlightenment of thoughts is pre-determined to be an illusion in practice. Early eco-socialists inclining to treat the man-nature relationship in isolation have generally charged the developing countries with European centralism when analyzing global ecological problems. When advocating the product quality and zero growth in economical development, they have neglected how the developing countries could manage to survive under the conditions when the gap between South and North was drastically increasing and their population was constantly growing.

Second, as for the exploration of socialist theories, their scheme for future ecological society still remains insufficient, or even utopian. On the one hand, in terms of evaluating the driving force which enables transformation from capitalism to socialism (the necessity of socialism), ecological socialists emphasize that the revolutionary transformation motive is rooted in human demands, rather than class contradictions. Putting the man-nature relationship on the first place, they dilute the class contradiction in the capitalist society. A number of ecological socialists narrowly reduce capitalist production to market economy and competition, arguing that it is the market logic that leads to the logic of the capitalist maximum profit pursuit. This conclusion obviously equalizes the market economy with the capitalist private ownership relation, and evaluates to reform current market rationality as the starting point of constructing the socialism. On this basis, when exploring and struggling along the road of ecological socialism, ecological socialists insist on human needs as the driving force of change; that is to say, only when people attain the consciousness that the requirements of the capitalist system are incompatible with the requirements of maintaining life, and it threatens the foundation of life as well as the meaning of life, then the elimination of capitalism will be regarded as an urgent task by the people. On the other hand, as for the leading force of realizing socialism, ecological socialists commission the historical important task to those groups (strata) in the ranks of the ecological social movement who are not those mostly harmed by capitalist alienated consumption, or with most strong "ecological awareness" as well as great revolutionary enthusiasm and who concern most about the future of the socialism. Apparently, this hypothesis does not hold water when we evaluate the long experience gained in the history of socialist practice. Third, as for the approaches and strategies of the social reform, ecological socialism also advocates non-violence, which is not completely different from other environmentalists and democratic socialists. Although eco-socialism does not oppose the Marxist class theory and agrees to combine political struggles with certain class struggles (like supporting strikes), on the other hand eco-socialism and democratic socialism have no fundamental distinction in terms of their approach to practical struggles. In other words eco-socialism advocates rigidly reduces revolutionary measures or practice in the scope of "education" and "demonstrating or exposing problems in real life", opposing revolutionary mass movements or violent revolution, which bears similar colors with the old Fabianism and democratic socialism. In all, whether in theory or in practice, eco-socialism fails to establish a feasible scheme.

REFERENCES

- Ben Agger: *Western Marxism: An Introduction*. Beijing: Renmin University of China Press, 1991.
- Peter Dickens: *Society and Nature*. Philadelphia: Temple University Press, 1992.
- John Bellamy Foster: *Marx's Ecology*. New York: Monthly Review Press, 2000.
- Xu Juezai: *Schools of Socialism*. Shanghai: Shanghai People's Press, 1999.
- Yu Keping: *"Socialism" in the Time of Globalization*. Beijing: Central Compilation & Translation Press, 1998.
- James O'Connor: *Natural Reason—Research of Ecological Marxism*. Nanjing: Nanjing University Press, 2002.
- Xun Qingzhi: *Green Utopia - Social Philosophy of Ecological Socialism*. Jinan: Taishan Publishing House.

CHAPTER VII

SOCIALIST FEMINISM

1 *Rise of Socialist Feminism*
2 *Basic Views of Socialist Feminism*
3 *Evaluation of Socialist Feminism*

CHAPTER SEVEN

INTRODUCTION

Socialist feminism is a quite influential trend of thought in the contemporary world. It came into being between the end of the 1960s and the beginning of the 1970s, as the integration of two schools: Marxist feminism and socialist feminism, which have emerged one after the other. As the outcome of combination of feminist ideology and socialist thoughts in the contemporary Western countries, this trend of thoughts reflects not only the Marxist influence on feminism, but also the interaction of feminist movements with socialist movements. The study of these thoughts is of great significance to understand the current feminist movements in our era as well as the trends in related social thoughts, especially socialist thoughts and their development in those countries.

250 CURRENT GLOBAL IDEAS AND MOVEMENTS CHALLENGING CAPITALISM

7.1 THE RISE OF SOCIALIST FEMINISM

The emergence of socialist feminism has its own social background and origins in theory and ideology. The oppressed workers, including large numbers of women in the class society, particularly in the capitalist society, suffer great oppression and exploitation. Socialist feminism has emerged under such historical settings. Socialist feminism came into being in the 1960s, when Western capitalist society met several social crises and turbulences, especially when the new social movements rose. The rise and evolution of feminist movements, particularly the climax of the second feminist movement between the end of the 1960s and beginning of the 1970s, were the direct causes for the emergence of socialist feminism. It was indeed based on the outcome of women's emancipation and rising self awareness in both socialist movements and the feminist movements, and united them to form their own theory and ideology.

7.1.1 EMERGENCE OF SOCIALIST FEMINISM

Thoughts of socialist feminism, as the outcome of the integration of feminist and socialist thoughts, were not only related to social settings of the feminist thought and movements, but also to social settings of socialist thoughts and movements. As a matter of fact, these two backgrounds were interrelated, making up social and historical settings for socialist feminist thoughts.

Exploitation and oppression in the capitalist society can be seen as the wide social source for the rise of socialist feminism. On the one hand, women are oppressed in the capitalist society, which has created conditions for feminist thoughts and movements. On the other hand, workers are also exploited and oppressed in the capitalist society, which has produced conditions for socialist thoughts and movements. These two conditions are interrelated. For example, female workers suffer oppression not only from males but also from capitalists. Therefore, the exploitation and oppression in the capitalist society has not only brought about feminist thoughts and socialist thoughts respectively, but also the combination of these two as socialist feminist theory and practice.

The rise of socialist feminism was set in the background where the oppressed and exploited in the capitalist society strived for their own emancipation (feminist movements and socialist movements). The feminist thoughts and socialist thoughts were both the outcome of capitalist society. Though women's oppression was a long and deep rooted historical phenomenon, there had not appeared, and could not appear, feminist movements and thoughts for women's emancipation prior to the capitalist society. Similarly, socialist movements and socialist thoughts as well, in a real sense, have emerged in the capitalist society to some extent on the prerequisite of capitalist development. Both feminist and socialist movements have emerged in large scale in the middle of the 19th century. From then on, they both have gone through a history of rises and falls. Additionally, they have shared the similar or same miseries in many eras. They have influenced each other and tended to approach to each other in the process of their development.

Feminist movements have started in the middle of the 19th century. This movement was known as the first-wave feminist movement, or first great leap of women's emancipation development. This period has lasted until the end of the 1920. In this great movement, women have fought for equal political and legal rights with men. Their criticism has directly aimed against capitalist states and those laws that excluded women from the rights of education, employment, participation in government and political affairs etc. The initiation of the U.S. feminist movements was marked by The Declaration of Sentiments, which was issued in July 1848. From 1890 on, feminists in the United States have made great efforts to organize women to participate in suffrage movements. In 1917, two women's emancipation organizations "National American Woman Suffrage Association" and "National Womens' Party" have jointly organized a 24-hour demonstration against the White House. In 1919, the U.S. Parliament was forced to issue The 19th Amendment to the U.S. Constitution, clearly prescribing that women had the right of suffrage. This feminist movement has gained fruitful achievements. Till the end of the First World War, women in several European and American countries have obtained rights of suffrage, property rights and rights for higher education. It is noticeable that the peak period of the first feminist movement was as well the time when socialist movements in capitalist countries were vigorously ascending. For example, in the middle of the 19th century the scientific socialism has emerged; Marx and Engels' Communist Manifesto was issued in February 1848, which was just a little bit earlier than The Declaration of Sentiments by feminists of the United States. Later on, the Paris Commune and the founding of proletarian political parties and their unions, particularly the Russian October Revolution in 1917, all have marked the climax and great achievements of socialist movements.

In the beginning of the 1930s, Western women's emancipation movement was at a low ebb. With the outbreak of the capitalist economic depression, prejudices against women's employment have sharply risen in the European and American countries. . In 1920ies, although the success of the Russian October Revolution has encouraged proletarian revolutions in several European capitalist countries, they had little success and failed to seize power one after another. Thereafter, capitalist states have brutally suppressed the proletarian movements. And after Hitler came to power in Germany, he launched the Second World War, crazily expanding globally, fascism and war has greatly destroyed women's organizations in some of the European countries. After the end of the Second World War, capitalist countries with the leadership of the United States have launched the policy of

"Cold War" against the communist parties and communism, suppressing feminist movements as well as labor movements. Particularly in the 1950s, movements against feminism have reached a crescendo in the United States, strongly restricting women's participation in public life. In this period a younger generation of American female intellectuals have forced to abandon their studies and their career one after another, retreating to the dream of "happy housewives" and aiming it as their top life goal. From then on, the momentum of feminist movements has completely subsided. At the same time, in this era the labor movement in capitalist countries as well receded towards a low ebb.

Especially after the Second World War, great changes have occurred in capitalism. By means of promoting the new scientific revolution, the Western countries have adjusted their policies in many spheres, particularly economy and politics, which have not only alleviated class contradictions but also greatly promoted economic development. Consequently, traditional labor movements in the Western capitalist countries generally fell into a decline; struggles of the working class for socialism receded to an ebb.

By the end of the 1950s and beginning of the 1960s, Western capitalist countries have begun to enter another turbulent period, causing the emergence of the New-Left movement against capitalist reality and as well the second rising tide period of the feminist movement. Reforms in capitalism during the postwar years could not eliminate the inherent contradictions of capitalism. Capitalist states could not overcome their drawbacks and evils, like long-term economic stagnation, militarization of economies, government's financial deficiency and high state debts, intensifying social bipolarization, deformed social development, increase of crimes, drug trading and use, widespread venereal diseases, prevalence of superstition, deep-rooted racial discrimination, increasing destruction on the ecological system and environmental pollution, rampant bureaucracy, ceaseless escalation of nuclear and conventional armament race, all of which arose great discontent among broad masses. It was with the intensification of these social contradictions and crises that the struggle against capitalist reality was fueled again. These struggles and opposition have attained different forms compared with the struggle of traditional labor movement. For instance, they were based on a wider and intricate social basis, which was loose, decentralized and unsteady. There was no common political ideology, and their organization forms were also amorphous, unsystematic and instable; there was no long-term objective, neither was there a clear class orientation. Those who participated in the movements belonged to different classes, stratums or parties, rather aiming or joining for the realization of a specific social goal; thus, which did not appear as a movement stamped by a certain class or stratum. The movement of racial civil rights of blacks, the anti-war and peace movement, the New Left movement, New Feminist movement and ecological movement have all supported each other. They have widely and increasingly spread in Western countries in the form of "Movement for a New Society", one wave after another.

Among those movements for a new society, the new feminist movement was a very important one. It has in fact originated from the "New Left" movement. In the large-scale mass movements exploding in the United States, the "New Left" which was based on the mainstay of university students and young intellectuals, had become an attractive political and cultural movement in the United States in the 1960s. They have supported blacks' movement against racism, actively participated in movements for civil rights, opposed the Vietnam War and the established system of schooling and education institutions, and fiercely attacked the U.S. social system. These left-wing student movements have also inspired women to struggle for their own emancipation. Many women who had actively participated in these movements hoping that they could find their position in the New-Left movements. However, they were disappointed by the reality they have faced in the New-Left movements, they have soon observed a strong andro-centrism in these organizations. The leaders of the New Left groups have viewed women as vase, or assigned them do odds and ends, like serving tea. They went so far as to express their backward ideas in public, "In the anti-war student committee, women can only be placed in such secondary positions, or, in other words, they behave obsequiously." This kind of attitudes have indeed irritated women in the "New Left". They have keenly realized: "It is more urgent and vital for women to emancipate themselves than struggle for blacks or for other aims", realizing that it was necessary for women to have their own emancipative movement.

During the "National New Politics Conference" organized by the "New Left" in the United States in August 1967, a female member was refused to read her article on women issues by those men in charge of the convention. A week later, women have decided to hold an independent meeting in Chicago, releasing "A Letter to Left Women", calling for them to unite in order to initiate a new "women's liberation movement". Thus the second feminist movement has emerged in the United States in the middle of the 1960s, and then spread to Western Europe and to entire capitalist world. Between 1968 and 1970, the new feminist movement has spread all over Britain, and has reached a new tide in France in 1968 due to the baptism of "Revolutionary May Storm". At the same time, in Northern Europe, like Denmark and Norway, the new feminist movements have also shown a vigorous development, women's emancipation organizations were being organized one after the other. The aims and scopes of this new feminist movement involved all aspects of women rights and demands, which has far surpassed the first movement both in depth and width. If the first feminist movement can be regarded as the one for political and legal rights such as universal suffrage, then we can say that the second feminist struggle was characterized as an all-round and multi aspect movement, including political, economic, educational and cultural spheres, and covering a range of problem areas in the society, family and schooling. Furthermore, the second feminist movement was even more radical. It has advocated a complete change in the social system to create necessary emancipative conditions for women, rather than reforming the society on the basis of the existing system through parliamentary legislation.

It was also in the second feminist movement that socialist feminism has emerged. In this second feminist movement, a variety of theories or schools could be distinguished such as, liberal feminism, radical feminism, Marxist feminism and socialist feminism. We will introduce in this chapter the latter two, Marxist feminism and socialist feminism which are subsumed as "Socialist Feminism".

7.1.2 IDEOLOGICAL ORIGINS OF SOCIALIST FEMINISM

The ideological origin of socialist thoughts for women's emancipation is intricate. To sum it up, there are two aspects: one is the thoughts on women's emancipation advocated by traditional socialism; the other is ideas rooting from traditional feminism.

7.1.2.1 WOMEN'S EMANCIPATION THOUGHTS

In the 19th century and beginning of 20th century, two utopian socialists Charles Fourier and Robert Owen, and existentialist Simone de Beauvoir were the first to definitely link women's emancipation with socialism. In the process of criticizing the capitalist reality and advocating the socialist ideal, they have clearly raised the idea of women's emancipation. De Beauvoir has pointed out that capitalism should be stamped as an unreasonable society if it did not concern the security of women, who covered half of the population in the society. In Fourier's view, the development quality of a certain historical era could be judged by the degree of women's liberty; "The degree of women's emancipation is the natural criterion to measure the universal emancipation." Owen has criticized the marriage in the capitalist society, advocating men-women equality with the attempt of realizing it in practice. To set an example of alleviating women's housework, he was the first to establish a kindergarten in the world. The exploration of those utopian socialists on women's emancipation was not only an important source for Marxist theory on this problem, but also for later socialist feminists.

Marxist theory on women's emancipation also constitutes an important source for socialist feminism. Most women's thoughts were more or less affected by Marxism. Some of them were true Marxists, who committed themselves to apply Marxist theory to explore women's emancipation problem in the capitalist society. Some of them did not declare themselves as Marxist when studying the feminist issue, and even criticized the Marxist viewpoint on women's emancipation.

However, whether they inherited or learned from, and approved or disapproved Marxism, it cannot be ignored that the feminist socialist concepts, thread and ideology is partly related to traditional Marxism.

What the feminist socialists adopted and developed from Marxism mainly involves two aspects: The first aspect includes some basic standpoints and methods expounded in Marx's social and historical viewpoints or works, like Marxist historical materialism, critic of bourgeoisie political economic theory and his analytical methods, class theory and also his early theories related human nature and alienation. These theories and methods do not directly relate with feminist problems, but they can serve that purpose as well. The second aspect includes direct Marxist thoughts on women problem and emancipation. Writers of classic Marxism have paid much attention to women's emancipation. This can be seen in Marx's *Economic and Philosophical Manuscripts of 1844* and Engels' *The Condition of the Working Class in England in 1844* and their co-authored works *The German Ideology* and *The Communist Manifesto*, also in Marx's *Capital* and Engels' *Origin of the Family, Private Property and the State,* all of which have to a degree dealt with issue of women's emancipation. They have revealed women's conditions in the capitalist society, specifically focusing on laboring women being exploited and her body and health ruined under heaviest working conditions, and formulated advanced thoughts on women's emancipation. For instance, in his book *Origin of the Family, Private Property and the State*, Engels had systematically demonstrated Marx's thoughts on women's emancipation. He had definitely pointed out, "As long as women are excluded from a broad participation in social production labor process and restricted to engage in private labor in the family, it is, or will be, impossible for them to be liberated or equal with men. Women's emancipation will not be possible unless they can participate in production and unless housework will occupy only a small part of their time. But this can be achieved on the basis of nothing but modern industry."[1]

German socialists have also developed important ideas on women's emancipation. Bebel, one of the outstanding leaders of the German Social Democratic Party, was the first to systematically explore the relationship between women's emancipation and socialism in his book *Women and Socialism*. This book reveals why and how women are enslaved in human history, with a systematic analysis of women's enslaved position in different historical periods from numerous aspects, such as physiology, psychology, culture and education, marriage and family, profession and morality. He has pointed out that in the capitalist society, especially in families of the propertied class, women are degraded to nothing but machines to produce legal children, as housewives or female wards of exhausted husbands indulged in sex. As long as the capitalist society remains, evils, such as money

---

1   *Selected Works of Marx and Engels*, Second Edition, Volume 4, p. 162. Beijing: People's Press, 1995.

marriage, infanticide, abortion, increasing divorce rate and prostitution will continue to exist and will even worsen. However, "women's complete emancipation and gender equality are one of the developing objectives of our civilization; there is nothing on earth that can prevent the practice for such a goal." As a movement aiming to eliminate the capitalist system and establish a new social system, socialism is directly linked with women's emancipation. "The future belongs to socialism, and first of all, it belongs to workers and women."[2] Clara Zetkin, an influential socialist as well as German politician, was the first to raise the proletarian flag for women's emancipation, and has devoted herself to socialist movements. She has pointed out that the reason why women have an inferior position for thousands of years is not related with the laws "formulated by men", but in their economic status and property relations. For emancipating themselves, women should step out of their houses, and participate in social production, workers' movements and socialist movements. As an important part of human emancipation, women's emancipation inevitably pushes the cause for the emancipation of labor from capital. It will be impossible for the proletariat to get liberated unless they unite without gender distinction. It is the same with the socialist cause; it cannot be victorious unless it unites a vast number of women to participate.

7.1.2.2 FEMINIST THOUGHTS ON WOMEN'S EMANCIPATION

Feminism is a quite influential trend of thought in modern society. It expounds the theoretical aspects on how and why women suffer oppression, and their problems as freedom and equality, and guides the struggle for women's rights and emancipation. Socialist feminists have also adopted a lot from several feminist thoughts prior or contemporaneous to them. Including liberal feminism, Beauvoir's feminist thoughts and radical feminism all have inspired socialist feminism.

Liberal Feminism:

Liberal feminism is the thought based on the theories of bourgeois liberalism. This feminist school can be traced back to the book *In Defense of Women's Rights* by Mary Wollstonecraft in the 18th century. In the 1960s, the book *The Subjection of Women* co-authored by John Stuart Mill, and his wife Harriot Taylor Mill a British feminist in 1869, is a classic of liberal feminism. Representatives of this school are mainly well-known feminists in the United States, like Betty Friedan. Friedan's book *The Feminine Mystique*, which was first published in 1963, is another classic of Western feminist movements after *The Second Sex* by Simone de Beauvoir, the French female writer. Liberal feminism generally worships the liberal principles of the European Enlightenment Movement and evaluates women's emancipation in line with individual liberties, self-independence, natural rights and emphasizes

---

2   Bebel, August: *Women and Socialism*, p. 471. Beijing: Central Compilation and Translation Press.

rationality. It asserts that women are born into rationality and have limitless potentials to develop and improve themselves, just as men do; if equal opportunities are given, they can also exert their wisdom and talent as men do. The disparity of roles and status between men and women lay in legal and political regulations. This kind of inequality is unfair. It is necessary for women to organize and struggle for equal political and legal rights to overcome the disparity. Once women obtain equal political and legal rights, they can emancipate themselves on the basis of everyone's joint effort. Liberal feminism was the mainstream thought in the first feminist movement, and has also influenced the second wave to a certain degree. Although socialist feminists have adopted several ideas and practices from liberal feminism, generally they have a critical and oppositional attitude towards it.

Beauvoir's book *The Second Sex* can be regarded as the feminist "Bible", which has made a great influence on feminist movement and established its theoretical base. Socialist feminists are also more or less influenced by this book. In her book, Beauvoir has made a profound analysis of women's living conditions, fiercely attacking the deep oppression over women by the bourgeoisie. She has sharply explored women's actual conditions from women's physiological, psychological, economic and historical aspects, and has boldly revealed women's social and life problems. Her sharp comment "One is not born, but rather becomes a woman" has made an unprecedented effect in the feminist history. According to Beauvoir, it is the society that produces the difference between men and women, which is the major source for women's subordinate position. If women strive for freedom and human dignity, it is necessary to eliminate this artificial distinction. The book *The Second Sex* was published in 1949, when the feminist movement faced a decline; in the period between the first and second feminist movements. As a result, this book has become an epitome in theory of the first movement, and theoretical preparation for the second feminist movement. When analyzing the feminist problem, we can see that Beauvoir is apparently inspired by Marxist thoughts and methods. Her critical attitude and perspective based on social history has shed much light on the development of contemporary Western feminist theories. Her approach includes similar characteristics with socialist feminism, thus we can easily regard Beauvoir as the pioneer of socialist feminism.

Radical Feminism:

Radical feminism is a "current" that has emerged in the second feminist movement at the end of the 1960s. This current has almost co-existed with socialist feminism, and they have largely impacted each other. Representative works of this school were Kate Millett's Sexual Politics and Shulamith Firestone's *The Dialectic of Sex*. Radical feminists have argued that women constitute a separate class, and this class is under several deep oppressions, among which men's oppression over women is the most primary one, and it is the basis and core of other oppressions.

They strongly reject the liberal feminist view that the source of women's oppression lies in their lack of political and civil rights; neither do they agree with the Marxist feminist view that the source of women's oppression lies in class oppression. They argue that its source is nothing but patriarchy and patriarchy is an institution advocating men's rule over women. This patriarchal system is characterized by power, rule and hierarchy. It has emerged prior to capitalist society and continued to exist and play its role in social history. Radical feminists assert that patriarchy primarily originates from division of labor based on sex. And it is the biological cause that leads to women's oppression and negative fate. Thus, radical feminists suggest that women should reject the "task of giving birth to and bringing up children". They, with the aid of science and technology — artificial reproductive technology— intend to expand this "task" to the whole society so as to emancipate women. Some radical feminists go so far as to advocate blurring up sexual distinction, establishing a hermaphrodite culture, adopting sexual separation, rejecting heterosexuality and support lesbianism. The radical feminism goes to extremes and generally has a minor impact among women. However, its criticism of patriarchy has shed much light on the later socialist feminism.

Additionally, socialist feminism as well has adopted some thoughts from the trend of "Western Marxism" thoughts, such as the criticism on the separation between public and private spheres in the late capitalism period expounded by Horkheimer, Adorno and Marcuse, and from Gramsci's thoughts on "cultural hegemony".

7.1.3 DEVELOPMETS STAGES OF SOCIALIST FEMINISM

As a trend of thoughts, socialist feminism has gone through two stages, which also demonstrate themselves in the form of two theoretical schools, the former as Marxist feminism and the latter as socialist feminism. Though different in form and their evolution, they are usually considered as two different schools. They are both influenced by Marxism, employing Marxist terms and analytical methods when exploring women's problems in contemporary capitalist countries. In their view, effort is necessary to combine feminism with socialism, and seek ways for women's emancipation on the road to socialism. Diachronically, they are in a sequential order. Marxist feminism has emerged in the beginning of the 1970s, while socialist feminism rose in the middle of the 1970s. The former has promoted and has given much enlightenment to the latter, while the latter has absorbed some ideas from the former to some extent and continued its exploration on this basis. Therefore, it is reasonable to study them together as integrated thoughts.

Members of Marxist feminism are mainly female scholars who believe and study Marxism, thus apply Marxist viewpoints to illustrate the feminist problem. Representatives of them are scholars, such as Heidi Hartmann, Lise Vogel and Lin James. They have openly declared that they regard Marxist theory on women emancipation as the source of their thoughts. They believe Marx and Engels' illustration on women's social position is a valuable source and have inherited the Marxist tradition emphasizing economic and class analysis, especially focusing on women's economic position and interests, besides problems related with women's working conditions. Above all, they have applied Marx's method, he used when analyzing the capitalist commodity economy in his work *Capital*. Marxist feminists have also adopted many ideas from Engels' work *Origin of the Family, Private Property and the State* when studying family and women problems including their studies related to housework women "have to do". On the basis of their analyses on housework, they have revealed from another aspect how oppression and restriction occurs in this kind of work and have included this problem in their strategy for women's emancipation.

Socialist Feminism:

Socialist feminists, besides adopting some viewpoints and methods of Marxist feminism, have as well absorbed the patriarchy hypothesis from radical feminism, and have strived to integrate those two sources when interpreting women's conditions and emancipation. Its representatives are mainly those from Britain like Juliet Mitchell, Zillah R. Eisenstein, Ann Fenguson, Nancy Folbor, Barbara Ehrenreich and Alice Jagger. Compared with Marxist feminism, the source of socialist feminism is a little more intricate; and its theoretical orientation also seems vaguer, and does not have a clear and pure linkage with Marxism as the former.

Between the end of the 1980s and the beginning of the 1990s, the feminist movement has entered a new stage, and socialist feminism has also faced with new changes and developments. In this new period Post-modernism has started to influence the feminist thoughts including socialist feminism. It was a dual effect: on the one hand, socialist feminism has gained some similarities with post-modern feminism in some aspects; and there occurred a tendency of convergence and further alliance between the two. On the other hand, post-modernism has caused a shocking effect in socialist feminism. This is because post-modern feminism negates macro analysis in theory or rejects general concepts, such as "society", "feminism" and "women". Their approach has caused a great confusion and dynamism in the existing feminist movements. Under such a mutual interaction socialist feminism has adopted a new approach. In the 1970s or 1980s, socialist feminists have applied general methods in the analysis of women's social reality but recently they have started to put more emphasis on the research of women's self-experiences and emotions in daily life and their rebellion to current reality.

7.1.4 BASIC FEATURES OF SOCIALIST FEMINISM

First, the majority of socialist feminists are female persons. As a trend based on female thoughts, feminism supports the ideas on behalf of women's interests and struggle for it. Those ideas are easily supported by most females. Therefore, feminism is still a kind of women's self thought and movement. Although there are male writers and social activists who advocate gender equality and women's emancipation and make their contribution to it, some view them as only supporters of the feminist movements, and not regard them feminists. In reality, the most renowned figures of feminism, including socialist feminism, are female writers, scholars and activists.

Second, socialist feminism is a trend or "current" in reality, and also a feminist movement in reality. Socialist feminism has emerged in the new feminist movement, and turned out to be a theory of the movement and has pushed the practice forward. Most of the renowned members of socialist feminism are female intellectuals making academic researches on women's problems from different aspects, and make an important contribution for the contemporary women's studies. Meanwhile, they are active public figures-activists- who advocate and take practical part in the movement, thus women struggle for their own rights. Some of them are in the front ranks of the struggle as leaders. Thus, it is not right to study this trend of thought merely in theory, but necessary to link our research with the practical feminist movement.

Finally, socialist feminism is different from those comparatively unitary schools. It integrates feminist thoughts with socialist thoughts, and strives to combine various feminist movements and demands with socialist movement. Socialist feminism bears a duality, can be regarded as either a kind of feminism or a kind of socialism which receives theoretical nutrition from different sources and attempts to integrate the analytical methods and achievements of both. Thus, in the illustration or theory of socialist feminism, there are some parts inconsistent with each other. Some put more emphasis on Marxism and socialism, while there are others highlighting feminism. Or it is related with the subject's practice, on certain occasions, his/her analysis on a certain problem leans to Marxism, while at other times it is close to feminism.

7.2 VIEWS OF SOCIALIST FEMINISM

There are various thoughts among socialist feminism; for instance, early socialist feminism has paid attention to the analysis of family economy, while late socialist feminism places more stress on non-economic spheres, like ideology and culture; the U.S. feminists incline to make macro exploration, while British feminists usually follow Marxist tradition. In spite of these, they share as well some commonality and consistency on their basic stand and viewpoints. Generally speaking, socialist feminists mainly conduct their research around those problems, we observe below.

7.2.1 WOMEN AND OPPRESSION

7.2.1.1 WOMEN AND MODERN CAPITALIST SOCIETY

Socialist feminist researchers usually start their studies on women problem from the analysis of women's conditions. They try to offer a diachronic review of women's social status and conditions in the history, especially in modern capitalist society. Though women make up half of the humankind, and are irreplaceable, the role they play in economy, politics and society is undermined, and judged as an inferior compared to men for a long time in history. Though the development of capitalist industry and technology provides solid conditions for women's emancipation and women have gained equal legal and political rights through women movements, they have not yet freed themselves from the severe oppression in the capitalist society. The oppressed women still exist extensively in the society and the oppression is comprehensive, tangible and intangible prevalent in all the walks of social life. In her book *Capitalism, Patriarchy and Job Segregation by Sex*, Heidi Hartmann makes an indisputable demonstration of it.

First, women's activity in the family is still limited and restricted. Socialist feminists argue that human society is for a long time in the segregation of two spheres: one is social production and public life which are men's world; the other is family and private life, which are under women's mandate. Social public sphere is thought to be vitally important, while the sphere of family and private life is considered secondary or even marginal. Men and women seem to live in two separate worlds with disparate social positions. Men engage in what seems more important and brilliant in the society, and they not only possess more income, but also enjoy higher social reputations, while women merely undertake seemingly trivial family labor thus women's activity area is restricted as a quite narrow range. They have little opportunity to break away from the familial restrictions and enter the broader social world; neither can they have the chance to undertake positions related to those social public affairs with high reputation. Though women have more access to jobs with the development of market economy, no essential changes have occurred in the range of their activities, and most of them remain in the familial sphere, which is considered their sole or basic activity space. Though some women have gained a majority in certain social professions, they are not free from or cannot give up family labor. As a matter of fact, they shoulder dual burdens of family labor and social labor.

Second, women are in a subordinate status in the family. In depiction of women's family role, socialist feminists hold the view that men are still masters of the family, who demand or even order women to do the family labor. Returning home after work, men pose themselves as the emperor of the family, expecting that he is bestowed with the privilege; that his wife should provide considerate family service for him. Though some husbands as well do some family labor at home, they do not regard it as their duty, but a passing fad. Even the wife herself considers family labor as part of her natural duty. In some families, wives even suffer from their husbands' violence. In Juliet Mitchell's view, there is a fallacy that is popular in the society for a long time: a "genuine woman" and family are symbols of peace and wealth; in the atomized and chaotic world, the family presents a piece of clean indestructible land, where people love each other and enjoy a safe and harmonious life. But In fact, women are both sufferers of violence and depression in the family.

Additionally, women live an alienated life in the family. Alice Jagger suggests using Marx's alienation concept in the analysis of women's condition under oppression. She has argued that alienation not only occurs in the sphere of production as traditional Marxists have asserted; it so seems that the family labor that women undertake does not bear alienation. But actually, observed in accordance with Marxist spirit, one can find that alienation also emerges in all aspects of women's life. For instance, when analyzing the love life of a woman, just as a worker is separated from the product he produces, she as well is alienated from her body. Although usually many women say that her diet, exercise and make-up are all for herself; but in fact, she does them just for men. When a woman trims her eyebrows, dyes her nails and has esthetical plastic surgery, her body becomes an object both to men and her. Additionally, just as workers competing against each other for a higher pay, women as well become rivals in pleasing men. Jagger, comments that motherhood is also an alienated experience for women. This is because how many kids a woman should have is not decided by herself, but by others or the society. Let alone gynecologists' use of complex technological means to manipulate women's delivery. Thus to bring up children as well turns out to be an alienated experience. Mother works day and night merely to bring up their children following the advice of alleged women experts', rather than in their own ways.

Finally, even though women have the opportunity to participate in social work, they remain still disadvantageous in labor markets. Socialist feminists have made comprehensive analyses on the conditions of women who participate in social work, and have concluded that though large numbers of women have already entered the ranks laboring forces in capitalist society, they still remain at the margin of social economy; their status and conditions are no better than housewives. This is because there is also discrimination by gender in labor markets; thus women are just forced to step into a particular "female labor market". They mainly join those professions that are viewed to be typically fit for females, like nurse, primary school teacher, and secretary and shop sales assistant. What they usually do is the extension of their family role. For instance, to be a primary school teacher actually reflects women's role as caring for children in the family. They are paid less for their work compared to men, and some earn just half of that of men's. Hartmann points out, "In labor markets, men's dominance remains as labor division based on gender. Woman labor is considered as non-skilled, including no technology, which can use less power in exertion and supervision, thus she should be paid low. [...] Women's inferiority in labor markets also intensifies their subordinate role in the family. In turn, their subordinate role in the family as well reinforces their inferior position in the labor market."[3]

7.2.1.2 CAPITALISM AND PATRIARCHY

Socialist feminists have not only depicted the status of oppressed women in the capitalist society, but have also made a further step to analyze the source for the oppressions.

7.2.1.2.1 Physiological and Social Oppression

Socialist feminists completely disagree that the source for women's oppression lies in their physical weakness. Mitchell has pointed out, "Most of the classic theories are all based on the supposition that women are too weak to shoulder heavy physical labor, and argue that this is the essential factor that leads to women's subordinate position. But in fact, this supposition is highly insufficient."[4] This is because it ignores the interaction between social oppression and labor division on the basis of physiological power. As a matter of fact, it is not a natural phenomenon, but the consequence of culture and result of social oppression, namely women being restricted in the family. "It is not because of her physical weakness that she is excluded from production activity, but due to her social inferiority that she is degraded to a slave in the society."[5] Thus, the laborer's muscle strength does not become that important under the conditions of capitalist machinery production, and modern new science and technology has diminished the role of direct live physical labor. However, women are not yet emancipated as some had expected.

Socialist feminists as well disagree with the view that women's physiological structure is the source for oppression. In the view of radical feminists, the reason why women are in subordinate position in the last analysis lies in their physiological structure, because they shoulder the responsibility of having a child, and are sexually different from men. To emancipate, it is necessary for them to reject bearing

---

3   Li Yinhe (compiler): *Women: Longest Revolution - Selection of Contemporary Western Feminist Theories*, p. 61. Beijing: SDX Joint Publishing Company, 1999.
4   *Ibid.*
5   *Ibid.*

children by the help of modern biological techniques, and even eliminate their sexual distinction. Socialist feminists have criticized the above view of the radical feminists arguing that though women undertake different roles in the division of labor compared to men; this does not necessarily mean that women are oppressed because of this very reason. As a matter of fact, women's physiological features cause their subordinate position but only as a part of oppressive social structure and social relations.

7.2.1.2.2 Sources of Women's Oppression

Influenced by traditional Marxism, nearly all socialist feminists have put emphasis on the analysis of the economic sources for women's oppression, and argued that women's dependence on men in economy is the key factor for their inferior position in the society. However, they do not regard the economic factor as the sole source for women's oppression. Apart from emphasizing economic reason, feminists have as well analyzed sources of women's oppression from other aspects, like political, cultural, and ideological factors as well as daily social life. Some have focused on the political analysis of private life, like family, revealing power relations in those spheres that result in women's oppression; some have focused on cultural and ideological aspects, and consider traditional or capitalist ideology as the key factor leading to women's oppression; others make a holistic analysis which combines family relations and relations in social production. Take Mitchell for example, she has put forth the concept of "general social structure" in her discussion on the sources of women's oppression, assuming that women's oppression in the capitalist society is comprehensive. The social oppression includes four aspects: production, having child, sex and children's socialization. Among them, production occurs in the economic sphere outside the family, while the other three, having child, sex and children's socialization, are components of the family life. To reveal the sources for women's oppression, one should make an in-depth analysis on the family structure, and examine the relationships and relationship modes among those above three components in the family structure, apart from researching oppression occurring in the social production sphere.

7.2.1.2.3 Labor in the Family and Reproduction Labor

Park Quick was the first to raise the proposition: "Reproduction of labor force is the source for women's oppression." She has argued that in the reproduction of labor force, namely, in the period of women's reproduction, like pregnancy, childbearing, lactation and later fosterage, the labor division based on gender intensifies women's oppression and discrimination. In the view of some feminists like Vogel, the material foundation of women's oppression lies in social reproduction; it is the very reason that women are oppressed in the class society. The physiological role women play in giving birth to a child results in their dependence on men in economic sphere, which cause the division of labor in the familial sphere and also sphere of social labor.

Employing the basic theories and methods Marx had applied in his works Capital, socialist feminists have made an analysis on the reproduction of labor force in capitalist society. They have studied the conditions and function of family labor as a part of capitalist production mode in order to reveal the economic reasons for women's oppression. They have concluded that the value of women's reproduction is not properly acknowledged and appreciated in the capitalist society.

In their views, under the conditions of industrial capitalism it is necessary to divide social life into two halves: "public sphere" and "private sphere". Because it is necessary for the labor force to go through the process of childbearing, fosterage and socialization. However, this process still cannot be effectively and completely realized in the public sphere, but in the family. Meanwhile, the process of basic labor is as well divided into non-related two halves: industrial labor and family labor. Properties of these two parts are fundamentally different. Family labor reproduces labor forces for the labor market, while industrial labor produces commodities and services for commodity markets. This difference between the two labor processes lead to a division in labor forces which is generally based on gender. Women undertake the labor process in the familial sphere, while men undertake industrial labor. Labor process in the latter is capitalist production, while the former belongs to labor force reproduction. Women's labor in the familial sphere plays a vitally important role in the reproduction of capitalist labor force.

In their view, the family labor of housewives' which reproduces labor force is as well a kind of labor which creates value. Commodities, like houses, food and clothing, which are exchanged against industrial labor wages, do not directly affect the process of reproduction of labor force (familial labor) and cannot reproduce labor forces. Thus another kind of labor, namely family labor is necessary to reproduce labor forces. When a housewife directly uses wages to buy goods, and change their forms when necessary, thus their familial labor becomes part of the universal necessary labor in the society (the term universal necessary labor was also studied by Marx in Capital). And when labor force is exchanged as a commodity in the labor market, the value they create is realized. However, in real life appearance, wages appear as the pay against the labor that is solely completed in the industrial labor process. As a matter of fact, truly wages are not paid solely against industrial labor, but for the labor that reproduces all the labor force in capitalist society. The reason why this illusive phenomenon occurs lies in that industrial workers appear as independent agents directly dealing with the capitalist enterprise, while familial labor which reproduce the whole labor force in the society is hidden behind the curtain. Socialist feminists hold the view that Marx had indeed revealed the deceiving secret of labor wages, but had ignored another aspect of its secret; namely neglected housewives' contribution to the whole process of capitalist production. In capitalism, housewives' labor is excluded from those deals occurring in the labor market between laborers and capitalists, and is completely ignored. Their labor is not considered as a genuine labor which produces value. The labor of housewives is concealed, and she cannot prove her existence through wages. Therefore, she has no ways to demonstrate her labor and herself. Consequently, she utterly relies on her husband materially who provides her necessary money for living, and lose her independence.

7.2.1.2.4 Combination of Capitalism with Patriarchy

Marxists argue that the source reason for women's oppression lies in capitalism, while radical feminists think that it lies in the patriarchy. Taking the two sides into consideration, socialist feminists hold the view that the source reason for women's oppression does neither lie in capitalism nor in the patriarchy, but in the combination of the two. As for such "combination", socialist feminists generally hold two different views. One regards capitalism and the patriarchy are in a correlative relation, and argue that combination of the two factors result in women's intensified oppression. This view is known as the "binary theory". The other approach holds that capitalism and patriarchy are integrated in a unity of one, and form the "capitalist patriarchy" or "patriarchal capitalism". This view is called "unitary theory".

Binary Approach:

Socialist feminists who advocate "binary theory" hold the view that patriarchy and capitalism as two different systems embody different forms of social relations and interest patterns. They coexist in modern capitalist society, and play their respective roles. Patriarchy has emerged in the very early history, and continues to exist and exerts its influence in capitalist society. It is the overlapping effect of capitalism and patriarchy that intensifies women's oppression. Socialist feminists with this view advocate that it is necessary to treat patriarchy and capitalism as distinctive and correlative phenomena in the analysis of the source reason for women's oppression. Heidi Hartmann and Juliet Mitchell insist on this binary assumption. In fact, they regard the patriarchy and capitalism as systems that function in two different spheres: patriarchy exists in the family and plays its role there, while capitalism moves outside the family and exerts its impact therein. Concretely speaking, in the family, occurs the sexual oppression, namely, male oppressing female; while in the social sphere outside the family, so it was, particularly in economic sphere, occurs the class oppression, namely, capitalist oppression and exploitation over laborers. By this differentiation they offer a unique approach and analysis on the patriarchy and its relation with capitalism. Heidi Hartmann views patriarchy as a structure in social relations system which has a certain material base, arguing that patriarchy is materially based on men's control over women's labor force. They limit women's economic sources and control their reproduction. Men's control over women's labor capability or capacity varies in different social formations and at different stages of human society. In the capitalist society, their control is exerted as the specific social institution like monogamy. In this institution, women are responsible for childbearing, bringing them up and undertaking housework, which results in their economic dependence on men. Different from Heidi Hartmann, Juliet Mitchell evaluates patriarchy mainly from two aspects as women's bio-sociology and ideological criticism. In her opinion, in some aspects family life is undoubtedly the result of changes in the economic base of the social formation and production mode. However, family is as well the outcome of women's bio-sociological concept and social ideology (particularly concept of sex). No matter in which direction the production mode changes, bio-social perspective of the family and sex concept will remain unchanged. Thus, Mitchell puts more emphasis on the ideological criticism of the current family concept, assuming that incomplete family awareness is an important reason for women's being tamed. She suggests employing Freud's psychological analysis when studying the issue of male-female relationship and the ideologies related to this relationship. As it is, Mitchell's view on patriarchy focuses on ideology, which transcends or by-passes history and time, and is not determined by the changes in the production mode.

The Unitary Approach:

Lise Vogel and Alice Young advocate the "unitary" theory. They oppose evaluating capitalism and patriarchy as two different things, but propose to view them as an integrated unity of "capitalist patriarchy" or "patriarchal capitalism". In their view, capitalism and patriarchy are inseparably integrated. This concept in essence is non- "class" approach because "class" is a concept which could discard sex differences, but "labor division based on gender" reflects the truth much better. In the view of Alice Young, the analysis method of labor division is better than that of class to explain why women usually are obedient and undertake dull work with low pay, while men give orders and undertake more lucrative jobs with higher rewards.

In their eyes, there is a close correlation between patriarchy and capitalism. In order to keep their traditional patriarchal privilege and maintain their position as males who financially "shoulder the existence of the family", and men also unite to protect their interests and support the legislation which restricts women's employment. Consequently, labor division based on gender difference and restriction of women's employment guarantees women's economic dependence on men, and force them to opt for housework as their career. Meanwhile, capitalism benefits from this arrangement in which women undertake housework because this is an efficient scheme for the reproduction of labor force. The "bargain" between capitalism and men mainly includes how to divide the time between two parties, but those two finally agree to keep women laboring at home for capitalist reproduction of labor force; women are forced to serve men by means of doing housework and bringing up children; in return, capitalist rulers offer men the privilege to enter into the social production sphere. Capitalism and patriarchy serve and fit best to support each other. Therefore, they have argued that women's subordinate position neither can be simply viewed as the outcome of capitalism, nor can it be separated from the capitalist system.

7.2.1.2.5 Ideological Aspect of Women's Oppression

In the view of socialist feminists, the combination of patriarchal ideology and the capitalist ideology has existed for a long period, and turned out to be a mighty power. It pervasively penetrates all walks of social life, people's mind and spirit, to maintain men's rule over women in the real society. This combined ideology defends the current situation in which women are oppressed, and provides some "rational evidence" for gender inequality. In this ideology, the concept propagated as "woman temperament" is an important item. As division of roles between men and women; people have always considered men should possess "male temperament", while women "female temperament". This was the God's truth. In the view of socialist feminists, men and women are not born into alleged "male temperament" and "female temperament", but acquire them later. Children are cultivated in the society with "male temperament" and "female temperament; boys are taught to be independent, brave, persistent and successful, while girls are told to be gentle, quiet and obedient. This ideology pervades the whole society, and is universally accepted. Not only males hold such a view, but also females themselves are deeply influenced by it. It is such an education as "female temperament" and ideological influence that counteracts women's ambitions and independence, weakens their self-awareness, and makes them unconsciously appendages of men.

Additionally, the dominant ideology in the capitalist society also fully misleads women's consumption; that is to say, it actually indoctrinates women with the notion of alienated consumption. The culture of humiliating and discriminating women pervades in the commodity consumption, and misleads women by all kinds of means. Commodities, from costumes, shoes and stockings to hairstyle and cosmetics, are designed with no exception to orient women as a sexual object and target. Advertisements are full of exaggerated marketing tricks promoting luxury commodities, and seduce women to follow the fashion. With "ideal woman" and "ideal family", ideology capitalists lure a large mass of women to seek unnecessary consumption. This kind of consumption is not only a direct economic exploitation but also a measure to retain women from awakening.

7.2.1.3 ASPECTS OF WOMEN'S EMANCIPATION AND ECONOMIC EMANCIPATION

Women's emancipation as advocated by socialist feminists includes many aspects, rather than few aims. Women in the first feminist movement have mainly strived for political emancipation; they have struggled for and won political rights, like universal suffrage. Then, in the second feminist movement, feminists, especially socialist feminists have realized that women's emancipation is not merely having political rights, but an overall comprehensive liberation, including economic emancipation.

Mitchell has focused her study on the holistic nature of women's emancipation highlighting its four aspects. In her eyes, women's oppression is caused by four factors: production, childbearing, sex and children's socialization. These four factors (structures) are closely related and jointly determine women's status and plight. "If one of the structures change, another will be strengthened and counteract to that the effect, but what only changes is the form of oppression or exploitation."[6] Thus, "ultimate solution can only be found by a strategy targeting all the structures that impact oppression and exploitation of women."[7] "It is necessary to do the revolutionary struggle based on the analysis of those structures; these structures develop in an unbalanced pattern, we should attack the weakest structure in that combination. Only in this way, can this combination be fundamentally destructed and we can accomplish a great transformation in women's conditions."[8] Mitchell believes that sex is the most vulnerable and the weakest link in the chain of those four structures, and is the key to solve other various contradictions; it is necessary to focus our attack against this structure. However, problems cannot be completely settled merely when we focus the struggle against the sex structure. As a matter of fact, if the revolution goes too far in this aspect, it may also cause several negative results too.

Women's overall and comprehensive emancipation includes such aspects as economic, political and ideological emancipation. In the economic emancipation, women should liberate from the dependence on men, and women working in the factory and family should be freed from overt or covert exploitation and be economically independent. In terms of political emancipation, women should not only obtain equal legal political rights as men and strive for the application of those rights in practice, but apart from socio-political sphere, the struggle for emancipation should cover the private sphere, like family, which is under the control of patriarchy. As for the ideological emancipation, women should sublate

---

6   Li Yinhe (compiler): *Women: Longest Revolution - Selection of Contemporary Western Feminist Theories*, p. 31. Beijing: SDX Joint Publishing Company, 1999.
7   *Ibid.*
8   *Ibid.*

patriarchy in their mind which restrict and dominate their awareness for a long time, women should be confident of their self-capability and powers, and develop their consciousness for self-esteem, self-confidence and self-reliance.

In women's overall emancipation, economic emancipation bears a special significance. Mitchell acknowledges that economic structure is ultimately determinative in the integrated social structure. Thus, any emancipation movement, including women's emancipation movement, should focus on the economic aspect. Women's economic emancipation concept proposed by socialist feminists is generally linked with women's economic independence from men. They offer several approaches to realize this aim. I can summarize them as follows.

1. Women in labor force market: In the view of Marxists, it is an important aim for women to break away from the familial restrictions and participate in social production for their emancipation. Some socialist feminists have inherited this view of Marxism, with the advocacy of women entering labor market and participating social production .By the development of capitalism, demand for woman labor force increases, and women start to enter labor market one after another in the capitalist society. Women's access to employment rights becomes an important aspect and a symbol in their struggle for emancipation. Women's access to employment indeed raises their position to some extent: on the one hand, some professions bring them an independent income, thus economically they do not completely depend on their husbands as before; hence the their position in the family rise; on the other hand, their participation in social work as well opens them a new horizon, and enables them to think beyond the traditional family affairs. However, some socialist feminists have argued that women are not really emancipated by participating in social production because women are still remain in a disadvantageous position in the labor markets, and they are paid unequally when compared with men.

2. Housework should be paid: Some socialist feminists propose that housework should be paid as wages. Housework itself is an indispensable part of social labor, and it is impossible to exclude this labor from social production. There is no distinction in regard to their importance; housework and the labor outside the family are both vital. Solution to this problem does not lie in whether women should give up housework and participate in social labor; it means struggle should aim the pay for their housework and make people acknowledge the value of housework.

Dana Kosta and Saima James, British socialist feminists, advocate that women's housework should be paid, public should adequately understand the difference between house labor and wage labor and support those women who struggle for housework pay. In their view, women should not be paid by individual men (husbands, fathers or boyfriends) but by capitalists. This is because women's housework, as it is the process of reproduction of labor force, does not benefit (men) their husbands, but capitalists who own all the production means in social production. If capitalists do not pay them, the state should do. This is because in the final analysis, the capitalist state benefits from women's housework. When calculating the pay for housework, equal criteria should be used with the labor outside the family; it is not right to view the housework as cheap labor and pay it symbolically. Some feminists have evaluated and developed standards to calculate the labor in the family, some calculations have shown that housework of a woman with two children equals to nearly ten thousand pounds a year in 2003. As a first step the pay for the housework must not take the form of monetary wages; it could also be paid as welfare allowances or other services for example overburdened mothers could be offered free childcare. Socialist feminists also insist that women should have the right to "strike" and stop the reproduction of labor force, and as struggle methods they could use divorcing, contraception and abortion if the state refuses to pay them.

There are also some socialist feminists who question the feasibility of the struggle for housework pay. They have argued that this struggle could legitimate women work in the family; and as a result, women will continue to remain at home, isolated from the outside world, their opportunities for other better jobs will decrease and this will consequently damage their struggle against labor division based sex in labor markets.

3. Housework should be socialized. In the view of Margaret Benston, British socialist feminist, the socialization of housework is a much more effective approach for women emancipation than women's participation in social work. Socialization of housework should precede women's participation in social affairs. She also admits that socialization of housework will mean that women will continue to undertake the housework they are already engaged in. However, even so, this could offer a kind of progress forward. The struggle may not free women completely from this kind of familial labor, but its significance lies in that everyone in the society will realize the vital contribution of this kind of labor for the society. Once people see how hard the housework is, they will not undermine women's labor in the family. Vogel points out "a main solution to alleviate housework is to socialize family affairs. For instance, it is possible to transfer such kinds of housework as dealing with clothing and home textile or dining or preparation and storage of food to social production sphere, and those services can also provide new businesses for capitalist enterprises. Public education and healthcare services can be broadened to include those functions which today are part of the housework and housework related to these could be reduced and state can take the lead in this step. As another step the cost of labor force reproduction by mothers can

be widely shared by the members of the whole society through a taxing system[9].

7.2.1.4 STRUGGLES AGAINST CAPITALISM AND PATRIARCHY

Socialist feminists hold that the society is actually divided into two halves: inside the family and outside it; thus, women's struggle as well falls into these two spheres accordingly. Struggle in these two spheres have different features and requirements. Women's activity is mainly limited in the familial sphere; as a result, the family is the major battlefield for the self-emancipation of women.

Struggle in the family is realized by each woman individually against patriarchy. In their co-authored book, *Contemporary Marxist Theory and Practice: A Feminist Critique*, Heidi Hartmann and Ann Markusen, have written; "women are in isolation, this is the same in their struggle against patriarchy, it is necessary for them to apply strategies different from the strategies employed against capitalists. The essential feature of this strategy is that each woman should fight against their men who command the patriarchal rule in the house; the struggle should take one-to-one form. Just as Gilman Grille has once mentioned, "all over the country, a revolution is taking place in the bedroom"[10] Women's struggle against patriarchy should mainly aim to take the control of the production means that are necessary for population reproduction, it is just similar to workers' struggle which aims to take the control of the production means. "Inside the family, the woman should strive for the right of abortion and contraception, and fight against her husband's will; in the sphere of local neighborhood communities, they should strive to transform community healthcare centers and control their operation aims thus oppose and change the medical healthcare system which operates under the rule of patriarchal institutions."[11]

Socialist feminists have also argued that it is necessary for women to establish a common strategy though it is necessary to fight individually against patriarchy in the family. Patriarchy has linkages and is part of the whole social system and its superstructure; thus, it is impossible for women to win the struggle against it separately without forming a common broad strategy. The goals of the common strategy should not be isolated from each other, but they should be properly combined. For instance, when a wife slaps her husband, it is possible for the husband to set up a new family with another woman to maintain his privilege, which equals to "firing" a worker and "hiring" another. This possibility could hinder the success of individual struggles in the family. In such a case, she will need other

---

9   Vogel, Lise: *Marxism and the Oppression of Women: Toward a unitary theory*, Rutgers University Press. New Brunswick. New Jersey, 1983, p. 74-75.
10   China Women Publishing House: *Anthology of Feminist Movements Abroad*. p. 28. Beijing: China Women Publishing House, 1998.
11   *Ibid.*

women to help, just as workers striking in a factory need to get the support of those in other factories.

The housewives' struggle needs support and help from women's groups and organizations. "The leading style in women's political organization should be different from that of workers. The tenet of women's political organizations is supposed to form and guide a strategy with consensus, give support to those women who are struggling in the family, and oppose both non-governmental and state departments with the aim of isolating and weakening patriarchy."[12]

7.2.1.4.2 Struggles against Capitalism outside the Family

Socialist feminists hold the view that the factory and state should only be secondary battlefields where women fight, but they should also pay attention to the whole battlefield in the society and engage in political struggles. Women should struggle in three spheres: economic, political and cultural.

As for the economic struggle, they should mainly strive for equal rights in economy. For instance, they fight for the equal pay for the same work as men do, for maternity leave and flexible working hours before and after the maternity leave in the workplaces. And they also fight against discrimination in the labor markets. Socialist feminists fight for equal access in the actual realization of right of work to overcome discrimination and strive to break down the system of wage bracket. Women are treated as a second-class labor force after they enter the labor markets. Even if they are employed by a job that demands the same qualifications, techniques and responsibilities required from men, mostly they only get the half pay compared with male workers. Advocates of this wage system claim that the market determines who will earn higher pay or the reverse according to their value contribution. Socialist feminists retort to this view, and argue that it is hard to observe whether the market really determines higher pay to those who contribute more. Additionally, no one can measure if the work one does embodies more value than another work made by another individual. Furthermore, even if the work women perform embodies less value from the work men do, it should not hinder women from earning a decent pay, just because of this. This is because women cannot live a decent life without a decent pay. For socialist feminists, the movement against wage bracket system and its elimination in fact targets capitalism because this wage bracket system is a feature of capitalism.

As to political struggles, they both aim social reforms and lead some radical revolutionary attitudes and activities. Some socialist feminists are rather strive for social reforms, such as wage increases, more social benefits, bestowing childbirth

---

12   China Women Publishing House: *Anthology of Feminist Movements Abroad*. p. 29. Beijing: China Women Publishing House, 1998.

liberty and free abortion, and advocate legal and ethical demands related same sex marriages. Some socialist feminists rather choose to participate in the broader movement of working class, and also criticize male workers' androcentrism. Some groups lead women to demonstrate their critics in their daily life, namely, they support micro political movements in a localized pattern. They usually organize women in a struggle community to take part in these movements, and struggle is generally restricted by the individual fighting capacity of that community organization. Some socialist feminists sharply oppose to those who pool women struggles social reformist aims, and advocate radical changes. Mitchell points out "Contemporary left reformists prefer the mildest attitude in their criticism, such mild which is far behind compared with the level of development of women's movement and demands; as a result, there is no progressive content in it."[13] Based on such a viewpoint, these socialist feminists advocate more active and deeper political struggles, and advocate both rigid organizational forms and struggles without any organization. The struggle within the family needs no organization, but it is necessary to have a rigid and efficient organization to mobilize and lead women to fight against the capitalist system and its state machinery, specialized fighting organizations are also necessary. They propose to set up a united revolutionary women front and establish a broader alliance with other oppressed groups, organizations and even political parties. Women's emancipation cannot be realized unless they organize and ally with organizations of other oppressed classes and stratums. Of course, women's organizations should be different from trade unions or political parties, and so it is with their movements. As a matter of fact, most women organizations are usually restricted to develop communication among women or promote friendly ties, transmit information about women's movement and exchange new ideas and viewpoints. Thus their current activities are far behind from being so revolutionary.

As for cultural struggle, socialist feminists strive to criticize capitalist and patriarchal ideologies. In their view, women's political and economic emancipation are external, while their ideological emancipation is an internal and a profound aim. This involves an in-depth ideological reform, which is a more difficult task. They insist on criticizing capitalist culture, the deep rooted cultural concepts which humiliates and undermine women as the second-class sex prevalent since old times, and the concept of alienated consumption that confuses and destructs women's awareness. They advocate and strive to lead a critical daily life; and emphasize to sublate or correct current concepts on equality, liberty, solidarity, sharing and political responsibility with socialist feminist values. They promote and support those women working in the spheres of culture and education to write books and their ideas which criticize capitalist culture and advocate women's values.

---

13   Li Yinhe (compiler). *Women: Longest Revolution - Selection of Contemporary Western Feminist Theories*, p. 3 Beijing: SDX Joint Publishing Company, 1998.

7.3 EVALUATION OF SOCIALIST FEMINISM

As a left trend of thought in the contemporary Western society, socialist feminism plays an important role in the struggle for women's emancipation and struggle against capitalism. Its theoretical exploration adds considerably both to the scientific analysis of woman issues and to the application of Marxism to women emancipation problem.

7.3.1 ITS SOCIAL PROPERTEIS AND EFFECTS

Socialist feminism has emerged in the movements which struggle for a new society. These movements are left wing social movements launched by the petty bourgeoisie and masses of lower strata which fight against the capitalist system. Among the movements for a new society, the new feminist movement has kept a certain distance from the traditional left organizations and "New Left", and has openly criticized the male chauvinism in these organizations. However, it still takes a similar political stance together with other left wing movements, but behaves slightly more radical compared to them. New feminist movement of the left wing is the outcome of combining the socialist thoughts with feminism, and bears strong features of socialism; this is particularly true for socialist feminism.

Socialist feminists have to a certain degree enriched and also expanded the influence sphere of Marxism, which has an extensive influence in those movements seeking for a new society; this includes the new feminist movement in the left wing. A number of radical intellectuals and young students enthusiastically keep seeking ideological inspiration and theoretical support from Marxism. It is also in such a background that some pioneers of female intellectuals have accepted the Marxist analytical method, and employed it in the analysis of women's issues under the condition of capitalism. Leaving aside whether they actually grasp the essence of Marxism or are in line with Marxist spirit, we can easily say that they expand the Marxist influence among the contemporary Western trend of thoughts.

Socialist feminists play an active role in revealing and fighting against capitalism. They, from numerous aspects disclose women's oppressed conditions that exist universally in capitalist countries. They demonstrate the realistic fact that capitalists do not only grasp the surplus value created by the workers, but also exploit the labor of housewives without compensation in the reproduction of labor force. Consequently, the socialist feminists have drawn the conclusion that the important source of women's oppression lies in the capitalist exploitation. Socialist feminists as well demonstrate the role that the dominant ideology in the capitalist countries plays in controlling and oppressing women. Among various trends of thoughts in the Western world, socialist feminism is prominent in politics, and features a relatively strong mass and militant character, and the role it plays in women's emancipation is unique compared to other schools.

Socialist feminism combines both the struggle for women's emancipation and the socialist future. In its historical development, it was inevitable for feminism to combine with socialism. Socialism aims the emancipation of proletariat and that of the whole humankind, including women's emancipation. Beginning from its inception, the socialist movement, including women's emancipation movement, has ceaselessly explored approaches to women's emancipation in its development process. The new feminist movement with its left leaning orientation is greatly associated with the socialist movement. In their view, "Marxism is remarkably consistent with feminism in both concept and aims. This provides a strong possibility and opportunity to establish an alliance between the new feminist movement and left movement". Sheila Benhabib, a socialist feminist, has once commented; "feminist movement presents some brand new approaches to re-launch a powerful socialist movement participated by masses", I think this reflects the right direction of the feminist development.

Of course, socialist feminists pay great efforts in their attempt to integrate feminism with socialism. However, observed from both their theoretical demonstration and practice, they actually fail to realize it. They still remain vague about the socialist aim and in their approaches on socialism.

7.3.2 EVALUATION OF SOCIALIST FEMINIST THEORIES

Inspired by Marxism, socialist feminists apply Marxism in the analysis women issues. Mitchell has underlined that it is necessary to analyze women emancipation issues with the approach of scientific socialism, and she has also employed this approach in her researches. It is true that socialist feminism inspired by Marxism offers more reasonable solutions on the women issues and brings more profound and systematic ideas on the problems of women's emancipation. By a general comparison we can see that they have broader social horizon, and give due emphasis on the economic aspect when analyzing problems, also develop specific views on various women issues and have a deeper understanding on the effect of ideology. Feminists of other schools when criticizing the current family they only offer a generalized approach; however, socialist feminists hold the view that this "general family", actually refers to the white families of middle class -mainstream bourgeoisie family – namely those white families that are comparatively wealthy, bi-parental and heterosexual. It is improper to restrict the studies on such families; additionally, it is necessary to take into account the class differences, races and nationalities. For instance, in the working class and most black families mothers do not feel that they have become housewives under oppression; on the contrary, mothers who work two shifts to earn a living naturally long to be housewives — an unattainable dream for them-. However, for black women, it is more urgent to eliminate racial discrimination than sexual segregation. For unmarried or divorced women, it is more urgent for them to alleviate poverty or lack of time than overcoming labor division based on gender. Additionally, families formed by homosexuals have similar different problems. Some socialist feminists have even fairly questioned the concept of "female temperament". For example, Greens as one of them has argued that the concept of "female temperament" is absolutely inapplicable for women belonging to certain ethnic people. "They first orient themselves towards social production, and their familial role is certainly secondary. The fact is that in most cases men-and-women relations in black families are cooperative rather than being contradictory, which may be regarded as guarding against social, political and ideological oppressions.

The active theoretical exploration by socialist feminists provides Marxists a positive enlightenment. This trend of thought explores women's oppressed situation in modern times and the new problems they are face. Their studies cover women's oppression from the perspectives of economy, politics, history, culture and physiology, practical strategies for women's emancipation, and in-depth analysis in certain issues. For instance, they apply Marxist theories on production and reproduction in the analysis of housewives' roles, which offer a mechanism to capitalists for the reproduction of new labor forces at the lowest cost and housewives also provide them cheap flexible labor force as reserve. Socialist feminists argue that this mechanism works on the basis that women rely on men's wages for their living, and this causes their dependence on men. As it is, this is a creative exploration to push forward Marxist theories. They lay emphasis on the study of culture and ideology, regard ideology as the important reason for women's oppression, and advocate fighting against the "invisible enslavement", which is also a creative and important idea.

However, socialist feminists have several grave problems in dealing with Marxism and when combining Marxism and feminism. As to treating Marxism, feminists quote Marxist phrases out of their context to serve their purposes. Some just borrow Marxist terms to decorate feminism, while some reverse Marxist research approach; others go so far as to openly criticize Marxism, especially the Marxist view on women. They pay painstaking "efforts" to supplement and rectify socialist theories with feminism. Lise Vogel has also commented on this point: "Generally speaking, in the view of socialist feminists, it is necessary to widen or completely change socialist theories with the insight provided by feminism in theory and practice."[14] In Alice Young's opinion, socialist feminism is featured as a "'marriage" between the essence of feminist fashion trends of thoughts developed between 1960s and 1970s and Marxist theories which aims to rebuild it."[15] On

---

14   Vogel, Lise: *Marxism and Women's Oppression*, p. 13.
15   Young, Alice: *Transcending Unhappy Marriage: Criticism of Binary System*, p. 85.

one hand, socialist feminists attempt to deepen feminism with Marxist theories and analyze the specific forms of women's oppression; on the other hand, they borrow a series of theories on patriarchy from radical feminists in analyzing these problems, in order to "supplement" and even to replace Marxist analysis. Thus several conclusions of their studies on patriarchy are unsystematic and insufficient in many basic aspects which cannot clearly illustrate the basic characteristics of patriarchy in the capitalist society. They really cannot organically integrate these two theoretical systems-Marxism and feminism— and combine them in their researches. Just as remarked by a representative socialist feminist, socialist feminism is "combination of traditional Marxism with neo-feminism, combines class differences with gender/sex differences, production with reproduction, and the public with the kingdom, which is its duality."[16]

REFERENCES

- China Women Publishing House (compilation): *Anthology of Feminist Movements Abroad*. p. 29. Beijing: China Women Publishing House, 2004.
- Alison Giger: *Political and Human Nature of Feminism*. New Jersey: Rowman & Littlefield Publishing Group, 1988.
- Yu Keping: *"Socialism" in the Era of Globalization*. Beijing: Central Compilation and Translation Press, 1998.
- Lise Vogel: *Marxism and the Oppression of Women*: Toward a Unitary Theory, Rutgers University Press. New Brunswick. New Jersey,1983.
- Xiao Wei: *Ethics of Feminist Concern*. Beijing: Beijing Publishing House, 1999.
- Wang Wei, Pang Junjing: *Western Marxist Thoughts in the 20th Century*. Beijing: Capital Normal University Press, 1999.
- Zhang Xiaoling: *Women and Human Rights*. Beijing: Xinhua Publishing House, 1998.
- Li Yinhe (compilation): *Women: Longest Revolution - Selection of Contemporary Western Feminist Theories*. Beijing: SDX Joint Publishing Company, 1999.

Boston: Southern Press, 1981.
16   China Women Publishing House (compilation): *Anthology of Feminist Movements Abroad.* p. 14-15. Beijing: China Women Publishing House, 1998.

CHAPTER VIII

MARKET SOCIALISM THEORIES

1 *Origin and Evolution of Thoughts of Market Socialism*
2 *Miller, Roemer, Schweickert*
3 *Evaluations of Market Socialism Trends*

CHAPTER EIGHT

INTRODUCTION

Market socialism is a theory endeavoring to combine public ownership of the means of production with a market economy to realize socialism. It has originally appeared in the 1930s, and was first systematically expressed by Oscar Lange, a Polish-American economist. In the economic reform of the socialist countries, including Soviet Union and East Europe, from the 1950s to 1980s, theories of market socialism were further developed by economists of those countries, and turned out to be the theoretical ground for the reform of the economic system in these socialist countries. At the beginning of the 1980s, there appeared a discussion among Western left scholars on how the advanced capitalist countries could shift to socialism. Under the influence of the market-oriented reform of the economic system in the Soviet Union and East Europe, Western scholars began to pay attention to theories of market socialism and put forth some models for market socialism with the purpose to make them feasible for the advanced capitalist countries. In the late middle of 1980s, socialist countries of the Soviet Union and East Europe had disintegrated one after another. However, in spite of this setback, the research of market socialism by left scholars has developed further. On the contrary, on the basis of reflecting on the failures of socialist construction in Soviet Union and East European countries, left wing proponents of market socialism have drawn a further conclusion that market socialism could be the only feasible program for the advanced capitalist countries to move toward to socialism. During the 1980s, they successively have established theories proposing various models for market socialism and published them in their books. I can say that more than 50 monographs and collections on market socialism were published and approximate 200 related papers were issued only in Britain and the United States since the middle of the 1980s; as a result, a new trend of market socialism has come into being.

After the 1990s, theories on market socialism have been quite influential among left scholars in the advanced capitalist countries, with the United States and Britain in particular. In the middle and later 1990s, left scholars held several international conferences, like the socialist scholars convention in New York in 1996 and the international conference in memorial of the 150th anniversary of *Communist Manifesto*, based on the theme of market socialism. In the view of Bertell Ollman, professor of New York University as well as renowned Marxist scholar, "market socialism, as it was, has become a topic which left scholars are debating worldwide." We will discuss in this chapter this trend occurring in Western advanced capitalist countries in the 1980s.

8.1 ORIGIN AND EVOLUTION OF THOUGHTS OF MARKET SOCIALISM

8.1.1 ON MARKET SOCIALISM

Who was the first to coin the notion of market socialism? Currently, there is no genuine answer to this question. It is generally believed that this notion of market socialism was first seen in the works of some U.S. scholars in the 1950s or 1960s, like *Journey to Poland And Yugoslavia* (Galbraith & John Kenneth, 1958), *The Firm in Illyria: Market Syndicalism* (B. Ward, 1958) and *Marxism-Horvatism: A Yugoslav Theory of Socialism* (1967), and the paper of "Market Socialism Revisited" by A. Bergson issued in *Journal of Political Economy* (Vol. 75, No. 5, 1967). All of those works above directly or indirectly were based on the notion of "market socialism".

Since the notion of market socialism emerged, it was frequently used by scholars, but it was usually bestowed with different meanings. The interpretation of market socialism by scholars in the 1980s may well serve as an example: based on the four factors of ownership, mechanisms of making decision, adjusting and stimulating. P. Gregory and R. Stuart defined market socialism as "an economic system featured in public ownership of production factors, decentralization in decision making and modulating socialism with market mechanism, and using material and spiritual stimulations to promote those involved to achieve the aim of this system."[1] Market socialists in Britain have based their definition of market socialism on the perspectives of the means and target, with the assumption that socialism should "use market to achieve the objective of socialism."[2] C. E. Lindblom, ex-president of the Association for Comparative Economic Studies in the United States, gave the definition of market socialism on the basis of two ultimate controlling forms of production, namely, consumers' preferences and government's preferences. With reference to private ownership and state ownership, he presented his criteria as consumers' decision or planners' decision. Using his criteria, he defined market socialism as a market system of consumers' decision on the basis of public ownership, namely, a market-oriented system of public enterprises distinct from market system based on private enterprises, or as the economic system based on planners' decision and public enterprises. However, according to the authoritative *The New Palgrave: Dictionary of Economics*, market socialism was defined as "a theoretical epitome (or mode) of an economic system; under this system, the means of production are possessed publicly or collectively, while the allocation of resources follows the law of market (commodity, labor and capital markets)." In terms of past practices in socialist economies, usually this notion was widely used to define the following two economic systems: firstly that of Yugoslavia which was established after 1965 was in a strict sense, close to this definition, and secondly the system which replaced the commanded economy and its material allocation for production— accompanied with financial adjustments and various stimulations employed as means of central plans—; namely the regulated market or reformed 'new economic mechanism' in Hungry in 1968)."[3]

From the various definitions of market socialism presented above, we can see that market socialism is generally considered either distinct from the "market capitalism" represented by the United States or the "planned economic socialism" practiced by the former Soviet Union as the representative models. Market socialism is generally featured as public ownership of the means of production (mainly collective ownership) and market mechanisms as the means of allocating resources. Currently, Chinese scholars generally follow Western scholars' use of this term above. Specifically, the theory of market socialism has its three features as follows:

First, the theory distinguishes forms of allocating resources from the social system itself, namely separates planning mechanism or market mechanism from socialism or capitalism. In the view of traditional Marxism, the resource allocation

---

1   Gregory, P & Stuaret, R:*Comparative Economic Systems*, p. 20. Shanghai: SDX Joint Publishing House, 1988.
2   Estrin, Saul & Le Grand: Julian. *Market socialism*, p.1. Beijing: Economic Times Press, 1993.
3   Eatwell, J., Milgate, M. and Newman, P.: *The New Palgrave: A Dictionary of Economics* (III), p. 363. Beijing: Economic Science Press, 1992.

system, either by planning or by market, was closely related to the social system, and was essentially one of the unique character of the social system. Thus, planned economy was the natural expression of socialism, while market economy was the natural expression of capitalism. From the perspective of Western classic economics, market economy cannot function unless under the private ownership of the means of production. Therefore, it is necessary to have private ownership of the means of production under market economy. On this point, market socialism differs from both traditional Marxism and Western classic economics. It assumes that market and planning are both means of allocating resources, and they have nothing to do with the nature of social systems. Consequently, socialism could have market economy, while capitalism could as well have a planned economy.

Second, it advocates public ownership of the means of production. The reason why market socialism was called socialism lay essentially in its advocacy of public ownership of the means of production, and opposing the private ownership of the means of production. In terms of this, Cohen, political philosopher of Oxford University as well as a prominent figure of analytical Marxism, has remarked that "market socialism is socialism because it overcomes the separation of labor from capital. In market socialism, there is not a capitalist class who is in the opposite side to the laborer who possesses capital."[4] Of course, different market socialists have different understandings of public ownership of the means of production; some regard public ownership as social ownership by the whole society, some consider public ownership as collective ownership, or collective ownership of laborers in each enterprise; some suggest public ownership as stock shares held by all citizens.

Third, it upholds market as the principal means of allocating resources being another characteristic of market socialism. However, proponents of market socialism have different schools and hold different views on several questions, for example, what range, to what degree and in what form the market should be used as the means of allocating resources.

8.1.2 THREE STAGES OF MARKET SOCIALISM

Market socialism has emerged in the 1930s. Up till now, it has generally gone through three stages.

The first stage was from the 1930s to 1950s, when the early market socialism theory came into being in Western countries with Oscar Lange, Polish-American economist, as the representative. At this stage, market socialism was featured as a theoretical exploration on its feasibility and rationality to combine market with socialism.

---

4   Cohen, G.A.: "A Few Questions about Market Socialism", from *Journal of Renmin University of China*, 2000(5).

With the victory of the October Revolution and the birth of the first socialist country in the world, the operational feasibility of the socialist economic institutions has started to catch people's attention. In April 1920, Mises, economic professor of Vienna University at that time and later known as "nonesuch" of the Neo-Austrian school, issued his paper titled as; "Economic Calculation in the Socialist Commonwealth". In his paper, Mises claimed that it was impossible to have a proper economic calculation under the socialist economic institution according to the practice of economic policy of "wartime communism" carried out in Russia at that time. He had expounded his hypothesis as follows: market and market pricing were the only effective tools to allocate resources, but "it is impossible to separate market and its role in pricing from the social function that is based on private ownership of the means of production."[5] In his opinion, "the socialist society has no choice but to delegate the right of controlling the capital to the state, or precisely, to those who work in managerial authority to execute the state affairs. However, this will lead to the elimination of market. As a matter of fact, this is just the essential aim of socialism."[6] Socialism has no market for the means of production and market pricing to allocate resources; as a result, it is impossible to have proper prices for production factors, therefore there was no objective measure to allocate resources properly. In all, socialism seems incompatible with market; "market is the core of the capitalist system as well as the nature of capitalism; only under the condition of capitalism, it is practicable; under the socialist condition, it is impossible to be artificially created. [...] The question is that only one of the two must be true; either socialism or capitalism."[7]

In the middle of the 1930s, F. Hayek, another outstanding figure of the Neo-Austrian school, compiled a book of *Collectivist Economic Planning*. In this book, he basically adhered to Mises' view, but gave some "partial amendments" to it. Different from Mises, Hayek had argued that socialist economic calculation, namely, rational socialist economic calculation was imaginable in theory, but impossible in practice. In his view, using simultaneous equations to express economic equilibrium, a centralized economic planning institute was theoretically unable to have an optimal allocation of social resources. However, it was necessary to have two conditions to work out this equation for economic equilibrium: one was that it was necessary to have a complete market mechanism; the other condition was the capacity to master dynamic data for a series of economic factors, like product quality and price, production coefficients, articles and services; that is to say, there must be a system to transmit and give feedback information for markets precisely and spontaneously. Since the socialist economic practice was unable to meet these two requirements, it was actually impractical to rely on a central planning institute to achieve a rational allocation of resources in socialist economy.

---

5   Bornstein, Morris: *Comparative Economic Systems*, p. 16. Beijing: China Financial & Economic Publishing House, 1988.
6   *Ibid.*, p. 64.
7   *Ibid.*, p. 165.

From 1934 to 1937, some Marxist economists and left scholars, in sympathy with the socialist system, retorted to Mises' and Hayek's hypotheses. Lange, Polish-American economist, issued a series of articles with the title of "On the Economic Theory of Socialism" in *The Review of Economic Studies* Vol. 4, No.1 (October 1936) and Vol. 2 (February 1937). In his articles, Lange had criticized Mises' and Hayek's viewpoints, making an exploration on the operation of socialist economy and putting forth his assumption on market socialism, which was known as "Lange model".

Lange model can be summarized as follows: (1) Practicing public ownership of the main means of production, but preserve the private ownership in small industry and agriculture; (2) establishing a partial market system; specifically commodity market and service market, but no market for the means of production or no capital market; (3) using multiple systems to make economic decisions, i.e., a triple-dimensional system as central planning, enterprise and family; (4) to have a dual pricing system: commodities and services could be priced through market, while the price of the means of production could be decided by the central planning institute with trial-and-error method analogous to market competition.

Lange model is of great significance. First, he had expounded that market was compatible with socialism. He had claimed that the allocation of resources in socialism was completely the same as that through pure market competition in capitalism; both of them determined their production scales in line with marginal cost price and combined production factors aiming the lowest costs. He added, "public ownership of the means of production itself does not dominate the system of distribution of commodities and services among people inherently; neither does it prescribe the principle of commanding commodity production."[8] This implies that he had evaluated market mechanism as a means of allocating resources that was separable from ownership. Second, Lange had illustrated that planning was after all compatible with market. In his view, the socialist economy could employ a mixture of planning and market; the central planning institute could invest, regulate the interest rate and distribute capital with the assistance of market stimulations. Consequently, such an economy could settle the contradiction between market and planning. Third, Lange had also expounded the complementariness between efficiency and equality. Lange had argued that socialism could get rid of the original old mode of distribution under the private ownership, set up a fairer mode to distribute consumptive property than capitalism, and as a result, can guarantee to achieve higher efficiency than capitalism. The socialist distribution of consumptive property consisted of two parts: wages and socialized dividends. Wages could be determined by market relations, which were closely related to the variation of the marginal value and marginal utility in the

---

8   Lange, Oscar: *On the Economic Theory of Socialism*, p. 9-10. Beijing: China Social Sciences Press, 1981.

industrial sectors or a professional labor department that laborers were enrolled. This could reflect the principle of market efficiency. The social dividend could be determined by relations of the public ownership of the means of production, which should reflect the socialist principle of equality. This was because efficiency has complementariness and unity with equality.

Although Lange model had apparently based mainly on planned economy, we can say that it had marked the birth of market socialism. It is widely acknowledged that Lange model established the concept of market socialism in modern economics, and has turned out to be the "theoretical base for those who have attempted to integrate planning with market in theory."[9]

The second stage was from the 1950s to the 1980s. During this period, market socialism emerged in socialist countries, like Soviet Union and East Europe. The most remarkable figures were those scholars, like Branko Horvat from Yugoslavia and Ota Sik from Czechia. At that time, market socialism has advanced with the economic institutional reforms in these countries. Its basic view was to give full play to market mechanisms under the frame of planned economy.

At this stage, Edvard Kardel, a Yugoslavian economist, was the first to put forth theories on market socialism. As early as in 1949, Kardel, an important leader of Yugoslavia as well as a theorist, had criticized the state ownership of the Russian model, appealing for more autonomy for enterprises. In 1950, Boris Kidric had claimed that it was necessary to liberate socialist commodity exchange to play its role. Thereafter, "market school" has emerged in Yugoslavia with Horvat as its main representative. This school has argued that it was impossible for economy to advance substantially unless it was based on market. They have assumed that market pricing could play its role in balancing demand and supply, rationally distributing rare resources, making economic behavior more rational and fair, and will provide an optimal economic structure. In 1961, Virlyn W. Bruce, a Polish economist, had published his book *Socialist Economic Operation*, systematically illustrating his hypothesis on market socialism. Proceeding from the point of internal relationships between the socialist division of labor and the law of value, Bruce held the view that the commodity-money relation could be an active tool to allocate socialist resources; therefore, the operational mechanism of the socialist economy was supposed to be a regulated market mechanism. He had for the first time formulated the model of "planned economy with adjustable market". Under this model, enterprises should interact through market, and the goal of enterprise's activity should be to achieve maximum profit. However, Bruce had also pointed out that it was impractical for economic activities to be totally adjusted by free market mechanism. This was because market mechanism

---

9   Turner, R. Kerry & Collis, Clive: *Economics of Planning*, p. 8. Beijing: Commercial Press, 1982.

itself had many drawbacks that are hard to overcome. Therefore, it was necessary to supervise the market in order to avoid its negative effects. In 1964, Ota Sik, Czechoslovakian economist, had published his book titled as *Commodity-Money Relations under Socialism*. In his book, he started from the analysis of macro and micro unbalances in the social production, highlighting the important role that market indeed plays in the socialist system, he had advocated modulating micro unbalances by market, while adjusting macro unbalances by planning. His proposition was later called the Czech model of "dispersed market economy under unitary control". However, in Soviet Union, where planned economy had originated, theories on market socialism lagged behind the researches in others countries and recorded little progress. Russian economists, like Leontief, Connick and Lieberman, had put forth their assumption of "socialist commodity production" arguing that socialist economy was a planned commodity economy; thus, it was necessary to adequately utilize market, and achieve the planned goals through market. Those theories were remarkably characterized by market socialism.

The third stage can be extended from the 1980s till now, debated mainly in Western capitalist countries, like Britain and the United States. Their theories on market socialism focus on the demonstrating that market socialism is the only feasible approach for capitalist countries to transform to socialism.

8.2 MILLER, ROEMER, SCHWEICKERT

During the 1980s, the Soviet Union and East European socialist republics had seen regime changes one after another. Some bourgeois politicians and right-wing economists in the West had successively declared that "socialism has come to an end", adding that "socialism does not exist anymore whether in reality or ideality." Facing their attack at socialism, Western left-wing scholars have firmly retorted them. Roemer, U.S. left-wing economist had pointed out, in his book *A Future for Socialism* published in 1994, "the collapse of communism in the Soviet Union and East Europe has encouraged some old arguments and produced as well some new arguments with the belief that socialism is impossible to exist either in the current world or in ideality. However, I wish to illustrate that socialism is still an ideal that deserves to be pursued, and it can possibly exist in the real world. In my opinion, arguments in agreement with socialist economy are necessary to be revised in terms of the basic stance on the components of socialism. Indubitably, socialism with the Russian model has failed, but this does not mean that other forms of socialism that were not on a trial were supposed to be buried with it."[10] While firmly resisting those fallacies put forth by the bourgeois politicians and right-wing scholars, many progressive scholars have started to rethink and review socialism in theory and practice. Carefully summing up the failures of the soci-

---

10   Roemer, J. E.: *A Future for Socialism*, p. 1. Chongqing: Chongqing Publishing House, 1997.

alist system in former Soviet Union and East Europe, they made their efforts to explore how advanced capitalist countries could realize socialism. It was in such settings that models for market socialism came into being in the 1980s. Among the models for market socialism proposed during this period, the foremost influential ones include "cooperative market socialism" established by David Miller, British scholar, "stock market socialism" by John Roemer, U.S. economist, and "market socialism with democratic economy" by David Sweet, U.S. philosopher.

8.2.1 MILLER AND COOPERATIVE 'MARKET SOCIALISM'

David Miller, professor of sociology and politics of Newfield School of Oxford University, UK, is one of the prominent exponents of market socialism. His works on market socialism include: *Market Socialism: Why and How?* (1987), *Market, State and Community: Theoretical Foundations of Market* (1989), *A Vision of Market Socialism: How It Might Work and Its Problem* (1991), and *Equality and Market Socialism* (1993). In his works, Miller has built a model known as "cooperative market socialism". His main views can be summarized as follows:

8.2.1.1 MARKET IS A MEANS OF ORGANIZING ECONOMIC ACTIVITIES, AND SOCIALISM NEEDS MARKET

Miller is a politician as well as a philosopher. He put forth his idea of market socialism with the purpose of defending market socialism in theory to oppose the criticism leveled against by traditional socialists, rather than formulate a specific program to practice it.

At the beginning of his paper *A Vision of Market Socialism: How It Might Work and Its Problem*, Miller wrote, "a question rose after the collapse of communist system of former Soviet Union and East Europe: is there a form of socialism acceptable and widely supported? More frankly, the failure of communism in practice implies that this kind of system cannot work without market."[11] Could socialism rely on market? In terms of this question, Miller had pointed out that socialism meant no market economy in the mind of traditional socialists. In a sense, this view was not surprising at all because, in the contemporary capitalist society, those who were wildly beating the drum for the advantage of market economy were usually right-wingers in politics who defend the policies of Premier Thatcher and President Reagan. Consequently, people usually regarded the struggle between left and right as the same thing as the conflict between exponents and opponents of market socialism. However, the arguments of the right-wingers were based on tricky statements, presenting it as a common means of organizing economic activities, which had no difference from capitalism. Undoubtedly, capitalism relies on market; it is characterized with the ownership of the means of production

---

11   Contend (US), 1991, summer, p. 6.

that is mainly in the hands of a small number of people, but the rest majority had nothing but to be employed by the minority as wage laborers. But left-wingers cannot perceive this. As a matter of fact, it could be quite possible to set up a market opposing capitalism. For instance, when a journalist found a market-oriented supermarket chain dealing with food, he might ask such a question: how could it be reckoned as socialism? The answer to this question is simple as well. If this supermarket chain was run in a democratic way, and its property was possessed by the society, how could it be excluded from socialism? As it were from Miller's exemplification, market was nothing but a means of organizing economic activities; it had nothing to do with the nature of a social system; capitalism could also use it, rather than being the market economy, the distinction between socialism and capitalism lies in who possesses the means of production.

Why did socialism need market? As for this question, Miller made an illustration from the following three aspects.

First, market could provide people with better and more material welfare. Miller has pointed out that market pricing was both an information system and a stimulating system. On the one hand, it signals to suppliers what consumers need; on the other hand, it stimulates commodity producers to manufacture what is short or more needed in the market. It is noticeable that the two functions of pricing could be separable. This is because even if those who feel high social responsibility and realized their management functions without any desire for selfish benefits, they still needed something to inform them what the most beneficial decision could be. Without market providing information, people could necessarily find other means to coordinate producers and consumers. However, in the current industrial society, the only feasible way was the state planning, namely, the planning departments allocating labor force for enterprises, prescribing varieties and amount of products, and setting price of commodities and services for enterprises to optimize the balance between supply and demand. But it has proved in practice that there occurs much difficulty for planned economy to settle these problems in reality. The practice of former Soviet Union and East European socialist countries might be well-served as a case for this view. As for inequality in distributing welfare in the capitalist countries, that was the problem of capitalism itself. And it was this problem that market socialists could rectify.

Second, the market could provide people with more liberty. In Miller's view, the view of socialist liberty was oriented with efficiency option as the core, namely, a free man was supposed to have more options, and these options must be practical rather than formal. How much freedom a society had, was closely related to how the social resources were allocated. In a liberal society, market inevitably played an important role because it allowed people to choose resources that were suitable for their specific life styles. As long as suppliers responded to the market stimuli and provided necessary commodities for the society, people could get whatever they needed: they could wear whatever clothes they wanted and enjoy whatever music they liked. Apart from these, market could as well provide people liberty to opt professions and liberty of speech. The goal of market socialism was set to extend these liberties beyond the limits of capitalism. However, socialist economy without market or with an insufficient market could not guarantee these liberties.

Third, market could better promote the process of democracy. In Miller's view, democracy fell into two categories: industrial and the political democracy. The industrial democracy means that members of enterprises had the right to make the decision about what and how they would produce. Only in a market economy could members of enterprises have such an autonomy, while in a planned economy, it was impossible to have such independence. Of course, market made the industrial democracy possible, but not inevitably. How much possibility there might be depends on the structure of the enterprise, among which the foremost democratic form can be the workers' cooperative. However, such an enterprise structure as workers' cooperative is not always the optimal option for other enterprises. This is because all people may not take industrial democracy as their first choice when they have free option between economic efficiency and industrial democracy. However, market socialism could undoubtedly provide democratic working circumstances for those who pay much attention to industrial democracy.

In all, Miller believed that market socialism was not worse than the current capitalism in terms of economic efficiency. As for equality, freedom and democracy, it was much more progressive than the contemporary capitalism and Russian socialism. Therefore, it was a feasible program to replace the temporary capitalism and the "state socialism" of the Russian model. He suggested that market socialism at least achieved these four goals: to gain economic profit through market in the process of production; to develop democracy practically by means of restricting the role of the state; to provide more equality in the initial distribution; to guarantee workers' autonomy. And to make these goals achievable, Miller has designed a model of "cooperative market socialism".

8.2.1.2 COOPERATIVE MODEL FOR MARKET SOCIALISM

In Miller's model for "cooperative market socialism", workers' cooperatives are in a leading position. The cooperatives will sell their products in an open market, pay the workers with what they earn from their sales. The cooperatives will be under a democratic management by the workers. It will have a great autonomy in making decision, such as what and how to produce, how to distribute income among the workers, amount of funds they would invest to a certain field, set prices for their products, and all the other affairs involving them. Under the conditions of market socialism, how much a worker can be paid will totally depend on the economic profit of the cooperative he works. The production capital of the cooperatives initially comes from public investment departments set up by the state. These departments should control the funds possessed by the whole society. Enterprises can also borrow funds to run their business from these investment departments. And these public investment departments have the right to decide which projects should be supported and the rate of interest these enterprises can afford.

Miller also made an elaboration on the basic principles the cooperative enterprises could follow. The first was the principle for the capital operation. Enterprises will borrow funds from the public investment departments on the condition of accepting a fixed rate of interest. The enterprises have the right to use the money, but do not have a free-ownership title of it. This suggests that enterprises should carefully manage their fixed assets, and the borrowed capital should not be used as income or dividend for cooperative members, neither should it be lent to other enterprises for a second time. The second was the principle of bankruptcy. Enterprises that are unable to provide their staff with the minimum income to maintain their well-being should announce bankruptcy. Their staff should be re-assigned to other enterprises. The third was the principle for enterprises' democracy. Every enterprise should implement democratic management, and each worker will enjoys equal rights to participate therein. If an enterprise wants to expand its scale and recruit new staff, there must be a consensus among the enterprise members. Of course, the enterprise can also decide on its internal structure for democratic management. For instance, in a small-sized enterprise, decision can be made through plenary sessions, while large-scale enterprises can implement more complex mechanisms to make decision, like expert committees and executive councils.

In Miller's model for cooperative market socialism, workers' cooperative always take the leading position, but there could be other forms of production enterprises at the same time, so the state plays an important role. Specifically, the functions of the state could include: first, it should be responsible for the adjustment of capital allocation, which will be implemented by the public investment institution (bank) set up and supervised by the state. The bank provides funds for existing and newly established enterprises. Its decisions on investments will be based to guarantee the soundness of the enterprise's business, but will also consider other overall factors, such as maintaining economic competitiveness, avoiding monopolistic trends in the market, and caring for regional balances related employment. Additionally, the investing institutions should also undertake such functions as providing enterprises with information related prices in the markets and other market data and trends; promoting establishment of new companies in the branches with higher demands; secondly, they should regulate the minimum wages. Third, they will regulate tax policies, adjust income distribution among the population in order to achieve fairness; fourth, the state departments should also provide public goods and services, like welfare services, in order to meet social and cultural demands. Miller has emphasized that his model does not blindly worship and totally depend on market, but he definitely clarified which products and services should be regulated by market, and which should be regulated by the state.

8.2.1.3 MARKET SOCIALISM: A FEASIBLE APPROACH TO PROMOTE SOCIALIST VALUES

Miller has argued that his market socialism model was faithful and committed to consolidating the core values of socialism. He has sharply commented that traditional socialists blindly and illusively pursued only a part of the socialist goals. They usually aim to exercise a conscious control or leadership over social activities, democracy, equality, liberty and value of community, but they generally neglect two aspects: first, there are certain controversies among these goals. For instance, conscious leadership over social activities need a unitary controlling center, which contradicts with extensive democracy idealized by socialists; socialists' belief collective community values can indeed be harmonized by individual liberties. Therefore, for the aim of community building, it is necessary to promote common moral values for the population. Second, traditional socialist have failed to develop a real socialist model that could totally integrate the five value goals mentioned above and they were unsuccessful to combine those values appropriately. Therefore, those who advocate and acknowledge various models for market socialism should be acutely aware that when they bestowed priority to goals, like democracy, liberty and efficiency, they should arrange other goals and choices accordingly. The reason why Miller proposed the model of "cooperative market socialism" lay in his attempt of settling the controversies among the goals mentioned above, in order explore a practical approach to realize the core values of socialism. His ideas to realize the core values of socialism can be summarized as follows:

As for democracy in "cooperative market socialism", the workers' cooperative enterprise should be an organization inside which economic democracy would be comprehensively exercised. This democracy should not be in contradiction with state's guiding role, thus realizing the unity between democracy and conscious leadership. Specifically, the holistic frame of an enterprise operation should be under the conscious leadership of the state, such as the enterprise's general structure, investment policy, consideration of balances within the parts of the society, while the specific economic activities of the enterprise, like what and how to produce, should be decided by the workers themselves through consideration of market circumstances.

As for the values of a community, Miller has suggested that market socialism does not negate socialist values; on the contrary, it enhances them. The notion of the community values refers that social relations should be characterized with cooperation and the individual should be subject to the collective, rather than being in unrestricted conflicts and competition. In Miller's view, the community values are the foundation of economic democracy and collective aims. But they should not be understood as a social consensus imposed by "communists", or a unitary collective identity without diversity or plurality. Market socialism should be understood as a complex society; accordingly and naturally there will be variety of relations and differences among the people in a community or society. Communities should be allowed to reflect and transmit their values from bottom to up throughout all levels; neighborhood, enterprise and society.

As to equality, Miller has suggested that market socialism should aim "social equality", thus, its aim cannot be limited as economic equality. The equality cannot be measured with numerical expressions, like Gini coefficient or other formula. Social equality means that people have equal status; that is to say, people have an equal starting point and equal opportunities in the society. In "cooperative market socialism", naturally there will be income disparities among the staff in an enterprise and also among different enterprises. But this disparity is often determined by their economic performances or similar structural differences and not based on any privilege like non-democratic reasons thus they can be evaluated as reasonable. Of course, such disparities should not be allowed to increase uncontrolled and arbitrarily as generally observed in contemporary capitalist societies; neither should they endanger the social equality and solidarity goals in the society. Market socialism aims to eliminate the private ownership of capitalism and the income resulting from the capital ownership. Meanwhile, the distribution among the workers in an enterprise is determined through democratic decision and wide gaps in distribution of incomes should not be allowed. Consequently, in regard to equality aim, market socialism could prove to be superior to capitalism or "bureaucratic state socialism" dominant in the former Soviet Union and East Europe.

In regard to justice, some scholars have criticized that there existed unfair elements in the market socialism model. Refuting this criticism, Miller has argued that social justice does not mean, economic equality in a strict and narrow sense, but means that each member of the society receives what he deserves according to her/his contribution to the community and society. For a fair economic style or institution, wages should be calculated on the basis of the individual's contribution. In market socialism, the income of an individual should be proportional to his contribution to the society, and this calculation could easily be determined in an open, non-arbitrary and tolerant patterns. When the economic income of few individuals or groups excessively deviates from the majority, the socialist government should intervene and find reasonable solutions to reverse those tendencies.

As for efficiency, whether cooperatives could achieve high economic efficiency when they are the main actors and determinants of social production is a quite controversial issue among economists. Some hold that cooperatives could only be suitable for smaller scale domestic industries, rather than modern advanced socialized production or international production; some argue that cooperative enterprises could not adapt to technological innovation, resulting to stagnation in production. In terms of this, Miller has offered some concrete examples from several small scale cooperative enterprises —with more than 500 staff – which had also achieved remarkable results, and has proved that they could also achieve high efficiency. Additionally, in the contemporary capitalism, big corporations do not choose internal expansion pattern but horizontal expansion integrating related numerous companies as branches of a big corporation. Inside that larger complex of corporation, the original companies can still be able to remain autonomous in production and other activities. This shows that cooperative enterprises can also adapt to modern socialized production because categorically there is no necessity that they should reject combinations or alliances with other enterprises. As for technological innovation, Miller has remarked that those who doubt cooperative enterprises could lack innovation and creativity baselessly attribute and limit those aims to highly motivated individuals. But in fact in a cooperative market socialism model an individual talent and his/her innovation and invention abilities can produce benefits for all the other staff in the enterprise. He/she will be supported and motivated by the whole community of the enterprise staff and be rewarded by his/her contribution. Therefore, there will always be a high motivation and a stimulating mechanism for technological innovation in cooperative enterprises.

8.2.2 ROEMER AND 'SHAREHOLDER'S MARKET SOCIALISM'

John Roemer is a well-known left-wing economist, Professor of economics at the University of California, as well as the leader of "Economics, Justice and Society" Program. He is also one of the most renowned figures of "analytical Marxism". After the abrupt changes in Soviet Union and East European socialist countries, Roemer has made remarkable efforts to defend socialist ideas and formulated his unique theories on market socialism. His masterpiece is *A Future for Socialism*, which was published in 1994.

In Roemer's view, one of the important reasons for the failure of Soviet Union and East European socialist countries lay in their planned economy pattern which was highly centralized. However, the private ownership is still continues to be the fundamental reason for the injustice in the contemporary advanced capitalist countries. Therefore, an adequate model of socialism can overcome the capitalist private ownership and the planned economy of Soviet Union and East European socialist countries, by combining public ownership with market economy. Public ownership can guarantee social justice, while market economy can provide economic efficiency. In Roemer's eyes, Soviet Union and East European countries had three basic distinctions compared to the Western capitalist society: political monopoly, centralized allocation of resources and public ownership of the means of production. In theory or from the perspective of modern history, this special combination was inefficient in economy, unstable in politics, and disastrous in morality. However, Roemer has not argued that it was impracticable or undesirable to combine public ownership of the means of production with democratic politics and allocation of resources through markets. In the preface of a collection of papers he had co-compiled with Bardhan, Roemer has pointed out, "in the view of many people, the collapse of communism (it is interpreted as a kind of political economic system, which is short of competition; the state directly possesses and controls enterprises, which is badly short of markets) in the Soviet Union and East Europe has strengthened a vulgar point of view that capitalism is still the only optimal system in politics or terms of economic development. But in the eyes of former communist countries, the advances in capitalism were always evaluated instable and deceptive. In this book, we hope to arouse people's interest in the study of market socialism again"[12]. Roemer has proposed his model of "stock market socialism" based above arguments. He made an elaboration of his model from the following aspects.

8.2.2.1 SOCIALISM AS EGALITARIANISM

Socialism was generally considered to be a society established on the basis of public ownership of the means of production, especially state ownership, either in Grand's model for market socialism in the 1930s; or in theories inspiring the model of Soviet Union and East Europe in the 1950s to 1970s. In terms of this, Roemer has proposed a different view. In his opinion, those who are for socialism should revise some basic concepts on socialism. The foremost important among them is: "It is better to interpret socialist objective as a kind of egalitarianism, instead of pursuing a specific property relation. In other words, what I mean is when socialists evaluate property relations, it is necessary for them to be able to provide certain egalitarianism in line with the property relations they evaluate."[13]

What does it imply to interpret socialism as a kind of egalitarianism? Roemer has not given a definite answer for this question. He has argued only that socialists needed to pursue for a self-realization, and equal opportunities in such three aspects; welfare, political influence and social status. This indicated that socialism was supposed to be a society that would have equal opportunity in these three aspects. The alleged equal opportunity, in a broad and general sense, means to

---

[12] Bardhan, P. & Roemer, J.E.: *Market Socialism*, p. 3. Oxford: Oxford University Press, 1993.
[13] Roemer, J. E.: *A Future for Socialism*, p. 113-4.

offer compensations to those who are in inferiority because they were restrained by the factors which are beyond their control. This is because these unfavorable conditions are not caused by them, but brought about by the factors beyond their control.

Why is it necessary to interpret socialism as a kind of egalitarianism? In Roemer's view, the criticism of capitalism by the traditional socialists was based on criticism of exploitation. But this criticism was actually based on the approach of self-ownership; that is to say, the value one produced with his labor should legitimately belong to him. He asked: can we limit ourselves with a fairness concept in which each who produces a value should possesses its fruits? Or should not everyone share the fruits? Judging from the classic self-ownership approach, the answer was nothing but the former one. But this proposition is almost identical with the principle of modern liberalism. But what socialists require is everyone should share the property. Therefore, the only correct principle for socialism can be a kind of egalitarianism.

On the prerequisite that socialism is a kind of egalitarianism, Roemer has criticized the view of linking socialism with the state ownership form of the public ownership .Since the socialist objective is to realize equality, the option for an ownership pattern is nothing but an issue of means. Therefore, the state ownership of public ownership pattern is not indispensable for a socialist system. "Socialists should take a compromising attitude towards property relations: there may be other patterns of ownership which can be more appropriate for the socialist objective than the traditional pattern of state ownership of the means of production."[14] What pattern of ownership on earth was more suitable to promote the socialist objective as he mentioned? Roemer commented "various patterns of property can be found everywhere in modern capitalist countries (rather than in socialist countries): non-profit enterprises, limited liability companies, cooperative enterprises, sole proprietorship enterprise, public ownership enterprise, social-democratic property, labor management enterprise, and community property. The optimal forms of property that could promote socialist objectives could be those enabling direct control by the public or the state over the means of production."[15] The notion of "direct control by the public or the state over the means of production" is still the pattern of public ownership in the last analysis. I should say that; in Roemer's remark the state ownership not a necessary condition of socialism refers to that of Russian model; although he emphasized egalitarianism should be the socialist objective and the public ownership is nothing but the means of achieving this goal; he did not intend to mean that the public ownership is not a necessary condition of socialism.

---

14   *Ibid.*
15   *Ibid.*, p. 6.

8.2.2.2 MARKET SYSTEM: APPROPRIATE TO ACHIEVE THE SOCIALIST OBJECTIVE

In his book *A Future for Socialism* Roemer wrote, "The mission of this brochure is to bring about a new model that combines the strength of market with the socialist system, which can produce a balance between efficiency and equality."[16] Apparently, he has argued that the market system embodies nothing but efficiency, while socialism embodies equality. That was to say, market system had nothing to do with the nature of social system. It could be applied either to capitalism or to socialism. This was the base for all market socialists to establish their theories. To highlight this point, Roemer has elaborated that from another perspective.

First, the success in economic development of the modern capitalism cannot be attributed to the capitalist private ownership, but the market mechanism that creates competition. Roemer has commented, "We have only a vague concept on the roles the private property and market plays because, till now, the two have actually co-existed. However, we have other cases — modern enterprises or maybe China's township enterprises — which help us to unmask those theories that used to be universally accepted and by which economic development is perceived as the right for ceaseless accumulation of private property; as a matter of fact, this ceaseless accumulation was attributed to the market competition."[17] That was a pedantic way of saying; the market and the capitalist private ownership play totally different roles.

Second, failure of Soviet Union's socialist practice should not be attributed to socialist system but to dismantling of the markets. Some people have argued that the disintegration of Soviet Union lay in that it did not properly settle the principle -agent problem like capitalism did. In terms of this, Roemer has argued that the economy of Soviet Union had made a great leap in those two decades during the postwar time and in the 1930s. If it was a fact, we could not simply regress to commission-agency assumption to interpret failure of this economic pattern in the 1980s. From the 1960s to 1980s, the growth of economic welfare was greatly determined by the economic reform capability, namely, the ability of applying new technologies. At this point, the Russian economic pattern had disappointingly failed to work. The fundamental reason for the occurrence of this situation lay herein: "Without market-driven competition from home and abroad the enterprises could get no incentives for reforming themselves; without the driving force of competition, and reforms could not happen, at least, it could not compete with the growth speed of foreign market economies as in the beginning."[18] Therefore, the fundamental reason for the failure of Russian economy does not lie in the socialist system, but in the fact that it had not practiced market economy.

---

16   *Ibid.*, p. 21.
17   *Ibid.*, p. 114.
18   *Ibid.*, p. 39.

MARKET SOCIALISM THEORIES 299

Why could socialism not be realized without a market system? In Roemer's view, if socialism cannot provide almost the same colorful life styles to its citizens as capitalism did, it will be instable. Apart from market system, people are unaware and know what other systems can perform. If this is the fact, the question socialists should answer is: can we design an economic system, under which technological reform can occur and the unique inequalities in the capitalist income distribution can be avoided? This system can be nothing but market socialism. Market system tackles the problem of efficiency, while socialism can solve the problem of equality; thus, market socialism is efficiency plus equality.

It is noticeable that Roemer did not totally expect market socialism could actually achieve the equality which he mentioned. He said, "I will not defend or argue for such a system to be the only one, in which people's income is in proportion with their skills, because individuals have unequal opportunities according to their skills and capacities, and this reality will remain that way for the next decades or may be also in the future few centuries. The prominent question is: Is there a better stage when we look with a long-term consideration in the transition period from capitalism to socialism other than market socialism patterns? In my opinion, there is not any."[19] That is to say, he meant that; though market socialism is unable to achieve equality in the short term; it was the only economic system that can be achievable and feasible, bit by bit toward the ultimate goal of socialism.

8.2.2.3 SHAREHOLDERS' MARKET SOCIALISM

What is market socialism? Roemer has defined it as: "The notion of market socialism, in my opinion, refers to various arrangements in economy that the most production factors, including labor, are distributed through pricing system, and profit of the enterprises (whether under the management of the workers or not) are equally distributed among citizens. The key problem is: Through what mechanism can such a distribution of profit be realized? And also in the meanwhile, it should not go so far as to result unacceptable losses in terms of efficiency."[20] To demonstrate the feasibility of market socialism, Roemer has designed a model known as "stock market socialism". This model of market socialism is generally featured in five aspects: First, stocks of all the state-run companies will be re-distributed, in order to offer each adult citizen stock shares per capita from the very beginning. With that share, they will each obtain- from the company–a share of capital bonus proportionally. When they pass away, their shares will be returned to the state. Once people get these shares, they could trade them with other stock holders, but they will not be allowed to sell them for money. As a result, it is impossible for the rich to purchase the shares of the poor and control or determine the economic

---

19   Ibid., p. 107-8.
20   World Socialism Institute of Central Compilation & Translation Bureau: *Contemporarily Abroad Socialism: Theory and Models*, p. 299. Beijing: Central Compiling &Translation Press, 1998.

interests of others. With the purpose of guaranteeing the implementation of this system, Roemer has established two kinds of currency, namely, cash currency and securities currency. The cash currency is used to pay for daily commodities, but it cannot be used to buy enterprises' stocks, while securities currency can acquire nothing but stocks, and cannot be exchanged for cash. Hence emerges the term: "stock market socialism". Second, all banks in the economy will be state-owned, which collect money from private depositors, and lend it to enterprises. Their running principles are no different from those of the capitalist banks. Third, managers of the companies are elected by the board of directors, instead of being appointed by the state. Generally they will be representatives of the main banks, from which these companies borrow funds. They are also representatives of the enterprises' workers as well as the company stockholders. Fourth, the government guarantees that there are significant investing programs, utilizing different rates of interest to encourage or inhibit some specific investments. Fifth, it will also allow having capitalist enterprises in the economy, even if they are run by individuals. But once these enterprises reach a certain scale or their founders pass away, they have to be nationalized via offering compensation so that their stocks will be re-distributed to working masses.

In Roemer's view, the model of stock market socialism is feasible economically. It can settle the basic contradictions that a central planned economy has. With this economic pattern, enterprises (including foreign enterprises) can compete against each other in the market circumstances. Consequently, problems of information exchange and stimulation mechanisms should be settled. There will be no tendency towards centralization because there will be no central planning institute to which enterprises are dependent on. The problem of enterprise reforms and innovations will also be settled from two aspects: on the one hand, competition will push public-owned enterprises to pay attention to innovate and produce new products and technology; on the other hand, there is also space for the capitalist enterprisers to develop under this economic pattern, although this room will not be large enough for them to assume a leading position in the economy.

Roemer has argued that his model could also settle the two basic problems in the capitalist economy: inequality in economy and irrationality in investments. As for inequality in economy, it will apparently decrease the income of the capitalist class (though not eliminate) due to the substantial reduction of the income that the capitalists possess by means of their possession on the means of production. On the whole, all citizens will equally share the social prosperity, thus, they will equally enjoy all the surplus benefits from the production. Property inequality which will be caused by the citizens' stock trade will not be allowed to go beyond their life years thus it means inheritance will be restricted as in the capitalist countries of today. This inequality will be suppressed in order to hinder capital accumulation and centralization of it, as it occurs under the capitalism. As for the irrationality of investments, Roemer's model definitely acknowledges that market is not an effective mechanism in deciding appropriate investments when evaluated from a long term aspect. Thus, the government's visible hand should be used to supplement the invisible hand as in the sense of Adam Smith. He said, the state's intervention in planning investments "is for nothing but two reasons: there is no efficient market that effectively distributes investments in market economy, and there are also exterior influences -to be exact, exterior factors, pollution is only one negative example – which is beyond the control of market."[21] However, the visible hand should also exercise controls over interest rates to lead the investment activities in the economy.

8.2.3 SCHWEICKERT AND 'ECONOMIC DEMOCRACY MODEL'

Among the models of market socialism occurring in the middle of the 1980s, Schweickert's "market socialism with economic democracy" is one of the foremost prominent models. David Schweickert, Professor of Philosophy at Loyola University, Chicago, as well as left-wing scholar, put forth this notion in his book of Against Capitalism, which was published in 1993. He expounded this model from the following aspects:

8.2.3.1 WHY MARKET SOCIALISM?

Like all market socialists, Schweickert has also focused on how to realize socialism in the advanced capitalist countries. He has argued that there is no other way for the advanced capitalist countries to realize socialism other than relying on market means. As to this, he has commented: "Various theoretical models of market socialism have been proposed in the latest few years, but all proponents of market socialism agree on four points: (1) Market should not be considered as identical with capitalism; (2) There are great drawbacks in central planning that is regarded as an economic mechanism; (3) Rather than other forms of socialism, it is the market socialism that is feasible and desirable. That is to say, market is an indispensable and feasible (though not perfect) mechanism to organize economic activities; (4) certain forms of market socialism are economically practicable, and can be more favorable than capitalism."[22] Schweickert has developed his ideas as follows:

First, market is not identical with capitalism. To illustrate this problem, Schweickert made a comparative analysis on socialism and capitalism. In his view, the capitalist economy is a kind of market economy featured as private ownership of the means of production and employment of labor force. Specifically, economic

---

21 *Ibid.*, p. 18-19.
22 Ollman, Bertell: *Market Socialism.* The Debate Among Socialists, p. 7.

exchanges of the capitalist society are predominantly under the control of the invisible demand-supply hands, namely under the control of market mechanisms; social means of production predominantly belong to private owners; most people are employed as laborers who are working for wages. Different than the capitalist economy, the market socialist economy, though still preserving the market mechanisms (despite it is highly restricted compared to that in capitalism) which will organize the major part of economic activities, it will replace the capitalist private ownership with the state ownership and with the workers' collective ownership. "The common state property will be a collective property under the control of laborers who are utilizing it."[23] Correspondingly, the workers' income will no longer be a contract based wages system any more, and the character of workers' labor changes it is no more employed or hired labor any more like in capitalism. In all, in Schweickert's eyes, the distinction between socialism and capitalism does not lie in the practice of the planned economy or practice of market economy, but in the public ownership or private ownership of the means of production. Hereafter, he made a further step to emphasize that "it was a fatal error for those arguing for the conservative laissez-faire approach and also the left-wing radicals arguing against market socialism by regarding capitalism as equivalent to market."[24] In defense of capitalism, the right wing usually advocates the advantages of market and the demerits of central planning, but they go around the issues of employed/hired labor and private ownership of the means of production. This is an effective strategy for the right-wing, because it is much easier to defend market than arguing for the employed labor and the private ownership of the means of production. The left wing radicals also base their criticism on market socialism focusing on market, particularly pointing to demerits and irrationality of the market. As a matter of fact, abstractly attacking at the market is more easily compared to defend it because market has both advantages and disadvantages. Those defending capitalism focus on the merits of market, while opponents of market socialism emphasize demerits of it.

Second, the central planned economy of Soviet Union and East European socialist countries had great drawbacks. In Schweickert's view, "The central planned economy is the one where a central planning department decides what should be produced, and then order enterprises to produce commodities imposing the quantity and quality as required. Such an economy has four apparent problems, namely, insufficiency of information to decide, lack of motivation, tendency of centralization and sluggish or no enterprise reform motivation."[25]

The primary problem for a centrally planned economy is insufficient information feedback. Schweickert pointed has out that efficiency was always a problem for

---

23   *Ibid.*, p. 15.
24   *Ibid.*, p. 7.
25   *Ibid.*, p. 8-9.

the Russian economy and economies with the Russian-oriented pattern. And this problem has aggravated in the course of further economic development. This was because the information problem is not difficult to tackle when a small number of commodities are produced and when more emphasis is given to quantity rather than quality. However, it turns out to be a critical and difficult problem when it is required to produce more variety of goods with better quality. Therefore, "once central planning economies have developed up to a certain level, market reformation had become necessary."[26] There was also insufficient motivation in a centrally planned economy. The practice of the former Soviet Union proves that if the production is decided by the planning department, the enterprise will have no motivation to produce what consumers actually need; if the input and output are both determined by the planning department, the enterprise is likely to submit a production scheme with low production complexity but high quantity, so that it can easily complete its mission; if the employment is guaranteed for workers and if workers' income has nothing to do with enterprises' operation or success, they will have no enthusiasm to work; if the planning department is responsible for the whole economy, it will not have any motive to shutdown those inefficient enterprises; this is because it will either increase unemployment or it has an extra job to arrange new jobs for the unemployed workers. There is also the problem of centralization in a centrally planned economy. This is because the planner grasps much power and authority, which inevitably contradicts with democracy. Finally, the problem of innovation arises. In a planned economy, enterprises are not under the pressure of competition; as a result, they have no drive for reform or innovation. They are never afraid whether they are unable to follow the pace of new technology, or whether they will lose the markets they already control.

Third, at the current stage of human development, market socialism is the only form of socialism both feasible and desirable. Schweickert has pointed out, even in the advanced capitalist countries, the economic development and growth does not suffice to implement the policy of distributing property in line with people's demand. The failure of Soviet Union and East European socialist practice reflects that the centrally planned economy was impracticable, so there is no other choice than to practice market socialism. It might be said that the existence of market socialism will inevitably result in competition, injustice and unemployment. Could it be regarded as socialism? In terms of this, Schweickert has argued, "Socialism is not equal to the advanced form of socialism which is communism. It is a new system just emerges out of the matrix of capitalism; so it has the traces of the old society it derives from. Socialism is not a perfect society. It is not totally a non-capitalist economic system, but it integrates the best achievements of capitalism and overcomes the worst demerits of it."[27] Market socialism belongs to socialism because it firmly opposes capitalism. It is based on the general insight that in

---

26   *Ibid.*, p. 10.
27   *Ibid.*

the modern world the role of the bourgeoisie, as the capitalist is out of time or bygone. It has become unnecessary for the bourgeoisie to cumulate capital, manage industry, create new products or develop new technology. Now there are better ways to realize these functions. Market socialism not only firmly opposes capitalism, but also embodies the best ideal and values of the socialist tradition. It is feasible to control the economy by producers, rather than vice versa. Market socialism is not "utopian" socialism. It at least acknowledges that our values cannot be perfectly realized today at the moment and we have to find a balanced reality. This approach is completely in conformity with the common knowledge of Marxism. Compared with market socialism, those forms of non-market socialism are economically infeasible or undesirable when judged from the aspect of norms of socialism.

Fourth, some models of market socialism are feasible economically, and are far more favorable than capitalism, for example, Roemer's model of "stock market socialism".

8.2.3.2 ECONOMIC DEMOCRACY

Schweickert called his model, market socialism with economic democracy because his model "places workers' self-management as the core of this system". In his view, the difference between his model and Roemer's model of stock market socialism lay in: the former puts stress on workers' self-management, while the latter highlighted egalitarian ownership of the means of production. Specifically, market socialism with economic democracy is featured by three aspects as follows:

First, it implements collective ownership of the means of production and workers' democratic management. Different from Roemer's stock market socialism, there are no stocks in economic democracy model; as a result, there is no stock market. Here, the common state property will be a collective property, which is under the control of the laborers who utilize it. Correspondingly, each enterprise implements democratic management, and workers legitimately enjoy the rights to elect the managers of the enterprise, each having one ballot. The ultimate right belongs to all the staff of the enterprise. Under economic democracy, enterprises are not possessed by their workers, but an association under their control. Except small-scale enterprises that implement direct elections for their managers, workers in large or medium-sized enterprises will choose their representatives to form a committee, and the committee will elect a manager for the enterprise and supervise him.

Second, it implements social control over investment. Different from Roemer's stock market socialism, under Schweickert's market socialism, the investment capital comes from the revenue of enterprises instead of private savings. That is to say, every enterprise must pay a capital levy in accordance with their capital volume. This tax can be regarded as a rent that is paid back to the society to increase the social property or social prosperity. From the angle of economy, this revenue is actually the interest of the capital — in this way this system avoids paying interest to private savers. Taxing enterprises, rather than "inducing" individual savings to collect investment capital not only eliminates the source of capitalist inequality, namely, paying interest to individuals as private owners of money, but also frees this economy from relying on savers and investors. The market socialism with economic democracy does not allow enterprises to reinvest with their "profit", thus "all profit" returns to workers. In a nutshell, all investment capital comes from the revenues of enterprises. The re-investment mechanism in market socialism is different from that of capitalism because the investment capital returns to the community which is made up of each individual (because each has his right). In this way, the capital flows back to the people, who are not imposed to chase the flowing direction of the capital. Once the investment capital flows back to the commonwealth, they will be "lent" to the enterprises of the commonwealth, or "lent" to the enterprise's collective association with the intention of starting new enterprises. This "loan" is conducted and decided through the public bank network and follows two principles: efficiency of planning and provision of jobs. Market principles only work at this stage.

Third, there are only markets for commodities and services, but no capital market and labor force market. Under this market socialism, enterprises cannot use their profit to begin new investments. Though there is still "capital property", namely, that production material under the control of the workers, there is not an abstract value of self-appreciation. Additionally, the social investment source of the enterprises comes from their revenues, which is decided in a democratic way, rather than imposed by market. That is to say, the overall rate of reinvestment is under the conscious control and decided through democratic discussions. Thus, there is no capital market, neither is there a labor force market; what the workers get are not contractual wages, but their income is part of the enterprises' profit. It is noticeable that in this model there are no "wages", in a strict sense, in those enterprises under the workers' self-management. All workers, including managers are paid from the "profit", rather than contractual wages or salaries. The calculation method of "profit" under the condition of market socialism is different from that in capitalism. In both capitalism and socialism, profit is the difference between sales revenue and costs. However, in market socialism, the workers' income cannot considered as cost but as surplus, namely, the "profit" in market socialism is the amount what is left after production material buying costs, depreciation cost and tax . Therefore, managers cannot increase enterprises' profit by forcing workers to accept lower wages, while the workers cannot insist for higher wages which will decrease the profit because it is these profits that constitute their "wages".

Schweickert has made a summary: "In all, this type of market socialism can be viewed as an economic system with three basic structures: self-management by enterprise workers, social control over investments, markets for commodities and services. These definite components are different from those of capitalism: employed hired labor, private ownership of the means of production, and markets for commodities, services, capital and labor force."[28]

8.2.3.3 FEASIBILITY AND SUPERIORITY OF MARKET SOCIALISM WITH ECONOMIC DEMOCRACY

In Schweickert's view, his model of economic democracy market socialism is feasible economically. From the perspective of enterprises, they are actually co-operative organizations due to their implementation of collective ownership and workers' democratic management, which provides efficiency for the enterprises. Practice has proved that cooperative enterprises have almost similar efficiency compared to capitalist enterprises, and often they can be more efficient. From the perspective of inter-enterprise relations and the enterprise-customer relations, and due to the macro circumstances of market economy there will be no such problems of information deficit and lack of stimulating mechanism as central planned economies had. Seen from long-term economic development aspect, the investments will be decided according to the market demand. Investments will have a higher quality of decision backing because decisions are not completely restricted by market impulses. And the problem of enterprise innovation is also settled because the competition pressure will force the enterprises to adapt to technological development in their spheres. Additionally, it is possible for workers to get more benefits from the enterprise, like more monetary income, less working times and better working conditions, which will as well motivate them for innovations.

Schweickert has also elaborated how market socialism is superior to capitalism. First, it ensures more justice because it gets rid of gaining profit income from property, by eliminating capitalists. Second, it is more democratic because it extends economic democracy down to factories, and up to policy makers for the management of macro economy. Specifically, the workers each have an ultimate vote in the enterprise matters. If the manager is deemed unfit or incompetent for his/her work, he/she can be "recalled" back from his/her position"; as a citizen, the worker enjoys his/her democratic rights for the investment scale and also can decide on the economic structure to be designed by the state. Therefore, they enjoy the democratic rights to direct overall development of the economy. Finally, market socialism adequately overcomes a most destructive feature of contemporary capitalism: the excessive mobility of the capital. With the development of newest technology and politics, the capital has become more mobile than it had

---

28   Ibid., p. 16.

ever been ever in capitalist history. It can swiftly flow to anywhere in the world that promises the highest returns, which results in lower wages and worse working conditions in less developed parts of the world, ruins the well being of those less developed societies and causes numerous drifting migrants. Economic democracy market socialism will fundamentally change this phenomenon. This is because workers in charge of the enterprise will not allow capital to move to those areas where wages are lower; also the public-owned capital will not go over national boundaries for higher profits; the investment capital, under the supervision of laws and which comes from revenues, will be returned to the commonwealth.

8.3 EVALUATION ON MARKET SOCIALISM TRENDS

Trends of market socialism schools have occurred in the settings when the socialist system in the Soviet Union and East Europe had disintegrated. It was also the result of left-wing scholars' resistance against right-wing scholars and politicians. After the disintegration of socialist system in the Soviet Union and East Europe, some bourgeois scholars have wildly beaten the drum that capitalism was the end of the history, and argued that socialism has proved it has no chance to exist whether in reality or in ideality. Facing the zealotry of the capitalist defenders, left wing scholars and Marxists in Western countries have firmly refuted them, and market socialists have actively involved in that resistance. As mentioned in the previous parts, proponents of market socialism have all agreed that the disintegration of socialism in Soviet Union and East Europe does not prove that no other social form but capitalism is the best one; on the contrary, market socialists have all argued that the current capitalist society is an unequal society without any appropriate democracy, while the socialist society is an ideal society people pursue for present and future. Various theories or models of market socialism are all markedly oriented by socialist values. In the settings when socialist movements are at low ebb worldwide, the revival of market socialism in capitalist countries has partly boosted up the confidence of world people that socialism was inevitably to take the place of capitalism.

The relationship between market and socialism has always been a significant issue in socialist theory and practice. In 1980s, various theories on market socialism have made a beneficial exploration on the possibility and ways of combining market with socialism. In terms of the view held by the traditional socialism; it was impossible for market to integrate with socialism, market socialists have refuted them and demonstrated their ideas from the following three aspects. First, they have raised that market and plan are both means, while socialism is the objective; second, market and plan are both neutral, and they can serve capitalism as well as socialism; third, the historical lesson taught by Soviet Union and East Europe demonstrates that market is superior to plan at the current stage of human development. They have also put forth various designs on how to combine market with socialism, and offered specific models for market socialism, with the attempt to turn market socialism from theory to practice.

Market socialists have insisted on the orientation towards socialist values, and made a beneficial exploration on the possibility and means of combining market with socialism, however they have also exhibited some misunderstanding on what socialism indeed is. Although they have all argued that socialism must implement public ownership or put public ownership to a leading position in the economy, they have advocated different opinions on the patterns of public ownership. Additionally, some of them have interpreted socialism as a system with more democracy, some have argued that socialism is a kind of egalitarianism, and also some have based their view on Marx's theories on socialism, but their interpretations are quite far from what Marx had demonstrated. Due to their insufficient understanding on some issues of socialism, these market socialists were unable to put forth a feasible approach to realize their ideal society, nor could they point the major subject to realize this society, although they depicted their beautiful outlook for market socialism they were perceived as "utopists".

The study on the trends of market socialism occurring in the 1980s is of vital significance both in theory and practice.

First, it is helpful to make a further step to clearly understand the relationship between market and socialism in theory, and deepen our understanding in China's practice of socialism and develop Marxist theories on socialism. Currently, China is still in the transition period from the traditional planned economy to a socialist market economy. To realize this shifting process smoothly and successfully, it is necessary to clearly understand market-and-socialism relations. On this problem, Marxist were for a long time constrained by traditional concepts, equating market with capitalism, while considering planned economy as socialism. But in practice it could possible to see the drawbacks of previous ideas. Deng Xiaoping was the first leader to put that idea in a clearer way in China and then theorists and people have tested the new ideas in practice and gradually formed newer and more advanced ideas on the issue. Today, there are still some people who doubt the possibility of combining market with socialism. In terms of this point, it is vitally important to study the profound research made by market socialist and assimilate useful ideas from their researches. This will undoubtedly widen the range of Marxist thoughts, and provide a new angle in research.

Second, this is also beneficial to learn and take in some ideas from the positive research achievements made by market socialists for the practice of socialist construction in today's existing socialist countries. Undoubtedly, the various models of market socialism formulated by market socialists in the 1980s are essentially different from the socialist market economy which is practiced in Vietnam, China or Laos. These differences are not only restricted to those ideas related socialism, but also covers another issue; namely market socialists have explored the ways to combine market with socialism in the advanced capitalist countries, while our exploration focuses on the combination of socialism with market at the primary stage of socialist society where productive forces were historically backward and original capitalism was weak or underdeveloped. However, these distinctions do not mean that their models for market socialism have nothing valuable for Marxists to learn from and take in, on the contrary both sides are facing the problem on how to combine market with socialism and there are valuable points which deserve our attention.

Third, this is necessary to correctly understand the new changes in socialist movements in the world after the abrupt changes in the Soviet Union and East Europe, in order to strengthen our confidence that socialism is inevitably to overcome capitalism. The viewpoints and researches on market socialism occurring in capitalist countries in the 1980s will enable Marxists to realize that the socialist disintegration occurred in Soviet Union and East Europe does not mean that the capitalist system is better. Socialism is still an ideal society that numerous people, including those in the advanced capitalist countries, are pursuing for. The occurrence of market socialism is convincing evidence. As it were, the emergence of market socialism, in a certain sense, is an indication that the socialist movements are in a process of revival and also that socialism has abundant vigor and vitality.

REFERENCES

- P. Bardhan & J. Roemer: *Market Socialism*. Oxford: Oxford University Press, 1993.
- Gerald A. Cohen: "A Few Questions about Market Socialism", from *Journal of Renmin University of China*, 2000(5).
- Saul Estrin & Julian Le Grand: *Market Socialism*. Beijing: Economic Times Press, 1993.
- David Miller: *Market, State, and Community: Theoretical Foundations of Market*. Oxford: Oxford University Press, 1989.
- Bertell Ollman: *Market Socialism: the Debate Among Socialists*. Beijing: Xinhua Publishing House, 2000.
- John E. Roemer: *A Future for Socialism*. Chongqing: Chongqing Publishing House, 1997.
- Christopher Pierson: *New Market Socialism*. Beijing: The Eastern Publishing Co. Ltd., 1999.
- David Schweickert: *Against Capitalism*. Beijing: Renmin University of China Press, 2002.

CHAPTER IX

THE THIRD WAY

1 *Reasons for the Rise of "The Third Way"*
2 *Basic Ideas of "The Third Way"*
3 *Evaluation of "The Third Way"*

CHAPTER NINE

INTRODUCTION

In the middle of the 1990s, a new trend of thought, the Third Way, rose in Western European countries. It was first put forth by the U.S. Democratic Party at the beginning of the 1990s and was pushed forward by British Labor Party. This trend of thought was widely accepted by parties of Western European countries, such as German Social Democratic Party, Dutch Labor Party and Italian Left Democratic Party. When they came into power, they have promoted this thought. For example, leaders of these parties held three forums on "the third way" between 1997 and 1999. Through their efforts, the principle of "The Third Way" was extensively spread or put into practice, which has made great influence. Following the Third Way, a powerful group came into being in politics. Known as "new European route", "the third way" has also caught much attention of people in the world.

CURRENT GLOBAL IDEAS AND MOVEMENTS CHALLENGING CAPITALISM

9.1 REASONS FOR THE RISE OF "THE THIRD WAY"

9.1.1 WESTERN WORLD IN 1990S

In the 1990s, with the abrupt change in Eastern Europe, disintegration of Soviet Union and end of the Cold War, great changes also took place in Western politics. "The Third Way", as a new political philosophy or theory, rose in Western countries.

It is noticeable that the first advocates of "The Third Way" were not left-wing parties of the European countries, but U.S. President, Bill Clinton.

In the U.S. presidential election in 1992, Clinton had oriented his election program to "putting people's benefit to the first place". He took a flexible centrist stand, instead of the rigid creed that democrats adhered to for a long time, in order to revive the domestic stagnant economy and tackle the intricate and tough social problems. He said, "The reform that we must take is neither laissez faire, nor conservatism. It is the combination of the two, but quite opposite to them. People in the town or countryside show no interest in formulaic utterance of the leftism or rightism, or liberalism or conservatism; neither do they have any interest in other political speeches rather than actions. The government is responsible to create more opportunities, while the people should be responsible to make full use of these opportunities."[1] Due to his thoughts transcending the dispute between the left-wing-wing and the right-wing-wing, Clinton's stance was titled as "radical centrism".

By implementing a mix of some left and right policies in domestic and foreign affairs, Clinton won the second general election in 1996. His success had greatly encouraged British Labor Party and Social Democratic Parties in other countries in Europe, and set up an example for them. Furthermore, Clinton had actively participated in discussing the issues of "The Third Way" himself. In September 1998, the G7 summit was held in New York. Clinton took this opportunity to discuss the Third Way with leaders of similar political orientation, such as British Premier Minister Tony Blair, Italian Prime Minister Romano Prodi and Bulgarian Prime Minister Petur Stefanov Stoyanov, in the "Forum for World Democracy" on "the Third Way" held in New York University. In the forum, they have ambitiously put forth the idea of establishing "world center-left coalition" on the basis of the third way ideas.

---

1   Yang Xuedong (compiling): *The Third Way and New Theories*, p. 6-7. Beijing: Social Sciences Academic Press, 2000.

Clinton's theory and action have affected the theories of Western European left parties. These left parties include Labor Party, Socialist Workers Party and Socialist Party, which all belong to the social democratic ideological system. They were marginalized in the period from the 1970s to 1980s, but started to rise by the middle of the 1990s in Western European politics. In Britain, Anthony Giddens, President of London School of Economics, wrote and published his book *Beyond Left and Right – the Future of Radical Politics* in 1994. This book was the third volume of his trilogy *A Contemporary Critique of Historical Materialism*, in which the author had planned to answer the question whether capitalism could surpass socialism under modern conditions, with the theme of contest "between capitalism and socialism".

Owing to the abrupt changes in Eastern Europe and the collapse of bipolarization, Giddens had become aware that a further discussion about this question bore no significance any more. However, he as well believed that in European countries, some major political parties "had exhausted their political plasticity, and hollowed their political ideology, and either communism or social democracy or neo-liberalism had lost their validity, and Marx's social radicalism to establish "a genuinely free man" had turned out to be a utopia. He rejected that socialism could take the place of capitalism; neither did he agree on the prediction of scholars, like Francis Fukuyama, that the socialist development had come to an end and that the existing liberal democracy combined with market would permanently go on. Therefore, he put forward his radical politics hypothesis. In his book *Beyond Left and Right – the Future of Radical Politics*, Giddens has criticized the existing socialism with Soviet Union as the representative, and the social democracy of Western European left parties. He also made an analyses on conservatism and neo-liberalism, with the attempt to transcend the left-right conflict and construct a unique system that embraced both left-wing and right-wing ideology. His thought turned out to be the theoretical foundation for "The Third Way". This has as well marked a theoretical turn in British Labor Party.

From 1995, Tony Blair, leader of British Labor Party, has frequently used the term "The Third Way" to account for his political philosophy in public, advocating that the Labor Party would transcend neo-liberalism and social democracy and construct a new thought. In 1997, Blair won the general election by an overwhelming superiority over his opponent John Major, Prime Minister, which brought the Labor Party into power again after it was out of power for 18 years. "The Third Way" became the slogan of the new government. In order to expound the meanings of the third way, Giddens wrote another book *The Third Way: Renewal of Social Democracy*, which was published in May 1998. In this book, he made a further step to enrich and illustrate the new thought of the Labor Party. In his view, "The Third Way" refers to a kind of thinking or policy-regulating framework, which conforms to the tremendous changes in the past thirty years.

The significance of "the third way" is to transcend the old social democracy and neo-liberalism[2].

In September 1998, Blair's book *The Third Way: New Politics for the New Century* was published, which expounded the Labor Party's leading idea. In the same month, he wrote an article with the title of "'The Third Way' Is the Best Way" for Washington Post (09/27/1998). He claimed that "'The Third Way' is the access to restore and successfully achieve modern social democracy. It is not simply a compromised way between the left and the right, but to seek for basic values mixing centrist and center-left lines, which is applicable in social and economic reforms worldwide and is not constrained by any outdated ideology." In Blair's view, his "basic view of values as center and center-left-wing lines" covered "those traditional concepts, like unity, social justice, responsibility and opportunity", while he rejected the outdated "ideological concepts dominated by left-wing ideology, which advocates state control, high taxes and producer-oriented benefits" and also rejected the outdated "right-wing laissez faire theory and its new version advocating that individualism and free market economy were able to solve every problems."

Blair has argued that his theory of "The Third Way" transcends not only the "old left-wing theory" advocating "state intervention in economy" represented by Western European social democratic parties, but also Reagan-Thatcher's "new right-wing" theory of "laissez faire". His theory was a new political philosophy or theory, which served the purpose of settling various problems in current modern globalization.

Just at the same time when Blair's book *The Third Way: New Politics for the New Century* was published, Gerhard Schroeder, German Socialist Democratic Party candidate had defeated Helmut Kohl, former chancellor of the Christian Democratic Union of Germany, who had been in power for as long as 16 years, and won the general election for the 14th federal parliament. In order to enable the Social Democratic Party to get away from the difficult situation and recover as soon as possible, Schroeder also put forth the position of "new centrist policy", and joined the chorus of "The Third Way", which was popular in European and American political stages. Blair congratulated Schroeder on winning the general election and declared that both British and German governments held the same viewpoint. Soon after, during Schroeder's visit to Britain, the two countries set up a Britain-Germany committee, which consisted of ministers of trade and industry. They were responsible for propagating and implementing of "Blairism" and "new centrism". Thus, Schroeder was known as "Germany's Blair" and general designer of "The Third Way" of Germany.

---

2   Giddens, Anthony: *The Third Way: Renewal of Social Democracy*, p. 27. Beijing: Peking University Press, 2000.

With European Integration Process speeding up, 11 euro zone countries, where members of Socialist Democratic Party were in power, have jointly issued a document of "New Road for Europe", apparently tinted with the color of Blair's thought "The Third Way". The issuance of this document indicated that it was widely accepted in Europe. In other words, the thought of "The Third Way" started to shift from theoretical discussion and proposal to a political program that was able to essentially influence European politics and economy. In November 1999, the forum "Scholars for European Social Democracy" initiated an international conference involving issues of "The Third Way" in Berlin, with the purpose of propagating it in a wider range and discussing problems occurring in its development. The theme of this conference was "varieties of 'the third way': convergence and deviation". Participants have held a full and hot discussion of its temporal features, basic contents and specific forms in different countries. "The Third Way" was known as a new policy that the Social Democratic Party put forth in conformity with the globalization tendency, which reflected a new combination of social democracy with liberalism. It was the third forum that the "Forum Scholars for European Social Democracy" initiated. The other two were respectively held in October 1997 and November 1998. In the forum that was held in 1997 with the topic of "Reforming European Social Democracy", participants had extensively discussed the social settings challenging the revival of European social democracy and various problems it faced in reality, such as European integration and nation state and future of the welfare states. In 1998, they had discussed the issue of "European parliamentary elections and government practices", focused on German and Sweden general elections and political practice of the European social democratic governments. And "The Third Way" was also the important theme in this forum.

Apart from Blair, other social democrats and the political leaders of the socialist parties have put forth similar positions on "The Third Way". For example, Lionel Jospin, Prime Minister of France, proposed to establish a "democratic socialism" between "communism and absolute liberalism". There were also proponents of "The Third Way", like former Italian Prime Minister Romano Prodi, the Swedish Prime Minister Goran Persson, former Prime Minister of Denmark Anders Fogh Rasmussen, Portuguese Prime Minister Antonio Guterres, and French Financial Minister Dominique Strauss-Kahn. On 20-21 November 1999, an international conference, with the theme of "Reformism in the 21st century" was held in Florence, Italy which also advocated "the third way", which was jointly organized by European University and New York University. State leaders of the United States and Western European countries had attended the conference. Because proponents of "The Third Way" were those parties in power, it increasingly turned out to be a mainstream thought in Western European countries. Nowadays, discussion on "The Third Way" is still an important topic in world politics.

CURRENT GLOBAL IDEAS AND MOVEMENTS CHALLENGING CAPITALISM

9.1.2 THEORETICAL ORIGINS OF 'THE THIRD WAY'

"The third way" was not a new term but was stated with different terms in the history, like "the Middle Way", "the Middle Standpoint", "the Third Force" and "the Third Universal Theory". This theory could be dated back as early as the end of the 19th century. At the end of the 19th century, a European bourgeois economist put forth the "middle way", combining laissez faire economy with planned economy; in fact this idea was first raised by Utopian socialists and was later accepted by some Marxists. He had attempted to create a "middle way" between the capitalist economy and the socialist economy. The alleged "third way" he raised was quite different from "The Third Way" in the 1990s, but that thought had a great influence on the formation and development of the currently existing "third way".

At the beginning of the 20th century, Eduard Bernstein, a German social democratic theorist, once had claimed to establish a "third way" between Marxist scientific socialism and the capitalism in reality. After the victory of Russian October Socialist Revolution, Rudolf Hilferding, prominent revisionist in the Second International, had proposed an "organized capitalism", arguing that a movement combining socialist advantages with capitalist merits of monopoly and parliament democracy, could both reform capitalism and be different from the mode of Russian October Revolution. Meanwhile, the centrist Socialist Parties in some European countries had also identified themselves as "the third force", advocating "the middle way", which was different either from the road of Second International to establish socialism with democratic methods, or from the Russian way through workers and peasants' revolution. Lenin had made a profound criticism on this proposition: "the reason why social democrats were short-sighted in theory and were captured by prejudice of the bourgeois and politically betrayed the proletariat is that they are unable to understand that when class struggle, the foundation of this society, was a little bit serious, there could not be "Third Way" except for bourgeois or proletarian dictatorship. The delusion of the third way is nothing but a reflection of reactionary paint of the petty bourgeois."[3]

From the 1920s to the 1930s, "the third way" of Western European Democratic Parties had made some progress and great influence. In 1929, an unprecedented economic crisis had occurred in the capitalist world. It had started from the most advanced capitalist country – the United States and hit not only the United States, but also other powerful capitalist countries in the world, which also greatly shook the structure of the capitalist system. Opposite to the crisis in the capitalist world economy, the newly-established socialist economy in Soviet Union had developed smoothly and also overcome numerous difficulties in its economic construction, and increasingly grew powerful. The socialism had begun to show

---

3   *Complete Works of Lenin* (Chinese edition). Beijing: People's Press, 1982.

its advantages. People in the world had started to make a comparison between the socialist economy and the capitalist economy, which had also aroused Keynesians' attention, and they began to doubt about the market's role being "self-adjustable and self-correcting" which was worshipped to be sacred by proponents of laissez faire economics. Faced by the capitalist crisis and successes of socialism, Western European Social Democrats had to change their stance toward Russian socialism and communism. They became proponents of the practice of "organized capitalism" in West, singing high praise for "middle standpoint" and raising the flag of "middle way". They have suggested establishing a democratic socialism, different from the capitalism, like the United States, or the socialism like Soviet Union. There were two important reasons, for which Western European Socialist Party raised the flag of "middle road": first, they could not dare publicly support the capitalism in the time of unprecedented economic crisis; and because the capitalism had launched the First World War and lost prestige among the people; second, they could not dare publicly oppose the increasingly powerful socialism because they would lose trust of some people if they did so. However, they had adhered to the supposed "middle standpoint" or "The Third Way", which could please the bourgeois because, on the one hand, they did not intend to abandon capitalism but reform it; on the other hand, they could deceive the proletariat by proposing a democratic socialism, which advocated taking in socialist advantages and discarding its disadvantages.

In 1932, the Sweden Socialist Democratic Party had won the general election and came into power by their election program formulated as "The Third Way", which was both different from socialism and capitalism, and got support from the masses. They began to practice "The Third Way". In 1936, Marquis Childs, an American journalist, wrote the book Sweden: *The Middle Way*, chronicling his research on the reform policies of the Swedish Social Democratic Party. He had expounded that the society life, economy, and politics of Sweden, greatly practiced "the third way". In 1938, Harold Macmillan, well-known economist of British Labor Party and former British Prime Minister wrote and published his book *The Middle Way: A Study of the Problem of Economic and Social Progress in a Free and Democratic Society*. In this book, Macmillan had made an overall demonstration of the necessity and possibility to practice "the middle way", arguing that "the third way" was to adjust the capitalism; and this adjusted capitalism not only promotes economy but also provides the people with some welfare. "The third way" had thus become a fashionable term then in Europe. Before the Second World War, Fascist intellectuals over the world had also appealed to practice "The Third Way", claiming, "Fascism is the third way between capitalist anarchy and communist dictatorship."[4]

---

4 Tony Judt. "The Third Way Is Not Access to Paradise". *The New York Times*, Sept. 27, 1998.

Influenced by "The Third Way" of Western Europe, Argentinean President Juan Perón had also put forth the similar proposal. His advocate of "theory of the third standpoint" had made much influence in Latin America. He argued, "Either the capitalism or the socialism was outdated. The capitalism exploits people by means of capital, while the communism exploits people through the state, both of which harm people through different social systems." "No matter what system we choose, it is unable to provide people of our country with merited welfare. Therefore, we decide to set up a third stand, which is neither capitalism nor communism."

With the formation of the cold war in the postwar years, members of Western Socialist Democratic International re-advocated "the third way". After Socialist Party International was set up in 1951, socialist parties of Western European countries took a stance of both criticizing capitalism and opposing communism, with an attempt to strengthen itself with a cloak of a "middle force" or "The Third Way" and follow "The Third Way", which would be neither capitalism nor communism. Furthermore, the Socialist International had strengthened its propaganda of "the third way" worldwide. Thus, it attracted numerous believers and parties in "the third world" and Eastern European countries. Thus "The Third Way" had evolved from ideology of the Socialist Party International into a quite influential thought and movement world-wide. In 1968, several social movements have gathered under the flag of "the third way", which would transcend the capitalism in reality and the real socialism, such as European youth movement, student movement, and other social movements affected by "the third way idea" but advocated the idea of grass-roots democracy.

From the 1950s to the 1970s, "The Third Way" took a further step, with more and more proponents in parties and academy. Apart from left-wing parties continuing with "the third way" in Western Europe, a European communism trend had appeared in European communist parties which also advocated a "The Third Way", different from democratic socialism or Russian-model socialism. In Eastern Europe, economists of socialist countries, like Czech Republic, Hungary, and Poland, had strongly advocated "the third way". Ota Sik, a Czech economist, specifically demonstrated "the third way" in his works, like *The Third Way, A Feasible Economic System, and Evidence for the Third Way*, with the purpose of seeking a model to replace the Russian-pattern socialism. In the Third World, there also appeared several versions of "third way" parties exploring a new road for national independence and road for development after independence. In Asia, the Indian Prime Minister Jawaharlal Nehru advanced to "establish a new-type socialism— a middle way between communism and orthodox practice of capitalist countries"[5] in 1956. In Africa, President of Mali, Alphonse Massanba-Debat, also presented his policy as "the middle way" and "blazing a new road in the valley between the slopes of

---

5   Jawaharlal Nehru. "Our Socialist Economy". *Economic Review*, Dec. 1, 1956.

the capitalist system and socialist system". Libyan President Omar Mouammer al Gaddafi had presented his unique "Third Universal Theory", and promised to follow the third way to establish a fair and equal society, which transcended capitalism and socialism under the guidance of Islamic creeds and based on Arabic tradition. Democratic socialism put forward by the Socialist International had rapidly spread in the Third World. For example, President of Panama, Omar Efraín Torrijos Herrera, put forward his "Panama Road", which was "neither the traditional capitalist road, nor communist road". In Venezuela's socialist movement, an idea was raised to establish "a socialist society with Venezuela style", neither capitalism nor socialism.

In the 1980s, "The Third Way" went forward a step further in Eastern Europe. In 1989, Lech Walesa, leader of Polish Unity Trade Union, claimed that Poland should walk along "The Third Way", which was different from the existing socialism or contemporary capitalism. During the course of abrupt changes in Eastern Europe, the communist organizations of those countries turned to social democratic parties one after another, and have advocated "The Third Way". Russia went so far as to establish a "Third Way Party".

We can draw at least two conclusions on the basis of the analysis above as follows.

First, "The Third Way" was not a new term, or a political "formula" in the 1990s. Though it is hard to fix the exact time when this concept had emerged, we can say that it has a history of more than one century. In the history, some Socialist parties, which form the left-wing tradition in Western parliamentarism, were proponents and practitioners of "The Third Way", and their policies and proposals had played a significant role in theoretical formation and development of "The Third Way" in Europe and other places in the world. Though there are many differences between "The Third Way" in the past and the one that was popular in Western Europe in 90ies, the former had made a great influence on the latter. A diachronic review of "the third way" reveals that the current theory of "The Third Way" has inherited approaches of reformism in the world socialist movement which was formed in the middle of the 19th century. It can also be said that "The Third Way" that was popular in Western Europe in 90ies was a kind of revision or "theoretical innovation" of that in the history. But we can say that the "The Third Way" in the history had never been as attractive as the current one.

Second, "The Third Way" is not a concept with clear definition. In the history, it had different meanings in different spheres. As a road of social development, it referred to "the middle road", which was different from capitalism and socialism, but integrated advantages and discarded disadvantages of the two; as an economic system, it was the middle way between the laissez faire capitalist economy and socialist central planned economy; as a socialist revolutionary road, it was different from both democratic socialism, which insisted on "peacefully entering socialist road", and the road of Russian style or other socialist parties advocating seizing political power with a revolution and implementing proletarian dictatorship; as a foreign policy, it kept a neutral stand between the capitalist camp under the leadership of the United States and the socialist camp led by the Soviet Union advocating an independent foreign policy without interference of Washington or Moscow. "The Third Way" we discuss today is a thought advocating a political reformation, to settle the current existing problems of Western European countries, such as Britain and Germany, in the settings of globalization. It aimed at transcending the left-right dichotomy, pursued binary convergent thinking models, and sought possibilities for the "revival of social democracy".

9.1.3 REASONS BEHIND 'THE THIRD WAY'

The reason why "The Third Way" has revived in Western European capitalist countries in the 1990s was quite complex with complicated international and domestic settings.

First, after the end of severe ideological conflict of the cold war, the left-wing political parties in the capitalist countries put forward "The Third Way" again to adapt to the new changes of the world situation, with the attempt to win more votes to get into power.

In the history, "the third way" was largely the result of the struggle between the capitalist and the socialist camps. In the past, Western European left-wing parties had advanced the "The Third Way" with the attempt to transcend the two rival ideologies and explore a social development road, which was neither the capitalism nor socialism. It had aimed to take the merits of capitalism and socialism, and discard the demerits of the two. After the end of the cold war, the global situation tended to be peaceful, and peace and development became main theme of the times worldwide. Particularly, in the later part of the 1990s, relations between great powers inclined to be more stable, affecting the mainstream of modern international relations, and cooperation and dialogue has replaced confrontation. Therefore, "The Third Way" that was popular in the advanced capitalist countries in 90ies was quite different from the one in the history. It did not intend to relate itself with the ideological and institutional conflicts between capitalism and socialism, but aimed to solve the internal conflicts related to traditional left-right ideological dichotomy and also reform the operational models in capitalist society and economy.

A review of the evolution of the political ideology and models of the left and right in advanced capitalist countries will be all too revealing: traditional left wing political parties, like the Socialist Party, Social Democratic Party and Labor Party,

THE THIRD WAY 323

have all attempted to combine the capitalist mode of production with social justice. Keynesianism and welfare-state thought aimed to meet this requirement. After the end of the Second World War, the advanced capitalist countries have established their political models in the form of welfare state, with the state intervention in economy as an economic operational pattern. In the 1970s, this political model was plunged into difficulty, resulting a hardship and decline with European political left-wing parties which was in correlation. The reason why those traditional left-wing parties has plunged into difficulty was intricate: first, the traditional model of welfare state they have led and advocated was in a predicament. Rapid and huge progress in science and technology and increase in productivity led to the growth of unemployment, and there were more and more people living on doles, but there were fewer and fewer tax payers. Great changes have occurred in the European demographic structure, which gradually forms an inverted pyramid shape: younger working generations have to support more seniors, who now have longer time to receive pensions with prolonged life span. With the improvement of medical technology, expenditures for medical care has become higher and higher. All of these have plunged the welfare states into financial difficulties, additionally, the economic globalization process sped up, but Keynesian economic policy was unable to meet the demands of economic globalization. The state over-intervention in economy has suppressed the role of market. These were the key reasons why the European economy entered into stagnation in the 1970s, and it was as well the important cause for the decline of the left-wing political parties. Third, in the 1970s, political indifferentism has risen in Europe. Ideologies had much more influence before the 1970s, but afterwards fewer and fewer people showed interest in politics. Especially, the youth were tired of factionalism, and they were greatly discontented with the political tendency of extreme conservatism and liberalism. They were reluctant to join political organizations with strong ideological and political colors, but rather tended to join neutral organizations, like environmental protection organizations and peace groups. However, left-wing parties used to be the parties that always put more emphasis on ideology. Last but not least, also changes have occurred in European social class relations. For example in Germany, the society took the form of an entity embodying different social groups, rather than old type classes with consistent value orientations. Among these groups, the number of people with high skills in service industry had risen overwhelmingly, while number of the traditional worker group had dramatically decreased, which had also weakened the social foundation of the traditional left wing parties.

It was for these reasons that the conservative right wing parties have assumed the power at the end of the 1970s. Neo-conservatism, represented by "Thatcher's Monetary School" and "Reagan's Supply-Side Economics" had swiftly expanded. The Neo-conservatism had emphasized that the "combination of individualism and laissez faire market economy could settle all problems". They also put forward a series privatization policies, which partly succeeded in correcting some defects produced by welfare-state models. On the contrary, measures of privatization and extreme emphasis on market competition did not help the capitalist countries go out of the "low-speed development" and high unemployment rates, but has intensified social polarization. The conservative parties in power could not bring about a new inspiration and prosperous economy as promised by them.

In between the end of the 1980s and the beginning of the 1990s, the disintegration of the Soviet Union and abrupt changes in Eastern Europe has greatly damaged left-wing political parties. Socialism, either as a thought or a movement, fell to the valley bottom. The left wing parties of Western Europe have suffered a total loss of prestige. To reverse this unfavorable situation, the left-wing parties had to find new ways, substitute their political strategies and theoretical basis, and seek for theoretical innovation and reconstruction. In the process of theoretical reconstruction, the left-wing parties have quickly made a "calculation" that it was a good time for them to take advantage from the disintegration of Russian-pattern socialism. They thought they could use Soviet Union as a negative example, but also could break through the traditional dichotomy of capitalism/socialism and left/right political division. They could bring about an innovation in politics and act more freely in policy making avoiding the pressure coming from left or right. Thus they would have more support for their revival and rise to power. It was in such settings that "the Third Way" of Western Europe rose.

Second, "the Third Way" reflects that its proponents responded to the new problems and challenges caused by the fast economic globalization process .With the advance of scientific revolution in the 1960s, in the 90ies world economic life was markedly featured in rapid economic globalization: either capital and financial globalization, or production, sales and market globalization reached an unprecedented level. On the one hand, this globalization prepared the foundation for international cooperation and harmony in the international society; on the other hand, the globalization tendency also had its negative effects: problems, like intensified international competition, unbalanced development, worsened ecological environment, international financial capital speculations, transnational smuggling, drug dealing, organized crime, regional conflicts, frequent occurrence of refugee waves, religious and cultural conflicts and moral degradation, have increased to an unparalleled level in history. Western capitalist countries, which were direct promoters of and beneficiaries of economic globalization process, lacked appropriate capabilities to deal with these new problems and challenges. More people have started to think that it is impossible for nation states themselves and West-oriented international organizations and mechanisms established in the cold war time to settle those new problems in the spheres, like economy, politics and culture without a wider participation or a reform in the international order. To solve transnational problems, like international hot money capital speculation, international crime, environmental protection, protection of human rights and eliminating poverty, it has become more urgent to establish a new global governance mechanism stimulating enthusiasm and initiative of nation states, international organizations, non-governmental organizations coordinating benefits for all parties, but also transcend differences of cultures, ideologies, social systems, and views of values. It has also become urgent to overcome problems caused by those who only pursue for their own short term benefits.

For Western European countries, the impact of economic globalization has caused three major problems: (1) Capital outflow has given rise to a downturn in economic growth rate; (2) It has raised the unemployment rate. From 1996 to 1998, the unemployment rate in 15 European countries had fluctuated around 10%, with a population of around 20 million jobless. The unemployment rate in the youth under 25 was as high as 20%. The enormous unemployment groups have put a heavy stress on the financial aspect of the social security system. As a result of this, the cost of welfare state policies have highly increased; (3) Contradictions between native population and immigrants and other domestic contradictions are becoming significant and have intensified. Separatism, exclusionism, crime rate and bankruptcies in small businesses and other worsening economic conditions have menaced the existing internal order and harmonious social relations. In such a challenging age with intensifying contradictions, governments are urged to seek economic vitality to become internationally competitive, strengthen macro-control to avoid destruction of laissez faire market, encourage domestic capital to invest in production abroad to bring down costs, fight against high unemployment rate to alleviate domestic contradictions, initiate reforms to adapt to constantly changing situation, and maintain social stability. Undoubtedly, the above scene had severely challenged the traditional left-wing theory as well as new and old right-wing theories. However, it was just for this reason "The Third Way" had claimed to follow "the middle road" which would "transcend the old left-wing and new right-wing theories" and break through the restrictions of these two models. "Flexibility", "innovation" and "modernization" were put forward as attractive new slogans to persuade the public.

Third, "the third way" was a kind of response to the changes in the class and societal pattern of developed countries which was caused by structural changes in the capitalist industry.

In the second half of the 20th century, the information technology has greatly affected societal transformation. Information technology developing with leaps has first changed the old structure of the industry, which was reflected in proportions of the three industries in the national economy. Proportion of the primary industry was greatly reduced. Currently proportion of agriculture in some advanced countries only makes up 3% of their GDP. It is only 2% in the United

States. Proportion of the second industry, however, has increased, with the exception of the United States. Proportion of the services industry has markedly increased, which make up over 60% of the GDP, and above 70% in the United States Among the branches of tertiary industry, information industry has shown the fastest growth. In 1996, the global trade volume of information industry products (computer, telecommunication equipment, chips, software and scientific apparatus) was more than 700 billion dollars, covering over 10% of the global trade volume. In 2003 this rate has increased to 24.3 %. Competition between countries increasingly focuses on hi-tech with information technology as the core, and scientific and technological competition has become sharper than ever. All the countries need to adapt to the development of information technology and constantly adjust their industrial structures accordingly to meet the challenge and avoid lagging behind. Information technology has changed the industrial structure radically, transforming the employment structure and working conditions in the Western advanced capitalist countries. In the past workers were roughly divided into two groups: "blue-collar workers", who did physical work, and "white-collar workers", who did office work. With the development of information technology, proportion of the former was constantly reduced, while the latter increasingly expanding. A statistic reveals that in the 1970s, the proportion of workers in industrial sector of the United States was reduced from 33% to 17% of the total labor force, while the number of "intellectual workers" has radically increased. In recent years, in the United States 90% of the new workers entering the job market are employed in the information industry as "intellectual workers". "Intellectual workers" are employed in production, business, investment, politics, military affairs, scientific research, education, entertainment, communication and culture, and other services etc. The main tools they use are computers and other equipments involving information technology; they generally process information such as data collection, analysis, process, integration, transference and delivery and greatly utilize Internet technologies and its facilities. These workers are well educated and possess high cultural skills, and also include several more skilled groups working in science and technology, economics, management and other fields.

Above changes in the employment structure has affected the class and stratum structures in Western capitalist countries. The capitalism in the postwar years has not developed in the direction predicted by Marxist classic authors. Another trend has occurred, accompanied by the intensification, centralization and monopolization of capital, more and more small and medium enterprisers has grown out from the proletarian class besides working class has kept expanding. Although these enterprisers and self employed individuals often face numerous difficulties by the monopoly trend to a degree they are also supported and protected by mainstream political parties and thus constitute a stable middle and middle-lower stratum in the society. The number of "blue-collar workers", who are directly involved in material production, has become smaller portion, while the number of "white-collar workers, employed in non-material production make up the largest part. Robert Reich, U.S. former Minister of Labor Department, has argued that the future social power would be in the hands of the rising "semiotic-producers". In the 1990s, human society has entered into an era of information and knowledge economy. A large number of individuals called as "middle strata" including intellectuals, hi-tech talents, enterprisers, self- employed, managers, managing posts, doctors, lawyers, professors and engineers play an increasingly important role in the society. Most of them come from the middle-low stratum of the society. Their individual success mostly relies on their talent and diligence. They are generally open-minded, innovative, and practical and can adapt to lifetime education and are able to face the challenges brought by new technologies. After gaining higher economic and social status they strive to defend their advantages demand democratization and more participation in societal and local affairs in various spheres, support equal opportunities and social justice. Opposite to the white collar "semiotic producers", who has become more powerful, those majority without technological skills or immigrants were pushed to an inferior economic status, are highly unemployed or partly jobless. Lifetime or full time jobs are getting fewer and fewer. These changes in class/stratum structures have also greatly impacted those trade unions that were organized in the second industry. The number of trade union members has greatly decreased, and the internal solidarity and collective powers of the original trade unions have weakened. The decline in the power of trade unions was also caused by the sudden attack of new-right policies.

In the past, left-wing parties had mainly relied on the working class. Proponents of "the third way" were keenly aware of the changes in the social class structures in contemporary capitalism. They have considered the fact that the "middle strata" increasingly gains a stronger position in the society, while members and organizations of the main force that they have relied on – especially the traditional working class had continuously lost its status and powers. These parties have decided to re-adjust their social bases to win more votes and get more supporters from the middle stratum. This was the reason why they have advocated "The Third Way and "new middle" in Germany and other countries.

Fourth, "The Third Way" was an inevitable outcome of a compromise among main ruling parties respecting each other's interest. The main ruling parties have converged their policies considering the process of global multi-polarization and democratization.

Though most European countries have multi-party system, the main left and right wing parties have led the governments alternatively for a long time in 20th century, which is also known as "bi-polar plus multi-party " political structure . When we compare their ruling styles and policies, these two parties have several unique characteristics. However, although the two contest sharply, inside their political platform there are mild, conservative and liberal schools or trends. Through long-term struggles between the two, they have also formed a unique relation. They believe there can be no single policy that could solve the complex problems in modern capitalist society; and that it is necessary for them to learn from or adapt some effective measures of other parties. And when they assume power, apply them in practice on the prerequisite of maintaining their original colors. Take British politics for example, when Conservative Party came into power in 1979 it hallooed to reduce the state intervention in economy, and implemented Thatcher's economic policy with privatization and market regulation as the core. However, they still bore in mind to preserve some political tools of the Labor Party – the state intervention in the economy, the welfare system, etc was not totally discarded. There was an important reason for the Labor Party re-gaining power in 90ies: it had discarded some extremities in its traditional theory or policies, with an attempt to "give up the old but seek new ways", but which, in the final analysis, was to "put on the old clothes of the Conservative Party", just as the British news media had commented. As a matter of fact, the orientation of the current world political civilization is increasingly characterized as the unity of diversities. The history of political struggles has also nurtured the art of compromise. The European continent is a unity of complex class structures, religions, psychologies and nations as well as diversities. Long-term experiences and ultimate outcomes of these diversities are reflected in politics which inevitably pushes compromises and correction of extreme policies. Parties eye certain degree of mutual benefits and interests, and practice interaction and convergence of opposite political programs are not seldom cases. The reason why Western European left-wing parties could rise again in the 1990s, and why "The Third Way" they have advocated has gained certain support by voters proves that they have adjusted themselves to the current trends; especially easing of international relations after the end of the cold war and the demand for democratization.

In all, it was not historically accidental at all that Western European left wing parties had put forward "The Third Way" in the 1990s. They have responded to the historical transformation occurring in the political and economic circumstances internationally and to the profound changes happening in the economic and social structure of the capitalist society, domestically.

9.2 BASIC IDEAS OF "THE THIRD WAY"

In order to respond to the challenges brought by the changes in the world political configuration and seek for development opportunities in the new century, the left-wing Western social democratic parties have revised their political programs in the 1990s. They have formulated their new line as "The Third Way" which can be summarized as follows.

9.2.1 WEAKENING IDEOLOGICAL COLOURS

Initiators of "The Third Way" have developed several new theories. They have argued that for a long period in history politics in Western society had taken the form of party and class struggles. Parties had long presented themselves as an advocate of a certain class which determined their identity. They have mobilized their supporters and voters with certain slogans and programs bearing strong class characteristics. The left/right dichotomy was the most prevalent yardstick to judge political schools and their stands. This kind of politics was indispensable and reasonable during the long period of industrialization epochs and when sharp and strict class divisions or boundaries had occurred and society almost periodically entered into social and economic crises which produced constant and deep conflict of interests. However, with the adjustments in the capitalist relations of production to adapt to constantly developing productive forces, several important changes have occurred in the aspects capitalist society. One of the results was the decrease in the proportion of the second industry in the production structure, and the increase of the tertiary industry. This industry is relatively characterized by dispersed structures and working conditions and also includes some branches with relatively flexible working conditions. This industry has largely surpassed the second industry with the number of employees and production value. Meanwhile, social systems, social life of workers and industrial relations in the Western countries were improved to a certain degree which have weakened and alleviated sharp class conflicts, deep income and opportunity gaps. All these have eroded the basis of some traditional theories that had reasonably advocated hard class struggles and class type political parties. In their view, the major political forces in Western political life after the Second World War–both the left wing social democracy and the right wing neo-liberalism – could not avoid class politics and the left/right division, and have mainly relied on one or a few social forces. Though they were in power and popular for long, they were not successful in satisfying their voters. Their programs and policies have not only separated the society, but also caused a discontent and loss of trust against that kind of politics and also produced an indifference. This pattern of politics has delayed or neglected necessary reforms and measures demanded by the economy and society which can also be defined as deviation from the real life of the society. And during the 1980s, the left wing parties, which have adhered to class politics, met severe difficulties, and lost their supporters. In order to regain their capacities and assume government positions again they were urged to abandon their traditional styles and ideas and seek reforms and adapt to certain realities.

In the view of proponents of "The Third Way", it was necessary to reform policies and party institutions, their organization structure and also change the leading ideology behind them in order to regain power and improve support of the voters and improve their political attraction. Their leaders have suggested several measures as follows: break through left/right dichotomy in political thinking, unite with several other social groups in the society especially those in the new middle strata. One of the reasons why the Labor Party under the leadership of Blair won the three successive general elections was that it had gained the support of the middle strata. To unite with different kinds of social groups, advocators of "The Third Way" had proposed to embrace diverse ideologies, to integrate demands of the different interest groups. Second, they had preserved their socialist core value as social justice. To seek for social justice is the consistent policy of the social democratic parties in Western Europe. Advocators of "the third way" had not only inherited this precious legacy, but also advocated using this legacy to strengthen the social cohesion in the society. Third, they had proposed to reform the political system and party's organizational system by making them more flexible and more open. After he assumed power, Blair started to reform the party program and constitution and also re-casted the party's rigid political image and reduced the ideological mix in party's original political style. In order to weaken the factions and opposition in the party, he advocated that the Labor Party should shift from a class party to a mass party, and strengthened the authority and power of the leading party organs and restrained the influence of the trade unions and basis or local party organizations on the party policy. He had defined his reform targets as the structural drawbacks of the traditional left party were successful to get support from the majority of the members. The report Partnership in Power, reflecting these reform thoughts was approved within the party .This report had clearly stated that it was unnecessary and irrational for the party leaders to yield to the pressure imposed by the party members: " we should bear responsibility for the people, the majority of the country and the parliament." …" the change that the new Labor Party brings is not only a change within the party, but also a "necessary factor for the whole British political reorganization"[6]. Apart from the reforms within the party, British Labor Party as well put forth a reform in electoral system of the country, and replaced the existing "First Past the Post (FPTP)" system with "Mixed Member Proportional (MMP)", to reduce political polarization and expand voter's choices. Blair reformed the cabinet forming system allowing other political party members participating to the cabinet for political efficiency.

---

6   Kennedy, Simon: "New Labor and the Reorganization of British Politics", *Weekly Review*, Volume 49.

In Germany Schroeder had praised his policies for being neither left nor right, and claimed that he would apply any policy which could produce optimal outcomes because "the old ideology has been overwhelmed by historical power. I am only interested in what works at present."[7]

9.2.2 INNOVATIVE ECONOMIC POLITICS

In the sphere of economy, traditional social democracy had advocated nationalization, to reform private capitalism with mixed economy; neo-liberal right parties had proposed market economy, abolishing the state-owned sectors of the economy. But both these two economic policies were unable to solve the burden of the social welfare and security system and the problem of stagnating economy, namely, they could not properly adjust the relation between justice and efficiency. The first was the problem of justice. From the 1980s on, Western advanced countries had continuously implemented Thatcher-Reagan's neo-conservative economic policies, cutting down public expenditures and social welfare and the social security system was radically weakened which had intensified poverty, widened the income disparity and led most people to a harder life. In the United States, the share middle strata earned from national income had fallen down in 1993 their share was reduced to 47% compared to 53.2% in 1970. Therefore, "Reaganomics" was called "robbing-the-poor-to-help-the-rich" policy. This problem was also an important factor that caused the British Conservative Party government to lose power. The second was the problem of efficiency. In the 1990s, Western countries had faced the most severe economic recession after since the Second World War. Apart from the United States, the economies of the other advanced countries grew only marginally. The economic stagnation in 1970s had led to the crisis of the Keynesian economics, and opened the era of neo-conservative liberal economic policies. But those policies could not lead the Western capitalist economies out of the low growth, which had revealed that undue emphasis on the state intervention in economy and unrestricted laissez faire policy do not work. It was necessary for people to reassess the integration of state intervention and market mechanisms in the economic operation. "The Third Way" was believed to be right orientation.

As for the relationship between justice and efficiency, advocators of "The Third Way" had proposed that attentions should be given to both. People needed social justice, but temporary efficiency was also badly needed and the problem was how to combine justice with efficiency. To settle the problem of efficiency, "The Third Way" had advocated building a "new economy", that is, to put economic growth to the first place and promote an "innovative vital modern economy". Blair had

---

7   Song Yimin: "Western New-generation Leaders and Socialist Democratic Thought", *Guangming Daily*, Dec. 25, 1998.

argued against those who emphasized social justice and pinpointed to economic growth. To push for economic growth, "the third way" had abandoned traditional ideological conflict between the state intervention and laissez faire market regulation mechanisms, and combined the two and implemented several adjustments in social welfare policies.

As for the ownership, "The Third Way" of the past had generally advocated public ownership, and "the social democracy should aim to change that condition in which a minority capitalist group controlled the ownership of the means of production. They proposed to expand public ownership, so that all the people could have more economic control rights. Nowadays, nearly no social democratic party in Western Europe puts emphasis on the change of private ownership and establish public ownership, but they advocate the mixed economic mode to produce optimal economic ends. In April 1994, Blair was elected leader of the Labor Party. With his suggestion, the Labor Party in its special party convention in May 1995 had abolished the Fourth Article the Fourth Item in the Constitution of the Labor Party, which was about the public ownership. In Blair's view, "the socialist ideology has died" the ownership should not be emphasized anymore, because in the settings of economic globalization any economic enterprise should compete and follow the competition rules in the market.

As for the relationship between the state and market, on the one hand, "The Third Way" had actually given up the state-ownership. However, it still held the view that it was necessary for the state to standardize or regulate the market order on some occasions. The state should create a favorable condition for economy, and clearly determine orientation of the nation's industrial development. However, the state should not take care of everything. Its role should be limited. On the other hand, "The Third Way" as well abandoned its ethical judgment that market is evil, adopting the belief that the market was neutral and an effective means of distributing social resources, but it was not almighty. Market without control was dangerous, so measures should be taken to partly intervene it. "The Third Way" believed that both market and state regulation are necessary means for adjusting economy. The key lay in institutional arrangements to organically integrate the two, to make this mechanism feasible in economy. "The Third Way" was an attempt for this integration. Blair clearly claimed, "in terms of economy, our view is that we shall adopt neither laissez faire economics nor the state intervening economy."[8] French Prime Minister Lionel Jospin believed, "there is no state, there is no market. Market economy requires rules, powerful institutions, stability and organization."[9] In order to better coordinate the relationship between the

---

8   Yang Xuedong (compiling): *The Third Way and New Approaches*, p. 26. Beijing: Social Sciences Documentary Press, 2000.
9   Yang Zhiqing: "Blurring Left-right Dispute, Focusing on Innovation and Practicality – Temporarily European Mainstay Social Thoughts". *Guangming Daily*, Dec. 25,

state and market, "The Third Way" had pointed out, the role of the government in economy was supposed to focus on stability of the macro economy, pay more attentions to market economic discipline, reduce the state intervention, should be engaged in a partnership with individuals and voluntary organizations; put more government input on scientific research and refurnish scientific research bases; improve education, implement life-long education programs to ensure that people have working skills in modern conditions; share responsibility and rights to carry on "new community politics" and settle unemployment issues, reform tax and encourage independent tax and welfare policy.

As for the welfare policy, it advocated reforming the previous welfare system, and constructing a "new welfare system". Reform of the welfare system was the toughest problem for Western countries, which no political party could solve when they were in power. Proponents of "The Third Way" took a "compromising" attitude toward that issue, with the attempt to establish a system that could concern benefits of all stratums. To establish such an optional system, they proposed: first, they should accept criticism of the welfare system from new rightists, because the welfare system that was "from cradle to grave" leads to alienation and bureaucracy, distorting the primary purpose of welfare system. Therefore, it was necessary to reform the traditional social democratic welfare system. Second, the key point of welfare reform was to redefine the functions of the welfare system. In Gidden's view, the welfare system needed to cleanse the Augean stables, but it was not for the sake of reduction, but to make it adapt to new circumstances. The reform should focus on cultivating individual's responsibility and independence and give full play to social organizations and institutions, so that they could actively make their contributions to welfare system. "The Third Way" emphasized that "if there was no responsibility, there would be no rights" and "responsibility was the foundation of a sound society". Individuals should actively repay the concern of the society and assume their obligations, so as to genuinely realize social justice on the basis of modern awareness – "offering and gaining", namely, sharing opportunity and rights, and risks and obligation. Blair had highlighted that the welfare reform would produce the outcome of combining gaining and obligation, that is to say, when individuals gained welfare security from the society, they should as well assume social obligations. Giddens hoped that by means of this kind of reform, the original welfare state would be turned into a "socially investing state", to establish an optimum mechanism of risk – security and individual responsibility – collective responsibility[10].

1998.
10   Giddens, Anthony: "After Leftists Paralyzed". *New Statesman*, May 1, 1998.

9.2.3 REFORMING THE GOVERNMENT SYSTEMS

In the 1980s, in the Western academia; the Civil Society Theory was proposed. Though there were different views on civil society, it was generally considered that it is a sphere that is opposite to political state, and it balances abuse of political power. After new theories were put forward, it was approved and supported by neo-liberalism, who was in power. However, with the economic and political changes, people gradually learned more about civil society. They began to realize that either an over-strong or over-weak civil society will hold back the social development. "Smallest possible state" assumption of neo-liberalism has gone to the extreme side, and its approach as overlooking the role of the state was more and more criticized. Therefore, Western European left-wing parties have explored how to coordinate civil society with the state and combine the strength of the two when they assume in power. In Gidden's view, "the general political aim of the third way is to help the citizens find their development orientation in the deep reform occurring in our age. These reforms include: globalization, changes of individual life and the relationship between men and nature."[11] In the political program of "The Third Way", social justice was still a core problem. To realize social justice, proponents of "The Third Way" suggested establishing a new relationship between individual and the society, and avoid the "dichotomy" of the state/civil society in practice. "The Third Way" had pointed out that, "the reform of the state and government should be a basic political polestar of 'The Third Way'."[12]

First, they had proposed to reorient the role of the state, to find a proper orientation for the state in a mixed economy. In Gidden's eyes, the largest difference between the new mixed economy and the previous mixed economy lay in that it should properly balance: control and anti-control, economic life and non-economic life, instead of balancing state-owned enterprises and private enterprises. In the new mixed economy, functions of the state should be: (1) to maintain competition when monopolies threaten economic competition; (2) to control natural monopoly process; (3) to develop and maintain the foundation of the market system; (4) to avoid public, political and cultural articles from being ill-purposely distributed in the market; (5) to realize medium- and long-term objectives by means of the market; (6) to avoid market fluctuation at the micro and macro level; (7) to protect workers' material conditions and labor contracts (8) to promptly respond to and settle natural disasters (including disastrous consequences that market caused). In the new mixed economy, assessment and adjustment of economic development should be done in accordance with extensive consequences of the development[13].

---

11 Giddens, Anthony: *The Third Way: Revival of Social Democracy*, p. 67.
12 *Ibid.*
13 Giddens, Anthony: "After Leftists Paralyzed". *New Statesman*, May 1, 1998.

Second, they proposed to implement governance "democracy", establishing interaction between government and civil society. It was supposed to cultivate civilism, motivate citizens to actively participate in political life, give full play to the initiative of non-governmental organizations to have them assume more appropriate responsibilities and participate in government decisions. The third way proposed "democratization" of the government, which should be more transparent, lawful, efficient and responsible, and should become a reliable public institution. Looking from the government side, "there is no authority without democracy." In Giddens' view, new democratic governments were supposed to have the following characteristics: decentralization, two-way democracy and policies for public sphere, transparency, administrative efficiency, direct democracy, and the government assuming the role of "risk manager".

Third, it proposed to change the relationship between center-local: improve the constitutional government system, extend more local autonomy, delegate power to the lower levels so that they could have more functions related to local citizens, and give full play to the activity, initiative and creativity of the local governments. The central government should provide necessary support to local governments. Additionally, "The Third Way" also believed that when "new democratic state" transfers power to the grassroots, it must also submit power to transnational institutions[14].

Fourth, it has also paid attention to coordinate the relationship between government agencies, to establish a "Totality of Government". The "Totality of Government" approach was coined by British New Labor in the course of government reform, which meant that government departments and agencies should cooperate rather than confront with each other.

Fifth, it has advocated being globally involved. The international and global governance means that the government should actively involve international affairs, regulate international and even global rules, coordinate actions among nations, sign cooperative agreements with international institutions and non-governmental organizations, and cooperate with them in all aspects, like fighting against transnational crime and terrorism, and related eco-system management.

9.2.4 NEW SOCIAL RELATIONS

Aiming at the new changes in class/stratum structure in the contemporary Western society, advocates of "the third way" have opposed divisions on the basis of class, but propagated to establish a new society with cooperation and inclusiveness, where everyone and every group could be socially involved, and where community awareness will be cultivated. In Giddens' view, "'inclusiveness'

---

14   Ibid.

means such a citizenship that all members of the society will have civil rights, political rights and corresponding obligations not only formally but also practically. It also includes opportunity and participation in public sphere.[15]"

The new type of social relations

First, it has advocated cultivating community awareness on the basis of respecting individual's value. Individuals were supposed to actively participate in public life of the community they live in, and make their contributions to it. In the 1990s, the influential approach of "community building" became an important theoretical support for "The Third Way". The core concept of this approach "community" became a significant term for "The Third Way". Additionally, terms of "citizen values" and "civil society" were also employed to illustrate the significance of community.

Second, it has coordinated the capital-labor relationship with the idea of sharing risks and benefits. "Stakeholder" approach was formulated to define the corporate/company administration pattern in the 1990s, and it was seen as opposite to the "stockholder" approach. It refers that: all staff and organizations should participate in corporate operations they should undertake both risks and share the benefits with the management."We must realize that the benefits/stakes of all sides are closely related".

Proponents of "the third way" employed this concept to their theoretical system, advocated establishing not only Corporate Governance of "stakeholders", but also extended it to the whole economy as: "stakeholder economy". When he paid a visit to Singapore in 1996, Blair mentioned in his speech: Nowadays, central and central-left economics should move to create a "stakeholder economy", which includes all the people, not merely the privileged minority .In this economy, the corporation should respect employees, customers and stockholders, and should be responsible for education of human resources. The government should support the development of the corporation by means of offering stimulus and control, and promote a corporate culture of sharing risks and benefits or stakes. "The Third Way" hoped to eliminate the confrontation between capital and labor.

Third, it has proposed to coordinate the relations between native people and immigrants. The government was supposed to cultivate an awareness of inclusiveness and oppose exclusive actions, to build a "harmonious country". In his speech given on the occasion to celebrate his election as the leader of Labor Party, Blair had said: "it is our mission to stimulate a national spirit, unite the people and rebuild a core common object that is consistent with one country." Additionally, it is necessary for the government to affirm the contributions that the immigrants

---

15 Giddens, Anthony: *The Third Way: Revival of Social Democracy*, p. 107.

make to the social economy, government should make efforts to fight against poverty, protect the basic rights and interests of the immigrants, and help them join the mainstay society, so that they could make more contributions to the society.

Aiming at a series of problems, like social bipolarization, unequal distribution that was the outcome of the policy of "robbing the poor to help the rich" of the right-wing parties, and reduction of social welfare and social security, advocators of "The Third Way" declared that they would pay more attention to social problems and adjust rights and obligations. For this purpose, the state should arrange new programs to support families to better balance family rights and obligations; the government should take measures to prevent and fight against crime, especially juvenile delinquency, highlight community spirit, so that individuals and the whole society shoulders responsibility when enjoying rights.

9.2.5 COOPERATION AMONG BIG POWERS

As for international issues, traditional left-wing political parties regarded nation states as a menace for international unity, while right-wing political parties overemphasized nationalism and chauvinism, with the advocacy of mixing nationalism with the their laissez faire market theories. However, in 1990s, "The Third Way" had argued that nation states constitute a more durable and stable force. Those, who are for nation states, should also care for more cosmopolitism, in this way large-scale wars among nations could disappear. In the new circumstances of economic globalization, it has no future to advocate protectionism or nationalism. Without an effective international cooperation it will not be possible to coordinate policies of different countries and promote harmonious global development. The unity and sovereignty of states should be maintained with more open ways; sovereignty should be open to international control. Thus, proponents of "the third way" coined the notion of "cosmopolitan nation". They have greatly appreciated "fuzzy nationalism" and "multiple sovereignty" and advocated constructing an extensive national identity, so as to organically combine individuals, cosmopolitan nations and cosmopolitan states.

In the view of proponents of "The Third Way", globalization not only refers to economic dependence, but also covers all spheres, like economy, politics, science, cultural life and ecological environment. Although economic globalization has actually emerged, economic globalization or financial globalization could not be the real theme of globalization. Adequate development of information technology promotes establishment of both-way direct association and communication between individuals, nation states and the world. People's social lives, the states' political and cultural lives, all are gradually globalized. "The Third Way" approach has argued that the globalization was a two-way movement. Powers and status of all states should be opened to its influence in the process of governance, economic and cultural globalization. On the one hand, power of the nation states should weaken, so that globalization can freely develop without being restrained by nation states; on the other hand, globalization should be allowed to penetrate downwards, to adapt to new demands and new possibilities for reconstructing local identity. Boundaries of countries continuously become obscure, but the nation state does not disappear. Generally speaking, the scope of government activities expands rather than diminish with the continuous advance of globalization. Despite economic globalization, the state still keeps more powers both domestically and internationally in political, economic and cultural spheres. The new state should be different from traditional one, should act more extensively, and change its mode of effecting the economy and society.

When carefully studying the characteristics and structural changes that globalization demands, "The Third Way" has also summarized and analyzed the European Union. In Giddens' view, "European Union had primarily emerged as an institution of bipolar world, but nowadays, it should be viewed or interpreted as a response to globalization process."[16] In the process of globalization, European Union should offer a set of social, political and economic models that transcend nation states and directly involve and reach individuals, and establish a new European Union idea – European Member States – as a political transnational system of Market Society and a single European Parliament. The European Union was set up through cooperation among central governments of its member states, but it goes far beyond a regional international organization. Although it has some problems in many aspects like deficits in democracy, it has achieved great success in alleviating strained relations and risk of war among European nations. And it serves essential interests of European countries. Additionally, the operational mechanism of European Union and its achievements in open governance policies have offered an example for global governance mechanism. Based on this, proponents of "The Third Way" has presented a model of global governance pattern, and offered several policies for reforming and transforming the existing international organizations, such as United Nations.

Inspired by organizational frame and principles of European Union, advocates of "The Third Way" have designed an organization chart for global governance mechanism as "a participation organ (parliament), an administrative organ (commission), an inter-governmental or an organ managing international relations (council) and a united juridical system (court of justice)". To reform the organization of United Nations, they proposed to set up a world conference or a world parliament as an additional institution. Furthermore, advocates of "The Third Way" also advised setting up an efficient International court of justice as counterpart of the world conference, and widely extend its jurisdiction to the states and world citizens.

---

16   Ibid., p. 148.

Proponents of "The Third Way" have argued that the international society was confronted with great risks and challenge. Problems, like global markets, financial crisis, regional confrontations, environmental pollution and organized crime are international issues. Solutions to these problems rely on the construction of powerful international organizations and strengthening transnational cooperation. Therefore, advocates of "The Third Way" have proposed to promote "cosmopolitanism" to meet the requirements of the age under the new global circumstances: the end of bipolar world and economic globalization; "We should actively and efficiently develop international cooperation and promote a global harmonious development".

9.3 EVALUATION OF 'THE THIRD WAY'

After "The Third Way" was put forward, people from all walks of Western countries held different views on its outlook. In the view of its designers, leaders and proponents of "The Third Way", "'The Third Way' was the best approach", and was the way to "establish a vital democratic society in the 21st century." For Anthony Giddens, "'The Third Way' is the only feasible political philosophy and theory in the new century in the contemporary West." He had predicted it would be popular at least for 20 years in Western world. However, opponents of "The Third Way" held the view that "The Third Way" had not offered the road to paradise; just as there were fashionable terms in every epoch, "The Third Way" was the catchword of current times. There were also some critics, going so far as to comment that "The Third Way" was "a blind alley" because it has no theoretical foundation.

Objectively speaking, "The Third Way" was a theoretical exploration by the "new-generation" leaders of Western European countries to adapt to changes in contemporary politics. Behind their speeches on "The Third Way", from Blair to Schroeder, there were a number of influential theorists and thinkers carefully pondering on and testing "The Third Way". They made their efforts to adapt to the new changes of the world, update the traditional political theories, offered a new analysis on the new problems in the contemporary age, and new ideas and policies for reforming welfare states. Many problems they explored were not only related to Western advanced capitalist countries, but also those faced by the whole world. Their exploration was of much significance both in theory and practice for many other regions and countries. However, we should make an analysis on the essence of "The Third Way" when we are learning from and taking in it.

Generally speaking, "The Third Way" was a constructive "solution" that the Western European left-wing parties have raised in the process of globalization, with the attempt to settle several real problems occurring in capitalist society, which reflects the right deviation of the left parties after the end of the cold war.

It was in essence a reformist thought for the capitalist society to meet the challenges of globalization, to overcome its drawbacks and keep its internal vitality. It has attempted to "transcend" left and right politics.

9.3.1 'THE THIRD WAY': NEW STAGE OF DEMOCRATIC SOCIALISM

Compared with several types of "third ways" occurring in the history, "The Third Way" in the 1990s had more new contents either in forms of expression or strategies.

First, "The Third Way" has responded to the specific demands of Western social development, raising a timely series of ideas. In the 1990s, the cold war was over, so was the conflict between two ideological systems, and scientific development and globalization had sped up. In these settings, the Western society had gradually built a hope of settling economic and social problems with several innovative thoughts and practices that transcend traditional political and economic policies. Figures who were born after the Second World War had come to power and started to play a leading role in political and social life, which has strengthened this trend of thoughts. It was in such settings that advocators of "The Third Way" had presented a series of proposals that surpassed the left-right dispute and which were based on common interests, and thus easily became attractive in public.

Second, "The Third Way" opted several new emphases on problems and tasks to be completed. Different from "the third way" in the history, "The Third Way" in the 1990s did not label itself as "center" or "mediator" between the communist ideal and the capitalist system; neither did it aim at the development of the Third World countries or reform of former Soviet Union and Eastern Europe. It has aimed to surpass the division of left/right parties inside the Western capitalist countries, and emphasized settling the real problems of contemporary society, especially those in advanced capitalist countries. It has freed itself from the dispute of parties and classes, with the attempt to give people the impression of concerning real interests and safe life for everyone.

Third, "The Third Way" has raised some novel thoughts that deserve our notice. As for specific social policies and measures, like advocacy of coordinating relations between native citizens and immigrants, it has integrated traditional ideas of Western leftists and rightists in settling social problems, especially reforming welfare states with the principle of "no responsibility, no rights". These fresh thoughts had indeed greatly surpassed "the third way" in the history.

Fourth, although "The Third Way" was a medicine prescribed to settle domestic problems by Western European left-wing leaders; it can offer some ideas for other societies of the world. Related to employment and welfare policies, things should be done to increase investment for education and training, help weak individuals and promote them for self-employment; to improve welfare policies. While emphasis is put on economic development and promote international competitiveness, it will be necessary to keep social justice and support environmental protection. When individuals are socially supported, individual's responsibility should also be emphasized, and powerful measures should be taken to fight crime.

Fifth, "The Third Way" highlighted reforms and innovations. When we read Blair's collected speeches in his book: *New Britain – My Vision of a Young Country*, we can find the word "new" appearing nearly in every line. For example: "New Labor, New Life of Britain", "New Labor, New Britain", "New Industrial Society", "New Economy", "New Community, New Individualism", "New Nation States" and also "new network and service", "new relationship between the society and individual", "new relationship between government and the people", "new principles and a new mode of public intervention", "new constituency system ", "new central-left economics", "new problems, new methods and new ideas", and "new Millennium". Blair has linked his general reform ideas with the reform of Labor party. In his view, a political party would die without reforms, and a political party cannot adapt to the changes of times or will lose its vitality unless constantly improves itself.

9.3.2 SUDDEN RISE BUT DRAWBACKS

The third way had offered some fresh points in theory and practice, but there were also many drawbacks in its system, which are markedly featured as immaturity. These drawbacks have shadowed its innovative character; thus we can say it has a long way to go. Generally speaking, its drawbacks are:

First, definition and political contents of "The Third Way" are obscure, and there are many fuzzy and indefinite concepts. Its affirmation and ideas on individual's value includes part of basic values of neo-liberalism, and basic values in Western society. The socialist core value it claims to follow is also vague. For example, equality is defined as "equal opportunities", rather than fairer society; adequate employment means to provide "opportunities" for everyone to have a job; thus socialism turns out to be a vague and abstract social "cooperation". The role of the state is shifted or reduced from pursuing all-sided political aims to only making market more dynamic. "The Third Way" actually consciously and unconsciously accepts the platform that neo-liberalism had constructed. It opposes the critical stand of the traditional radical left, but it tries to avoid an extreme critic to it and adopts a more constructive critic and also borrows some ideas from neo-liberalism when establishing that critical line. Just as many critics point to:

"The Third Way", is merely a pseudo-philosophical coating concealing the interests of multi-national corporations and offers a governance mode for capital moving freely world-wide. Several critics were raised against it policies: "It is an old policy with a new label."[17] "What it provides us is nothing but a recurrence of Roosevelt's New Deal before the war, and that policy mixed with New-Thatcher's economics and blended with Victorian hypocrisy."

Second, it seems that "The Third Way" covers every sphere, but it is weak in its logical setup, which weakens its theoretical system and endangers feasibility of its political measures. Leadbitter, who had attended a seminar chaired by Blair in May 1998, pointed out: "if the third way becomes a leading policy and builds a consensus, it will have to answer four key questions: is it indeed clearly outlined or defined? Can it inspire people? As it is a government scheme, could it be a scheme of civil society? Can it develop economic potentials and capacities to improve welfare? But it seems that "The Third Way" fails to do so"[18].

Third, "The Third Way" does not have a series of systematic theories to settle tough problems. In Leadbitter's view, any political view that had lasted long in British history, such as Keynesianism and Thatcherism was based on economics, but "The Third Way" apparently lacks support of definite economic theories. If "The Third Way" aims to be a leading political theory, it must settle the problems of a modern market economy, develop a kind of economy based on human capital, and clearly advocate the view that British economy has entered into the post-industry age. In practice, "The Third Way" should put emphasis on integrating universities with enterprises, financial circles with enterprises, to establish a comprehensive institution that combines public ownership with private ownership, and knowledge with financial capital. Leadbitter had pointed out, "'The Third Way' must be mid-wife of this knowledge economy. It must be a kind of political theory, through which all the tensions and conflicts brought by the "new knowledge economy" can be settled, such as: intellectual property rights, values, taxes, competition, ethics and ethnics."[19] In short, "The Third Way" must have its own economic theory.

Fourth, there are quite different interpretations on "The Third Way", which reflects that left wing political parties do not have consensus on some important issues. Due to specific conditions of each country, they have developed different interpretations on "The Third Way". Although the British Labor Party has similar views with the German Social Democratic Party, it focuses on different aspects. Blair puts emphasis on breaking with conventional left ideas, emphasizing

---

17   Daniel: 'New Centralist and the Third Way". *Diplomacy Century*, 1998 (12).
18   Harrington, Patrick: *The Third Way - An Answer to Blair by Patrick Harrington*. Yang Xuedong (eds. compiling). *The Third Way and New Theories*, p. 163.
19   Leadbitter, C.. "Fatal Weakness of the Third Way". *New Statesman*, May 8, 1998.

a compromise with liberalism on the issue of state intervention; he has praised enterprise spirit and the role of market economy. But Schroeder had emphasized means of achieving basic values: "vitally important is to keep balance, that is to say, how to keep the balance between social modernization, economic modernization and social security", and he advocated a "new middle approach" on economic efficiency, social solidarity and sustainable ecological environment. The French Socialist Party has argued that it is necessary to give a careful consideration to the risks of the market economy and pointed to the significance of strengthening market management or regulation. FSP has underlined: "no market economy, no market society" and also advocated integrating market economy with state intervention in economy. However, socialist parties in Northern European countries, like Sweden, generally adhered to "the Sweden-pattern economy", and have put emphasis on social welfare reforms. They have tried to analyze changes in labor market and developed several policies to improve laborers' skills to enable them adapting knowledge economy. Based on their interpretation on "The Third Way" and ideas on new development modes, political parties can be generally divided into three groups: radicals, moderates and centrists. M. Pierre Mauroy, former President of Socialist International as well as the former Prime Minister of France, has claimed that "The Third Way" refers to the middle way between the capitalism and communism, and it should not to be redefined. Currently, the dispute on "The Third Way" among socialist parties generally focuses on the interpretation of socialist democracy, and also differences have arisen on how much the state should intervene to change the orientation of the economy, its functions in social life and welfare system.

Because of the immaturity of "The Third Way" that it is difficult to know how it will develop in the future. Apart from its drawbacks, more important question is whether Western European leftists can make achievements that will satisfy all sides when they are in office, and maintain voters support in future election campaigns. I think the future of "The Third Way" largely depends on the left's competence in settling economy related problems and the electorate campaign when they are in power.

9.3.3 'THE THIRD WAY' AND CAPITALISM

Superficially, the theories of "The Third Way" was put forward in Western Europe to serve three purposes: first, it has tried to establish a neo-left identity with creative thoughts, differentiating itself from old left and right and establish a new image as neo-leftism; second, it has attempted to re-construct the constituency foundation for the left political parties and recover its political power to seize power; third, it has aimed to find solutions for the domestic economic and global problems. But essentially, the content of "the third way" was to seek ways for further development of capitalism.

CURRENT GLOBAL IDEAS AND MOVEMENTS CHALLENGING CAPITALISM

For over 50 years after the Second World War, Western capitalist countries had a rapid development in economy, stability in politics and certain improvements in social spheres. But the nature of capitalism has not changed. The inherent contradictions of capitalism have still existed and caused constant economic and social crises. There was not only an overproduction crisis, but also a financial crisis and a monetary credit crisis, which had led to overproduction and inflation. To get out of those difficult crises, capitalism has constantly adjusted itself. Keynesianism advocated by the traditional left wing political party and neo-liberalism of Conservative Party have both served the purpose of settling the internal contradictions of capitalism and promoting its further development. In the 1990s, "The Third Way" was put forward with the attempt to answer and settle the contradictions and problems of further development of capitalism when it was confronted with new circumstances: post-cold war new developments and rapidly deepening globalization. On the basis reviewing Keynesianism and neo-liberalism, advocators of "The Third Way" have presented a series of new proposals, like combining traditional social democracy with neo-liberalism, adhering to principles of balance, like the state and market, supply and demand, justice and efficiency, and rights and obligations. They have attempted to build a new economy and welfare system and promote new policies to seek new ways for development.

There were many differences between "The Third Way" that Western European left wing parties have put forward in the 1990s from "the third way" that had occurred in the history. But in terms of views of value, methodology and general political stand, it had no essential differences from democratic socialism that had emerged in the Second International. A general analysis on its basic ideas reveals that "The Third Way" is essentially consistent with democratic socialism in the following aspects:

(1) Methodological eclecticism: No matter of its given images, either its claim to transcend left-right dispute or spokesman of "non-class people", the only central method "The Third Way" employs is to recognize and settle practical problems by integrating diverse ideas and proposals through mediation in order to achieve some compromise.

(2) Viewpoint based on Pragmatism values: All the ideas and proposals of "The Third Way" in the 1990s have served one practical purpose, namely, to expand its political base and exert its influence on the constituency of different stratums to take the power. Therefore, its basic principles, political ideas were quite arbitrary and temporary. If ideas were favorable for their aims, they could be qualified to advocate and publicize.

(3) Reformist social practice: That is to say, "The Third Way" had attempted to

enable the machine of the capitalism work forever through governance measures on condition that the current capitalist system remains intact. From this viewpoint and to make a comparison; if we can say that democratic socialism had waved the flag of "socialism" in its history, the current "third way" has totally pulled down this flag.

Meanwhile, it is also necessary to point that although the advocators of "The Third Way" emphasized to play down class, its theories possess a markedly class color. It has attempted to utilize the concept of "universal theory of democracy" to the current re-divided classes and society and have tried to unite them by means re-constructing democracy reversely in various ways. Today, many observers point to the reverse changes in the democratic life of Western Europe due to increasing poverty, dis-empowerment of trade-unions and unemployment. They have tried to blur class boundaries and alleviate class contradictions with hypocritical capitalist democracy to bridge the class differences and gaps which has increasingly widened. They have hoped to enhance social cohesion and inclusiveness and improve internal social stability in the capitalist society, coordinate the relationships between capitalist countries and protect interests of the bourgeoisie.

Therefore, "The Third Way" in the 1990s was closer to the needs of the bourgeoisie, and paid more attention to serving the capitalist class. As a result, the left wing socialist parties were transformed to a moderate political party for the bourgeoisie. In order to have a realistic idea on "The Third Way", it is necessary to grasp the capitalist reformist nature of its ideas and propositions.

9.3.4 GLOBAL GOVERNANCE MECHANISM AND 'THE THIRD WORLD'

The global governance theory advocated by "The Third Way" advocated is established on the basis of a hierarchy: individual – family – community–civil society – nation state – global governance organization. Its purpose was that the capitalism, with the advanced capitalist countries as its main body, should govern the world in a Western style, and exert power politics and hegemony thus governs the world under the guise of democracy. Conventional left parties had adhered to pacifism in international diplomatic policy and advocated to maintain peace even under those conditions when Europe was faced by actual military from Soviet Union in the cold war era, or they had advocated similar views to that of pacifists'. But current left parties have raised the flag of "the third world". On the one hand, they appeal peace, beating the drum that "war should not be a diplomatic means any more, diplomacy should aims to eliminate wars"; on the other, they declare that "countries without enemies" would establish a global governance mechanism in a democratic way, under the leadership of the Western ideology. There is no enemy due to the victory of Western democratic system in the world after the fall of socialist camp and socialism. However, we can say that the colonialism and expansionism, which capitalism was born with, either in economy or politics has not changed a bit. When Western European left parties take power, their new-generation leaders advocate human rights as a diplomatic principle, frequently accompanied by economic sanctions, and forced foreign governments to accept their view and practice of human rights. They extend it so far as to put forward queer theories like "human rights are superior to sovereignty"; "human rights have no boundaries"; "sovereignty is outdated", in defense of intervention and infringement upon the sovereignty of other countries. When Bosnian and Kosovo crisis occurred in 1999, social democrats advocating "The Third Way" have firmly supported NATO's bombardment and military intervention against the Federal Republic of Yugoslavia. They did this totally under the guise of fighting against "enemy". In this process, leaders like Blair have also put forward the theory – "New Interventionism" in defense of NATO, and adapted this concept into the frame of "The Third Way", and this idea turned out to be the core of "New Internationalism". Therefore, it is reasonable to think that "limited sovereignty of states "approach" and advocates of "The Third Way" formulated as establishing global economic norms, humanistic criteria and ecological standards have partly become a fig leaf of Western powers indoctrinating their view of values, power politics and hegemony. Thus European left-wing parties have gradually shifted from "pacifism" to a kind of "new imperialism".

It is not long since "The Third Way" was put forward, and some of its policies were already tested in practice. Its influence on the society was not as remarkable as anticipated, and it is hard to guess its future course. However, the future development of "The Third Way" not only concerns the fate of European new left-wing parties, but also the future development and outlook of advanced capitalist countries.

REFERENCES

- Anthony Giddens: *The Third Way: Revival of Socialist Democracy*. Beijing: Peking University Press, 2000.
- Anthony Giddens: *The Global Third Way Debate*. London: Political Press, 2001.
- Anthony Giddens: *The Third Way and Its Critics*. Beijing: Party School of the Central Committee of C.P.C. Press, 2002.
- Chen Lin, Lin Deshan: *The Third Way: Western Political Reform in the Turn of the Century*. Beijing: World Press, 2000.
- Yang Xuedong (eds. compiling): *"The Third Way" and New Theories*. Beijing: Beijing Sciences Academic Press, 2000.
- Wang Zhenhua (eds. compiling): *Rebuild Britain: Blairism and "The Third Way"*. Beijing: Chinese Social Sciences Press, 2000.

ABOUT THE AUTHORS

Duan Zhongqiao, born in 1951, has studied philosophy at Nankai University and Renmin University of China; he earned his Ph. D. at the University of Essex, United Kingdom between 1991-1994 and continued teaching at the Renmin University of China . Between 1997 and 1999 he joined Oxford University, All Souls College as a visiting fellow. Duan Zhongqiao has written numerous articles and three books titled as Marx's Theory of the Social Formation (English) in 1995; A Course in History of Marxism (Chinese) published by Higher Education Press in 1998 and Contemporary Social Trends of Thought Abroad (Chinese) by Renmin University Press of China in 2001.

www.ingramcontent.com/pod-product-compliance
Lightning Source LLC
Chambersburg PA
CBHW031139020426
42333CB00013B/438